WAR
MOVIES

The Belle & Blade Guide to Classic War Videos

Gary Freitas

with Foreword by Steve Mormando — "The VideoGuru"

Robert D. Reed Publishers
P.O. Box 1992
Bandon, OR 97411
Phone: 541-347-9882 • Fax: 9883
E-mail: 4bobreed@msn.com
Web site: www.rdrpublications.com

Book cover by: Julia A. Gaskil

Editing by: Grace LeForge

ISBN 1-931741-38-7

Library of Congress Catalogue Number: 2003095796

Manufactured, Typeset, and Printed in
the United States of America

53727296

"Men are at war with one another because
each man is at war with himself."
F. Meehan

CONTENTS

Gary Freitas

Gary Freitas is a writer and life-long war movie enthusiast. He served four years in the US Air Force (1970-74) and has a Ph.D. in clinical psychology. He is currently a practicing forensic psychologist residing in Phoenix. A student of military history and social conflict, he has authored books on violence (*Defusing Violence in the Workplace*) and relationships (*Relationship Realities*).

Steve Mormando

Steve Mormando holds a masters degree from New York University and served in the US Navy from 1973-1978. He is a 14-time US National Fencing Champion and represented the US in the Olympic games in 1984, '88 and '92. Steve has coached the New York University fencing teams for 25 years and has been inducted into the Rutgers University and Toms River Halls of Fame.

FOREWORD
Steve Mormando, President of Belle & Blade

I grew up at a time when a telephone call was a dime and a theater ticket cost a quarter. A 'mobile phone' was a rotary model with a long cord, and a laptop was where the cat would lie while you were watching one of the two TV channels broadcasting then (four if you were lucky). Multi-tasking was reading a book and watching a movie while dreaming of being the hero. We kids could not wait for the school year to end and, somehow, summers seemed to last forever.

Saturdays at the movies. You could watch cartoons during the early hours, and The Little Rascals right after (political correctness had not yet been invented), followed by The East Side Kids. Then came the 1 PM movie that was usually a costume adventure featuring heroes such as Robin Hood or Zorro. Between the 1 PM and 3 PM feature I would rush to the store to get milk and eggs (and a paperback for myself). At 3 PM the theater played a war movie and at five a serious movie for my parents. After the war movie, I raced home to finish my chores so that I could read my comic and adventure books in the apple tree out back.

At twilight, when it had cooled down my real adventures would begin. I would break off a strong branch and duel with the trees and shrubs by myself or play war when the gang was there. I was with Horatio at the bridge and Leonidas at the pass. Davy and I fought off the Mexicans, and I went around the world with Fogg in 80 days. When it got dark and my grandmother would call me in, I would go reluctantly.

My youth was a golden time full of dreams and adventures. Books and movies nurtured these dreams and helped me determine the direction my life was to go. Costume adventures and battling trees made me want to learn how to fence with a sabre. However, mastering this art was delayed a bit by the US Navy, since swords were now passé on Navy ships. After the Navy and during college, I picked up the sword with a passion. Eventually, I was to compete on three Olympic teams and win a World Championship.

Unfortunately, being an amateur athlete proved to be a poor career choice, and I had to figure out a way to make a living. When videos first appeared, I started collecting all my old favorites. This hobby of collecting videos turned into a career of selling videos, and my company, Belle & Blade, was born. I had tons of help from others who believed in my dreams, and I was able to amass one of the largest collections of war and history films around. Now I get to watch movies and talk about them for a living—a dream come true!

When I was a boy, I thought that all of the films I saw were great. Since then, I have watched many old favorites and now realize that some do not hold up well. The truth, however, is that no matter what I say or what any critic says about a movie, it is what the viewer himself thinks and feels that is most important. I have heard critics give 'thumbs down' for *The 300 Spartans*, *Pride of the Marines*, *Zulu*, *Waterloo*, *God Is My Co-Pilot*, *Casablanca*, and *The Alamo*, but I've loved all of them.

Reenactors and gamers enjoy many of the films that the rest of us may not because these films help them reconstruct battles. History buffs enjoy *Gods and Generals*, while many action film guys and 'regular Joes' hate it for being so windy. Many a lesser aviation film is treasured because it might be the only film in which a particular aircraft appears. One of my customers loves *Zulu Dawn* because the mountains in the background are so accurate he can use them as a reference in creating his dioramas. One man may prize a film because it helps recall a first date with his future wife or a cherished moment with his dad.

While keeping the above in mind, you may appreciate that this book on war films takes a critical look at many of the old and new films. Personally, I tend to be very forgiving. If a movie can take me on a ride to a place I've never been, then I am quite happy. Movies provide high adventures, laughter, dreams and hopes. They take us back to those long summer days, living room floors, and heroic times under and in the apple trees.

PS. Please e-mail me at **video.guru@verizon.net** if you would care to discuss any movie with me.

INTRODUCTION

"God is always on the side of the big battalions."
Turenne

You may already believe you have seen most of the great war movies, and are simply browsing this book to confirm your knowledge and judgment on the subject. You are just the person for whom this book was written. I started this project with a similar assumption and quickly came to realize that I had not seen all the best war films. Chances are you haven't either. This book is an attempt to save you time and point you to outstanding movies you won't want to miss.

Presented here are 347 concise reviews of modern war movies, from 1940 through 2004, that will hopefully stir discussion and provoke debate among war movie fans. However, this book is more than a review of war movies. It also attempts to rate them and compare them across a wide variety of categories. Perhaps you, like me, would like to know—what are the best submarine or prisoner-of-war movies or the twenty-five best combat films of all time?

These reviews will hopefully provide some retrospective on sixty years of war filmmaking. Often a movie is reviewed when it comes to theaters or is shown on TV and is never reviewed again. In time, however, many of the "so-called" good or great movies appear very average, and an overlooked film has grown so much better. For many movies, this book provides a chance for another look when it's nearly impossible to see or even know about every war movie ever produced. For the avid war movie fan, here is an opportunity to make up for any oversights.

This book simply asks the question, should you spend your time and money on this video? As a result, the book is a serious revision of existing war film criticism. To that end, the reviews give little consideration to whether a film has been popular at the box office, a critical success, an award winner, designated a "classic," has historical significance or carries the weight of a generation's nostalgia. The focus of this book is on whether a war movie can successfully compete with all the other video options occupying space on store shelves.

With the goal of defining the best war movies, I was confronted early on with the realization that there are really two types of war movie enthusiasts out there—the *action-junkies* and the *drama-buffs*. By no means are the two types of interests mutually exclusive but, clearly, some viewers are drawn more to action movies, such as *Black Hawk Down, Full Metal Jacket* or *Hamburger Hill*. Others seek out war movies that have compelling characters and stories with underlying themes, including movies such as *Patton, Breaker Morant* or *The Thin Red line*. I enjoy both types of movies and tried to give equal weight to both types of viewing experiences.

This book also differs from other war movie books in one other important way. Every effort was made to research relevant historical and military facts regarding each film. Because of this focus, there is less emphasis on who starred in the movie or on outlining the plots in great detail. While there's some attention to movie trivia and gossip, this book is primarily written for dedicated war film fans.

"Classic" War Movies

Perhaps the most controversial aspect of this book was the decision not to include older war movies and to focus almost exclusively on war films produced after 1950. Having watched many of the early war movies in preparation for writing this book, I concluded that war films of the silent era and talkies of the 1930s are too simple to be seen as compelling film viewing today. I suspect this decision will outrage many film critics and pundits, but for the filmgoer it probably reflects reality.

While nearly all the war movies of the 1940s were "flagwavers" that served as Hollywood propaganda for the war effort, they still need to be honored for their time. I have reviewed many of the so-called "classic" 1940s flagwavers. However, they are no more the best war films than "Steamboat Willie" is the greatest cartoon, "Pong" the greatest video game, or the "Spad" the greatest fighter plane. I also realize that I may have lost some of you at this point. Try not to be disappointed but rather be willing to reexamine your nostalgia for these films.

Perhaps you sat enthralled in front of the television watching *Dawn Patrol* or *Wake Island* on a late Saturday night; but unless you are a film historian, movie critic, or student of film, proclaiming these old movies as great war films simply doesn't wash. The fact is that film making has gotten much better over the years by using a blend of new technologies, more sophisticated techniques, and more complex storytelling. As a result, the modern movie is superior to its predecessors.

Looking back over 90 years of filmmaking, one sees each generation demanding that it be seen as "special" and insisting that a few war movies be designated as "classics" in order to give meaning to its experiences. And while the curators of these early movies implore us to watch these great films—no one is really listening or, more importantly, watching. We are too busy trying to define our own experiences. The sense of adventure and/or horror about war these films generated are, for the most part, lost on the next generation.

What Is a War Movie?

When I started this project, I never anticipated that having to decide what constitutes a war movie would be the hardest part. I thought I would automatically recognize a war movie when I saw one. I was wrong. By my estimation, and depending on one's definition, there are probably more than 3500+ war-related movie titles. Obviously, it's not practical to review all of them.

Not only are there a lot of war movies, but there are many different types of war movies. In order to determine which films to include in the book, I decided to categorize them. But I then discovered that most war movies do not fit easily into one category, making this process even more difficult. For example, a common genre crossover is war and journalism, as in *The Killing Field, Salvador, Year of Living Dangerously* and *Welcome to Sarajevo*. The following is an attempt to classify war films by their basic subgenres:

> • combat • spy and espionage • assassination, terrorist, antiterrorist, paramilitary or mercenary groups • occupation, guerrilla, partisan, underground and resistance movements • missing in action (MIAs) • prisoners of war (POWs) • internment camp, concentration camp or Holocaust experiences • Hitler and Nazism • political thrillers • military legal dramas and scandals • "coming home" stories of postwar veterans • war era and "homefront" experiences • documentaries and biographies • war journalism • prewar and postwar military life •

peacetime war games • Westerns and samurai • epic action adventures and period dramas • exploitation actioners • futuristic sci-fi wars and post-apocalypse survival • satires and comedies • wartime romances, musicals and cartoons.

The focus of this book is on the combat movie—war films about the experiences of men in combat. From this experience all other war-related films have to be understood. Combat is the elemental experience that defines the war movie genre. However, defining which movies are "combat" movies, and which are not is complex, because most war movies mix themes. Determining categories was also made more difficult because the "combat" movie, with few exceptions, is defined by modern war. The experience of men in combat, as a separate and unique story, begins with movies about WW I. Movies about wars that predate WW I generally focus more around romance, heroes and large battles.

I am convinced that all the best "combat" films have been reviewed for this book. It is my hope that there are a large number of combat films here that you are not familiar with and that are well worth your time. If some of your favorite films are not listed, please accept my apologies. For the most part, any combat movie not reviewed was probably of the "B" movie variety, or was not available on video or has gone out of print.

Of all the categories excluded for review as war movies, the one that posed the most difficulty was the epic-adventure-historical drama. Many of the all-time most popular movies fall into this category—*Ben Hur, Braveheart, Gladiator, Lawrence of Arabia*. While all of these movies are about war, and feature spectacular battles and awesome combat scenes, they do not tell the story of the combat soldier. However, in order to satisfy your lust for these entertaining movies, I have made a separate ranking of the best epic-adventure-historical dramas.

Types of Combat Movies

There are many ways to categorize combat movies. The most traditional manner is to divide them up by wars, such as WW I, WW II, Korean Conflict and Vietnam War. However, all combat movies also tell an underlying story, separate from the particular war that is taking place. To help clarify the focus, combat movies will also be identified by the story they tell.

Combat Themes

Combat Hell Portrays the impact of war on soldiers. The focus is on the savageness of combat and the hardship soldiers face—surviving, bonding, confronting death.

Unit Conflict Focuses on individual soldiers. Conflicts revolve around personalities, rank, race, class, ethnicity and nationality.

War is Crazy Reveals the absurdity, senselessness, futility, immorality, irrationality and tragedy of war, often with dark humor, biting satire and devastating ironies.

Combat Duels Typically features a *cat and mouse* struggle between individual soldiers, combat units or commanders.

Military Command Examines the leadership of soldiers and the personal conflicts of leading or sending men into combat.

The Big Battle Shows the operational command and strategic planning of war as a large-scale battle unfolds.

In addition to the combat movie, this book takes a long look at prisoner-of-war movies, military legal dramas, war humor-satire and military life. As you can see, many subgenres were not seriously considered or were only included because they crossed over genres. I attempted to search internationally for important films that were available (dubbed or subtitled) to American audiences. Some films are here simply because they were on the video shelf, and I reasoned that war movie watchers will run into them and be curious about them, as was I.

Reviewing War Movies

While the critics are generally perceptive about the very best and worst films, their opinions often leave a lot to be desired. If you go on-line, the babble of opinions about war movies can become insufferable. Because they're only human, critics can be influenced by all the studio hype surrounding a movie's release, and much of it is directed at them. (Don't kid yourself, well-known critics are lavished with attention by the big studios.) Critics pay attention to the box office receipts published in the trade papers and occasionally have to pander to their audiences and publishers. Critics also have a lot of movies to review and, in some cases, may have little interest in war movies. I am also certain that some critics do not see all the movies they review, particularly those who write for the large video guides.

There is no doubt that critics often get caught up in the movie myth-making process and the power of their words to define a movie's success or its legacy. As a result, many critics too easily dismiss movies or simply go along with the preformed and safe judgments of the past. What the critics can't offer is a reasoned approach to the entire body of contemporary war filmmaking, which this book attempts to do.

Perhaps the most disappointing finding was that many critics tend to dismiss made-for-television movies as not good enough to review. This is unfortunate because many of the very best war movies are made for TV (*Band of Brothers, Gettysburg, A Rumor of War, When Trumpets Fade*). Also, smaller films and foreign movies are often slighted.

Recognizing that reviewing movies can be a subjective process, I have attempted to standardize my criticisms and add balance by utilizing the works of respected critics. Under the heading **References** at the back of the book are listed the eight video guides consulted for the **What the critics say** portion of each review.

"War Realism" in Movies

Obviously, war films are not war, rather they are commercial and artistic enterprises whose primary goals are to make money and entertain a mass audience. This often limits a film's ability to tell us about war. As a war movie "junkie," the most moving portrayals of war, for me, come from watching documentary footage of war. These detached images tell a profound story about war that no movie has ever achieved, as far as I am concerned.

However, war movies offer something both more simple and complex than the documentary. They attempt to tell an entertaining story that revolves around individual lives and experiences with which the audience can identify. At the same time, they attempt to us tell something about the nature of war. How well they do both of these determine if they are great war films.

The single greatest failing of most war movies, and the one that separates the great ones from the average ones, is that the worst films tend to oversimplify their story. The characters are stock, the situations cliché; focus is on patriotism over ambiguity, heroism over ambivalence; and the rich, complex themes of life are reduced to overly simplistic formulas. Many critics will argue that these films are jingoistic or escapist. Many times, I suspect, they are just bad films.

There is one final criterion for judging war movies, and that is what I call "war realism." With the advent of television, news cameras and camcorders, a demand for a higher degree of realism has evolved. The images created for the viewing public with modern technology have also reinforced the already strongly held belief that war is hell. Every review of war films has to take this into consideration. Today, the baseline for evaluating a war film is always how realistically the film portrays "war as hell." This focus takes us up close to the soldier in combat and what he has to endure—the common denominator for all wars and, therefore, for all war films.

Movies that fail to convey that war is hell, that oversimplify war, make it more exciting and glamorous than it is, that minimize the destruction, or sanitize the experience—are often judged to be more propagandistic. At best they may be seen as great escapist entertainment, but not as serious war films. This is one reason that period dramas and action adventure films are not considered war movies for the purposes of this book. All the films reviewed here will be judged by their degree of realism; i.e., "war is hell." Films that simplify this reality lack the realism necessary for a great war film.

War Movies as "Propaganda"

When you watch a war movie and are in awe of the panoramic shots of an aircraft carrier or marvel at the complex helm of a nuclear sub or at the beauty of an F-18 firing an air-to-air missile, do you ever ask, who makes all this available to film producers?—the military! When movies feature thousands of extras all in uniform, with submarines, tanks and artillery, do you ever think about who is paying for all this?—the military!

In the US each military branch of service has an office actively engaged in consulting, participating in and financing war moviemaking (providing the script is acceptable). However, there

15

is a *quid pro quo* for the military's cooperation. In return, the director gives up some degree of editorial control, mutes criticism of the military, deletes an objectionable scene, or chooses not to question strategy or policy. This practice has been ongoing since the 1930s.

The truth is, war films are about more than simply entertaining an audience. They should be viewed as a mixture of entertainment and as an attempt to influence public opinion. In fact, propaganda and entertainment have become so intertwined that it's nearly impossible to separate them, particularly in the best war movies.

From film's earliest beginnings in Europe and the US, producers and directors attempted to influence public opinion towards WW I. In the US, the earliest war films were pacifist and isolationist in their sentiments. Two years later they had become openly hostile to Germany, painting the Kaiser and German soldiers as barbarians. By the 1940s the governments of Germany, England and the Soviet Union were actively using war films as propaganda to influence public opinion at home and abroad. In the US, the collaboration between Hollywood and the Office of War Information in the production of war films was virtually indistinguishable.

Governments have always banned, censored, blacklisted and protested war films for fear of their ability to influence public opinion. Either directly or indirectly, governments have financed and assisted films that furthered their political agendas. Attempts by governments to gain public support for war efforts and to help military recruitment have been and continue to be ongoing.

Writers, producers and directors, independent of the government, have their own unstated political agendas in making a war film. Their views might be "hawkish" or "dovish," "left" or "right," motivated by patriotism or contempt for the establishment, but the war movie as a form of entertainment is rarely a serious attempt to be factual or objective. Ultimately, it is more important that war movies be entertaining than truthful, making most war movies nothing more than a form of disinformation. It is important to keep in mind that when fact and fiction are mixed, the result is always fiction. Because directors and producers hide behind the claim—"it's just a movie"—all movie fans should keep a realist's eye toward the bitter truth—war never takes place in a political or moral vacuum, and is never entertaining.

Sometimes truth-telling in war films can only take place years after the fact, similar to declassifying secret documents. In some cases the facts aren't known; other times the truth isn't considered entertaining. But more often than not, directors and producers are concerned that controversial, fact-based films will not do well at the box-office. This partially explains why Hollywood failed to make movies about the Vietnam War until well after the war.

Unlike Hollywood, however, television has stepped forward to examine military controversies. Responding to the public's demand for contemporary stories and to competition from rival networks, television has, by far and away, done the best job with movies such as *Afterburn*, *A Glimpse of Hell* and *Thanks of a Grateful Nation*. (In the **War Movie Tables** section checkout "Fact-Based Military Scandals.")

"Antiwar" Films

The modern belief regarding war is that while some wars may be more just than others (self-defense or to protect others), all war is ultimately absurd and immoral at some level. Hence, a strong "antiwar" theme in films has been handed down to us from WW I. It is important to note that not all times and places shared this view of war. There were times in human history when war was seen as more noble and justified as a means to an end than it is today. To die in war was heroic; one's afterlife would be more glorious, and those who survived more honored. War was a rite of passage for young men or a chance to move up socially, politically or economically.

The truth is, a nation's or people's motives for war are enormously complex and are still not well understood. Are we genetically programmed? Are there broader biological-and evolutionary-based determinants? Do economic and resource acquisition models better explain this form of social competition and destruction? Or what about the psychological programming that allows so many individuals to conform to such a destructive process? Yes, the political and bureaucratic decision-making process is impersonal, filled with ambition and ineptness.

However, simply having an antiwar sentiment may not be enough. Yes, war is destructive, but is it wrong? Attempts to portray war as irrational and absurd may not provide us a complete understanding. While it's fashionable to talk about the "end of history," it is premature to talk about the "end of war," which appears to a "tragic necessity" for the foreseeable future. Balancing the hope of peace against the reality of war is a struggle every outstanding war movie confronts.

In order to know how people of a particular historical epoch felt about war, we would probably need to know how they felt about death, because the one unwavering fact about war is death. Our modern belief system is strongly defined by an "individualism" that results in less identification with an all-powerful deity, charismatic leader, great cause, holy war or a nation's manifest destiny. Without an overriding identification with something greater than one's self, death becomes increasingly meaningless and without real purpose. As a result, war has become increasingly meaningless and irrational—and all war movies have become antiwar tracts, no matter what the personal tragedy or patriotic message.

Today, audiences understand that war is a hellish and absurd experience, but they also realize it is often a realistic and tragic necessity. The very act of enjoying war in the safe confines of the movie theater partially testifies to this reality. As a result, films that explore the complex stories of soldiers and the broader sense of the absurdity and immorality of war, in conjunction with the soldier's need to understand his war experience and his possible death, achieve the highest goals of filmmaking. I will point you in the direction of the war movies that come closest to achieving these goals.

War Movie "Heroism"

War movie fans watch war movies for the simple pleasure of safely experiencing war vicariously. All efforts at looking deeper into this experience, while intellectually interesting, are of a second, third or fourth order of importance. Audiences enjoy going to war movies for much the same reason they enjoy going to amusement parks—to escape daily routine and to experience thrills without risk. Trying to impart greater meaning to the war movie experience beyond this is presumptuous and risky.

The most significant criticism leveled at war movies, next to the accusation of being propaganda, is that they distort the experience of war by making it look more exciting and adventurous than it is, and minimize the impact of the death and destruction it causes. The worst movies appear to revel in creating mayhem—the hero casually killing dozens if not hundreds of anonymous soldiers as a meaningless gesture of his omnipotence (sometimes this can be a lot of fun to watch).

While it's not really possible to judge whether these films are harmful (numbing audiences to violence or making some individuals more violence prone), they are often vacuous and predictable and seldom, if ever, convey anything important about the experience of war (which is the most important criticism that can be made).

The real problem, for critics and sophisticated audiences alike, emerges under a closer examination of war films that strive for greater authenticity. The fact is, even these war films unintentionally make war appear falsely heroic—including antiwar films. This is truly a conundrum. War movies create protagonists in dramatic and often tragic events, rendering them larger than life on the screen and in the consciousness of the audience.

No matter how stupid a war or meaningless a death from war, the soldier's sacrifice has a heroic element to it that cannot be denied. The act of watching a war movie in its own small way honors this sacrifice and enables viewers to confirm their own nobility by identifying with the tragic but heroic death. More importantly, the audience, through its identification with soldiers on the screen, shares in their celluloid immortality. All of this gives a heroic (and sometimes tragic) unreality to the experience of war, no matter how well portrayed, on the screen.

This doesn't mean that war movie fans should stop watching and enjoying war movies. On the contrary, it's important that these stories be told and watched over and over. War films are an important mechanism for the overwhelming human need to give meaning to our lives and our deaths—much as ancient ritual conferred this protection on our ancestors.

What does this all mean? If a film portrays the enemy as bad or even evil, so be it. In war we tend to dehumanize our enemies. If a film chooses to focus on the heroism of soldiers rather than on the inhumanity of war, that's okay. There's a great deal of heroism and sacrifice in war. Many films do not look at the failures of command or the politics behind the scenes or never allude to the complexities of waging war. I would simply say that there's room for all of these films to be enjoyed as well. There's glamour and excitement in war that cannot be experienced in any other way. There is triumph and elation that can only be achieved with the death of one's mortal enemy. I sometimes want these experiences in a war film. Perhaps it's the totality of all these experiences that tells us the most about war. Although all war movies fail to convey the real horror of war, it's ultimately going to be up to the audience to balance this experience.

Final Thoughts

Early on in writing this book, I stopped telling people about it. Inevitably, they would tell me about their favorite war movies, and I would soon find myself becoming quiet or diplomatic. I discovered that among movie fans, war movie enthusiasts are among the most passionate. Beyond a small handful of films, it was nearly impossible to gain any consensus on the best war movies, and even harder to agree on which ones were bad. Everyone had their favorites; everyone seemed to be seeking their own experiences from these movies, and they all varied.

This book is not an attempt to deny war movie fans the pleasures of a so-called "bad" war movie or judge their boredom with a supposedly great war film. I tried to see all these movies, as if for the first time, and judge them as contemporary films. I asked—do these films speak to today's audience in a meaningful way? With this objective in mind, it became readily apparent that all war movies are a product of their times. Ultimately, no film transcends its epoch, the best are simply appreciated a little longer, and then forgotten by the public.

If you are anxious to see which movies are considered the best in their class, turn to the section titled **War Movie Tables**. Here you will get an opportunity to debate the best war satires, movies about Nazism or films about journalists at war. For those interested in how Vietnam War movies are different from WW II movies, or how war movies evolved or changed based on the conflict being portrayed, turn to **About War Movies: WW I to Vietnam**. At the very end is a **War Movie Index** classifying all the films reviewed by the war they represent and their subgenres.

I hope you enjoy this book. It was fun to research and write. More importantly, I hope you find a few new war movies that you really enjoy. If you have comments or suggestions please contact me at **gyalf@aol.com**. PS. For those who are impatient and want to find out immediately which movies are considered the best, the "25 Greatest Action War Movies" and the "25 Greatest War Dramas" are listed on the next two pages.

—Gary Freitas
Phoenix, Arizona

25 Greatest Action War Movies

ANZACS *1987 AUS tv*

Band of Brothers *2001 USA tv*

Das Boot *1981 GER*

Beast, The *1988 USA*

Black Hawk Down *2002 USA*

Blue Max, The *1966 USA*

Crimson Tide *1995 USA*

84 Charlie MoPic *1989 USA*

Full Metal Jacket *1987 USA*

Gettysburg *1993 USA tv*

Glory *1989 USA*

Hamburger Hill *1987 USA*

Light Horsemen, The *1987 AUS*

Platoon *1986 USA*

Battle for Port Arthur, The *1986 JAP*

Pretty Village, Pretty Flame *1996 GRE/YUG*

Rumor of War, A *1980 USA tv*

Saving Private Ryan *1998 USA*

Shot Through the Heart *1998 USA/CAN*

Stalingrad *1993 GER*

Thin Red Line , The *1998 USA*

Three Kings *1999 USA*

317th Platoon *1965 FRA*

To Hell and Back *1955 USA*

When Trumpets Fade *1998 USA tv*

25 Greatest War Dramas

Andersonville *1996 USA tv*

All the King's Men *1999 GBR tv*

Attack! *1956 USA*

Battle of Algiers, The *1965 ITA/ALG*

Behind the Lines *1997 GB R*

Breaker Morant *1980 AUS*

Born on the Fourth of July *1989 USA*

Bright Shining Lie , A *1998 USA*

Capitaine Conan *1996 FRA*

Catch 22 *1970 USA*

Come and See *1985 RUS*

Dr. Strange Love *1963 GBR*

The Hanoi Hilton *1987 USA*

Human Condition, The *1959 JAP*

Judgment at Nuremburg *1961 USA*

Man Escaped, A *1956 FRA*

No Man's Land *2001 BOS-HRZ*

Patton *1970 USA*

Piece of Cake *1989 GBR tv*

Prisoners of the Sun *1990 AUS*

Seven Days in May *1964 USA*

Twelve O'Clock High *1949 USA*

Underground *1995 SER/FRA*

Welcome to Sarajevo *1997 USA*

Winds of War *1983 USA et al.*

WAR MOVIES A-Z

"Only God has seen the end of war."
Plato

Above and Beyond

1952 USA b/w d. Melvin Franks/Norman Panama

WW II: Pilot Who Dropped Atom Bomb   3.0

How is it that one of the most interesting and important stories of the Second World War somehow devolves into a struggling and unhappy relationship. Yes, Hollywood is at it again! This rather conventional 1950s biopic of Col. Paul W. Tibbets (Robert Taylor), the pilot who dropped the first atom bomb (on Hiroshima), is unable to separate the wheat from the chaff. What would you rather watch, Tibbets working as a test pilot in the development of the B-29, or him and his wife Lucy (Eleanor Parker) arguing over the fact that they have only been together seven week during their five-year marriage? (He's a busy guy. I mean it's wartime; can't a guy ever catch a break!) Tibbets was a B-17 pilot with 25 missions over Europe when he was selected to work on the development of the B-29. From here, he was chosen to operationalize the 509th B-29 Squadron and prepare it for dropping of "The Bomb." Security issues surrounding this program, flight crew selection and training, and the development of tactics for delivery could be really interesting. Instead, we get Lucy upset that Tibbets has completely cut her out of his life, and appears to be totally indifferent to their two children. (We all know that this top secret mission allows him to be a jerk—hey! this is 1945.) But where this movie really let's us down is in its failure to explore any of the complex moral, political and military issues associated with this monumental event. What Tibbets felt or believed remains unknown to us beyond the conventional wisdom that this weapon would shorten the war and save American lives. The movie's best moment comes when the bomb is delivered and the crew understand for the first time the enormity of the destruction and the unworldly power of this weapon. *Above and Beyond* would have us believe that Lucy and Paul lived happily ever after. I suspect that the real story, for Col. Tibbets, was just beginning.

What the critics say Critics rate this movie 1.0 to 4.0. "Overstretched flagwaver...of little real interest then or now."[1] "Good performance by Taylor...exciting sequences of the mission itself."[5] **Final Word** The B-29 flown by Tibbets was named after his mother Enola Gay. An even worse 1980 TV remake came out titled *Enola Gay: The Men, the Mission, the Atomic Bomb*.

Above Us the Waves

1955   GBR   b/w   d. Ralph Thomas

WW II: British Minisubs	2.0

The famous British stiff upper lip may well have reached its apogee (or perhaps stasis), in this rather listless war-actioner. Based on true events in 1943, the British are desperate to sink the German battleship KMS *Tirpitz* to prevent it from disrupting their merchant shipping lanes in the North Atlantic. The only problem is that the *Tirpitz* is anchored 60 miles up a Norwegian fjord and nearly impossible to bomb from the air, due to the steep mountainsides. It is also impenetrable from the sea, due to shore batteries and air cover. But the ever ingenious British have a plan. Led by Commander Frasier (John Mills), they develop two Mark 1 Human Torpedoes—open cockpit minisubs manned by two men in diving gear. The minisubs are to be towed to within a mile of the *Tirpitz*, where they will submerge and attach mines to the German ship. Unfortunately, the minisubs sink in heavy seas. But, by some miracle, the British Admiralty immediately produces three minisubmarines that are self-contained, with a crew of five men each, and truly submersible. This rather documentary-style movie, filmed mostly in the dark, never explains how these rather sophisticated weapons (X-Type submarines) were suddenly developed. No effort is made to suggest any training is required to operate them. But what really stops this movie in its own cavitation, is our having to follow the crews of all three minisubs. This is akin to watching three slow-moving submarine movies at the same time. Events also tend to blur at the end. One sub is sunk and the crews of the remaining two are captured, but not before they attach mines to the *Tirpitz*. While the mines damage the *Tirpitz,* they do not sink it. In fact, this movie never explains whether this ship is sunk by the minisubs. There are no subplots or characters to really speak of in this British flagwaving effort. The movie's one refreshing deviation from British war dramas is the absence of class or rank conflicts here—there are only heroic men risking their lives.

What the critics say Critics rate this movie 2.0 to 4.0. "Disappointing action sequences and jumbled continuity."[1] "Fine cast in exciting submarine drama."[2] "Doesn't do the action justice."[8] **Final Word** For those who are interested, the British sank the *Tirpitz* from the air later in the war.

Aces High
1976 GBR color d. Jack Gold

WW I: Aerial Combat	2.5

This movie fires a lot of shots at mostly unmoving targets and somehow manages to miss just about every one. A popular play by R.C. Sherriff, *Journey's End*, about British soldiers surviving trench warfare (made into a movie in 1930), was adapted to this story of aerial warfare. In 1917 newly trained fighter pilot Lt. Croft (Peter Firth) joins the 76th Squadron of the Royal Flying Corps in France, ten miles from the front. He's a naive and idealistic, young pilot who admires the Squadron Commander, Maj. Gresham (Malcolm McDowell), a fighter ace and war hero. Both had previously attended the same public school. What we are really entering into with this squadron is the snobbish social world of the British class system, where nearly all the pilots came from privileged families. This could be Oxford or Cambridge at war with Germany as much as the RFC. The drama is over the fact that most new pilots have an average life-expectancy of 14 days. Gresham, now drinking heavily in order to cope, is ambivalent about protecting his young protégé, and fearful of becoming overly attached. Mostly we get a long burst of club camaraderie—singing, dancing, drinking and carousing over a seven-day period. The story fires a few rounds at the emptiness of putting on a good front (the stiff upper-lip thing). In one scene a captured German pilot, of upper-class origins, is treated as more of an equal than the British enlisted men. The movie also fires a few rounds at British command for its refusal to issue parachutes and to treat pilots as expendable resources, while the generals partied and indulged social lives. Ultimately, this movie rings hollow with its simple character-izations. With all the interesting conflicts raised here, it would have been more satisfying if these pilots had been forced to confront these issues. Simply getting drunk is not enough. While we get to see some good footage of SE-5s, the action is mostly average, and the German planes are not as authentic as the British planes.

What the critics say Critics rate this movie 2.0 to 3.5. "Spirited if rather unnecessary remake of *Journey's End* transposed to the air war, which makes it identical to *The Dawn Patrol*."[1] "Strong antiwar statement, solid cast...exciting aerial dogfights."[2] **Final Word** British public school boys find out that dying is neither a game nor glamorous.

Action in the North Atlantic
1943 USA b/w d. Lloyd Bacon

WW II: Merchant Marines	2.5

The video-box proudly proclaims, "Heroic, one of the most rousing propaganda films of the 1940s." Damning praise indeed. After the fourth or fifth patriotic speech, you quickly realize that all these points could have been better made by making a good movie and not preaching to the audience. Raymond Massey (Capt. Jarvis) and Humphrey Bogart (Lt. Joe Rossi) star in this story of the Merchant Marines, the men who manned the freighters and cargo ships that delivered war supplies to America's allies during WW II. While the risks and dangers associated with Allied efforts to break the German blockade of the Atlantic are conveyed here, the movie lacks compelling storytelling or great action. The best part of this movie is the first fifteen minutes, when the *Northstar* is torpedoed by a German U-boat. We watch as the frantic efforts of these men to rescue their ship quickly turns to saving themselves, as the ship is about to go down. When the U-boat captain rams their lifeboat, you know the propaganda war is on. The rest of this film never quite lives up to the opening. After the crew is rescued, there's a long sequence comprised, mostly, of Bogart reprising his tough-guy role of Sam Spade and marrying a club singer. Then the movie starts all over again, but this time on a new ship with the same crew in convoy to Murmansk in the Soviet Union. Here a *cat and mouse* game ensues with a German submarine, with long action sequences of subs torpedoing freighters, and subs getting depth-charged in return. The point of view of this film is completely lost for a half-hour, and the viewer is hearing so much German that one might begin to wonder which country this was propaganda for. The special effects are continually distracting as the models keep losing perspective. Overly long, poorly plotted, and with a crew of walking, talking clichés, the film is clearly a propaganda vehicle.

What the critics say Critics rate this movie 3.0 to 4.5. "Efficient propaganda potboiler; studio-bound, but stills works as an actioner."[1] "Rousing tribute to WW 2 merchant marine."[2] "Though conceived and produced as unvarnished propaganda...this sea-going adventure is still enjoyable as nostalgic entertainment."[6] **Final Word** Strictly for the nostalgic war movie kind of guy who can't sleep late at night.

The Affair

1995 USA color tv d. Paul Seed

WW II: Race-Based Drama 3.5

How much viewers enjoy this movie may well depend on whether they believe the facts of the story. The prologue states that this movie was "inspired" by real events (which is somewhat vague). In 1944 a Black-American GI, Travis Holloway (Courtney Vance), while stationed in England, is court-martialed and hanged for the rape of a married, white English woman, Maggie Leyland (Kerry Fox). The movie makes it clear that the two are, in fact, having an affair while her naval officer husband is at sea. When the officer discovers them having sex, he beats Holloway, because he believes his wife is being raped. Initially, Maggie goes along with this story until her husband discovers the truth. He then threatens to divorce her for adultery and take their child if she doesn't perjure herself and claim she was raped. Later, when Maggie realizes that the sentence is not just a few months in the brig but death, she goes to the army and recants her testimony. However, the army ignores her and hangs Pvt. Holloway. This movie also suggests that Travis had a letter from Maggie that would have exonerated him, but instead of presenting this evidence Travis keeps it to himself out love for Maggie. Many things are done well here, but the constant nagging concern about what the real facts are is disconcerting. If the facts are accurate—this is a powerful story. If not, it's very manipulative. The first half of this movie is a superior depiction of Black soldiers dealing with racism in the army and anticipating combat. Confronted with being in a foreign country for the first time, they are having difficulty reading the cultural signals about England's toleration for Black men and white women. The performances are solid and the script is thoughtful in creating interesting and real people. The idea that Travis sees a better possibility for the whole world in his relationship with Maggie adds a bitter twist to this film. The pervading sense of doom that foreshadows this tragic event makes for heavy but involved viewing.

What the critics say Critics rate this movie 1.0 to 4.0. "Bittersweet story of forbidden love...surprisingly honest racial drama."[1] "A disappointing attempt to address an interesting and much overlooked subject."[8] **Final Word** The fact is—Holloway, sentenced to hang, was dishonorably discharged thanks to anti-lynching protests in the US.

Afterburn

1992 USA color tv d. Robert Markowitz

Military Life: Air Force Cover-Up 3.5

Yet another military scandal. How many times can these bureaucracies get it wrong without learning a thing? In 1979 Capt. Ted Harduvel (Vincent Spano), an Air Force F-16 fighter pilot, lost control of his plane and crashed. A formal investigation attributed the cause of the crash to pilot error. This movie focuses on Janet Harduvel (Laura Dern), his wife of six years, and her efforts to clear his name. Dern excels in this role. Janet Harduvel then proceeds to do the unthinkable—take General Dynamics, the manufacturer of the F-16, to court. Her attorney (Robert Loggia) makes it clear than no one has ever successfully sued a major defense contractor. Her odyssey to bring General Dynamics to court is astounding, to say the least. Rejected by most of her Air Force friends and financially broke, she begins to accumulate detailed information on the planes electronics and get experts to analyze the data. Equally important, an officer sends her a copy of the confidential accident report. In court it is demonstrated that there was a design flaw in many of the early F-16s, which resulted in the wiring chaffing from protruding screws, which short-circuited the planes electronic guidance system. A jury awarded Janet Harduvel 3.5 million dollars and cleared her husband's name. On appeal, the award was overturned on the grounds that government contractors are "protected from liability." An epilogue noted that from 1979 to 1992, 140 F-16s had crashed. While much of the early part of this movie is overly focused on the Harduvel's romantic relationship, when it gets to the main story, it packs a wallop.

What the critics say Critics rate this movie 3.5 to 5.0. "Doesn't get much better than this scathing indictment."[5] **Final Word** Check out these real military scandals and cover-ups: *A Glimpse of Hell* (explosion on the USS Iowa), *Mission of the Shark* (scapegoated naval officer), *The Pentagon Wars* (defense contractor overruns), *Serving in Silence* (lesbianism), *Sgt. Mattock vs. the US. Air Force* (homosexuality), *Thanks of a Grateful Nation* (Gulf War Syndrome).

Air Force

1943   USA   b/w   d. Howard Hawks

WW II: Classic '40s Flagwaver	2.0

Directed by Howard Hawks and based loosely on actual events, this movie opens with an introduction to the crew of the B-17 "Mary Ann," who are a swell bunch of guys from all over the country. We meet their lovely wives, their doting mothers, the nervous rookie and the veteran crew chief (Harry Carey). All the officers are handsome and confident (Gig Young, Charles Drake, John Ridgely and Arthur Kennedy). There is a bad apple (John Garfield) with an attitude that the war straightens out. The "Mary Ann" and a flight of eight B-17s are on their way to Hawaii, and arrive as the Japanese are bombing Pearl Harbor. After a hazardous landing, they are immediately ordered to Manila by way of Wake Island. Most of this movie revolves around the interaction of the crew while in the air and as they survey the destruction at each landing. Somewhere along the line they add a cute dog (no orphan children this time, I guess). Upon arriving in Manila, the crew is sent on a bombing run in which the pilot is wounded. After an interminable death scene the movie does something peculiar—it keeps going for another half hour. The death was truly the end of the movie, but Hawks decided to turn the story into an actioner and give the audience a happy ending. The crew escape Japanese soldiers, accidentally discover the Japanese fleet and radio its location, and safely crash-land in Australia. We last see them taking-off to bomb Tokyo. Lots of things don't work here. The movie has really bad special effects, but more importantly, it keeps repeating itself, and you eventually tire of this plane landing and taking off without the plot being advanced. There's almost nothing remotely interesting about this crew, and the one guy with the bad attitude gives it up too easily. In ending this movie twice and extending it to nearly two hours, director Howard Hawksdeprives it of energy and focus.

What the critics say Critics rate this movie 2.0 to 5.0. "Tough to stomach at times...but generally exciting, well done."[2] "It is gripping, informative, entertaining, thrilling."[4] "One of the finest of the WW II movies."[5] "This is essentially wartime propaganda."[8] **Final Word** Movies such as this served the vital function of maintaining public morale during the war. It's hard to imagine them doing anything less, but the temptation to pretend, today, that they were good films is probably misplaced sentiment.

All Quiet on the Western Front

1930   USA   b/w   d. Lewis Milestone

WW I: War is Crazy	3.0

This is the most famous and honored of all war movies. It won the Academy Award for best picture in 1930, and the American Film Institute calls it one of the top 100 films of all time. Based on the book by Erich Maria Remarque, himself a German soldier wounded on the Western Front, this epic cost an enormous amount to produce at the time—$1.25 million and a cast of 2,000 extras. In 1933 the book was banned in Germany, forcing Remarque to immigrate to the US. The movie is the archetype for nearly every war movie that has followed. An attempt to portray the horrors of modern war, *All Quiet on the Western Front* was not a "combat" movie, but clearly a vehicle for critical commentary about war itself. There's no attempt to involve us in this war in terms of strategy or command decision making. We see it only from the viewpoint of the soldier fighting in the trenches. One of the main themes focuses on how the elite classes in society use propaganda and hysteria to rally the populace to war against peoples in other countries. This is shown as we watch seven young, naive and patriotic students enlist in the German army in 1914. The focus is on Paul Bäumer (Lew Ayres) who is a particularly bright and sensitive young man. We watch as the young men are quickly disillusioned and ultimately killed. In between, we are shown the horrors of trench warfare, with a number of outstanding combat scenes bringing us up close to the mindless futility and destruction wrought by machine guns and artillery. This movie clearly reflects much of the populist sentiment of the Depression Era, with its "aw shucks" naiveté and portrayal of the innocence of the "common man." As a result, there's very little character or story development. We follow these young men, but don't learn much about them. The film preaches a message when it could better depict it. At times, the movie lapses into a sentimentality that would certainly embarrass modern movie goers, as it uses many overly-dramatic moments to highlight a point. Much of what was original to this movie will now appear cliché today.

What the critics say Critics rate this movie 5.0. **Final Word** Should be seen as a movie of great historical interest, rather than a compelling war drama for modern audiences. The film was remade for TV in 1979.

All the King's Men
1999   GBR   color   tv   d. Julian Jarrold

| WW I: Antiwar Drama | 5.0 |

This Masterpiece Theater drama, derived from a book by Nigel McCrery, is based on true events. In 1915 Capt. Frank Beck (David Jason) organized a volunteer company of soldiers comprised of young men, with some as young as 14, working on the royal estate of George V and Queen Margaret. Capt. Beck, manager of the royal estate and a decorated hero of the Boer War, has grown bored with the bucolic paradise he has created in the English countryside. More importantly, he has grown vain from praise for his earlier heroism and in his belief he can duplicate the past. Too old to serve, he uses his influence to obtain active duty for his volunteer company who are immediately assigned to serve in the Dardanelles Campaign—otherwise known as Gallipoli. What Beck slowly comes to realize is how absolutely foolish he has been, particularly in his unquestioned belief in the infallibility of the British army. He has remembered war through the eyes of a young man. He is totally unprepared for the chaos and the sheer ineptness of British High Command. An utterly horrific scene of two soldiers being killed while searching for snipers has an immediacy and visceral quality that you will never forget. The story has any number of interesting and thoughtful subplots. In the end, the company is ordered to march on a Turkish position and is never seen again. While the story of their disappearance soon becomes myth, a postwar investigation by the British army confirms that these men had been captured and massacred by Turkish troops, and then buried to hide the fact. For political reasons the British army did not tell the public, as they wanted to leave the "miracle" intact. Although somewhat slow moving in the beginning, this is a deeply moving and thoughtful film that shows us youthful innocence and paradise lost due to the aging vanity and restlessness of a good man. Poet Siegfried Sassoon, writing about war, is quoted in the epilogue—"and pray you'll never know the hell where youth and laughter go."

What the critics say Critics rate this movie 3.0. "The storyline is muddled and it's not easy to distinguish one youthful character from another (although the veterans do a notable job)."[5] **Final Word** One of the best war movies this critic has ever seen, but only for serious war drama guys. Absolutely rent this one!

All the Young Men
1960 USA b/w d. Hall Bartlett

As war movies go, this low-budget actioner is indistinguishable from dozens of Korean War movies, except for one detail. This movie will get a footnote as one of the first to star a Black male lead (Sidney Poitier), and to make racial prejudice an important theme. The fact that it doesn't do a very good job is disappointing. (Prior to this movie the only war film to star a Black male lead was James Edwards in *Home of the Brave* in 1949.) *All the Young Men* opens in Korea in 1950, with a Marine platoon on patrol with orders to occupy a farm house at a key mountain pass, and to hold it at all costs until a Marine battalion is able to move up. Ambushed by North Korean soldiers, they take heavy casualties. When the lieutenant is wounded, he appoints Sgt. Towler (Sidney Poitier) in command just before he dies. This does not sit well with the platoon who trusts Sgt. Kincaid (Alan Ladd). Right from the get-go Sgt. Kincaid and Pvt. Bracken (Paul Richards) make race an issue, as they refer to Towler as a "black boy," and disrespect him. When Towler orders them to hold the farm house and not try to make it safely back, Kincaid questions Towler's ability to lead—"See, they're just not able to do it. They're not born to do it." Towler responds one-dimensionally. He aggressively asserts his authority and takes charge. This is where the movie basically fails, in its depiction of rather simple characters with limited responses to this crisis. There's also some odd casting—heavy-weight boxing champion Ingemar Johansson sings a Swedish folk song and comedian Mort Sahl improvises schtick that falls flat. Holed up in the farm house, while mostly shooting-the-bull, they fight off the attacking North Koreans. In the movie's best moment Kincaid (the white guy) has his leg crushed by a tank. Its worst moment immediately follows when he undergoes a transfusion with blood from Towler (the Black guy). This feeble attempt at irony makes for a happy ending but not a satisfying movie.

What the critics say The critics rate this movie 1.0 to 3.5. "Hackneyed Korean War story...mouthing the same old platitudes."[2] "Fairly powerful men-uniting-in-battle story."[5] **Final Word** In the same year *Sergeant Rutledge* came out starring Woody Strode. Hollywood taking its time. Black male leads would not really appear until the 1990s.

35

The Anderson Platoon

1967 FRA b/w d. Pierre Schoendoerffer

Vietnam War: Documentary	5.0

This grainy 65-minute black and white documentary was made and narrated by Pierre Schoendoerffer, a Frenchman who had previously served in the French army in Indochina. He states that he returned to Vietnam to revisit what he left. The title is derived from Lt. Anderson, a Black West Point graduate who leads a 1st Air Cavalry platoon of 33 men. Beginning in November 1966, Schoendoerffer chronicles events surrounding this platoon for six weeks. You are immediately aware that what you are seeing is much more serious than any fictional war movie. The camera lingers on the faces of the men as they are introduced by name, rank and home town. Unlike WW II documentaries, in this unique film you are much closer to the individual soldiers. Their faces are recognizable, and the pace of events is much slower. From the moment the camera starts, the scenes are intense and involving, ultimately giving you haunting and powerful images of men in combat being wounded and dying. This film also provides a close-up view of the Vietnamese people, the soldiers frequent contact with children, and the involvement of the villagers in supporting the Vietcong. There is no doubting this film maker's intentions, given the editing and the music that accompanies the images. This is a strong antiwar statement by a French soldier who had already experienced the folly of it all. The question has to be asked, where are other great documentary films on the Vietnam War?

What the critics say Critics rate this movie 4.0 to 4.5. "Vivid striking images."[2] "Harrowing documentary...a fascinating film that finally produces overwhelming sadness for the embattled young men."[3] "A rough, unpolished, direct look at the early days of American involvement...attempts no grand statement, no conclusions."[6] **Final Word** Four of my references did not mention this film, which won the Academy Award for Best Documentary in 1967. This unique war film has no equivalent. I highly recommend that you see it. Warning. This is for students of war, not action movie junkies.

Andersonville
1996 USA color tv d. John Frankenheimer

Civil War: Prisoner-of-War	4.5

This unremittingly grim and unflinching look at the inhumane conditions in the notorious Confederate military camp at Andersonville, Georgia, is the second of Ted Turner's made-for-television Civil War blockbusters (the first was *Gettysburg*). The movie opens at the battle of Cold Harbor, Virginia, and the capture of Union soldiers from the 19th Massachusetts Volunteers in June 1864. Told through the eyes of Cpl. Josiah Day (Jarrod Emick), we descend into a hell where survival is the only law. The camp, a walled enclosure with guard towers, was designed to house only 8,000 prisoners. However, in its 14 months of operation, its standing population grew to over 30,000 and, during its entire course of operation, it housed over 45,000 men. The slight stream that ran through the camp was polluted with effluents and could not be used for drinking or bathing. Soldiers had to capture rain water in order to drink. There were no facilities to house the prisoners, no clothing, no bedding and only limited food rations. During this nightmare, 12,912 soldiers died. Cpl. Day and a handful of soldiers from his unit were completely unprepared for what they were about to face. The very first night they are severely beaten and robbed of all their possessions by a band of criminally organized soldiers who terrorize the camp. We are also given a glimpse of the camp commander, Capt. Henry Wirz (Jan Triska), who comes across as a bureaucratic weasel. His rationalization of the atrocities he oversaw apparently wasn't good enough, as he was hanged at the end of the Civil War (see the review for the excellent *Andersonville Trial*). The cast, comprised of relative unknowns, give excellent performances throughout. While this movie is too long and fails to involve us fully in the lives of its characters, don't hesitate to rent it. An outstanding movie about human courage and dignity.

What the critics say Critics rate this movie 3.0 to 4.0. "Testament to the moral heights—and depths—man can attain."[3] "Harrowing Civil War drama...powerful, hard-hitting performances and a tough, literate script."[7] **Final Word** This is one of the best in the POW genre. Nearly all the films that preceded it have been too cute and too contrived.

Andersonville Trial

1970 USA color tv d. George C. Scott

Civil War: Legal Drama   4.0

The only Confederate soldier hanged for "war crimes" at the end of the Civil War was the superintendent of the Andersonville military camp for Union POWs at Andersonville, Georgia. This play, adapted from the Pulitzer Prize-winning book of the same name by MacKinlay Kantor, shows us the trial of Capt. Henry Wirz (Richard Basehart), which took place in Washington, D.C. in August 1865. Tried by a military commission, Wirz was charged with criminal conspiracy to destroy the lives of soldiers in violation of the laws and customs of war. The facts are not in dispute. During Andersonville's fourteen months of operation, its prison population grew from 10,000 to over 32,000 men, of which 12,912 died from hunger, disease, deprivation and abuse. The camp was an inhumane and hellish experience. The defense attorney (Jack Cassidy), argues that this is nothing more than a political show-trial, and that four months after Lincoln's assassination his client could not receive a fair trial. The Judge Advocate (William Shatner), realizing he couldn't make his case solely on the basis of criminal conspiracy, and not wanting to be party to the same mentality that enabled Wirz to be so callous to the POWs, seeks to convict Wirz for crimes of conscience. He argues that Wirz's defense of "following orders" was not sufficient in the face of the terrible atrocities he oversaw at the camp. In truth, it appears that this was nothing more than a show-trial and that Wirz's fate was predetermined. This well-done but flawed play probably tried to tell us too much. While the performances are outstanding throughout, its lengthiness makes any attempt to follow the subtlety of the arguments extremely demanding. However, the movie's biggest failure is its predictability and failure to make coherent Wirz's guilt. The dramatic ending, to which this entire play points, is anticlimactic and, at times, unclear. The fact was, Wirz was an overseer of these atrocities because he was passive and fearful in the face of authority. This was the case the play should have laid out.

What the critics say Critics rate this movie 4.5. "This is one of the great accounts of the Civil War."[7] **Final Word** The Union POW camp for Confederate soldiers at Elmira, NY, known as the "Andersonville of the North" contained 9,400 prisoners of which 3,000 died.

ANZACS

1985   AUS   color   tv   d. George Miller

WW I: Combat Hell	4.5

ANZACS is an acronym for the Australian/New Zealand Army Corps, a volunteer force that fought with the Allies against the Central Powers during World War I. This movie follows a handful of volunteers, in 1915, from civilian life through basic training and a disastrous landing at Gallipoli, to finally the Western Front in 1918. Of course, we know from having watched other outstanding Australian war films that the English are the real enemy. The commanding British general characterizes the ANZACS as "colonial hooligans" and suggests they shoot a few to set an example. He is upset when informed that the Australian army banned the execution of its soldiers because the British had done this during the Boer War. Near the war's end, all five ANZACS brigades are united under Australian command. The Australian commander tells a junior officer—"Its a pity about the British. They draw their officers from a narrow social class. Oh, sure some of them are good, but in a war like this there is not enough to go around. It has cost them dearly." In the many excellent battles scenes the film portrays of the horrors of trench warfare. These scenes are highly realistic and sobering. If there's truly one underlying theme in this movie, it's the spirit of the ANZACS soldiers and their loyalty to one another, from generals down to privates. (There is no doubt that if you couldn't fight in the American army, the Australian army would have been your second choice.) What keeps this from being a truly outstanding war film is its editing. Because the film started as a miniseries, it was edited down to two hours and forty-five minutes, or 45 minutes too long. The result is a movie that begins to lose emotional and plot focus, as it appears to start over several times. There is also a rather perfunctory romance that never takes off, a "stirring" speech that should have been edited out, and a silly moment near the end, featuring Paul Hogan (Pvt. Pat Cleary), that doesn't work.

What the critics say Critics rate this movie 4.0. "Well made Australian TV miniseries."[5] "Emphasis is upon friendship and loyalty among Australians. A powerful war film that dwells on the people involved, not the machinery."[7] **Final Word** A very good movie that, unfortunately, seems to have been forgotten. Check it out, mate!

Anzio

1968   ITA   color   d. Edward Dmytryk

WW II: Battle of Anzio   3.0

This story is loosely based on the memoirs of war correspondent
Wynford Vaughan Thomas, and stars Robert Mitchum as Dick
Ennis, a war correspondent covering the Allied invasion of Anzio.
The title is misleading, since the movie is mostly about a squad
of Army rangers trapped behind German lines, and not about the
fighting that took place on the beaches at Anzio. On January 22,
1944, American and British troops staged an amphibious assault
at Anzio in an attempt to outflank the Germans, who had
stalemated Allied forces at Cassino. While the assault initially
surprised Field Marshal Kesselring, the German commander-in-
chief. The battle quickly bogged down into a bloody stalemate. A
breakout didn't occur until May. Allied losses totaled 7,000 dead
and 36,000 wounded. This movie, through the Mitchum
character, has some tough talk for the American commanders. In
a battle surrounded with historical controversy, the film criticizes
military command—something very rare in American war-movie
making. The case is made that American commanders had been
overly cautious and had failed to take advantage of having
surprised the Germans. As a consequence, the Germans were
able to reinforce their positions, which resulted in significant
Allied losses. As Mitchum puts it, "He walked them into a park
and left them in a graveyard." "Ain't it a bitch. A dumb, dirty,
stupid, useless bitch." While this is not a great movie, it's not as
bad as the critics have suggested. This film demonstrates a
strong empathy for the "grunts" who paid the price with their
lives, and Mitchum gives a good performance as a war cor-
responent who is not afraid to tell the brass the way he sees it.
There are also a number of excellent combat scenes and no
false heroism. The movie fails in the meandering storyline that
tries to be a little of everything, with long, unrelated soap-opera-
ish interludes and digressions.

What the critics say Critics rate this movie 2.5 to 3.0.
"Undistinguished retelling of Allied invasion of Anzio."[2] "Suffers
from flat writing, stock performances, uninspired direction and
dull pacing".[4] **Final Word** You might want to read *Anzio: The
Gamble That Failed* by M. Blumenson. This author makes the
case that Churchill's ill-conceived plan had no impact on the
war's outcome.

Apocalypse Now
1979   USA   color   d. Francis Ford Coppola

Vietnam War: War is Crazy   4.0

This movie opens with Captain Willard (Martin Sheen) of the 505th Battalion, 173rd Airborne on a second tour of duty in 'Nam in 1969. In reality he is a CIA assassin, given a mission to "terminate without prejudice" a renegade American Special Forces officer, Colonel Kurtz (Marlon Brando), who has gone native in Cambodia and is conducting his own private war. Kurtz is worshipped as a god by Montaguard tribesmen. The movie follows Captain Willard on a lengthy patrol boat journey upriver to Cambodia to find and kill Colonel Kurtz. However, this movie has far larger pretensions than to tell a simple story. At a ponderous pace, with dark images that are at times surrealistic (based loosely on Joseph Conrad's *Heart of Darkness*), the film leads us to believe that this journey and climatic showdown between Willard and Kurtz will tell us about the Vietnam War and perhaps about war itself. All I can tell you is that the movie doesn't deliver. While there is much brilliance in this film, it becomes weighted down with artistic statement and self-importance. The final confrontation is anticlimactic and confusing. This film delivers many vague messages: war is madness; war is bureaucratic bumbling; war must be waged beyond morality; war will create a madness of the soul. The best reason to watch this movie is for the 20-minute sequence starring Robert Duvall. He plays Lt. Col. Kilgore, an air cavalry commander. This is the only part of the movie that truly comes alive. Wearing a Union Civil War hat, blaring Wagner's *Die Walküre* from his attack gunships, obsessed with surfing and war ("someday this war will end" he notes with ironic-sadness), he becomes a brilliant metaphor for American machismo in war. And to think that this is what the film could have been about!

What the critics say Critics rate this movie 4.5 to 5.0. "Pretentious war movie."[1] "A mind blowing, semi-hallucinating examination of the insanity of the Vietnam War."[3] "Epic vision of war."[5] "An exceptional war film in every sense."[7] **Final Word** The American Film Institute (AFI) rates it as one of the top 100 films. Twenty years later this film is honored more for what it attempted to achieve than for its success. If you have not seen it, check it out. It's a lot of fun.

Assault at West Point
1994 USA color tv d. Harry Moses

| Military Life: Race-Based Scandal | 3.5 |

This historical drama casts a pall not only on West Point and the US Army but on the nation itself. Based on a book by John F. Marszdek, *The Court-Martial of Johnson Whittaker*, the prologue states, "This is a true story" and notes that events have been substantiated by more than 12,000 pages of documents at the National Archives. The facts are as follows: Whittaker (Seth Gilliam), born a slave, was the first Black-American admitted to West Point. For four years he was ostracized by the cadets who never spoke to him except to issue an order or command. Two months before he was to graduate, in 1880, he was assaulted in his room, hog tied, and suspended from his bed by his feet and left unconscious. The Army charged him with "conduct unbecoming a cadet and gentleman," and court-martialed him for assaulting himself. His motive? Fear of failing a philosophy exam to be taken in several months. This movie focuses primarily on the legal drama. Johnson was represented by Daniel Chamberlain (Sam Waterston), a southern attorney, and by Richard Greener (Samuel L. Jackson), a Harvard-educated Black attorney. The conflict between the two attorneys is the substantive story here. Greener sees immediately that while Chamberlain may have an enlightened attitude towards Blacks, he's still racist and presents a defense too concerned with "upholding the honor of the academy." It's also evident that prosecution witnesses are perjuring themselves, and that the overall pejorative view of Blacks as inferior ensures a finding of guilty. Whittaker was court-martialed and dishonorably dismissed from the academy and sentenced to a year of hard labor. A year later the President set aside the sentence, but Whittaker was not graduated, having failed philosophy. In an attempt to put the justice system and military on trial, this well-acted and well-scripted presentation fails to tell us about Whittaker.

What the critics say Critics rate this movie 3.0 to 3.5. "Interesting case but a shallow production."[5] The story never connects."[7] **Final Word** Still packs considerable punch, and provides insight into racism in the 1880s that should shock contemporary sensibilities.

Attack!
1956   USA   b/w   d. Robert Aldrich

WW II: Intense Unit Conflict   4.0

Edgy, intense, compelling drama, this movie by director Robert Aldrich is one of the first serious attempts to examine the potentially fratricidal conflict within a combat unit. Clearly, this is the anti-1940s flagwaver—the antithesis of the "work together" mentality of nearly every previous WW II movie. Based on the play *Fragile Fox* by Norman Brooks, the film has an outstanding ensemble cast headed by Jack Palance. As Lt. Joe Costa, Palance gives a mesmerizing performance as a highly competent platoon leader who's unwilling to sacrifice more of his men due to the incompetence of the company commander, Capt. Cooney (Eddie Albert). Set in 1944 during the Battle of the Bulge as the German's counter-attack, Capt. Cooney fails to lead his men in support of a squad that is under heavy fire, that results in numerous casualties. Lt. Costa is disgusted by the inaction of Capt. Cooney and threatens his life if he ever repeats his failure. The complexity of this story lies in Cooney's boyhood friendship with Lt. Col. Bartlett. As Bartlett, Lee Marvin is a manipulative and ambitious officer who needs the patronage of Cooney's father to advance his political career. While Bartlett condescendingly tolerates the obsequious and cowardly Cooney, he's unwilling to transfer him to headquarters, fearing he would be an even greater liability there. From the opening combat scenes to the end, you know where this film is heading, and when Capt. Cooney leaves Lt. Costa hanging without the promised support—combat realities suggest that Cooney has to be killed. Filmed with a stark-realism that gives it an edgy tension from beginning to end, the combat scenes are well-done and have a graphic realism that foreshadows movies to come. Structured much like a play, it employs many of the dramatic artifices of a play. As with many plays, there are too many twists and turns at the end, and in this case, a fragile moralism prevails that may leave you vaguely dissatisfied.

What the critics say Critics rate this movie 3.0 to 4.5. "High pitched, slick, violent and very effective war melodrama."[1] "Entire film...is treated with a hard realism that pays off in gutsy entertainment."[2] "Terrific, gritty, antiwar movie."[7] **Final Word** This is one tough war movie that is worth watching. Jack Palance gives an over-the-top performance you do not want to miss.

Attack and Retreat

1965 ITA/RUS/USA b/w dubbed d. Giuseppe de Santis

WW II: Italian Army on the Eastern Front 3.5

Attack and Retreat is the only movie I have come across about the Italian army operating on the Eastern Front. The storyline parallels that of the outstanding 1958 German movie, *Stalingrad*. We are introduced to a range of characters, enlisted men and officers, as the Italian 8th Army, under the command of the German Wehrmacht, push towards Stalingrad only to be halted in the streets. Field Marshal Paulus' Sixth Army is encircled by the Soviet army and annihilated in the Russian winter of 1942. Of the 250,000 men who fought in this campaign, only 6,000 returned home. Hitler's *Operation Barbarossa*, intended to be a three-month undertaking, underestimated the Soviet army's capability and overestimated the Wehrmacht's mobility. The result was a complete disaster. The film, in part, has to incorporate this truth in telling us about these events. In this movie's best moment, a young Italian soldier, who was a farm boy before the war, is lost in a sunflower field somewhere in the Ukraine. Awed by the vast expanse of these fields, we hear his thoughts (paraphrased here), "I soon die in a field just like this, does my Papa know yet, and who won the war?" Sublime moments like this set high expectations for this film, but it finally gives in to sheer stupidity. Peter Falk is given a cameo role as a doctor half-way into the film, stopping the movie in its tracks. His dialogue consists of condescending wisecracking that parodies his television roles. Fortunately, he is killed. This movie consistently portrays the Italian soldier as taken aback by the atrocities and brutality of the German soldiers, and often is at complete odds with them. It portrays the elite Italian forces ("black-shirted super-men") as shirking combat duty—and their commander as a ruthless fascist ideologue who is a coward at heart. The battle scenes are realistic and well-staged. There is no heroism or escape from fate. Often touching, with several sublime moments, the film rambles and ultimately tumbles into a lesser film.

What the critics say Critics rate this movie 4.0. "Expansive chronicle of Italian-Russian warfront."[2] "An Italian epic."[8] **Final Word** To quote the film, "War teaches a man one thing, what we are not and what we don't want." (Is that two things?) A decent war film that will be hard to find.

Attack Force Z
1982 AUS color d. Tim Burstall

| WW II: Australian Spec Ops | 2.5 |

This film features a young Mel Gibson before he became a charming and roguish caricature, and a young Sam Neill before he became a fine character actor. Both actors star as Australian Z Special Forces assembled from Allied forces to conduct secret operations. The film purports to be a tribute to the 284 missions Z Special Forces conducted and to provide an "honest and unflinching account of the types of operations carried out." You should probably be suspicious of both claims. The story opens in 1945 in the southwest Pacific as a team of five Z special forces, commanded by Capt. Kelly (Mel Gibson), kayak from a submarine to a Japanese-held island. Their mission is to reach a crashed airplane before the Japanese and secure a defector, a military attaché from the Japanese War Ministry. This will, however, prove to be the least covert mission ever conducted by Z forces, as dozens of Japanese soldiers stand about and get killed. I might add there are numerous cute kids, our standard treacherous Japanese officers, and a young, beautiful Chinese woman. In the film's only unexpected moment, John Phillip Law gets the girl (but he also dies at the end). Yes, there's a Buddhist temple scene. And in the film's most unbelievable moment, the Z Forces murder one of their own wounded team members, just in case he is captured and forced to talk, This is absurd, of course, since every single person, including the kids, knows about this mission. While there's some decent action at the end, the film is mostly slow and tedious, particularly when it takes 10 minutes for Law to bandage the hand of a young Chinese woman. Her father, by the way, a martial arts expert and leader of the local resistance movement, doesn't approve of his daughter with Law (probably preferred Mel Gibson!). These special forces guys sure know how to have it all—women and adventure. The ending is downbeat, however, as four of the team members are killed, the father and many villagers die, and the Japanese defector is killed as well. Why Gibson survives is the film's only mystery.

What the critics say Critics rate this movie 1.0. to 3.5 "Downbeat adventure."[1] "Taut little war drama."[2] "Talented cast is effectively directed in low-key adventure."[5] **Final Word** Mel Gibson's first special operations mission behind enemy lines was apparently a failure in more ways than one.

Away All Boats

1956 USA color d. Joseph Pevney

WW II: Naval Combat Command	2.0

Away All Boats tells the story of a Navy attack transport and the heroic efforts of its captain and crew. It's also a patriotic yarn that is more typical of the 1940s than the 1950s. With good special effects and the cooperation of the Dept. of Defense and Navy, we get to watch the early shakedown of the newly commissioned USS *Belinda*, an attack transport ship designed to carry 1,400 combat troops in an amphibious assault on island beachheads. However, what this movie is really about is the rigors of command and what it takes to make a ship combat worthy. At the center of this uninteresting story is Capt. J. S. Hawks, played by Jeff Chandler (matinee idol of the early fifties), who brings all the charisma of an anchor at rest on the ocean floor. He's a decorated combat officer and by-the-book type of guy who is obsessed with his ship having the highest performance ratings. Later we are let in on the "loneliness of command" and get to watch Capt. Hawks come to respect the lowly attack transport, although he had hoped for command of a cruiser. The main problem with this movie is that nothing happens until the last twenty minutes. There is a sappy opening homage to the seaworthiness of the attack transport. Capt. Hawks is piped aboard and assumes command. The crew train and we get to share their boredom and, finally, there are a few humorous asides and some conflict between crew members. That's about it. Oh! At the end, the ship is struck by three Japanese planes that make a kamikaze attack. This is truly a movie without dramatic tension, either among the characters or in the storyline. The real question remains—Why was this film made? As a tribute to the officers and crew of attack transports? As a public relations effort by the Navy? Perhaps as an attempt to explore ship command? Relax, you won't be tested. This movie is not good enough for you to be concerned about why it was made. To find the answers to these questions, you may have to read the original novel by Kenneth M. Dodson.

What the critics say Critics rate this movie 2.0 to 2.5. "Exciting, inspiring story of battle action in the Pacific Theater."[2] "Lackluster war drama."[7] **Final Word** Unless your father or grandfather served on an attack transport, don't bother to rent this movie.

Ay, Carmela!

1990 SPA/ITA color subtitles d. Carlos Saura

Spanish Civil War: Humor-Satire 3.5

Of course, it's not possible to describe briefly what the Spanish Civil War (1936-1939) was about. Even today, no one knows. On one side were the Nationalists—fascists and traditionalists, aided by Italy, Germany, Portugal, and Irish Catholics and French Monarchists. On the other side were the Republicans—socialists, communists, Trotskyites, anarchists and separatists, aided by the International Brigade—mostly left-wing supporters from around globe (much like Berkeley, CA today). In the end the Nationalists won. As far as I can tell, this was mostly an international free-for-all for anyone with an ideological bent, and a bloody mess that resolved nothing. This movie, with serio-comic overtones, gives us a duo of vaudevillian performers, Paulino (Andrés Pajares) and Carmela (Carmen Maura), who are entertaining Republican soldiers. As they travel between shows, they are stopped and arrested by Nationalist forces and held in prison awaiting execution. However, a young Italian lieutenant who fancies himself a theatrical director, learns of their talents and enlists their support to provide propagandistic entertainment for Nationalist troops. There really isn't any more to this story, except for the wonderfully, rich personalities of our performers. Carmela is a preening and aging hysteric who craves attention and is full of emotion, while Paulino, her passive and amorous lover, simply wants the show to go on regardless of the politics. Carmela, attracted to a young Polish POW, begins to suffer a moral quandary about putting on a show that would humiliate him. There's lots of singing, dancing and poetry reciting that brings us to a dramatic and ultimately tragic finale. Without subplots or real metaphor, the impulsive, inevitable and violent conclusion does not provide us much insight into this civil war. This is primarily a drama of personalities and circumstances that is slyly humorous and quietly entertaining.

What the critics say Critics rate this movie 2.5 to 4.5. "Very watchful but flawed political film with a bungled ending."[1] "Clever, rapier-witted farce...both funny and poignant."[2] "Offers insight and entertainment, but...generates few sparks."[7] **Final Word** A limited story filled with outstanding performances. The movie has very little to say about the Spanish Civil War, but makes it clear that war is a pretty stupid affair.

Back to Bataan

1945   USA   b/w   d. Edward Dmytryk

| WW II: Classic '40s Flagwaver | 1.5 |

Back to Bataan is an unabashedly sentimental tribute to the people of the Philippines and their resistance to Japanese occupation. It's also a reminder that references to these 1940 war movies as "flagwavers" and "propaganda" are a criticism as well. John Wayne stars as Col. Joe Madden, commander of the Filipino "Scouts" serving in the US Army. The Philippines, invaded by the Japanese in December of 1941, fell in April of 1942. The movie opens with American and Filipino forces holding out just prior to surrendering. Madden has been ordered to help organize armed resistance to the coming occupation. It would also be fair to say that Col. Madden is not a model of organizational efficiency, spending most the movie shooting the bull with whomever will listen. He philosophizes with a hobo, and puts up with spinster school teacher and taskmaster, Miss Barnes (Beulah Bondi). Right out of the midwest "Depression-Era," she knows a thing or two about what's right and wrong (I think we're still in Kansas, Toto). He finds time for a young boy who idolizes American baseball. Madden also provides too much emotional support for resistance leader Capt. Andres Bonifacio (Anthony Quinn), who is melancholy over his girlfriend's supposed collaboration with the Japanese. There are many speeches about the heroism of Filipinos and their glorious history of fighting for independence. The movie is interspersed with a few uninspired combat scenes as well. The Japanese are appropriately brutal and treacherous, and the entire movie looks and feels as if it were shot in a Pasadena garden center. It also opens and ends with a parade of former American POWs. Even though the US was a colonial power occupying the Philippines since 1900, the Filipino people were smart enough to know that the Japanese were not their liberators. To our credit, we granted the Philippines independence on July 4, 1946.

What the critics say Critics rate this movie 2.0 to 3.5. "Modestly made and rather dislikeable flagwaver."[1] "A fun World War II action film...good script, photography, acting, and battle action."[7]
Final Word MacArthur campaigned to retake the Philippines even though it had no strategic importance. The decision was costly, resulting in 62,000 American and 250,000 Japanese casualties.

Band of Brothers

2001   USA   color   tv   d. Steven Spielberg

| WW II: 101st Battles for Europe | 5.0 |

This is truly an epic war movie. A ten-hour (ten-part) made-for-television series by Steven Spielberg, *Band of Brothers* follows the infantry paratroopers of the American 101st Airborne Division. We watch from their inception and training in 1942 to their landing behind enemy lines during D-Day. The middle story focuses on their participation in the ill-fated "Operation Market Garden" in Holland, to their entrapment by the Germans at Bastogne in Belgium, through the Battle of the Bulge. The final chapter shows us their occupation of Germany. Based on the book by Stephen Ambrose, this is Spielberg's best work and is probably the finest statement about the experiences of the combat soldier ever put to film. It's clear now that *Saving Private Ryan*, Spielberg's well-done and popular war film, was a warm-up. Gone are the maudlin sentiments, the contrived plot and cliché moments. In their place we get war realism and the picture of a true soldier, Lt. Winters, commander of 2nd Platoon. Many elements of this film standout—the intense, chaotic combat scenes, shot at angles that give you the soldier's point of view, with a camera motion that depicts realistic movement. The screen can be filled all at once with pinging and whining bullets as tracers flash, arcing across the screen. The action has never been done better and may never be done this well again for a very long time. More importantly is how it focuses on the men of the 2nd Platoon. Gone are silly subplots, improbable incidents and false heroism of past war movies. In their place are real people coping under the most intense circumstances life has to offer. While surviving appears to be everything, it's often not as important as the bonds that form between the men. As this movie hones in on these relationships, the realities of the battlefield emerge—the problem of incompetent officers, men too shell-shocked to fight, the constant wounds and deaths due to friendly fire, fear, and stupidity. But most of all, the indomitable will of so many soldiers, not just to survive but to prevail.

What the critics say Critics rate this movie 4.5 to 5.0. "The battle scenes are bracing, harrowing, and well-constructed, and the quiet moments serve to underscore the bond that develops between the men as they become battle hardened."[5] **Final Word** Keep a copy in your bunker—one of the great war movies.

Bataan
1943   USA   b/w   d. Tay Garnett

WW II: Infantry Combat Hell   2.5

This movie is one of a handful of 1940s classic WW II flagwavers that is honored mostly out of nostalgia today. Derivative of John Ford's 1934 WW I movie, *The Lost Patrol, Bataan* tells the story of a squad of 13 American and Filipino soldiers who die one by one defending a bridge against advancing Japanese troops. A box office hit, the film was released a year after the fall of the Philippines on April 9, 1942, and claims to be reality-based. Clearly this was an attempt by Hollywood to give the public a moral victory over the Japanese by asserting the heroic and just efforts of our soldiers. The squad is a melting pot reflecting American society; there's a Black, a Hispanic and a Jewish soldier. The leader of this motley squad, pieced together from available and inexperienced soldiers, is Sergeant Bill Dane (Robert Taylor). Clearly the common man's touch is at work here, when the sergeant takes charge and is deferred to by two officers. These soldiers know, along with the audience, that their fate is sealed, so the only question is how they will die. Well, they die fighting like hell and taking out as many "Japs" as they can (perhaps a few too many for reality). The ending itself is right out of a comic book, with Sgt. Dane yelling at the "Japs" to come and get him—50. caliber machine gun blazing. This is a low budget, backlot production that has very little action and too many talking soldiers with very little to say. While the action is pretty grim and realistic and many of the special effects well done, the question that kept arising was, should they retreat when it became obvious they couldn't hold the bridge? The fact was Gen. MacArthur had been ordered to escape, and 80,000 American troops surrendered. Holding actions such as this, while heroic, were in vain when no reinforcements were forthcoming to the Philippines.

What the critics say Critics rate this movie 3.0 to 4.5. "Stereotyped characters and much flagwaving. Very dated."[1] "Realistically made drama...good combat scenes."[2] One of the best films about WW II."[7] **Final Word** Not much here that would interest a contemporary audience—mostly for those who remember it on late night TV and want their kids to share the experience.

Battle Circus

1953 USA b/w d. Richard Brooks

Before Robert Altman's *M*A*S*H* there was *Battle Circus*, a light romance-drama about the 8666th MASH (Mobile Army Surgical Hospital) unit during the Korean War. It's probably fair to say that this film was the genesis of Altman's very successful film. *Battle Circus* stars Humphrey Bogart (Maj. Jed Webbe) as a disillusioned Army surgeon and June Allyson (Lt. Ruth McGara) as a naive and very sweet Army nurse intent on rescuing Bogart from himself. Despite the star power, this is pretty much a low-budget, studio-bound "B" movie of very little depth. The sole focus of this film is a silly-romance with too much cute repartee between the two miscast leads. It's more than the lack of chemistry between them; neither of them is right for the role. Bogart comes across as lacking the energy and command the role calls for and Allyson comes right out of a Doris Day comedy into a Korean War MASH unit—something too incongruous to contemplate, let alone watch. (I thought June Allyson was married to Jimmy Steward in *Strategic Air Command*. How could she be fooling around with Bogart in Korea?) There are many predictable scenes such as the rescue of a Korean boy, a wounded North Korean soldier with a grenade, and an emergency evacuation. More to the point, there is no urgency or poignancy to the medical emergencies these doctors and nurses are attending. The constant medical crises they deal with and have to learn to cope with are completely ignored. Perhaps the film's most interesting element is watching how mobile the MASH units are as they pull up tents and move the entire unit in a day. The movie makes no comment about the war itself, and the scene with the North Korean waving a grenade portrays him as frightened and not dangerous. Okay! let's get real here for a moment. Lt. McGara is seeking commitment and Maj. Webbe wants a few moments of pleasure—and all we get in this battle of the sexes is a happy ending. I would like to know whose unhappy illusion prevailed.

What the critics say Critics rate this movie 1.5 to 3.0. "Sappy drama...weak script and uninspired performances don't help this depressing story."[5] "It's a curious film—flawed, but more good than bad."[6] **Final Word** The romance and humor needed to be more edgy in order to succeed under such dire circumstances.

Battle Cry
1955 USA color d. Raoul Walsh

WW II: Wartime Romancer   1.5

This 1950s potboiler and box office success, from the novel and screenplay by Leon Uris, comes closer to the popular teenage romance movies of this era than to a war film. Of epic length, 2.5 hours, the movie's first two hours are devoted almost exclusively to the love lives of Pvt. Danny Forrester (Tab Hunter) and Pvt. Andy Hookens (Aldo Ray). The only interruptions are a few brief and routine scenes indicating they have just enlisted in the Marine Corps. Just when you think something about the war is going to breakout, these soldiers get leave and start chasing women all over San Diego and New Zealand. Each character appears to have been specially created by Uris to represent a stereotype that the audience can easily identify with. As a result of this not so clever device, nothing that transpires on the screen could possibly have any dramatic significance. Incidentally, our young "gyrenes" are in a communications battalion commanded by Maj. Huxley (Van Heflin) and run by MSgt. Mac (James Whitmore), who narrates the film. Both are military professionals who want to whip these young men into the best battalion in the Corps, which seems to run the gamut from intensive drilling to baby-sitting them through the emotional trauma of relationships breaking-up. Finally, at the very end, the overly sincere Van Heflin, at the risk of insubordination, convinces the commanding general to assign his battalion to the beachhead invasion of Saipan rather than conduct mop-up operations. Some Marines are killed, but the two heroes, Danny and Andy, are wounded and live happily ever after. The battle scenes are limited and appear to have been lifted from earlier movies (they look very familiar). The fact that these Marines have been trained as communications specialists is not important to this story, as it turns out. The movie is pretty much a flagwaving salute to the Marine Corps and the war effort. Besides, without a war what excuse would the producer have had to make this movie?

What the critics say Critics rate this movie 2.0 to 4.0. "Interminable cheapie epic with both eyes on the box-office."[1] "Amatory, rather than military, action."[4] "A two and a half hour...recruiting commercial."[6] **Final Word** Even if you suffer a rare genetic mutation resulting in a gene that makes you a fan of war-romances, I cannot recommend this movie.

Battle Force

1977 GER/YUG color d. Umberto Lenzi

WW II: Europe and North Africa   1.0

While I have given up proclaiming any one picture the worst war-movie ever, I can confidently say that *Battle Force* is the most incoherent and confusing war movie ever made. The director has patched together dozens of unrelated scenes, given them dates and places, and has Orson Welles narrate the transitions by telling us how the war is progressing. We get a brief opening scene in Berlin, October 1942, between Stacy Keach, a German army major, and his half-Jewish wife. Then we are in Los Angeles watching Henry Fonda, an American general, struggle in his relationship with his youngest son. Next we are in Crete viewing a failed British commando raid—then on to London and Greece (as Keach reluctantly executes a captured Greek partisan). After Berlin comes Plymouth, England, and Le Havre, France (where a woman prostitutes herself to a German officer), and then on to Normandy, France (with Fonda's son on a commando operation). The story picks up at West Point, NY, then North Africa and so on until we reach Los Angeles on March 30, 1943, where Fonda attends the funeral of his son killed in action. Unfortunately, none of these events appear to be connected to any other. There's just Orson Welles droning on about the progress of the war or Keach now commanding tanks in Rommel's Afrika Korps. There are two stories of a sort here: Fonda, the father of two sons serving in the military, and Keach, separated from his wife, who's trying to survive in Germany on her own. However, this movie is not about either of these stories and doesn't really connect them. The two stars, Fonda and Keach, are probably on the screen a total of fifteen minutes. How and why they ever agreed to participate in this project would be worthy of a short indie documentary itself. While this movie is in English, you always have the sense it was dubbed. It's hard to believe that anyone ever sat down and watched this movie from beginning to end, especially the director.

What the critics say Critics rate this movie 1.0 to 2.0. "Amateurish muddle combines tired vignettes with well-known actors, dubbed sequences...a waste of everybody's time."[2] "Passable World War II adventure."[7] "Dreadful mish-mash."[8]
Final Word Did I mention that John Huston even makes a lame and lackluster cameo appearance as well?

The Battle for Port Arthur
1980 JAP color dubbed d. Toshio Masuda

Russo-Japanese War: Big Battle   4.5

Produced on a scale to match any similar American movie (*The Longest Day* or *A Bridge Too Far*), but far superior is this outstanding Japanese antiwar epic by Toshio Masuda. The Russo-Japanese War from 1904-1905 was a battle of two expansionist powers seeking influence in the Far East. With the Russian occupation of Manchuria and Port Arthur (Korean peninsula) years earlier, the Japanese launched a preemptive strike without formal warning against Russia. The parallels between this strike and Pearl Harbor, in 1941, are startling. Japan, fearing their territorial ambitions were threatened, attacked a much larger nation, hoping to gain a strategic advantage through surprise, and negotiate a peace settlement. Done in a semi-documentary style with narration, battle-order, dates and maps, the epic shows the problems of military command and the personal and political conflicts this war engendered. The gruesome and harrowing depiction of combat on this scale makes a powerful antiwar statement. This war was also a dress-rehearsal for WW I—extended fronts and protracted battles led to trench warfare, the first time use of machine guns, grenades, mines, barbed wire, mortars, submarines, indirect-fire and radio transmissions. The ineptness and callousness of Japanese commanders, and their willingness to sacrifice soldiers for questionable strategic objectives or for issues of personal honor, are presented unflinchingly. This is especially true of the powerful and tragic figure of Gen. Nogi (Tatsuya Nakadai), the Japanese army commander. The parallels to the Western Front in Europe during WW I are chilling. The realism of this movie, along with its uncompromising examination of the failures of the Japanese Imperial Army, has no American equivalent. The images of war here are compelling and horrific, with a great deal of humanity expressed for both Russian and Japanese soldiers. Like most epics, *The Battle for Port Arthur* can be slow moving and incoherent at times, in trying to tell too many stories, including the story of a young and idealistic school teacher who is drafted into the army and separated from the woman he loves.

What the critics say No available reviews. **Final Word** This is a very human film that closely examines the conflicts of command. You will have to go on-line or to a specialty store to find this one.

Battle for the Falklands

1984   GBR   color   tv

British Wars: Documentary.   1.0

Argentina's right-wing military junta, led by Gen. Galtieri, made a power grab for the Falkland Islands (what the Argentines call the Malvinas) in 1982. These barren, windswept islands, the size of Northern Ireland and inhabited by no more than 1,800 people mostly of British descent, have been a British protectorate since 1833. Prior to this, the islands had been occupied by Britain, Spain, France, the US and, yes, by Argentina, which makes a historical claim to them. In response to the thugish junta's "liberation" ploy, the British drag out the last gasp of jingoistic, colonial empire nostalgia and attack. In order to uphold international justice and the rights of self-determination (the British were probably the good guys here), 1,000 soldiers are killed and 2,000 wounded, so that the 1,800 inhabitants could continue to drink tea and drive on the wrong side of the road. Unfortunately, this documentary is a "bloody bore" and a one-sided propaganda piece concocted from British news coverage of the conflict. There is nothing of interest here and only some of the truth. More damning is that there is no discussion of war planning and strategic issues facing the British military. In fact, there is no military film footage or cooperation with the film. This documentary also tends to whitewash the real damage inflicted on the British navy, and fails to help viewers grasp how close Britain came to being defeated by a second-rate military power. If a few Exocet missiles had not been duds, the world might have been shocked at how vulnerable the British navy was to modern air and missile technology. Equally important, the British sailed nearly 8,000 miles from home and were not prepared or equipped to establish air superiority once they arrived. Basically, they lucked out, but you have no clue about this from watching this documentary. Better yet, read *The Battle for the Falklands* by Hastings and Jenkins. It's clear that the war was a diplomatic failure on the part of the British to settle this dispute after 17 years of negotiation.

What the critics say No available reviews. **Final Word** While we can't let the thugs rule the world, what the hell are the British doing 8,000 miles from home on an island the size of Disney World? A pint of ale all around.

Battleground
1949 USA b/w d. William A. Wellman

WW II: Infantry Combat	1.5

This low-budget, back-lot movie has very little action and, for the most part, borders on a comedy rather than a serious war drama. The film, a box-office success when it was first released, won two Academy Awards (screenplay and cinematography), and gives us the war from the perspective of the GI on the battlefield. In one of the most significant battles of the Second World War, the 101st "Screaming Eagles" are cut off and surrounded at Bastogne (in Belgium) by a massive German counter offensive. By holding out against enormous odds in the middle of winter, these soldiers helped to break the back of the offensive, and bring a quick end to the war. No doubt this movie's box office success was due primarily to the audience's complete understanding and appreciation of what these men experienced, as well as the significance of what they had accomplished. However, watching this film fifty years later, you would have no clue about the peril they faced or the miracle they achieved. It's probably not a coincidence that the film script, by Robert Pirosh, followed his earlier success with a Marx Brothers comedy. The constant banter and slapstick-humor keeps the audience from getting to knowing anything about the star-studded squad of men they are following, who for the most part are characters without biographies (usually a problem for a drama). We mostly see them eating, sleeping, digging fox holes, reading mail, complaining and joking around. Near the end, several brief and lackluster combat scenes are inserted along with some documentary footage. Then, we are back to the silliness. The "Battered Bastards of Bastogne" deserve a better memory on the screen than this one (which is why you should see Spielberg's *Band of Brothers*). Perhaps 1949 audiences needed a break from the realities of war. This film's success may have made it a model for every bad Korean War film to follow.

What the critics say Critics rate this movie 4.0 to 5.0. "A tightly conceived picture of WW II character drama."[5] "Beyond the inevitable stereotypical characters these guys are real."[6] "One of the best ever devoted to WW 2's European theater."[8] (Say what!) **Final Word** There is obviously a nostalgia for these old war movies to be better than they are.

Battle Hell

1957   GBR   b/w   d. Michael Anderson

Cold War: Naval Incident on the Yangtse   2.0

If you have seen one British naval war film, you have essentially
seen them all. The films contains very little action and no
dramatic tension. Everyone is good-spirited (jolly-good show and
all that sort of rubbish), and the movies are low-budget. This
movie is based on an actual incident, in 1949, between Chinese
Communist forces and the British frigate HMS *Amethyst*. (The
modern frigate is slightly larger than a destroyer and was
originally designed to escort convoys.) The British claim that the
Amethyst was minding its own business in a peaceful and lawful
manner while sailing up the Yangtse River to resupply the British
embassy at Nanking. Chinese Communist artillery shelled the
ship at near point-blank range, causing it to run aground on mud
flats. Serious damage was done to the ship and 22 crewmen
were killed. The Communists claimed that the *Amethyst* was
intruding on their territorial waters without authorization and had
open-fired without provocation, killing 250 Chinese soldiers. The
Communists wanted to negotiate, but only if the British would
publicly make a formal admission of responsibility and regret
(they wanted an apology). The actual HMS *Amethyst* was used,
and its commander, Lt. Cmdr. J.S. Kerans, was consultant to this
movie which was based on a book by Lawrence Earl. The
opening battle sequence is well done but then, for the next hour,
this film fails to produce the necessary dramatic tension out of
the endless and unproductive negotiations that took place. There
were also three failed attempts to rescue this ship. The only
character of note is Richard Todd, the ship's captain, who
orchestrates the British escape. Filmed at night, the escape itself
is somewhat anticlimactic as there's really nothing to see.
However, with a measure of good luck and lots of pluck, the
Amethyst does a hell of a job of evading artillery and shore
batteries by running a 140-mile gauntlet to the sea (it's what the
British call a "sticky wicket").

What the critics say Critics rate this movie 2.0 to 2.5. "Stalwart
but not very exciting British war heroics."[1] "Pretty standard war
flick."[7] "Dull exposition of an interesting incident."[8] **Final Word** If
you are scanning the channels late at night, you could do a lot
worse than this sincere effort. Also released as *Yangtse Incident*.

Battle Hymn

1957 USA color d. Douglas Sirk

Korean War: Inspirational Biopic 2.5

The true story of Col. Dean Hess gets the full Hollywood makeover. You can almost always tell a movie is in trouble when it opens with the "Battle Hymn of the Republic," followed by a USAF general introducing the movie as an "affirmation of the essential goodness of the human spirit." The movie stars none other than Rock Hudson as Col. Hess, a WW II fighter pilot haunted by his accidental bombing of a German orphanage. After the war, Col. Hess turned to his faith and became a minister to help assuage his sense of guilt. With the start of the Korean War, he voluntarily returned to the Air Force as commander of a unit to train Republic of Korean (ROC) P-51 fighter pilots. However, as the war escalated, children were abandoned on a scale that became a problem at Hess's base. Insisting that his men help the children, this movie focuses on the Colonel's eventual efforts to help build what became "The Orphan's Home of Korea." This overly sincere effort shows how Hess's crisis of conscience and faith were resolved by saving hundreds of children. There are also several undeveloped subplots in the movie. A young Korean woman (Anna Kashfi), who's in love with Hess (he's completely oblivious), inspires him to become involved with an orphanage. There's an old war buddy (Don DeFore) who's a loose cannon. Most surprising is the prominent role of a Black fighter pilot (James Edwards), who, though not a major character, is prominent throughout the movie in a manner that was rare for the time. Because this movie attempts to be a little bit of everything, it fails to get at the heart of what had to be the real struggles in establishing this orphanage. There's also little focus on the plight of these children. Because everything is accomplished so effortlessly, it becomes clear this movie was simply made to let the audience feel good about itself. Hudson appears completely miscast as the chronically sincere and forlorn Hess. The combat scenes and special effects are decent.

What the critics say Critics rate this movie 2.0 to 4.0. "Earnest, somnolent, biopic...is indigestible despite professional handling."[1] "A decent if slightly hokey Hollywood drama."[7] **Final Word** A sincere but uninspiring effort to show us how the efforts of a few good people can make a significant difference.

The Battle of Algiers
1965 ALG/ITA b/w subtitles d. Gillo Pontecorvo

FRA-ALG War: Algerian Independence   5.0

How is it possible that a film made in Algeria, subtitled and in black and white with an Italian director (Gillo Pontecorvo), with only one paid actor and banned in France, is one of the best and most important war movies ever made? This movie, shot in a grainy, hand-held documentary style (*cinema verite*) shows us Algeria's struggle for independence from France from 1954 to 1960 (achieved in 1962). What the film really focuses on is the National Liberation Front (FLN), a terrorist organization that is assassinating French police and bombing French civilians in Algiers. As the conflict escalates, French paratroopers commanded by Col. Mathieu (Jean Martin) are deployed. Mathieu immediately begins a policing effort to hunt down and identify members of the FLN. He is also candid about the use of torture as part of the interrogation efforts. The film's most chilling moment is watching women terrorists casually plant bombs in restaurants and nightclubs. In its own way, while supporting the independence movement, this film acknowledged the logic of both sides in employing violence to achieve their aims. There has been much discussion about the style and techniques used in making this movie, which has fascinated critics for years and has been much copied. But what is most important about this movie is that it's a blueprint for nearly every important conflict of the past fifty years (N. Ireland, Lebanon, Balkans, Palestine) and a harbinger of conflict for the next 100 years. Its message is simple—you cannot oppress people and deprive them of their fundamental human rights without paying the highest price. Even then, you won't succeed. This is a revolutionary film Americans will implicitly understand. It is interesting to note that Yacef Saadi, a former FLN leader, coproduced the film and played himself.

What the critics say Critics rate this movie 4.5. to 5.0. "Brilliantly recreates the...events that led up to Algeria's independence...astonishingly realistic movie masterpiece."[3] "Makes most political films seem ineffectual by comparison."[5] "It has grown more impressive with age."[6] "A remarkable achievement in film."[8] **Final Word** Not for everyone, but for the war movie *realist*.

The Battle of Blood Island
1960 USA b/w tv d. Joel Rapp

WW II: Survival Drama	1.0

This low-budget actioner takes place on an unnamed South Pacific island in late 1945. As a platoon of American soldiers attempt to come ashore and reconnoiter the island, they are ambushed by a small force of Japanese soldiers. Unfortunately, for the audience, two soldiers survive. These two GIs, Ken (Ron Kennedy) and Moe (Richard Devon), are a miserable, odd couple who quickly get on each other's nerves (and, I suspect, those of everyone watching this movie). Ken, the younger of the two, is paralyzed from the waist down as the result of a wound. His dependency on the mirthless and neurotic Moe is at the heart of this small and inane psychological character study, penned as a short story by Philip Roth. The men also have to contend with Japanese soldiers. In the first half of the film there are any number of improbable confrontations in which the two manage to kill isolated soldiers. They then watch the remaining soldiers commit mass suicide for no apparent reason. Mostly this means these two characters get to move into more comfortable quarters. With most of their basic survival needs met, they can now really turn on one another. In one scene, the already wounded Ken attempts suicide after the two argue. Unfortunately, he only manages to wound himself. This suicide gesture is so bizarre that even the ending of this movie makes sense in comparison. After nearly seven months on this island these guys have regressed into obnoxious and self-absorbed individuals constantly at each other's throats. While this movie develops a certain intensity, it's hard not to believe that survival issues would have preempted this nonsense. If the director is suggesting this conflict helped the men survive their isolation, then either one of them would have been better off alone. These GIs are eventually rescued by soldiers who land on the island to ready it for an upcoming atomic test. The exact significance of this is completely lost, except that two guys who continually bitched about their fate get another undeserved break in the end.

What the critics say Critics rate this movie 1.0. "Dreadfully scripted, directed and acted."[8] **Final Word** The perverseness of two soldiers more at war with themselves than the enemy will keep you watching it long after you should have pressed the off button on your remote.

The Battle of Britain

1969 GBR color d. Guy Hamilton

World War II: Air Combat/Command   2.5

The story is simple, dramatic, and based on historical fact. In 1940 the British army suffered a terrible defeat in France, and the German army was poised to invade Britain. The only defense Britain had against an invasion was the Royal Air Force's air supremacy over the English channel. As noted in the movie, Britain had 650 fighter planes against the German Luftwaffe's 2,500 aircraft. It was estimated that RAF pilots would have to shoot down Luftwaffe pilots at a rate of 4-1 to prevail. *The Battle of Britain* was a big-budget attempt to tell this epic war story, with a *Who's Who* of British cinema and stage actors. Unfortunately, this story has been told better in documentaries and in the 1988 British television miniseries *Piece of Cake*. The failure of this movie is due to a lack of direction. It tries to tell too many stories from too many points of view—from the German as well as British point of view, both at the command and the pilot level. As a result, there is no coherent story with which the audience can identify. There is no drama at the personal level. This movie's failure to create drama during events leading to Germany's defeat in the air, while time was running out for Britain, is beyond comprehension. However, this film does have one crowning achievement. The filming of the aerial combat sequences are probably the best ever in a war film. The opportunity to see Spitfires, Hurricanes, Stukas, Bf109s and Heinkel 111s (borrowed from the Spanish air force) is spectacular. Unfortunately, too many important stories are not addressed in the movie. What about the development of radar ground control and tactical air combat strategies by the British to combat German aircraft? The movies fails to tell the audience about the critical time frames to train pilots and produce planes to hold the Germans back, not to mention the pilots' stories. While much of the above is alluded to, the movie fails to focus on the critical stories behind this important victory.

What the critics say Critics rate this movie 3.0. "Interminable dogfight sequences. On the ground, things are even duller."[1] "Superb widescreen aerial sequences."[2] **Final Word** Every true war-geek savant should probably see this film. It will be tough to get through, but the rewards are high for those who are into air combat.

61

Battle of the Bulge

1965   USA   color   d. Ken Annakin

WW II: Really Big Battle	2.0

Least we forget, Henry Fonda (Lt. Col. Kiley), Robert Shaw (Col. Martin Hessler), Robert Ryan (Gen. Grey), Charles Bronson (Maj. Wolenski) and Telly Savalas (Sgt. Gruffy) didn't really fight in the Battle of the Bulge. This is yet another big-budget, star-laden Hollywood effort to give the audience a command view of one of the most significant battles of WW II. In reality, Hitler ordered the German Ardennes offensive (popularly called the Battle of the Bulge) in an effort to split Allied forces and recapture the port of Antwerp. The attack, launched on Dec. 16, 1944 along an 88-mile front, caught a complacent Allied command completely by surprise. After the weather cleared on Dec. 22, Allied air superiority inflicted severe damage on German armor, which was already short of fuel. The German effort was a desperate gamble by Hitler, which had no real chance of success. In terms of depicting the basic problems confronting Allied and German command, this movie does a very good job, particularly in showing the confusion among Allied troops retreating in the face of the German offensive. There are many excellent large scale tank battles. But where this movie struggles is in trying to tell the story from a personal point of view. On the American side, we have an annoying and persistent Lt. Col. Kiley (Henry Fonda), an intelligence officer who accurately predicted the German offensive but was ignored. On the German side is Col. Martin Hessler (Robert Shaw) who is considered their best tank commander. Rather than being the typical "evil" Nazi, he is an evil, war-mongering fanatic, who revels in keeping the war going. Shaw is so flat and one-dimensional as Col. Hessler that you almost begin to appreciate Telly Savalas' comic relief. As with every similar film, the characters are not developed and the point of view changes so often that there's simply no coherent story. Unfortunately, movies such as this tend to be overly long and boring, despite many good action scenes.

What the critics say Critics rate this movie 2.0 to 4.5. "Bloody and unbowed war spectacle."[1] "Over inflated war drama...cannot overcome a banal script."[2] "An archetypal studio war movie (with)...ridiculously unrealistic Hollywood heroics."[6] **Final Word** If you are a traditionalist and like the sprawling epics, this is for you.

The Battle of the Last Panzer

1968   SPA /ITA   color   d. José Luis Merino

WW II: Dueling Tank Action	1.0

This is not the worst war movie ever made, only because it never tried to be very good to start with. Made in Italy, and poorly dubbed, the film plays like a bad spaghetti Western. The story revolves around a German tank crew who are ambushed by American artillery. Able to salvage one tank, the fanatical German commander, Lt. Hunter, insists they complete their mission to destroy an Allied fuel dump. Sgt. Schultz, a seasoned veteran, is immediately in conflict with the lieutenant and wants their crew to return to German lines. The action takes place in late 1944 on the French-German border (although it appears more like southern Italy). So far so good, even with poorly staged battle scenes, the producer has mustered up four American Mark IV tanks and painted iron crosses on them. However, things take a turn for the worse when the Germans enter a French village and the lieutenant takes three civilian hostages, including the innkeeper's attractive young wife. The young woman later volunteers to help, but only if the Germans release the other hostages. She then is squeezed into the close confines of a tank with five very sweaty and horny men who keep checking out her thighs and cleavage. Later that evening the lieutenant jumps her only to suffer: a. penile erection dysfunction, b. guilt, or c. performance problems related to war-trauma. You choose. But after having taken his shirt off and flexed all day, the lieutenant should feel lousy about not ravaging her, especially since she wanted him to. Are you still with me? Unfortunately this movie is not lurid enough to be entertaining. Now it becomes even more improbable, as our idiot lieutenant becomes a nice guy, makes up with the sergeant, lets the woman go only to find that the dastardly Americans have a trick up their sleeves. They have taken a captured German tank, put an American crew in it, and given it the same markings as our stalwart German crew. As a result the German crew is mistakenly shelled by their own forces and killed. If all this isn't confusing enough, the American soldiers appear to be wearing Italian army uniforms.

What the critics say No available reviews. **Final Word** This film was reviewed because it was available at a local video store, which means there is a good chance you might run into it and want to avoid it.

Bat 21

1988 USA color d. Peter Markle

This rather talky, slow-moving and not particularly involving war-rescue drama, shot on location in Borneo, was based on a book by William C. Anderson. *Bat 21* tells the true story of Lt. Col. Iceal Hambleton, a USAF missile intelligence officer, who was shot down over South Vietnam while conducting highly classified electronic-counter measures (ECM). In an effort to protect B-52 bombers, specially equipped planes were used to suppress ARVN air defenses by jamming the guidance radar of surface-to-air missiles (SAMs). (It might be noted that during the Vietnam War only one aircraft was lost for every 120 SAMs fired.) Hambleton's rescue took on a special urgency because of all the classified information he possessed. His story is actually very compelling, but just not told well. While this 53-year-old officer had been a desk-jockey his entire career, his attempts at survival are ingenious, and sometimes brutal, as he comes face-to-face with the horrors of war. At this point the movie takes on a decidedly antiwar theme, as Hambleton confronts war at a personal level. Unfortunately, the movie has another mission—to tell the story of Capt. Clark (Danny Glover), a forward air controller who flies a Cessna 0-2A Skymaster and targets air and artillery strikes. With two weeks to go before he heads back home, Clark takes on the mission of rescuing Hambleton. This split point-of-view ultimately detracts from either man's story being told with much depth or detail, and results in a lot of radio chatter between them. There is also an improbable final rescue attempt that appears to be a desperate measure to add drama to a story not very well told. Unfortunately, by the end of the movie, we don't know anything more about these guys than when it began, as it degenerates into a sort of "buddy-movie." There's an unintended irony in this film's antiwar message in that Hambleton not only becomes an efficient killer and survivor, but appears to thrive on it as well.

What the critics say Critics rate this movie 3.0 to 4.0. "Effective and suspenseful drama of the muddle and moral expediency of war."[1] "Rather routine action film."[3] **Final Word** Disappointing because all the pieces were here for something more significant.

The Beast
1988   USA   color   d. Kevin Reynolds

Soviet-Afghanistan : Hunting Soviet Tank   4.0

In a very powerful and disturbing opening sequence, we watch three Russian tanks decimate an Afghan village. As the Russians are attacked by women with rocks, they release nerve gas. Soldiers then descend using flame throwers and machine guns to kill the villagers and their animals, and then poison the well. It's 1981, the second year of the Soviet Union's intervention in Afghanistan (their Vietnam), and the hate and revenge atrocities that have begun to occur between these two enemies know no limits. Opposing the Soviets are the Mujahadeen, a loose organization of Muslim sects, factions and militias that have been at war for several thousands years. Based on the play *Nanawatai* by William Mastrosimone, which was beautifully filmed in Israel, the story revolves around a band of armed villagers hunting down a tank crew that gets lost. What ensues is a fascinating *cat and mouse* game between the five-man crew of the Russian tank and the Afghan rebels. The tank (the Beast), a destructive machine of modern perfection, is impervious to bullets—equipped with poison gas, flame thrower, machine guns and a cannon. But the rebels have a RPG (rocket propelled antitank grenade launcher, effective at short range and able to penetrate 11.8 in. of steel armor), and so the hunt begins. However, there are also conflicts within both groups. The Russian tank commander, Daskal (George Dzundza), a paranoid and unthinking soldier, soon attacks his own crew. First he kills an Afghan serving in the Soviet army and then turns his focus on Koverchenko (Jason Patric), a former student and peacenik turned tank driver. The first half of this movie is compelling and outstanding. The second half has a number of contrived and predictable plot twists, that make for interesting action, but prevent this from being a truly outstanding war movie. The arid land and rugged mountains bring a haunting physical reality to this story. This is an intense story with riveting action.

What the critics say Critics rate this movie 2.0 to 4.5. "Dull, violent, unilluminating movie."[1] "A harrowing tightly focused war film that becomes a moving, near biblical allegory."[4] (Did they see the same movie?) **Final Word** Well worth watching for war movie fans. It also has a great deal of relevance in today's geopolitical climate.

Beau Travail

1999 FRA color subtitles d. Claire Denis

Military Life: French Foreign Legion   4.0

A minimalist story with an emphasis on images, *Beau Travail* presents a provocative and, at times, mesmerizing contemporary look at a platoon of French Foreign Legionnaires. Stationed in the African desert nation of Djibouti, this arid country on the Gulf of Aden has a haunting emptiness that serves to highlight the lonely existence of these soldiers. The Legion is home and family to these men. Lost, running away, with no place to return to, they are accepted into this fraternity of warriors from every country without question, if they can withstand the hardships and obey the rules. Their Spartan life of physical hardship—exercising, combat training, field exercises, attending to the routines of camp life borders on the monastic—always waiting for an order that will take them to a potentially violent and deadly conflict. Based loosely on Herman Melville's *Billy Budd*, this movie, by director Claire Denis, is unusual in its sensual and nearly mystical focus on the physicality of the men. The camera shows us soldiers stripped down to their short khaki pants and boots in the hot desert sun, and choreographs the physical grace of their practicing for war or attending to mundane chores around camp. Denis creates a sensual beauty out of their masculinity. The story centers around a new Legionnaire who has joined the squad. Tall, quiet, handsome, Sentain (Grégoire Colin) is immediately liked by the other soldiers and establishes his natural leadership. Sgt. Galoup (Denis Lavant), who narrates this story in a quiet and understated manner, is unsettled by Sentain. Galoup's entire existence is the Legion, and his Commander, Forestier (Michel Subor), who serves as his symbolic father. Galoup, for reasons he doesn't understand, feels threatened by Sentain at some primitive level. It's as if his entire world is under attack. Galoup's unraveling is subtle and calculated as he seeks to destroy this threat. Well-acted, well-directed and beautifully photographed, this film looks at the beauty of soldiers' sub-mission to authority and the price they pay.

What the critics say No available reviews. **Final Word** Not a film for action-junkies, but rather for those seeking an intro-spective examination of military life. Warning. The sensuality may be too threatening for some.

The Bedford Incident

1965 GBR b/w d. James B. Harris

Cold War: Hunting Soviet Subs	4.5

This highly realistic drama about a possible Cold War meltdown exceeds its better known and contemporary counterpart *Fail Safe*, both as drama and as a realistic exploration of how a policy of "mutually assured destruction" (MAD) could fail. Set in the middle of the North Atlantic in the early 1960s, Richard Widmark (Capt. Finlander) is commander of a sub-hunting destroyer engaged in *cat and mouse* tactics with Soviet submarines. He's a driven commander (*a la* Ahab in *Moby Dick*) who seeks to "hunt to exhaustion" Soviets subs, forcing them to surface and lose political face. At his right-hand is a former German U-boat commander, Commodore Schrepke (Eric Portman), now a NATO officer onboard the *Bedford* as an observer. Rather than being the obvious fascist, Communist hating war-mongerer, he's a quiet thoughtful officer who has seen enough fanaticism bred by war and officers like Finlander. Into this mix comes photo-journalist Ben Munceford (Sidney Poitier) who is fascinated by Finlander. He sees Finlander as smart and competent, but distrusts his instincts as an officer. Filled with many excellent secondary characters, particularly Martin Balsam as the ship's doctor, this is a high-seas adventure fraught with tension between the personalities onboard the *Bedford* and the realities of Cold War gamesmanship. Finlander runs an exceedingly tight ship, and he commands the absolute respect of his crew, or as he tells Munceford: "I keep them interested with the hunt." Chasing and surfacing these subs is more than a game for Finlander, it is an obsession in which he's unable to tolerate anything less than success. This ultimately becomes a scenario in which the stakes keep escalating, as neither side is willing to give in. What truly make this movie, adapted from the book by Mark Rascovitch, exceptional is the intelligent script and outstanding performances, particularly by Widmark and Portman.

What the critics say Critics rate this movie 3.0 to 4.0. "Gripping mixture of themes...very tense and forceful, with excellent acting."[1] "Strong Cold War story...cast excels in intriguing battle of wits."[2] "Exciting Cold War thriller."[3] **Final Word** A great find that appears to keep getting better with age. Right up there with *Dr. Strangelove* and *Seven Days in May*.

Behind Enemy Lines

2001 USA color d. John Moore

Balkan's Conflict: Action-Adventure   3.0

Behind Enemy Lines is a solid effort that should provide a rush to all war movie action-junkies. With great special effects and the obvious cooperation of the US Navy, Lt. Burnett (Owen Wilson), a Navy F-18 Superhornet navigator, and pilot Lt. Stackhouse (Gabriel Macht), take off from the USS *Carl Vinson* in the Adriatic Sea on a NATO-authorized reconnaissance mission over Bosnia in the early 1990s. They veer off course into a non-flyover zone and photograph a site where Serbian soldiers massacred a civilian population. Then, in what may be the most exciting aerial combat ever on film (worth watching just for this sequence alone), their F-18 is chased and finally brought down by a SAM (surface-to-air missile). From here, the action takes place on the ground as the air crew attempts to evade capture. There are many appropriately menacing and blood-thirsty Serbian soldiers tracking them down. Meanwhile, back on the aircraft carrier, Admiral Leslie Reigart (Gene Hackman) attempts to rescue his air crew by tracking their movement through high-tech satellite infrared imaging. However, Hackman reports directly to a NATO commander who doesn't want to risk sensitive cease-fire negotiations by attempting an immediate rescue. The NATO commander wants the crew to hump it to a safety zone miles away. (If you think this all foreshadows questions of conscience and brass balls for Hackman, you are on the right track.) The action on the ground is intense and fast, providing a realistic view of the chaos and destructive violence taking place in Bosnia. However, plot weakens as too many improbable escape efforts succeed, concluding in a highly jingoistic shoot-out between US and Bosnian forces. Too often the simplistic assumptions of this movie undermine its credibility, particularly when Admiral Reigart is made out to be some kind of hero for defying the establishment (when he screwed up big time).

What the critics say Critics rate this movie 2.0 to 3.0. "Action yarn delivers a lot of excitement...corny finale seems to have come from a lessor-grade Hollywood movie of decades past."[2] "Cartoonish...video game approach to war."[5] **Final Word** This movie is a virtual remake of *Flight of the Intruder*—but considerably better.

Behind the Lines

1997   GBR   color   d. Gillies MacKinnon

| WW I: War is Crazy | 5.0 |

This is a thoughtful if not outright poetic film about soldiers suffering "war neurosis," otherwise known as "shell shock." Today we call it post-traumatic stress disorder. For those who require a lot of action, this is not the film for you. This intense, interpersonal drama tells the story of three British soldiers hospitalized at Craiglockart Hospital, in Scotland in 1917, who have suffered mental break-downs due to combat. Two of the patients are not ordinary soldiers. One of the soldiers is renowned British poet Siegfried Sassoon (James Wilby) and another is soon-to-be-famous British poet Wilfred Owen (Stuart Bunce). The third soldier, Billy Prior (Jonny Lee Miller), however, is the real emotional focus of this story, as he is deeply ashamed of having broken down in combat. The movie revolves around each soldier's relationship with their treating psychiatrist, Dr. Rivers (Jonathan Pryce). Adding to the story is the fact that Sassoon, also a highly decorated soldier, has requested to officially protest the British military's conduct of the war before Parliament. As a result, the Army has had him institutionalized in the "loony bin" in order to discredit his protest. Further, they do not want to court-martial him and give him a stage for his views about the war. The doctor has been asked to change Sassoon's mind about protesting the war. Ultimately, this becomes a struggle of unanswerable questions about war. What role should a doctor play in healing a man in order to return him to combat? How does any one individual protest the insanity of war and not betray his country? Rivers, a thoughtful and humane doctor, finally begins to suffer his own *war neurosis* as a result of over-identifying with these soldiers. This movie, in its own way, is a shocking look at war. It is also well acted, intelligent, filled with many poignant moments of its own, and a near perfect blend of poetry and film.

What the critics say Critics rate this movie 2.5 to 4.0. "Strong acting and superb cinematography enhances this talky, stagy adaptation of Pat Barker's prize winning novel."[2] "Powerful WW I drama. It's the interior battles that keep this import alive."[5] **Final Word** This is an outstanding war drama, nominated for many British Academy Awards but, understandably, will not appeal to most action freaks.

The Best Years of Our Lives

1946 USA b/w d. William Wyler

WW II: Post-War Vets   4.0

This is the most acclaimed and beloved American war movie ever—a classic that earned seven Academy Awards, including Best Picture, Best Actor (Fredric March) and Best Supporting Actor (Harold Russell), and an AFI top 100 film. Its success, in no small part, is due to its release one year after the war, and addressing the struggle of veterans returning to their communities. Based on a novel by MacKinlay Kantor, the film shows the lives of three vets returning home to the same midwest city. The first third of this movie rings most true and honestly examines the fears, anxieties and struggle of war veterans. The vulnerability of each man is truly poignant. Fredric March, a sergeant, returns to his wife (Myrna Loy) and two grown-up children. Portraying a banker from the upper middle class, March gives an outstanding performance as a man estranged from those he loves and befuddled by the relative normalcy of life around him ("Last year it was 'kill Japs', this year it's 'make money.'"). Dana Andrews, a B-17 navigator and war hero, has to deal with returning to a job at a drug store, while his beautiful wife (Virginia Mayo) lusts for life in the fast lane. Then there's Homer (Harold Russell), a Navy vet who lost both hands in combat (Russell had lost both hands during the war due to a grenade explosion), who struggles with how people react to his disability. The tone of the movie changes considerably in the middle, focusing on a relationship between Andrews and March's daughter, Peggy (Teresa Wright). At this point the movie becomes strictly melodrama. However, it's the ending that is least satisfying, with an overly optimistic conclusion that never addresses most of the issues raised. This uplifting moral sentiment, attached to this very real social issue—hardened vets now becoming vulnerable men—carried a potent emotional wallop. Today, however, the film seems a little too innocent and simplistic to carry the original impact.

What the critics say Critics rate this movie 5.0. "A superb example of high quality film-making in the forties."[1] "A landmark war film."[3] "The most critically acclaimed film following the post-war years."[6] "Eloquent, compassionate film."[7] **Final Word** While still compelling entertainment, its voice is beginning to fade.

Between Heaven and Hell

1956   USA   color   d. Richard Fleischer

WW II: South Pacific Actioner   3.0

Going beyond the predictable flagwaving of earlier WW II films, this late 1950s picture attempts to show us how the war and the military became a class equalizer in American society. Robert Wagner plays Sgt. Sam Gifford, a southern landowner whose family plantation dates to pre-Civil War days. Gifford is portrayed as a self-absorbed and arrogant young man who mistreats the white sharecroppers who farm his land. When his state national guard unit is called up and he is shipped to the South Pacific (in 1945), Gifford ends up serving side-by-side with many of the men he had contemptuously looked down upon. Combat, however, changes all this as many of these men prove to be exceptional soldiers, and their lives come to depend upon one another. His relationship with Pvt. Willie Crawford (Buddy Ebsen) cements his personal transformation. At times sentimentally heavy handed, the two men's quiet mutual respect has its touching moments. There is, however, another completely irrelevant story here. Unfortunately, it's a metaphor. Broderick Crawford plays a company commander who insists his men call him "Waco." He runs his isolated company as if it were a southern plantation, as he struts about, bellowing and browbeating his men. He also has two armed bodyguards who walk around without shirts, carrying submachine guns. This unfortunate analogy to southern plantation life initially makes you think you are watching an episode of *The Twilight Zone*. But our southern dandy does get a taste of his own medicine. Crawford is over the top and fun to watch. There are some decent combat scenes, but over all the movie is slow-moving, particularly with a long flashback of Wagner courting a young woman (Terry Moore). While this film is on target—there was an important shift occurring in American society—the film's liberal sentimentality about an emerging classless society was premature.

What the critics say Critics rate this movie 1.0 to 4.0. "Disjointed psychological drama."[2] "An interesting if talky war drama."[3] "A good hard-hitting action film."[5] "This one is closer to Hell, mainly because it's all talk and no action."[7] **Final Word** At least this film tried to say and do something different than the hundreds that came before it.

The Big Red One

1980 USA color d. Samuel Fuller

World War II: Infantry Combat   1.0

It appears that producer/director/writer *extraordinaire* Samuel Fuller has attained cult status for making low-budget war movies, of which *The Big Red One*, a retro 1940s flagwaver, is considered his opus. It's the last of a quartet of truly bad war films (*The Steel Helmet, Fixed Bayonets* and *China Gate*). *The Big Red One* is an autobiographical movie that follows a five-man rifle squad (16th Infantry) led by Lee Marvin (carrying the symbolic title "The Sergeant"), from North Africa in 1942 to the liberation of a concentration camp in 1945. The film is narrated by the whiny and obnoxious voice of Pvt. Zab, (Robert Carradine). This is a movie without any sense of dramatic tension because it's obvious from the beginning that this squad is invulnerable to the war and they know it. There are so many low-camp moments it is not possible to mention them all. In one scene, the "Bad Nazi," hiding at the top of a large wooden cross, sets an ambush by having 35-40 German soldiers play dead. Needless to say, our heroic squad of five ends up killing all the German soldiers. Then a motorcycle races up with a pregnant woman in the sidecar. In order to deliver the baby the men put her in a tank where they just stabbed three German soldiers to death. They rig stirrups for her spread legs with 50 cal. ammo belts, and the soldier who delivers has a rubber on each finger because he doesn't have gloves. All the while, they are shouting "pussy" at the woman, trying to encourage her to "push," hoping she understands "French"?! In another completely incomprehensible scene, Marvin tries to get a starving Jewish boy—a concentration camp survivor—to eat. Finally, while the boy is eating a piece of fruit, Marvin accidentally knocks the fruit out of his hand as he puts the boy on his shoulders. Marvin stares at the fruit for a moment and walks off with the boy. I know this film is a low-budget effort but this scene needs to be reshot!

What the critics say Critics rate this movie 4.5 to 5.0. "A rich, realistic and poetic film."[2] "Fuller is unequaled in revealing in intimate detail the individual's struggle against the panorama of monumental cataclysm."[3] "One of the most telling (movies) ever made about the war in Europe."[8] **Final Word** I am still in shock and nauseous, and have nothing more to say.

Black and White in Color

1976 FRA/SWI/IVC color subtitles d. Jean-Jacques Annaud

WW I: Antiwar Satire   4.0

Mostly antiwar moral fable, this movie has a biting take on racism, European colonialism, Christian missionaries and the small mindedness and stupidity of people everywhere. It's hard not to like this movie! Directed by Jean-Jacques Annaud and filmed on location in the Ivory Coast, the setting is a sleepy trading post in French West Africa in 1915. This rather dusty and blissful setting is turned upside down when late arriving mail informs the colonialists that France is at war with Germany. Struck by a patriotic fervor, the French colonists quickly organize an amateurish military adventure against three German soldiers at a nearby outpost. What follows is a farcical examination of all manner of folly that war entails: patriotic speeches, hysterical fears, the inevitable call to organize and take action, parades and a belief in their own infallibility. Friends became enemies because of something that happened thousands of miles away. In fact, the intellectual of the group, the young geographer, Fresnoy (Jacques Spiesser), speculates that for all they know the war may already be over, but this does not deter them. This war is a break from the boredom and routine of their daily lives. Surrounding all the war hysteria is a barbed look at the relationship between the native black peoples of West Africa and the colonialists. In one scene Catholic missionaries trade cheap religious icons for native art, which they later burn in an egregious act of blasphemy (much of it probably priceless today). The colonials are arrogant and constantly belittling the native people—that is, when the men are not having sex with the native women. This turns around wonderfully when Fresnoy assumes command of the French efforts to raise and train a native army and elevates his "negress" lover to the status of queen in the colony. The colonists efforts at war parallel much of the folly seen in Europe, only in this case the natives are dying.

What the critics say The critics rate this movie 2.0 to 4.5. "Curious mixture of...comedy and mordant satire."[1] "Powerful...explores the horror and absurdities of war."[3] "A cutting crucible pic...about man's inhumanity to man."[4] "Nothing more than antiquated French farce."[8] **Final Word** A surprising range of critical opinion. For those who enjoy irreverent satire, this is a must see film.

Black Hawk Down
2001 USA color d. Ridley Scott

Somalia Conflict: Spec Forces Ops 4.5

Directed by Ridley Scott (*Alien* and *Gladiator*) and adapted from a book by reporter Mark Bowden, this intense and riveting combat film is based on real events. The film open in 1993 in civil war torn Somalia, as Army Ranger and Delta Forces plan to abduct the two top lieutenants of a Somali warlord, who are secretly meeting in the Somali capital of Mogadishu. Somalia has been at war with itself since the late 1980s. With numerous UN humanitarian missions to relieve wide spread famine, UN and American peacekeeping forces have been deployed to ensure the security of food deliveries. This kidnap mission, which ultimately fails, was an attempt to stop the hijacking of food shipments. Part of what makes this movie a standout is the infusion of realism. The filmmakers had the complete cooperation of the US Army, as Humvees convoy into the city and above them Black Hawks and Little Birds hover, directing operations, repelling troops and providing an immense amount of firepower with gatling guns and rockets. However, the mission quickly escalates into a major confrontation as 123 American soldiers now face thousands of armed Somalis. There's no backup plan because UN troops had not been alerted about the operation. On the ground confusion reigns, and when two Black Hawk choppers are shot down the mission is altered in order to rescue them. At the center of a limited personal story is Ranger Sgt. Matt Eversmann (Josh Hartnett), a young soldier who has never faced combat, suddenly confronted with having to take charge. Let's cut to the chase. We don't really get to know the soldiers here beyond their incredible bravery and heroic efforts. The movie does very little to examine the politics of this region or to look at command decisions surrounding this event. However, we do get as close to combat as you are likely to experience on the screen. The epilogue states that 18 American soldiers were killed (70 wounded) and 1,000 Somalis died.

What the critics say Critics rate this movie 4.0 to 5.0. "Harrowing dramatization...ferocious battle scenes recreated in brutal detail."[2] "Action, which is fierce, intense, and non-stop...brilliant visuals...fine ensemble cast."[5] **Final Word** A terrific combat film that will leave you physically drained.

The Blue and the Gray

1982   USA   color   tv miniseries   d. Andrew V. McLaglen

Civil War: Epic Drama   2.5

In perhaps the most conventional attempt ever to portray the Civil War on an epic scale, this television miniseries meets all the key criteria—6.5 hours long, lavish sets, elaborate battle recreations, well-known actors in cameo roles, and a huge cast of extras (6,300). The story focuses on a farming family in Virginia and their close relatives in Pennsylvania. In 1859, shortly after the insurrection at Harpers Ferry by abolitionist John Brown, 18-year-old John Geyser (John Hammond) rejects his family's farming way of life and joins the staff of his uncle in Pennsylvania as an illustrator for the family's newspaper. When war breaks out, John decides that he cannot fight for the South because he opposes slavery, nor for the North because it would mean taking up arms against his family. The war and the key events are shown through the conflicted loyalties of this young man who becomes a war illustrator and correspondent. Where this miniseries succeeds is in bringing home the impact of the Civil War on families with mixed and divided loyalties. It also focuses on the soldiers in the field—their fears, naiveté, and the violent outcomes of war (battle scenes have excellent period detail and realism). A key figure is Union officer Jonas Steele (Stacy Keach), who befriends John and alternately mentors and protects him. As much melodrama as war story, the romantic relationships that John and Jonas find during the war bring home both the tragedy and hope of this conflict. Unfortunately, this miniseries is on the wrong track right from the start. By portraying innocent and one-dimensional characters whose stories have predictable outcomes, the series loses touch with the darker aspects of the war. Ultimately, there doesn't appear to be a story here, as events are randomly pieced together in unrelated ways, as the film follows the course of the war to its conclusion in 1865.

What the critics say Critics rate this movie 2.5 to 3.5. "Epic television mini-series about love and hate inflamed by Civil War."[5] "Star-studded saga...polished, if occasionally sanitized version of the bloodiest conflict in U.S. history."[7] **Final Word** *The Blue and the Gray* tells a better story and brings the war better into focus than the more lavish and truly epic 1985 television miniseries *North and South*.

The Blue Max

1966 USA color d. John Guillermin

WW I: Air Combat   4.0

This lavish, big budget Hollywood production gives us a close-up look at a German fighter squadron serving on the Western Front in 1918. Adapted from Jack D. Hunter's novel of the same name, and with an outstanding musical score by Jerry Goldsmith, it has the best aerial photography of any WW I film. There are large numbers of Pfalz D-IIIs, Fokker Triplanes, Fokker D-VIIs and SE-5s. There are also the best large-scale aerial scenes of combat on the ground you will ever encounter. At the center of the story is Lt. Stachel (George Peppard), a former infantryman who was ambitious and smart enough to become a pilot. He is also obsessed with obtaining the Blue Max, the German medal awarded to pilots with twenty kills. For Stachel, this award is proof that he is at least the equal of the aristocrats who serve as pilots in the German Air Corp. As a "commoner" he quickly experiences the disdain and snobbery of these pilots, as well as their false sense of chivalry about the war. Peppard is not a nice guy (more antihero than hero). He will do anything to prove himself, and this is played out against four other excellent performances. Jeremy Kemp plays Willi von Klugermann, the pilot Stachel competes with for kills and the girl. Karl Michael Vogler plays Heidemann, the squadron commander, and Ursula Andress stars as Kaeti, in a surprisingly good performance. James Mason is a manipulating Prussian general, Count von Klugermann, who makes Stachel a national hero for propaganda purposes. This film is about ambition and the politics of war that existed in Germany's class-ridden military. While the movie has been criticized for its lack of plot, this reviewer found it interesting and intriguing, and—for a change—the romantic interest was truly central to the story. Stachel's ruthless ambition, played out against the chivalry and treacherousness of the Prussian officer corps, makes this an outstanding war film.

What the critics say Critics rate this movie 3.0 to 4.5. "Fantastic aerial photography and memorable...score."[2] "More enjoyable as simple escapism than as a serious war film."[6] **Final Word** After watching enough war films, you begin to crave a real story with interesting characters. This movie has that, plus fantastic combat scenes. Geeks! The critics are Prussian snobs. Put your video games down and go rent this one.

Bombers B-52

1957   USA   color   d. Gordon Douglas

Cold War: Peacetime Melodrama   1.5

Imagine, an entire movie devoted to the Air Force's concern about retention of senior non-commissioned officers at the height of the Cold War. Or, better yet, with a subplot about a young, and—may I add—very hot! Natalie Wood, who is disappointed that her father is only a Master Sergeant, when he could be making the big bucks in the private sector. Imagine my surprise that *Bombers B-52* tells both stories. Yes, this movie manages to toss in some rather perfunctory and uninspired aerial shots of B-52s, but it's not about the planes or the pilots—it's about a ranting Karl Malden (Master Sergeant Chuck Brennan) waiting up late at night for his daughter to return home from a date. Yes, that date is with Col. Jim Herlihy (Efrem Zimbalist, Jr.), whom Brennan hates (a long story I won't get into here), but his wife has the right attitude as she explains to Chuck that his daughter, Lois, is old enough to take care of herself and knows about the "birds and the bees." As best as I could discern, the old lady appears to be tossing her daughter at the Colonel. And why not. Her husband completely ignores her and obsessively dotes on their daughter. When they go to a night club, Malden dances with his daughter, not his wife. When he wins a contest, he buys his daughter a new car. But this discarded wife understands because she chose the Air Force way of life. And, curiously, there's no mention made of the age differences between Lois and the Colonel. Natalie plays a girl of about 19 and Efrem has to be in his early 40's. Hmmm! It's all the more incestuous when Malden comes around at the happy ending and gives the relationship his blessing. As a rule I rarely reveal how a movie ends, but I feel a responsibility to the Cold War effort to let you know that Master Sergeant Brennan, in a patriotic gesture, decides against going to work for Boeing (or was that Northrup or McDonald-Douglas).

What the critics say Critics rate this movie 2.0 to 3.0. "Glossy domestic melodrama punctuated by aircraft shots."[1] "Ordinary love story...intertwined with good aerial footage."[2] **Final Word** This is the worst of the early Cold War "big-bird" movies, which include *A Gathering of Eagles* and *Strategic Air Command*.

Born on the Fourth of July

1989 USA color d. Oliver Stone

Vietnam War: Coming Home Drama   4.5

Tom Cruise stars in this emotionally powerful film about disabled Vietnam War vet Ron Kovic, who co-wrote the screenplay with director Oliver Stone. In 1965 Kovic, an 18-year-old boy from a blue collar community, is uncertain what to do after high school. He decides to enlist in the Marine Corps as a chance to prove himself and do something important with his life. His experiences in 'Nam forever change him. During his second tour of duty Kovic is involved in the accidental killing of women and children and—in the confusion of a firefight—kills one of his own men. Subsequently, he's wounded and medevaced to a field hospital where he's given last rites. It's really from here that the odyssey of Ron Kovic begins—in the rehab program of a VA Hospital in 1968. The hospital is rat invested, decrepit, chaotic, depressing and has an indifferent staff. In this setting Kovic learns he's paralyzed from the chest down. At home he's confronted with the antiwar movement and the world's complete indifference to the sacrifices he made. Slowly, he spirals into rage and depression, fueled by alcohol and self-pity. Suffering flashbacks, Kovic feels guilty for his actions in the war and foolish for having gone. In this film's most memorable scene, he is drunk and confronts his family about the lies that brought America into the war and that are at the center of his family's dysfunction. In tears, he finally says it all—"I want to be a man again," and poignantly adds, "who's going to love me?" By 1970, feeling lost, he runs away to Mexico, but begins his recovery by visiting the family of the soldier he killed. In a heartbreaking scene, he confesses he killed the family's son. Kovic then becomes radically involved in the antiwar movement. There's so much to like in this film, particularly Cruise, who gives the best performance of his career. But there are flaws. Stone tries to make this film a metaphor for America's experience of the war and, in the end, he becomes politically clumsy in seeking blame for the war.

What the critics say Critics rate this movie 3.5 to 5.0. "Relentlessly realistic and powerful."[2] "Stone shows America to itself in a way it won't forget...gripping, devastating."[4] "At heart, its propaganda."[6] **Final Word** The best of Stone's Vietnam war trilogy, which include *Heaven and Earth* and *Platoon*—and one of the great Vietnam War films.

The Boys in Company C

1978 USA color d. Sidney J. Furie

Vietnam War: Unit Conflict	2.5

The Boys in . . . follows five recruits from their arrival at the Marine Corps induction center in San Diego, CA, in 1967, through their first month of combat in Vietnam in 1968. This film operates on two levels. On the one hand, it is a conventional war film following a combat unit from basic training through its first month of combat. At this level the movie embodies almost every stock moment a war film could have and has very little to say that is new. The problem is compounded in the last fifteen minutes, where the film degenerates into emotional clichés. The natural leader of the group emerges as a transformed hero; the nice guy sacrifices himself and dies for his buddies and the nearby children. The obnoxious and ambitious captain is justifiably killed. The corrupt Vietnamese official gets it, and the "good ole American boys" win the soccer game because they are willing to risk possible death rather than lose. In between this action this company of Marines get the clap, overdose, are wounded, killed, get high on marijuana, loaded on alcohol, argue and bond—well, you get the picture. On a second level this film is an indictment of military command. It offers a terse and biting perspective on ambitious and inept American officers willing to sacrifice men for promotion, and shows us corrupt and murderous Vietnamese military officials. In this movie these are the real enemy. Time and again, as seen from the viewpoint of the grunt in the field, the Marines' lives are sacrificed for meaningless political and personal goals unrelated to winning the war. Unfortunately, this point is hammered at you in every way possible. Perhaps the film's best accomplishment is how it allows the audience to feel the sheer chaos and confusion that surrounds soldiers in combat.

What the critics say Critics rate this movie 2.5 to 4.0. "Crude action melodrama."[1] "Good tough film focuses on stupidity of military brass and demoralization of soldiers."[2] "Spotty but okay popcorn trade drama."[4] "A frank, hard-hitting drama."[5] "Comes close, at times, to being the powerful film the subject of the Vietnam War suggests."[7] **Final Word** If you are a hardcore war-movie type of guy, then check it out, it has its moments.

Bravo Two Zero

1999 RSA color d. Tom Clegg

Persian Gulf War: Special Forces   3.5

This compelling war film, adapted from the book by Sergeant Andy McNab, tells the true story of British Special Air Services (SAS) during the Persian Gulf War. In January 1991, an eight-man SAS team was inserted into Northern Iraq to cut communications between Baghdad and Iraqi mobile scud launchers. Choppered into "scud alley" at night and carrying 210 lb. packs, the team was immediately detected by Iraqi soldiers. Their efforts to cross 170 kilometers of desert to the Syrian border, after they lost communications, is a remarkable story of endurance and heroism. Heavily outnumbered, the SAS team engaged in numerous fire-fights, killing over 100 Iraqi soldiers and wounding an equal number. Crossing 85 kilometers of desert in one night, they then commandeered a taxi to get within a few miles of the Syrian border, only to be captured. While this movie starts slowly, and fails to develop characters, or to put events in a military or political context, it gets better as the story unfolds. As the mission unravels and the SAS team attempts to escape, they become separated. The story then focuses on Sergeant McNab (Sean Bean), who is eventually captured and tortured by Iraqi secret police. The film provides a graphic portrayal of his brutal torture and his refusal to give in to his torturers. Scenes of his teeth being extracted and his being fed urine and feces are difficult to watch, but his courage in the face of this sadism is remarkable. Ultimately, five of the eight SAS soldiers survived. This relatively unpublicized film provides many well-staged fire fights, and highlights the aggressive nature of the special forces and their ability to survive and prevail against overwhelming odds. After a brief and somewhat slow introduction, *Bravo Two Zero* quickly becomes a serious war movie with an important story to tell.

What the critics say No available reviews. **Final Word** Poorly titled, but well worth watching, this little known film is the best war movie to date about the Gulf War. These events are also chronicled in the book *The One That Got Away* by Chris Ryan. The SAS is considered the best special forces program in the world and is the basis for the US Army Delta Force, which it helped train.

Breaker Morant

1980   AUS   color   d. Bruce Beresford

Boer War: Military Legal Drama   5.0

Breaker Morant is one of the best war movies ever made. It is beautifully filmed, and every performance is richly nuanced. Based on an Australian award winning play by Kenneth G. Ross, this is a true story that takes place in South Africa during the Boer War (1899-1902)—a small war that pitted the British army against the Dutch settlers (Boers) in South Africa. The Boers engaged in guerrilla warfare and waged it with a civilian population, utilizing "hit and run" tactics." In response, the British organized the Bushfeld Carbiniers to fight the Boers on their own terms. The movie centers around three Australian officers in the Carbiniers who are facing court-martials for the execution of Boer prisoners of war and a German missionary. Through a series flashbacks, we are shown the many layers of what had transpired. There are outstanding performances by Edward Woodard (Lt. Harry "Breaker" Morant), accused of ordering the executions and by Jack Thompson (Maj. J.F. Thomas), the inexperienced defense attorney who attempts to try the military as well. The film explores two important issues: it examines a military cover-up of orders that resulted in atrocities, and it questions if soldiers can be judged by civilian law and morality during times of war. Or, as Maj. Thomas states during the court-martial, "War changes men's nature. The barbarities of war are seldom committed by abnormal men. The tragedy of war is that these horrors are committed by normal men in abnormal situations." This movie is also an indictment of British Commanders, and portrays Lord Kitchener (commander of British forces) and his staff as guilty of creating a sham court-martial. There is a strong suggestion that the Australian and British governments executed these officers for political purposes. While the movie's sympathies are clearly with the three officers, it in no way condones the brutality of their actions. This is a great film that examines the larger issue of moral responsibility during war time.

What the critics say Critics rate this movie 4.5. to 5.0. "Beautifully filmed...profoundly moving."[3] "It approaches masterful and is extremely effective."[4] "Riveting...antiwar statement."[5] **Final Word** Stop watching reality TV and go rent a movie that will help you transcend reality!

Breakthrough

1978   GER   color   d. Andrew V. McLaglen

WW II: German Western Front   1.0

Here is a formulaic war movie that only goes through the motions. It's also a sequel to the very average *Cross of Iron.* Whereby James Coburn, as Sgt. Feldwebel Steiner grinned his way across the German eastern front in *Cross of Iron,* here Richard Burton reprises Steiner, only on the western front and sans the grin. Attempting to cash in on the success of *Cross of Iron,* the producer went with even more big-name stars in the sequel. It's safe to say that these stars, collectively, give the worst performances of their careers (Richard Burton, Robert Mitchum, Rod Steiger and Curt Jürgens). By far, the worst performance is Burton's—53 years old when he made this film (he dies at the age of 59), he looks 70 years old, bloated and lifeless as he walks through his role. It's sad to see a once great actor wasting away like this. Steiger, who has only a few scenes as an American general, seems to be in a completely different movie. He is given to bizarrely intense outbursts with a southern accent, as if he were hallucinating scenes from *In the Heat of the Night.* Robert Mitchum (Col. Rogers) stands deadpan in front of him as if Steiger were nuts (it's high camp but probably not why you are watching this movie). There is a story of sorts. German generals are plotting to assassinate the Führer and want to negotiate a surrender to the Americans. Steiner is asked to make contact with the Americans, and to set up a meeting between German and American generals. Obviously, Hitler was not assassinated, and this planned meeting turns into a trap to knock out American tanks. Are you still with me? Sgt. Steiner, doing the right thing, turns against the German army, shoots the major he doesn't like, foils the ambush, saves Col. Rogers' life and rescues civilians in a nearby town. Did I mention that he also has sex with his commander's girlfriend while on leave in Paris? The opening large-scale action scenes are not bad and have a number of Russian T-34 tanks. However, the movie becomes a rather dull, bloodless affair after this.

What the critics say Critics rate this movie 1.0. to 1.5 "Superficial sequel...particularly disappointing considering cast."[2] "Average at best."[5] **Final Word** Another paean to all the "good" German soldiers in WW II. Is a "good German" soldier one who fought bravely for his army or one who helps his enemies?

The Bridge

1959 GER b/w subtitles d. Bernhard Wicki

WW II: War is Crazy	3.5

Based on an autobiographical novel by Erwin C. Dietrich, this film take us to a small rural German town just days prior to the end of the war in 1945. Young men throughout Germany are being drafted and hurried to the front lines in a desperate effort by Hitler to halt the Allied advance through Germany. We watch as seven 16-year-old boys, all close friends, get drafted into the German Wehrmacht. The boys are immediately assigned to defend a bridge leading into their town, under the command of an army corporal who is later mistakenly shot as a deserter. What transpires at this point is a poignant and brutally realistic depiction of young boys thrown into war. The first half of this film plays much like a Depression Era movie about small town life. The sketches of people and place are relatively simple, showing us rather naive and innocent adolescents who have all been militarized by German society. Each boy, in his own way, is filled with idealistic and heroic images of war. All are also at a vulnerable age and eager to separate from their families in order to prove themselves in the world. In many ways this movie is a WW II version of *All Quiet on the Western Front*, (a WW I novel and movie about a group of idealistic young boys who are drafted and sent to the Western Front in the last months of the war). The results are the same—death and wasted young lives. While this is a good film, it's predictable from the outset. The director's efforts to emphasize the youth of these young men goes to unreasonable lengths, particularly at the end, with an American soldier trying to help them. The first half is extremely unsophisticated filmmaking that glosses over any chance of bringing us close to these boys as individuals, but rather filling us with generalities about adolescence. The second half is excellent, and the depiction of the battle to defend the bridge is realistic and well done.

What the critics say Critics rate this movie 3.0 to 4.5. "Painful but memorable war vignette."[1] "A strong antiwar film...you won't soon forget".[3] "Emotional antiwar film."[7] **Final Word** This is a solid drama that lacks sophistication. Today, the forcible conscription of young men into armed forces is a serious world wide problem.

The Bridge at Remagen

1969   USA   color   d. John Guillermin

WW II: Infantry and Armored Combat   3.5

This is a surprisingly well-done WW II combat-actioner based on real events. In March 1945, seven months before the end of the war, the German army in the west is in full retreat, and Allied forces are racing to get to Berlin before the Russians. There's only one remaining bridge over the Rhine river, the Ober Kassel, and Hitler has ordered it blown up. Shown from both the American and German viewpoints, this film focuses on the command view of war. The Americans, at first, want the bridge destroyed in order to prevent 75,000 German troops from escaping entrapment. Later the Americans decide to try and capture the bridge. On the other side, a number of German officers resist blowing the bridge until their remaining army can escape across it. We watch the American soldiers under Lt. Hartman (George Segal), a battle hardened and cynical commander of an armored infantry company, trying to do his job and keep his men alive with the war near its end. Hartman's unit has been assigned to race ahead and destroy the bridge. On the German side is Maj. Kreuger (Robert Vaughn), one of the officers who has agreed to disobey Hitler's order and keep the bridge open. This movie is filled with intense and highly realistic combat action. If you like machine guns, tanks and German 88s wailing, then this is a good one for you. The pace of action is good, though it has a few digressions. And, there is an interior story going on here as well. Lt. Hartman realizes that his men are being driven to the limits of their endurance and then sacrificed in an effort to save the bridge. He understands the politics of this effort but questions it as a military objective. On the German side, the issue is how much they should resist and sacrifice in a lost cause. There's a happy ending for the Americans, as Lt. Hartman and Sgt. Angelo (Ben Gazzara) appear to be killed but survive. This little twist at the end detracts from what could have been an even harder hitting combat film.

What the critics say Critics rate this movie 3.0. "Disenchanted, violent war film...adroitly staged."[1] "Solid World War II drama...well-done action sequences."[7] **Final Word** Filmed in Czechoslovakia, the actors and crew had to flee in a "fleet of cars" when the Soviets invaded in 1968. The East Germans charged that the production was a CIA sponsored operation.

Bridge on the River Kwai

1957 GBR color d. David Lean

| WW II: Prisoner-of-War | 3.5 |

This critically acclaimed movie won seven Academy Awards, including Best Picture, Director (David Lean) and Actor (Alec Guinness). Based on the novel by Pierre Boulle (and his experiences as a POW), the movie is a AFI top 100 film. The question is, how does this movie hold up 45 years later? Shot in Ceylon (Sri Lanka), the story takes place in Burma, in 1943, as British prisoners of war are conscripted to build a railway bridge for the Japanese army. The British soldiers are commanded by Col. Nicholson (Alec Guinness), who is a stickler for doing things by the book. It also becomes apparent very soon that things are slightly askew with this officer when Nicholson makes the case that because they had formally surrendered, they cannot legally attempt to escape! The commander of Camp 16, played rather flatly by Sessue Hayakawa, is Col. Saito, a brutal and sadistic officer whose own honor and life are on the line if this bridge is not completed on time. A battle of wills between these two officers ensues. At this level the movie is fairly compelling drama, with many ironic moments as Guineas ultimately prevails and builds "a proper bridge," demonstrating British moral superiority. However, this is only half the movie. The second half, which stops the movie dead in its tracks, is about Maj. Shears, played by William Holden, an American POW who escapes and later returns to help blow up the bridge. Unfortunately, Holden's role is predictable, having played it many times. Also, it's difficult to explain his constant erotic interludes with native women while on this mission! But perhaps what most damages the film, is a highly contrived ending that undoes all the drama and ironic moments that had preceded it. This movie is not a realistic look at a Japanese POW camp, and it ultimately abandons being a serious drama for an escapist adventure. (British POWs were conscripted to build a bridge in Thailand', as part of the notorious "death railway." Today it's a popular tourist attraction.)

What the critics say Critics rate this movie 5.0. "Ironic adventure epic."[1] "Stands out as one of the greatest and most powerful films ever made about war."[3] "A war movie masterpiece...brilliant action picture."[7] **Final Word** What can I tell you. The times have changed. Average, at best, and often silly and distracting when it gets into the jungle.

The Bridges at Toko-Ri

1954 USA color d. Mark Robson

Korean War: Naval Air Combat   2.5

When this film was released in 1954 it had "Blockbuster" written
all over it. Adapted from a novel by James A. Michener, the
movie stars William Holden, Grace Kelly, Fredric March and
Mickey Rooney. It also features a close-up look at an aircraft
carrier and jet fighters. Holden plays Navy Lt. Harry Brubaker,
who was called up from reserve status to fight in the Korean
War. A veteran combat pilot of the Second World War, Brubaker
is now a married attorney with two children and does not want to
be fighting this war. The movie opens with him stationed aboard
an carrier flying combat missions off the coast of Korea in 1952.
What dramatic tension there is (and there is not much) is on
Brubaker's realization that their upcoming mission to bomb the
bridges at Toko-Ri will be extremely dangerous. This movie is
part 1950s romance soap-opera (Grace Kelly), part comedy
(Mickey Rooney), part close-up look at jet fighters taking off and
landing on a carrier, and fifteen minutes of action at the end. It's
slow moving, talkative, and has no serious character or plot
development. Except for a few well-filmed flight sequences of
Grumman F9F "Panther" jet fighters, this movie does not
succeed at any level. Midway through the film Fredric March, an
admiral, tells Grace Kelly (the wife of Brubaker): "If we don't stop
the Koreans here, they'll be in Japan, Indochina, and the
Philippines and then on to Mississippi." He then tells her, "You're
ignorant and defenseless." This scene is meant to prepare her
and the audience for the necessary death of Brubaker. His death
is not an antiwar statement but rather is justified to stop
Communism. The film provides very little sense of the war. We
are not privy to the feelings or motives of the pilots, there is no
discussion of air combat tactics, and almost no combat until the
last few minutes. Even Holden's death at the end feels
gratuitous—an attempt to add *gravitas* to a light weight film.

What the critics say Critics rate this movie 4.0 to 4.5.
"Ambitiously staged action thriller...taut, thrilling, top flight."[1]
"Powerful Korean War drama."[3] "Topflight war spectacle."[4]
"Rousing war epic."[5] **Final Word** I suspect these reviews reflect
the public's need for escapist entertainment in the 1950s. You
should ignore them. This is a movie who time has come and
gone, unless you want to check out vintage 1950s jets.

A Bridge Too Far

1977   GBR/USA   color   d. Richard Attenborough

WW II: Big Battle   2.5

In the 1960s and 1970s movie studios had an obsession with star-driven, big-budget epic war movies. They include *The Battle of Britain, In Harm's Way, The Longest Day*, the four-hour epic *Waterloo*, and an eight-hour version of *War and Peace*. It can also be safely said that every one of these movies failed because of their length and inability to tell a compelling story. *A Bridge Too Far* has been jokingly called "a movie too long," and at 2 hours 57 minutes it truly requires a director's cut. This lengthy movie is a potentially impressive war film, that was not realized. It also goes where no war film has previously gone. For many years now Australian war movies have been bashing British military command, but now we have the British highlighting their own military incompetence. This movie shows us Field Marshal Montgomery's attempt to upstage Gen. George Patton by politically prevailing with Eisenhower with "Operation Market Garden." Montgomery's plan was to drop 35,000 paratroopers 64 miles behind enemy lines, in Holland, in an attempt to capture three bridges along the Rhine. The main battle is for the bridge at Arnhem. While the paratroopers held the bridges, they were to be reinforced by tanks within 48 hours. It was expected that the Allies could then quickly enter Germany and end the war. The plan was a monumental failure of military planning. This movie suggests that Montgomery grossly underestimated enemy strength and that the plan had too many high-risk contingencies to ever succeed. The movie itself simply tells too many stories from too many points of view and fails to focus on its main story—the politics behind this operation. In the end, the film never really nails down this failure or its cost in lives. It turns out that more lives were lost in this operation than in the landing at Normandy. While there are many outstanding battle scenes, the $9 million spent on actors' salaries was a gross waste.

What the critics say Critics rate this movie 2.0 to 3.5. "Its sober intent conflicts with its roster of guest stars."[1] "Richard Attenborough's lifeless, over-produced version of the fine Cornelius Ryan book."[2] **Final Word** You can get a beer, fix a sandwich and go to the bathroom and still not have to hit pause on your remote.

A Bright Shining Lie

1998   USA   color   tv   d. Terry George

Vietnam War: Military Command   5.0

Based on the 1988 Pulitzer Prize-winning book by Neil Sheehan, this is the true story of American army officer, Lt. Colonel John Paul Vann (Bill Paxton). This film chronicles his arrival in Vietnam in 1962 as a military "advisor," and follows him until his death in a helicopter crash in 1972. At the time of his death he was a civilian Major General running the war for South Vietnam. Vann is portrayed as a brilliant and highly ambitious military strategist who early on resigns his commission because of his outspoken views about the war. As early as 1962, Vann begins to see the South Vietnamese government as extremely corrupt, and high-ranking Vietnamese army officers as highly political and incompetent. Behind the scenes, he believes American generals are supporting the political corruption and helping distort the public perception of the war. As the war escalates in 1965, Vann returns as head of the State Department's Civilian Aid Program. What becomes immediately evident to him is that General Westmoreland has no overall strategy for fighting and winning the war. The film opens with a strong statement—"We went there believing in freedom and democracy, but somehow we lost our moral compass. How did it happen?" This, however, is not an antiwar film. While it never shies away from showing us the mistakes made by the US in entering and conducting the war, it also gives us a complex and troubling character who does not, in the end, accept the opening statement. Vann doesn't believe this war is wrong or immoral, but, rather, that the US is not fighting it effectively. This movie is unflinching in showing us the war as well as this one soldier. Documentary footage inserted into the film adds to its realism. It is well acted, well-scripted and has many intense scenes of the war. In a riveting and entertaining manner, the film shows us ten years of this war from the perspective of the decision-making inner sanctums.

What the critics say Critics rate this movie 2.5 to 4.5. "Middle-of-the-road cop-out...dramatically hollow."[3] "Controversial expose of the Vietnam War...paints a grim picture of a war America clearly didn't understand."[7] **Final Word** This is another excellent HBO production. Without doubt one of the best movies about the Vietnam War. Take a few of your precious war movie hours and watch this one.

Buffalo Soldiers

1997   USA   color   tv   d. Charles Haid

Indian Wars: Black Cavalry Regiment   4.0

In 1866 Congress authorized the formation of two all-Black US cavalry regiments (led by white officers), the 9th and 10th, to help subdue Indian tribes in the southwest. Circa 1870 the Cheyenne began calling these troops Buffalo Soldiers because their dark skin and curly hair reminded them of buffaloes (this is one of at least three different explanations for this name). This fictitious story takes place in 1880, in the New Mexico Territories, as the 10th is attempting to suppress an uprising by Mescalero Apaches. In a well-acted, intelligently scripted and beautifully photographed movie, Danny Glover plays First Sergeant Washington Wyatt, a former slave who now commands a company of cavalry soldiers. He's a no-nonsense, hard-as-nails soldier who has the respect of his men. What evolves here is a compelling examination of the personal conflict these Black soldiers faced—suppressing American Indians while under the command of white soldiers who are openly racist towards them. It's clear that the Black soldiers are not far removed from the circumstances of the Indians, who are also seen as less than fully human. The catalyst for this conflict of conscience comes in the form of a cavalry scout, John Horse (Carl Lumbly), who is half-Black and half-Seminole, who confronts Wyatt—"The army bears you no love. None of you. They endure you...they wipe all the tribes from the slate with our blood. You have no pride, sergeant." This is a graphically violent film that pulls no punches in portraying the life and death struggle occurring on the frontier. As Black soldiers are killed, it becomes less clear what they are fighting for. Initially, the cause appeared to be for their own self-respect and to prove themselves as free men, but when confronted with massacring an entire tribe, they are forced to redefine themselves once again. While the ending is a little too pat and probably isn't consistent with the hardcore nature of the rest of this film, this is a first-rate movie.

What the critics say Critics rate this movie 3.0 to 4.0. "Full-blooded, often violent...powerful, well-acted tale."[2] "Danny Glover rides tall in the saddle...a decent cast and strong direction."[7] **Final Word** The whitewashing by Hollywood of how the West was won has slowly begun to unravel. Black soldiers fought in Cuba, the Philippines and on the Mexican border.

The Burmese Harp

1956 Japan b/w subtitles d. Kon Ichikawa

WW II: War is Immoral   2.5

The Burmese Harp is an elegy for the Japanese war dead in Southeast Asia. The film's portrayal of Japanese soldiers as basically heroic and noble, with no mention of their aggression and atrocities, left this viewer profoundly disturbed by the historical revisionism. We follow a company of Japanese soldiers along the Thailand-Burma border a few weeks before the war's end. The fact that the commander is a former music teacher who teaches Pvt. Mizushima to play the Burmese Harp and turns the rest of the company into a chorus that periodically sings Christian religious hymns may strike some as odd. From here, the story plays out in a uninteresting and slow-moving fashion. After the surrender of his unit, which features a joint chorus with British soldiers?, Pvt. Mizushima is sent to convince Japanese soldiers who are holding out to surrender. Out of a sense of honor they refuse and are subsequently killed, while Pvt. Mizushima is wounded. Nurtured back to health by Buddhist monks, he begins a long and arduous physical and spiritual odyssey to rejoin his unit, now at a British POW camp (Mudon). However, along the way he encounters the mass grave of Japanese soldiers, which leads this young soldier to a profound religious conversion. The remainder of this movie portrays the soldiers in Pvt. Mizushima unit as obsessing about him (it makes no sense whatsoever). In the end, Pvt. Mizushima decides to stay in Burma and tend to the souls of the unburied Japanese war dead. Only in this film's final moments is there the slightest hint that there were other tragedies in Asia as well. In a letter, Pvt. Mizushima refers to himself as a "penitent wanderer," implying, however obliquely, that the Japanese had a greater moral responsibility beyond their own war dead. This is an emotionally manipulative film, full of nonsensical moments that will leave you shaking your head in disbelief. The movie strove for something very profound but missed by not finding the truth.

What the critics say Critics rate this movie 4.5. to 5.0. "Deeply impressive and horrifying war film."[1] "Extraordinary antiwar drama is affecting and memorable."[2] A magnificent, poetic piece of film making."[3] **Final Word** If you watch this film and are not offended by it—when you wake up, remember to turn off the TV and rewind the film.

By Dawn's Early Light

1990   USA   color   tv   d. Jack Sholder

| Cold War: WW III Nuclear Thriller | 4.0 |

This gripping nuclear war thriller, adapted from William Prochnau's book *Trinity's Child,* covers familiar dramatic ground with new excitement and energy. We watch as renegade Soviet army dissidents launch a mobile nuclear missile from Turkey, making it look as if NATO has launched a first strike against the Soviet Union. Almost simultaneously, the Soviet Union launches a retaliatory strike at American military sites. When the Soviets realize what has really happened, they contact the American President (Martin Landau). The Soviets suggest three possibilities—America accepts its losses but not launch a retaliatory strike; launch a strike of equal destructive force (which they will accept); or escalate the war, forcing each side to destroy the other. These events are viewed from several perspectives. We watch the President, in the war room with his advisors, agonize over the best course of action, while issues about succession to the President arise and create more disorder. We watch the conflicts of a B-52 bomber crew heading towards the Soviet Union once they realize what has happened. There's also a politically correct element to this film as the copilot, a woman (Rebecca DeMornay), has a relationship with the pilot (Powers Boothe). We also watch the SAC E-4 airborne command post, commanded by James Earl Jones, who has the responsibility to execute the final orders to either call back the bombers and stand down the nuclear subs or order an all-out retaliatory strike. This action is all undertaken with a high degree of realism. The interesting angle the film takes is that the massive destruction has already happened. Now, how do both sides step back from total annihilation? There's chaos all about and mistrust on both sides. The film does a good job of focusing on how individual choices ultimately determine the outcome. While there are a few dramatic lapses, there are enough twists and turns to keep you glued to your set. The acting is excellent throughout, and the ending is not at all obvious.

What the critics say Critics rate this movie 3.0 to 4.5. "Cold War thriller...taut adaptation."[2] "Classy, edge-of-your-seat thriller."[3] "Slick adaptation...unfolds like an updated *Fail Safe.*"[6] **Final Word** Probably the end of the line for Cold War nuclear confrontation on this scale, but compelling drama nonetheless.

Cadence

1991 USA color d. Martin Sheen

Cadence is one of those movies which you root for to be good, but know you are going to be let down by in the end. Based on the novel *Count a Lonely Cadence* by Gordon Weaver, the film was directed by Martin Sheen, who along with his son Charlie Sheen, stars in it as well. We watch as a troubled young airman (C. Sheen), stationed in Germany in 1965, searches for direction in his life and finds it in a stockade with five Black soldiers who have been charged with serious crimes. The possibilities are endless and intriguing here but become too predictable to produce real drama. Adding to this movie's unreality is the miscasting of Martin Sheen as a racist, redneck, bullying stockade sergeant with a severe alcohol problem. While the Black dudes play the man's game, Charlie Sheen is defiant, and while he eventually earns the respect of his stockade mates, the stockade sergeant becomes increasingly erratic and threatening until it all gets very stupid at many different levels. Charlie Sheen, who mostly frowns his way through his movie, is not particularly effective in this role. However, the five Black inmates bring life to this movie and are truly interesting—particularly Laurence Fishburne as "Stokes" and Michael Beach as "Webb." This movie's best moments are when these five Black inmates are marching and break into a marching dance while singing Sam Cook's great hit "Chain Gang." At the end, the Charlie Sheen character has under-gone a subtle transformation from his stockade experience, but we are never quite sure what was at the heart of it. His 90-day sentence is commuted and, as the lucky one, his unit is immediately shipped to 'Nam. However, it all becomes less believable when everyone of the Black inmates is innocent of the rape, murder and armed robbery charges they face. This movie would have been better realized if a few really bad dudes, and not just victims, had taught Sheen some lessons about life and himself.

What the critics say Critics rate this movie 1.5 to 2.5. "Overwrought and insignificant."[2] "Characters and situations are intriguing but not rendered effectively."[5] "More notable for good intentions than dramatic power."[7] **Final Word** I recommend that everyone buy a CD of Sam Cook's greatest hits.

The Caine Mutiny

1954   USA   color   d. Edward Dmytryk

| WW II: Court-Martial Drama | 2.5 |

This is another "classic" movie that does not live up to its acclaim. *The Caine Mutiny* is based on the Pulitzer Prize-winning novel by Herman Wouk about a mutiny on a Navy minesweeper. At the center of this mutiny is the commander of the *Caine*, Captain Queeg, played by Humphrey Bogart. Bogart's performance as the obsessive and paranoid ship's captain is what truly elevates this otherwise average movie. Having served in combat in the North Atlantic, Queeg comes to a "beaten-up tub" that appears to reside in the backwaters of the Pacific in 1943. There's immediate conflict between his by-the-book approach and a crew that appears to have seldom taken being in the Navy seriously. The important story here, however, is watching Queeg unravel in a crisis and turn on his officers and crew. Soon he begins a delusional search for a non-existent key to the ship's refrigerator in the belief that someone has stolen a few ounces of strawberries. The climax comes when Queeg freezes during a typhoon that nearly capsizes the ship. Executive Officer Steve Maryk (Van Johnson) steps in and relieves the Capt. of command. Later, in response to his humiliation, Queeg brings court-martial charges against Lt. Maryk for mutiny. Unfortunately, this movie is often distracted from its intriguing story. There's a boring opening twenty minutes before Queeg is even introduced as a character, a happy musical score, silly humor and an irrelevant romance carried on by Ensign Keith (Robert Francis). But this film's biggest flaw is the ending. It races through the dramatic courtroom scenes and then adds a dubious twist as the defense attorney (José Ferrer) accuses the officers of disloyalty and mutiny, after they are acquitted. Their attorney suggests that, had they been loyal, the mutiny would not have occurred. This clever attempt to turn the tables at the end sink this entire film into unbelievability. The story was made into a more watchable 1988 TV movie, *The Caine Mutiny Court-Martial*.

What the critics say Critics rate this movie 3.0 to 5.0. "Decent if lamely paced version of a bestseller which was also made a successful screenplay."[1] "An absolute must see...beautifully done, a terrific movie."[7] **Final Word** There has never been a mutiny in the history of the US Navy.

Call To Glory

1984 USA color tv d. Thomas Carter

Cold War: Cuban Missile Crisis · 1.5

If you were to read the back of the box for this video, you would probably think it was about U-2 pilots during the Cuban Missile Crisis. You would be half-right. This pilot for a short-lived TV series is really more about middle-class angst among military families in the early 60s, than about the brief nightmarish incident in 1962. Now you ask, "How does he reach that conclusion?" The answer is simple. As Col. Sarnac (Craig T. Nelson) accepts dangerous high-altitude missions (4080th Strategic Reconnaissance Wing) over Cuba, we watch his teenage daughter become anxious about her prom. When documentary television news footage shows us Kennedy addressing the nation about medium-and-intermediate range Soviet SS-4 and SS-5 nuclear missiles being deployed in Cuba, the movie focuses on his young son refusing to talk. When Adali Stevenson, US Ambassador to the UN, pointedly asks the Soviet Ambassador if they have deployed missiles in Cuba, and he refuses to answer, and Stevenson tells him, "I am prepared to wait for your answer until hell freezes over," the movie cuts to his wife being upset about their daughter wanting to learn to fly. But mostly we know this isn't about nuclear brinkmanship between Krushchev and Kennedy because the movie ends without telling us the outcome of the crisis. Minimally, there could have been a brief epilogue telling us how the crisis was resolved, but no, we get a spirited discourse about duty and honor among military personnel. There's some excellent footage of the U-2 spy plane (but no details about the plane itself). There's no exploration of the operational requirements of the plane's high priority missions over Cuba or focus on the pilots. One U-2 is shot down by a SAM during a flyover of Cuba. Kennedy ultimately decided on a maritime blockade of Cuba, and for six days there was an international crisis. Krushchev ultimately agreed to dismantle the missiles and, secretly, the US removed its missiles from Turkey and agreed never to invade Cuba.

What the critics say Critics rate this movie 2.5 to 3.5. "Engrossing pilot episode...taut script...uniformly well-acted."[7]
Final Word U-2s became operational in 1957 and are still in service today. They have a service ceiling of 90,000 ft. and a range of 4,000 miles.

Capitaine Conan

1996 FRA color subtitles d. Bertrand Tavernier

World War I: Combat/Legal Drama 4.5

This scathing indictment of French military command opens along the Bulgarian border in Sept. 1918, two months before the Armistice is signed ending the war. Capitaine Conan (Philippe Torreton) leads an elite group of commandos who infiltrate enemy lines and create an enormous amount of havoc. They are extremely skilled in the "killing arts" and appear to relish not only their elite status but the killing as well. From here, many subplots evolve, but the focus is on Capt. Conan and his friend, Lt. Norbert (Samuel Le Bihan), an aristocrat and educated man who volunteered for the infantry. Norbert later becomes a prosecuting attorney in the French army. By war movie standards, it does not get any more complex than this one. The two main characters, Conan and Norbert, are wonderfully nuanced, with an inevitable conflict developing between them. This film also explores what happens to men who are adept at killing (many are psychopaths) when the war ends and they are unable to conform to a peacetime code of conduct. The drunkenness, disorderliness and violent criminal acts that follow are examined in light of the great bravery the men exhibited during the war as well as their enormous contribution to winning it. This movie is also a critical examination of the French military command as it attempts to impose order on soldiers, often imprisoning and sometimes executing them for menial offenses. This movie suggests an overall contempt by high command for the soldier, as it explores class issues in French society. There are excellent combat scenes, with outstanding realism, and tense courtroom moments, in this well-acted and well-directed Bertrand Tavernier drama. Perhaps this movie's only real serious failing was the director's decision to film it almost entirely in dark, murky and shadowy tones. Overall this is an outstanding movie that is richly complex in characters and themes.

What the critics say Critics rate this movie 4.0. to 4.5. "Powerful indictment of militarism and false heroism."[2] "Sweeping indictment of man's capacity for savagery with finely etched, sharply honed portrayals."[3] **Final Word** This is a very good film but not for everyone. Subtitled, darkly filmed and, at times, hard to follow. However, it is very rewarding as a "thinking" war-buff's kind of movie.

Captain Corelli's Mandolin

2001 USA color d. John Madden

WW II: Wartime Romance-Drama	2.5

The impact of this movie is similar to receiving a postcard with a beautiful picture on the front and nothing written on the back. Shot on the picturesque Greek island of Cephallonia, the film is predictable from sappy beginning too happy ending—at times bordering on romantic-fable. Unfortunately, the real world doesn't intrude until near the end, but not in time to give author Louis de Bernières' story any emotional punch. This film opens with the Italians and the Germans occupying Cephallonia in 1941, with Capt. Corelli (Nicolas Cage), an officer in the Italian army, falling for the attractive Pelagia (Penelope Cruz), the daughter of a meddling Dr. Iannis (John Hurt). Cage manages to go through his entire repertoire of sad and happy faces until he and Cruz inevitably succumb to the needs of the plot (if you get my drift). But there's the small matter of Pelagia cheating on her fiancé and fraternizing with the enemy. This never really becomes an issue, which adds an air of unreality to this movie. The director's attempt patch up this problem doesn't wash. After the Italians surrender to the Allies, in 1943, the Germans seek to disarm them, but many Italian soldiers fight with the Greek partisan movement (the movie is dedicated to these men). There's a brief and intense battle scene near the end, but nothing really special. This is primarily a relationship flick produced in a style better left to the Italians—*Mediterraneo*, *Night of the Shooting Stars*, *Seven Beauties*. If the film is any statement about the Italian army, it's easy to see why they proved less effective than the Germans in combat. Capt. Corelli's entire company is comprised of soldiers who sing and prefer Verdi to Wagner, drink lots of vino and romp on the beach with prostitutes (I think I would have enjoyed the Italian army). Finally, there's the death spiral of every romance, a lack of chemistry between the principles (and in this case we are not talking about the Germans and Italians).

What the critics say Critics rate this movie 2.0 to 3.0. "Characterizations are inconsistent and the love story...is never as gripping as it's meant to be."[2] **Final Word** This movie is based solely on the audience's preconceived notion of the entire story and setting, so that the director didn't really have to do anything but color in the numbered areas along with the audience.

Carrington V.C.

1955   GBR   bw   d. Anthony Asquith

| Post-WW II: Court-Martial Drama | 3.0 |

This is a tightly wound courtroom drama with a few good twists that, unfortunately, ends in a safe and predictable manner. David Niven stars as Major Carrington, a winner of the Victoria Cross (V.C.) during WW II. He also has a high-maintenance wife, Valerie (Margaret Leighton), who has expensive tastes and is a real pain in the derriere. By the way, he's having an affair with Alison (Noelle Middleton), a young and fetching army captain who's in love with him. Did I mention that the commander of the royal artillery regiment, Lt. Col. Hennike (Allan Cuthbertson), is extremely jealous of Carrington's combat heroism (the colonel, of course, was never fortunate enough to see combat). Carrington, never one to stand on protocol, takes money from the mess fund to pay some of his personal expenses. He is owed the money by the army, which has been slow to pay him. He also claims that he announced his intentions to Lt. Col. Hennike in order to "advertise his grievance." Regimental Commander Hennike now sees an opportunity to court-martial Carrington, claiming he stole from the mess fund. Claiming complete innocence, Carrington decides to represent himself at the court-martial, simply wanting to tell his side of the story and clear everything up. Based on a play by Dorothy and Campbell Christie, this somewhat contrived mid-fifties melodrama is engaging in fits and starts. Carrington's claims of innocence aren't supported by the facts, particularly when his jealous wife takes the stand and perjures herself. Perhaps the most interesting part of this film is listening to the officers who sit on the court-martial board adjourn to discuss Carrington's case. While Niven is excellent in this role, his character is a little too chipper for all the chaos he creates, innocently or not. The most disappointing aspect of this movie is that there's very little emphasis on military life.

What the critics say Critics rate this movie 3.0 to 4.0. "Good cast, superlative Niven performance."[5] "This is a solid, engrossing drama."[7] **Final Word** This movie is not a bash at the military, as is typical today. There's no cover-up or conspiracy or hidden political agenda by the military higher-ups here—rather it's a low-keyed clash of personalities. No one would make this into a movie today, unless there was a murder or more lurid details.

Castle Keep

1969 USA color d. Sydney Pollack

Many will find *Castle Keep* to be a self-consciously arty and intellectually pretentious war movie, confused on many different levels. Others will just turn it off. Based on a fantasy novel by William Eastlake, eight weary American soldiers, led by Major Falconer (Burt Lancaster) replete with eye patch, arrive at a 10th-century Belgian chateau in the Ardennes forest, days prior to the Germans offensive that will become the Battle of the Bulge in 1944. What transpires at this point is a matter of conjecture— dream of the dead, fanciful magical-realism or your simple allegorical tale (New World saving the Old World from the barbarians)? Many strange and unbelievable events begin to take place as reality is distorted to make a point. Sgt. Baker (Peter Falk) moves in with the baker's wife and runs the bakery. Maj. Falconer beds the beautiful Countess with the Count's permission, Capt. Beckman (Patrick O'Neal), a art historian, discovers art treasures beyond his wildest imagination; a soldier falls in love with a Volkswagen; and the rest find the bordello of their dreams. Aspects of this movie suggest our squad of misfits is suffering a crisis of faith or perhaps an existential crisis (we are in Europe). The war is being fought on such a large scale and the actions of each soldier are so irrelevant to the outcome that each is forced to find his own meaning for fighting or not fighting. Ultimately, defending the castle becomes the agreed upon reality. Only the American soldiers will have to destroy the castle in order to save it (irony). Much of this movie is filled with scenes and dialogue that pretend to deeper meaning, and Lancaster is continually offering up cryptic, all-knowing statements. Adding to the confusion is the absence of any real characters we can identify with. There's only the montage of many different scenes with many different people, with no story. Now that may be the film's intention, but it's not compelling enough to hold an audience's interest or to make a larger, more-telling point.

What the critics say Critics rate this movie 2.0 to 4.0. "Never seems quite sure, and the uncertainty finally deadens it despite careful work all around."[1] "Pretentious adaptation...film has no coherency."[2] **Final Word** I would highly recommend *King of Hearts* and *A Midnight Clear* if you have a taste for the truly whimsical and surprising war movie.

Casualties of War

1989 USA color d. Brian De Palma

Vietnam War: Unit Conflict	4.5

Set against the backdrop of soldiers in the bush fighting for their lives, this is a tense psychological drama about the moral ambiguity of war. Based on a book by Daniel Lang, this story first appeared in the *New Yorker* in 1969. The movie opens in Vietnam in 1966, with a newly arrived Army private (Michael J. Fox) assigned to a squad of hardened veterans led by a tough and temperamental sergeant (Sean Penn). While on a long-range reconnaissance patrol, four of the five squad members, led by Sgt. Meserve (Penn), kidnap, brutally rape and later murder a young Vietnamese girl (Thuy Thu Le). This story is effective on many levels and pulls you into the complex interplay of forces at work here. The story's focus is on the dehumanizing aspect of war on soldiers, and the reality that if you kill enough, and those you care about are being killed, one more life in the scheme of things is not important. This squad is imploding in a personal war of retribution and revenge. Filled with rage and despair, the Vietnamese people have become the enemy for these soldiers. Pvt. Eriksson (Fox), a new arrival to the war and the squad, begins to rightly fear for his life after he refused to participate in this crime. Ordered to murder the girl in order to make him an accomplice, he refuses. Later, when a member of his squad attempts to frag him, Fox goes to his commander who ignores him. The complex interplay of loyalty and morality is very effective, and in some ways this movie by director Brian DePalma has more to say about the nihilism of war than *Apocalypse Now,* for all its artistic intent. There's a high degree of realism and a number of excellent combat scenes. What makes this film effective is the interplay of personalities and emotions that threatens the lives of everyone. While this movie tends to over simply events in the courtroom, with a tendency to preach, it goes beyond a simple morality play. It explores a complex war time event in a substantive manner.

What the critics say Critics rate this movie 2.5 to 5.0. "Jumbled, detached feel to it."[2] "Harrowing fact-based story...superbly directed."[3] "Thought provoking...brings home the horror of war without purpose and heroes without valor."[4] "Morality play."[5] **Final Word** An outstanding war movie that tells us an important truth about all wars and all soldiers.

Catch-22

1970   USA   color   d. Mike Nichols

WW II: Antiwar Satire   5.0

Directed by Mike Nichols and adapted from Joseph Heller's best-selling novel, this controversial film is always being compared to the novel. Thirty years after the film's release the time has come to evaluate it on its own. The setting is a fictional island off the coast of Italy where a B-25 bomber squadron implodes into raucous nihilism. What if the whole world was crazy, and you were the only one to know it? That is the plight of Capt. Yossarian (Alan Arkin), who believes that people are out to kill him. Meanwhile, the squadron commander, Col. Cathcart (Martin Balsam), continues to slowly raise the number of missions the crews have to fly from 25 to 80 before they can rotate back to the states. Yossarian wants out and asks the base doctor to diagnose him as crazy. But then Catch-22 is explained to him. Yossarian takes us through it—*Let me see if I've got this straight. In order to be grounded I've got to be crazy. And I must be crazy to keep flying. But if I ask to be grounded, that means I'm not crazy anymore, and I have to keep flying.* Running parallel to his neurotic and hapless pleadings is Lt. Milo Minderbinder (Jon Voight), who forms a black market syndicate that takes military supplies and trades them on the open market, while issuing shares to the officers. While on a bombing mission, Yossarian discovers that Milo has taken their silk parachutes and bartered them for Egyptian cotton. At the end of the movie, Milo is directing the bombing of the American base by their own planes, as part of a deal with the Germans to take the cotton off his hands. The scope of madness that is occurring is hard to convey; the movie employs flashbacks, many surreal images of death, slapstick humor and, ultimately, a dark and morose irony that there may be no hope for humanity—that it's all profits and death, and that everyone is using everyone else. It's a troubling image in which only a small ray of hope for escape is offered. This is a potentially disillusioning film filled with many powerful images and ideas.

What the critics say Critics rate this movie 3.0 to 5.0. "Brilliant screen adaptation...powerful and subversively funny black comedy".[3] "A biting antiwar satire...both humorous and disturbing."[5] **Final Word** It all makes so much more sense after Vietnam. A must-see movie.

China Gate

1957   USA   b/w   d. Samuel Fuller

Indochina War: Commando Operation   1.0

This studio-bound melodrama—written, directed and produced by Samuel Fuller—was probably shot in two weeks and came in under budget. It stars Angie Dickinson ("Lucky Legs") as an alcoholic, Eurasian adventuress with a small child, and Gene Barry (Sgt. Johnny Brock), as a mercenary who has rejected her and his child because the child looks Asian. We know this because the priest with one leg and every member of Brock's squad personally takes him aside and attempts to shame him. The setting for this actionless war film is Vietnam, 1954. French Legionnaires are cut off defending the city of Toy Sun in North Vietnam, near the Chinese border. We know they are cut off because every animal in the city has been eaten. Meanwhile, the Communist Chinese are supplying the Vietminh with Soviet weapons stored in a mountainous region called the China Gate. (Not to be confused with the song, *China Gate*, sung twice by Nat "King" Cole. You will eventually begin to hope this movie is a musical, because the best thing about it is Cole's singing.) Lucky Legs also happens to be having an affair with a Chinese officer, Maj. Cham (Lee Van Cleef). She moves easily between the lines as a blackmarketeer distributing alcohol and sex to Chinese soldiers, and has also agreed to help a French commando team infiltrate the Chinese ammunition dump. Are you still with me? Lucky Legs is doing this on the condition that her child is taken to America. I am not sure how much more of this plot I should reveal. Closer to soap opera than war movie, the film does do a good job of warning us about the "Red Peril" and the potential "rape of Asia." Oh, what the hell—they eventually blow up the ammo dump, Angie is killed, and Gene takes the kid with him to America. The outcome of the war is never mentioned or even the immediate fate of the city of Toy Son. No, the real story is the reuniting of father and son (or is it bad girls get killed). I am all confused.

What the critics say Critics rate this movie 2.0 to 3.5. "Dynamic action story, with early view of Vietnam's internal strife."[2] "Fuller gives his indie good production values."[4] "Conventional fare bolstered considerably by director Fuller's flair for action."[5] **Final Word** The only thing more absurd than this movie are the above reviews.

The Civil War

1990   USA   b/w-color   tv   d. Ken Burns

Civil War: Documentary:	5.0

Producer-director Ken Burns' award winning 9-volume set, which runs nearly ten hours, is an epic film *tour de force* chronicling America's most devastating war. It is also quite simply the finest war documentary ever made. Its rich collage of photographs, letters, diary entries, wartime dispatches, newspaper accounts, and critical commentary by historians and Civil War writers is unparalleled. Without benefit of modern film, Burns uses strong narrative voices and period music to bring alive the early photographs of the war. But even more impressive, Burns is able to get at the emotional heart of what took place. The poignant and evocative stories told by Americans through their letters has no modern equivalent. The first-hand sources, clear, simple, eloquent and from the heart, convey the full burden of war to everyone watching and listening. It's also clear that the passions underlying this war transcend anything known to us in contemporary times. The "idea" of America illuminated the world of this recently immigrated nation with a fervor that has not been touched in us since. There were more war-related deaths, 620,000, than in any American war. The Civil War is clearly the most important event in American history. This was also the first modern war, with its emphasis on logistics, communications and transportation, and an attritional strategy that favors the side with the largest population and greatest industrial resources. And the introduction of the rifled musket (fired a Minié bullet to a range of 1,000 yards) had a devastating effect on the battlefield, leading to trench warfare and minimizing the use of cavalry. Standing alone and above this tragic event in American history is Abraham Lincoln. He lterally willed this nation to survive and did whatever he believed it would to take hold the states together. Without Lincoln it's unlikely there would be a United States today. While this documentary will primarily satisfy the history buff, you will never see and hear more honest and harrowing accounts of war than told here.

What the critics say No available reviews. **Final Word** I cried through most of these 9 volumes and was forced to watch it alone so as not to embarrass my family. Burns' ability to show us the whole war from the inside out, from the big picture to the soldier in the field, is the genius of his work.

Cockleshell Heroes

1955   GBR   color   d. José Ferrer

WW II: Commando Operation	2.0

This is the story of a commando operation only the British could have concocted. Train eight men to paddle 70 miles in kayaks to the heavily guarded French harbor at Bordeaux, after having crossed the English Channel in a submarine. Then have them attach small "limpet-mines" to freighters that are helping the Germans break the British blockade. When the mission is completed, the commandos have to get back on their own. This could only be a true-life British commando operation, much like the minisubs that attacked the German battleship *Tirpitz* in *Above Us the Waves* or the Lancasters that bombed the German dams along the Ruhr in *The Dam Busters*. Unfortunately, the best part of this movie is the rather humorous misfits who volunteer for a dangerous mission character of the first two-thirds of this movie (yes, there's a brawl in a pub). More compelling is the interview of Bill Sparks DSM in the introduction to the film. He was one of only two members of the commando team who survived. The story he tells of their efforts to get back to Great Britain makes the story told in the *Cockleshell Heroes* look dull in comparison. It's obvious that the real adventure and misadventures were ignored in this rather conventional war story. José Ferrer (Maj. Stringer) directs and stars along with Trevor Howard (Capt. Thompson). Maj. Stringer goes about forming and training this commando team along his own rather somewhat misguided, if not naive, democratic notions of how to motivate soldiers. This, of course, leads to considerable conflict with Capt. Thompson, an elite commando officer who believes discipline is at the core of competence. A compromise of sorts is reached. The action is limited and not very interesting, as only one, two-man kayak is able to successfully mine the German freighters. The movie isn't clear about whether any serious damage was inflicted.

What the critics say Critics rate this movie 2.0 to 2.5. "Absolutely predictable semi-documentary war heroics, with barrack-room humour turning eventually into tragedy."[1] "Taut script...completely avoids the pitfalls of false heroics."[4] **Final Word** This must have been among the first British war films shot in color. It's also a nice break from the overly serious tone of most British war films at the time.

The Colditz Story

1954   GBR   b/w   d. Guy Hamilton

WW II: Prisoner-of-War	2.5

The critics suggest that *The Colditz Story* is among the best of the many British POW films. One flushed critic describes it as "one of the best films of all time."[7] First off, let's set the record straight—there are no great British POW films. However, there are many very average films, of which this is one, and include *Break to Freedom*, *Bridge on the River Kwai*, *The Captive Heart*, *Danger Within*, *The Password is Courage* and *The Wooden Horse*. The two very best are *The Hill* and *The McKenzie Break*. *The Colditz Story* is a based on a novel by Maj. P.R. Reid, who was a British POW at Colditz Castle in Saxony, Germany during WW II. This castle was supposedly a high-security camp to house Allied officers who attempted escape from other POW camps. While this film tends to portray German officers as fat, stupid, and incompetent, there may be some basis in reality for this, if the epilogue is correct. Apparently, more prisoners (56) escaped Colditz Castle than from any other German POW camp in either WW I or WW II. The movie is standard British POW genre, shot in a 1940s noire style, with lots of hijinxs and plenty of British contempt for everyone else's incompetence, including French, Polish and Dutch POWs housed at Colditz. Because the film plays out as a drawing room melodrama, one forgets that there is a war going on. Void of any real suspense or drama, most the characters are stereotypes everyone will recognize from previous British POW dramas. Unfortunately, many of the escape attempts have a rather "Three Stooges" quality about them, and one can't help but believe that the purpose of these films was to further humiliate the Germans, even after their defeat in the war. In this, and many movies like it, escaping a German POW camp became more of a game for the bored than an attempt to further Allied war efforts.

What the critics say Critics rate this movie 2.0 to 4.5. "Probably the most convincing of the British accounts of POW life."[1] "Super-solid POW saga."[2] "Easily one of the best prisoner-of-war yarns to come from a British studio."[4] **Final Word** Reality TV shows have more reality than most POW movies. The British preoccupation with POW films probably results from being a small island nation.

Come and See

1985   RUS   color   subtitles   d. Elem Klimov

WW II: German Atrocities in Belorussia   5.0

In what can only be described as a cinematic masterpiece, director Elem Klimov shows the German Army's reprisals against the Slavic peoples of Belorussia (White Russia) in 1943. Based on the memoirs of writer Ales Adamovich, the movie opens on the border of Poland and Russia, with Flor (Alexei Kravchenko), a young adolescent boy, searching for a weapon among the debris of an earlier battle. He has to have his own rifle before he can join the partisan forces fighting the Germans. Later, despite the protests of his wailing and beseeching mother, Flor leaves and begins a horrifying journey that will take him from innocence to a numbness towards death and killing. Shot in a grainy, dark and foreboding manner, with many sequences bordering on the dreamlike and hallucinogenic, the screen becomes a stark portrait of the horrors of war. At times the accumulation of these scenes is difficult to watch due to their intensity. Carried along by events Flor meets a young woman, Glasha (Olga Mironova), who has been so reduced as a human being that she can only spout vague ideas of what a woman should be. Flor, shell-shocked and near deaf from an artillery barrage, returns with Glasha to his village, where he refuses to see the massacre of his family and villagers. The second half of the movie then becomes less shadowy as we see the morning fog slowly burning off across farmlands and the figures of German soldiers appearing. In the light of day we are invited to "come and see" as the soldiers round up villagers and execute them. We bear witness to their panic and helplessness and to the complete indifference of the soldiers. In one haunting scene we watch an officer pause with several soldiers to have his picture taken with his pistol at the head of Flor. This movie gives war a horrific and unforgettable face. Based on true events, over 600 villages were destroyed and the inhabitants systematically murdered during the German occupation from 1941-1944.

What the critics say Critics rate this movie 4.5 to 5.0. "Thoroughly mesmerizing...an extraordinary film."[1] "Remarkably powerful Russian film...told with a barrage of electrifying imagery"[3] "Harrowing, unnerving epic."[4] **Final Word** May be the most intense and haunting portrait of war ever achieved by a movie.

Command Decision

1948 USA b/w d. Sam Wood

WW II: The Politics of Command   4.0

Command Decision is a thoughtful and well-executed movie that closely examines the pressures and politics of military command. In 1943 the Army Air Force committed the 8th and 15th Air Forces to the long-range precision daylight bombing of Germany. Initially, without fighter support, daylight bombing into Germany was controversial, and it resulted in high losses. This movie, adapted from a successful play by William Haines, stars Clark Gable (Gen. "Casey" Dennis), who is an air operations commander confronted with the daily task of putting bomber crews in the air and determining their targets. With his commander, Gen. Kane (Walter Pidgeon) away, Gen. Dennis makes the controversial decision to implement "Operation Stitch," a plan to bomb the German production sites of the Me-262 jet fighter. The result is a loss of 48 bombers on the first day, and 52 on the second. Immediately, many unexpected problems arise, including a visiting congressional delegation, a highly decorated pilot who refuses to fly, and Gen. Dennis' rival, Gen. Garnet (Brian Donlevy), arrives on an information gathering visit. Realizing that the bombers missed their target on the second day, Gen. Kane, a cautious and politically minded officer, becomes fearful that continued losses will lessen political support for bomber command. Gen. Dennis, adamant that the losses are acceptable given the possible long-term gains, puts his career on the line, and says to hell with politics. This is a well-acted movie filled with thoughtful and often acrimonious debate that takes us beyond the pressures of putting air crews at risk (*Twelve O' Clock High*), and shows us the politics behind the decision making. There's still considerable debate about the effectiveness of daylight bombing in 1943-1944. Many believe the enormous losses were not justified due to its limited impact on German wartime industrial production. While this film raises the issue, it strongly supports the decision to implement daylight bombing.

What the critics say Critics rate this movie 2.0 to 4.5. "Taut, engrossing...intriguing look at the behind-the-scenes politics."[2] "A gripping and thoughtful war adventure."[3] "A literate war drama, presented with a class touch."[4] **Final Word** On a daylight bombing raid on a ball-bearing factory in Schwenfurt, Germany, in 1943, the 8th AF lost 147 of 376 bombers.

Commandos Strike at Dawn

1942   USA   b/w   d. John Farrow

| WW II: Classic '40s Flagwaver | 2.0 |

Directed by John Farrow, with the story by C.S. Forrester and the script by Irwin Shaw, the only thing this movie has going for it is its good intentions. Churned out in the 1940s with dozens of other films about partisan and resistance efforts, Paul Muni (Erik) plays a humble and soft-spoken meteorologist whose sleepy Norwegian fishing village (Vancouver Island) has been occupied by the Germans in 1940. As the Nazis grind down any sense of dignity and freedom these people have, the chronically forlorn Erik organizes a resistance effort, and gives numerous patriotic speeches about the German "gangsters and thugs." The German soldiers burn books, conscript labor, and physically abuse and murder suspected collaborators. Erik, not the brightest light in Norway, gathers the villagers together in order to convince them to organize—those who don't want to are free to leave (so much for secrecy). Then, completely out of the blue (and out of character), Erik stabs the local German commander to death. On the run he discovers a hidden German airfield (what are the odds?) and escapes to England to report his finding (the German planes are being used to spot convoys heading to the Soviet Union). The last part of this movie involves Erik leading a British commando raid on the airfield and attempting to rescue his young daughter. While this movie has collaborators betraying the resistance movement, and Germans reprising civilians for resistance activity, these drama laden events are completely ignored, making this a very simple and uninvolving action movie. There's a final scene in which the villagers are safely on board a British warship—to make the audience feel better (it's not like every Norwegian could live in England). Warning, the opening twenty minutes of this movie revolves around a tepid romance which turns out to be completely irrelevant to the story. With all the talent involved here this is surprisingly inept movie making. But when you are in a hurry and on a mission that can happen.

What the critics say Critics rate this movie 2.0 to 3.0. "Dated propaganda angle lessens impact today."[2] "Frequently slow, sometimes belabored, and occasionally unbelievable in its sentimental dramatics."[4] **Final Word** In the 1940s, Hollywood produced two other movies about the Norwegian resistance *The Moon is Down* and *Edge of Darkness*.

Corregidor

1943 USA b/w d. William Nigh

WW II: Classic '40s Flagwaver	1.0

Movie audiences had some difficult emotional choices to make while watching this film in 1943. Are they more upset that the Japanese are attacking the Philippines or that Dutch and Pinky, an American nurse and Army sergeant, may not live long enough to get married? Does the heroic stand by American soldiers for twenty-seven days on the island fortress of Corregidor, which stands at the entrance to Manila Bay, move them to a wartime commitment to beat the Japanese, or does the romantic triangle between three doctors, Jack (Otto Kruger), Royce (Elissa Landi) and Michael (Donald Woods) leave them too melancholy to care? *Corregidor* is a cheaply made film shot on a backlot. The limited action consists mostly of documentary footage of Japanese bombers and a few American soldiers impatient to mix it up with the Japanese. There's also a lengthy epilogue that consists of purple prose to arouse the audience to a righteous indignation toward the Japanese. However, the director, at some point, decided that the best way to tell the story of the defense of Corregidor, and of the eventual surrender of the American garrison, was to give us a 1930s style romantic triangle. We get one doctor (Jack) obsessed that his new wife (Royce) is still in love with another doctor (Michael). Despite the protests of Royce and Michael that there is no basis to his fears, he obsesses beyond all reason, until he is killed in a bombing raid. (So much for his concerns, which appear to have been unfounded. Well that's not completely true, Michael is still in love with Royce, but she has moved on.) Throughout the film the Americans are of good cheer in the face of great adversity. We are not shown the Americans surrendering or their subsequent mistreatment by the Japanese. Instead, we are left wondering if there's still a spark between Royce and Michael. The US doesn't retake the Philippines until 1945.

What the critics say Critics rate this movie 1.0 to 2.5. "Feeble wartime quickie, inept in almost every respect."[1] "Routine WW 2 melodrama focusing...on a corny love triangle."[2] **Final Word** You may be wondering—what was the US was doing in the Philippines? Well, we won it fair and square during the Spanish-American War (1898). The US paid Spain $20 million dollars, and took possession after quelling local rebellions.

Courage Under Fire

1996   USA   color   d. Edward Zwick

Gulf War: Postwar Drama	3.0

Courage Under Fire is a cynical post-Gulf War morality play that advances the politically correct notion that women can perform capably in combat. It stars Denzel Washington as Lt. Col. Serling, who has been assigned to investigate the merits of medevac chopper pilot Capt. Karen Walden (Meg Ryan) being posthumously awarded the Medal of Honor. The investigation is explored in a retrospective manner as each of the surviving crew members is interviewed by Serling, and each produces a story with conflicting details. There's a great deal of political pressure to ensure that Capt. Walden is the first woman soldier to receive this award. Six months earlier, Serling had been the commander of a tank squadron during the Gulf War and was responsible for destroying an American tank and killing its entire crew, which was covered up by the Pentagon. Part of this movie is devoted to Serling's suffering from posttraumatic stress disorder, which is also what's making him more determined than ever do the right thing regarding this investigation. Unfortunately, this film doesn't really deal with either of these stories. We never get to know Capt. Walden. She is primarily an empty character for a politically correct agenda about women in combat. The movie is not about Denzel Washington's character, as none of his issues are addressed in any substantial manner. Based on the novel by Patrick Duncan, we get a confusing, feel-good message-movie. On the one hand, this film appears to congratulate itself on portraying women as competent, if not heroic combatants, while the real story that unfolds supports the Pentagon's contention that male-female issues will result in command problems in the field. The acting is generally good, but the repetition of events as told by each surviving crew member truly becomes tedious. Ultimately, the film is too pat and simple.

What the critics say Critics rate this movie 3.5 to 4.5. "Intelligent, multilayered story about integrity, personal honor, and public hypocrisy."[2] "A carefully conceived, dramatically honorable picture that treats its subject with clarity and intelligence."[4] **Final Word** In the coming remilitarization of our society, we will see women dying as combatants as well.

The Court-Martial of Billy Mitchell

1955 USA b/w d. Otto Preminger

| World War I: Post-War Legal Drama | 3.5 |

In 1925 the Dept. of War court-martialed Brig. Gen. "Billy" Mitchell for "conduct prejudicial to the good of the service." Based on true events, Mitchell was an aviation visionary who had become dismayed with the antiquated Army Air Corps he headed. He strongly believed that the outcome of future wars would be determined by air superiority, and that the US had seriously fallen behind in developing a modern air force. Out of frustration, Mitchell goes to the press to make his case. He suggests that the Depts. of War and Navy are guilty of "criminal negligence" in this matter, and that their actions border on "treasonable." Needless to say Mitchell understood that he would be court-martialed, but saw this as an opportunity to make his case to the American public. During the course of the trial, Mitchell predicted long-range bombers, paratroopers, 1000-mph jet fighters, an independent air force and, most importantly, the Japanese attack on Pearl Harbor. It's intriguing to see Mitchell's attorney attempt to try this case in the press and manipulate public opinion to his benefit. Rod Steiger sparkles as the prosecuting attorney. Where this movie seriously fails is in casting Gary Cooper as Gen. Billy Mitchell. Cooper appears to reprise his role as Sgt. York, a humble and honorable person who does not want to hurt the military, but has a duty to protect America. By 1955 this was a hero of another era and no longer fit the more edgy contemporary hero that was emerging. Casting Cooper and turning Mitchell into a folk hero deprives this important story of its dramatic edge. Director Otto Preminger may also have had in mind the recent McCarthy hearings and "red-baiting" that had taken its toll on the national psyche, as Cooper makes an eloquent case for a higher duty to conscience over blind obedience to authority. This movie does a good job in taking on military command as well as the ineptness that can be inherent in military bureaucracy.

What the critics say Critics rate this movie 3.0. to 4.0. "Adequate recreation of historical incident."[1] "Low-keyed drama...slowly paced film."[2] "The picture is a real kick in the shins for the cult of blind military obedience."[4] Terrific courtroom drama."[5] **Final Word** An entertaining movie of historical relevance.

The Court-Martial of Jackie Robinson
1990 USA color tv d. Larry Peerce

Military Life: Racism in the Army   4.5

For all the talk about Jackie Robinson being the first Black-American to break the color barrier in professional baseball, the lesser-known incident in this movie tells us more about his character than his baseball career ever will. What is clear is that Robinson was a very bright individual, a leader and a truly exceptional athlete. In 1945 he starred in four sports (football, baseball, basketball and track) at UCLA. But, before he graduates, Pearl Harbor is bombed and Robinson enlists in the Army. After basic training Robinson applies to Officer's Candidate School, but is refused admission. However, with the help of an attorney and a national sports writer, the Army's "old boy network" is persuaded. Once in the Army, Robinson found a segregated institution riddled with racism. The incident detailed in this movie involves his refusal to sit at the back of a bus as demanded by a civilian bus driver at Fort Hood, Texas. Robinson correctly pointed out that military regulations didn't require him to sit in the back, but this provided the excuse many racists had been looking for to drum him out of the Army. Eventually charges were dropped to refusing to obey a lawful order, not for the bus incident but for Robinson's conduct during the inquiry. He was eventually exonerated of all charges but resigned his commission, disgusted by his treatment. A high-profile athletic figure long before he played for the Dodgers, he was befriended by boxer Joe Louis while in the Army, and was well known to the press and sports agents. The racism Robinson experienced in the Army creates a tense picture, at a time in which racial conflict was extremely overt. At times Black soldiers suffered not only overt discrimination by policy, but were subjected to considerable verbal abuse and physical threat as well. Andre Braugher gives an outstanding performance, and this film's willingness to show us Robinson, flaws and all, makes for compelling drama at the highest level.

What the critics say Critics rate this movie 3.5 to 4.5. "Intriguing drama...hits a homer, thanks to Braugher's forceful perfor-mance."[2] "Well-made television drama."[7] **Final Word** This thoughtful character-study clearly outshines nearly all Hollywood efforts to focus on either racism in the military or to tell compel-ling personal wartime stories.

Crimson Tide

1995   USA   color   d. Tony Scott

Cold War: Submarine Doomsday   4.5

Crimson Tide is a suspenseful World War III, doomsday thriller, played out onboard an American nuclear submarine, the USS *Alabama*. The film stars Gene Hackman as Capt. Frank Ramsey, commander of the sub and Denzel Washington as a Harvard-educated but inexperienced executive officer Lt. Cmdr. Ron Hunter. A nerve-wracking battle of wills is foreshadowed right from the beginning, with Hackman giving a Capt. Queegish performance, *à la* Bogart in The *Caine Mutiny*. The relationship eventually explodes into mutiny over an order to launch a nuclear strike. Rebel forces from the breakaway Russian republic of Chechnya have captured 25 ICBMs and 4 nuclear attack submarines, and have threatened to launch a retaliatory nuclear strike at the US. After receiving a message to launch a first strike at the fueling rebel-held ICBMs, the USS *Alabama* comes under attack from a Russian sub. While having to dive and evade torpedoes, the American sub loses radio contact and receives only a partial message regarding the missile launch. Capt. Ramsey is convinced they need to launch their missiles immediately in order to prevent a rebel launch. Executive Officer Hunter wants to wait and confirm that the second message is not an order to stand down, fearful their launch may trigger a nuclear war. This movie has many things going for it. The special effects are truly outstanding and the attention to military protocols onboard a sub and in preparation for a missile launch are exceptionally realistic. The underwater shots of torpedo launches are nothing short of spectacular. But what really drives this movie is the tension between Hackman and Washington. The voltage is turned up when Hackman violates a basic order and Washington moves to have him arrested. The second half plays out rather formulaically as an action thriller, and the ending is a complete cop-out. However, this film is even better than *The Hunt for Red October*.

What the critics say Critics rate this movie 4.0 to 4.5. "A thriller that grips and entertains."[1] "The torpedoes, missiles and testosterone levels are all in red alert."[4] **Final Word** The type of doomsday hysteria that the Cold War and *mutually assured destruction* provoked is really entertaining. Drop your drawers, turn your head and cough. We're all signing up for sub duty!

Cross of Iron

1977 GBR/GER/YUG color d. Sam Peckinpah

WW II: German Retreat from Stalingrad   2.5

Following the earlier critical success of director Sam Pechinpah's *Wild Bunch*, this movie is a major disappointment. The choreographed violence for which he became famous appears to be overwhelmed by the chaos and savagery of war. More problematically, this film never figures out what it wants to tell us about German soldiers retreating from Stalingrad in 1943. The first two-thirds of this movie has nothing to do with the story that evolves. There is an unrelated bit on homosexuality (replete with an officer dressed for a gay leather bar), a young Russian boy interjected as irony, a sequences with Sgt. Steiner (James Coburn) in a hospital. Later there are nude Russian women soldiers, one biting off the genitals of a soldier (Steiner gives her a gun to finish him off). There are, however, at least five intense and realistic combat scenes, but they could have been inserted interchangeably anywhere, at anytime. In the last half-hour of the film, the real story finally emerges as a conflict of personalities between Sgt. Steiner and Capt. Stransky (Maximilian Schell), his company commander. Steiner is a tough guy who doesn't ask for and doesn't give any quarter, while Stransky is an arrogant, aristocratic Prussian dandy who is obsessed with being awarded the Iron Cross. Eventually, this "duel on the steppe" leads to Stransky twice attempting to have Steiner killed. When this fails, Sgt. Steiner shoots the gay sycophant who does the Captain's dirty work, and confronts the Capt. In order to make a film about German soldiers more palatable, there are no Nazis here. In fact, Sgt. Steiner hates the Nazis, all officers, the German army, and the uniform and what it stands for. These soldiers are all clean as far as a war crimes tribunal is concerned. This film appears to be less about the war and more about the pissing contest between Steiner and Stransky, replete with moronic ending. One would think that with a German army of 260,000 men in retreat, in which only 6,000 will survive, these two idiots could have put aside a little animosity.

What the critics say Critics rate this movie 2.5 to 4.0. "Represents the director's decline and is only intermittently interesting."[3] "Affirms director Sam Pechinpah's prowess as an action film maker."[4] **Final Word** For the action-adventure junkie who has had too many brewskies.

113

The Cruel Sea

1953   GBR   b/w   d. Charles Frend

WW II: Convoy Escorts in the N. Atlantic   2.0

Despite this movie's box office success, critical praise, having been taken from a successful novel by Nicholas Monsarrat and adapted for the big screen by Eric Ambler, there is nothing here to recommend it to an audience today. This is a slow-moving, earnest British effort that tells us about life on a corvette, providing convoy escort duty in the "Battle of the North Atlantic," from 1939-1945. The movie stars Jack Hawkins as Capt. Ericson, a quiet but clearly in-charge commander of the *Compass Rose*. He's the only experienced officer on the ship, as he commanded a merchant vessel before the war. Shot in "glorious" black and white, the film has a documentary feel as Hawkins narrates events. As a result we only get a command point of view, and for the most part nothing ever happens. Yes, life is wet, cold, cramped and difficult onboard ship. While the *Compass Rose* rarely encounters German U-boats, having sunk two in five years of operation, it has the important mission of rescuing survivors of torpedoed freighters. There are occasional shore-leaves in which crew members visit family, wives and girlfriends. There is mild tension between officers, but none of this is compelling, dramatic or of interest to the audience. We simply never get the chance to know who these people are in a movie which is primarily about people. We watch them go through their difficult and sometimes monotonous motions and, before we know it, the war is over. This movie is a salute to the men who sacrificed to perform an important and demanding job. It also has the look and feel of a 1940s flagwaver. The film was dated before it was ever produced and appears to have been churned out without much thought as to how film-making and views of war-films has changed. It's very much a companion piece to *The Sea Shall Not Have Them*.

What the critics say Critics rate this movie 4.0 to 4.5. "Well-conceived documentary style account."[2] "Recalling the 1940s classic British war film in both its pacing and structure."[3] **Final Word** This last critic hits the problem on the head. This type of film wasn't very good to start with. (A corvette is a small, heavily armed warship displacing between 500 and 1000 tons developed during WW II for antisubmarine warfare.)

The Dam Busters

1954 GBR b/w d. Michael Anderson

WW II: Secret Bombing Mission	3.5

The Dam Busters is a very dated but still stirring war movie about a secret British operation in 1943. Based on the books *Dam Busters* by Paul Brickhill and *Enemy Coast Ahead* by Wing Commander Guy Gibson, the mission ("Operation Chastise") was to bomb six dams, including the Möhne and Eder dams on the Ruhr river in Germany. By taking these hydroelectric plants off-line, the British could disrupt wartime industrial production. The problem was twofold. There was no simple way to get at the dams from the air. This was solved by a British scientist, Dr. B.N. Wallis (Michael Redgrave), who developed a bomb that would skip along the surface of the water and, upon striking the dam, would submerge and explode. Wallis said he got the idea from reading about Admiral Lord Nelson's technique of bouncing cannon balls off the water in order to gain even greater momentum before they struck a ship. The science involved in this is presented in a truly interesting manner. The second part of this mission required a squadron of sixteen Lancaster bombers to fly precisely 240 mph, drop the bombs at exactly 60 feet altitude, 600 yards from the dam, at night! (Each bomb weighed 11,380 lbs.) This near-impossible feat was solved in a variety of ingenious ways that in itself makes this film fun to watch. While the acting is fine, today we would see the two main characters as stereotypes. Dr. Wallis is played as a rather simple and somewhat eccentric individual, and Wing Commander Gibson (Richard Todd) is strictly a by-the-book nice guy who is motivated by duty. The movie has a few other things going for it as well—there are no romances, very limited attempts at humor and no distracting subplots. The bombing raids are suspenseful and the special effects are well done throughout.

What the critics say Critics rate this movie 4.0 to 4.5. "Understated British war epic."[1] "Exciting and intelligent film."[2] "Told with painstaking attention to detail and overflowing with the British quality of understatement."[4] "Now quite dated, sentimental."[8] **Final Word** Two dams were destroyed in this raid, while eight Lancaster bombers were shot down. Short on action but intelligent. Well worth a look.

Darby's Rangers
1958 USA b/w d. William A. Wellman

WW II: US Army Rangers   1.0

After watching this movie you will be tested. Q. Why were the US Army Rangers formed during World War II? 1. To spear-head American invasion forces or 2. To seduce and impregnate as many women as possible. The correct answer is 2, if I correctly understand what the director intended. Now, given this answer, you would think it's obvious why the charming James Garner is cast as Major William Darby (appointed to head up the formation and training of an Army Ranger battalion in 1942). Wrong again. In fact, Garner is the only member of the Rangers not obsessed with women; he's only obsessed with his men. You do learn a few interesting things about the Rangers. They were an all-volunteer outfit—an American version of the very successful British commandos who trained them. They were utilized in the Allied landings in North Africa and Sicily (the movie somehow forgot to mention the Normandy Invasion), and they were not disbanded, in 1944, as this movie indicates, but in 1953. There are also a few extremely lame battle scenes that were enhanced by the sparse use of documentary footage. This film starts out full of "happy" music, as if it is going to be a patriotic salute to American Ranger forces, but quickly digresses into a soap opera. Garner, while earnest, is not very convincing as the nice-guy leader of this elite force. The Ranger Corps eventually reaches a strength of 6 battalions—used primarily as "shock troops," rather than commandos. In 1953 they were disbanded and many of their missions were transferred to the Special Forces. However, after the Vietnam War, three new Ranger battalions were formed. These battalions (606 men) are a volunteer force selected from airborne troops and are used for reconnaissance raids and special operations tasks. (Take a look at *Rangers in World War II* by R. Black.)

What the critics say Critics rate this movie 2.0 to 3.0. "Standard WW II actioner."[1] "WW II potboiler."[5] **Final Word** Due to the shortcomings of the regular British army in fighting the French and their Indian allies, light infantry units were formed in 1775 to harass the French under the command of colonialist Robert Rogers. They were called "Rangers." The British remained contemptuous of these colonial militias right until the end, when they got their butts kicked in 1783.

Dark Blue World

2001   CZE/GBR/GER/DEN/ITA   color   subtitles   d. Jan Sverák

WW II: Air Combat   2.0

The elements are here for a dramatic storytelling that never materializes. Beautifully filmed, with some great shots of Spitfires and Me-109s, and very good special effects, this film never rises to the level of cliché. With some vague allusion to the darkness (Nazism, Communism, war, prison camp) that has choked Czechoslovakia for the past sixty years, and the sense of pessimism and hopelessness this invokes, the movie lurches from one scene to the next unable to connect them into a story. Unfortunately, this movie is not nearly as complicated as the storyline. With the surrender of Czechoslovakia in 1938, we have expatriate Czech pilots joining the RAF to fight the Nazis. This story centers on two pilots, Franta (Ondrej Vetchy) and Karel (Krystof Hádek), who impatiently wait their chance to fly, all the while indulging the stodgy English who have doubts about their flying abilities. The real drama revolves around a young English woman (Tara Fitzgerald) whose attraction to the older Franta tests his friendship with Karel, particularly after she had a brief affair with the naive and love sick Karel. All of this is narrated by Franta, who is a political prisoner in a Communist labor camp in 1950. We know nothing more about these characters than we find out in the opening scenes. We learn nothing of the struggles of Czech pilots in the RAF or in prison camp. That leaves friendships and love affairs that exist only as backdrop to a moody and atmospheric movie. In fact, the only thing one can say for certain is that Franta seems to have a closer relationship with his dog than with the woman he's in love with. In the end, the missing husband of his English girlfriend returns. His girlfriend in Czechoslovakia marries and keeps his dog. This guy is getting slammed, but he has nothing to say about it. He just rests quietly in prison, having just found out a friend had tried to involve him an escape attempt so he could turn him in to be beaten. Circumstances don't get much bleaker than this.

What the critics say Critics rate this movie 2.5 to 3.0. "Not much to distinguish this capable but uninspired yarn from hundreds of other WW II dramas."[2] "Hackneyed story and unfocused structure."[7] **Final Word** Shot like a Hallmark television special, but without the sentiment or happy ending.

Dark of the Sun

1968   GBR   color   d. Jack Cardiff

| Post-Colonial Africa: Mercenaries | 3.0 |

Adventurism in Africa has never been more violent or embued with misguided idealism than in this Wilbur A. Smith story of soldiers of fortune seeking to recover diamonds in the Congo. In the early 1960s, shortly after the Congo received independence from France, the Simba-rebel army seeks to overthrow the government. In desperation the country's president hires two mercenary soldiers, Capt. Curry (Rod Taylor) and Sgt. Ruffo (Jim Brown) to retrieve 50 million dollars in uncut diamonds before they fall into rebel hands. For $50,000 the two mercenaries, with forty hand-picked Congolese soldiers and their psychopathic ex-Nazi commander, Capt. Henlein (Peter Carsten), board an armed train heading 300 miles into rebel-held territory, on the pretext of rescuing colonial civilians. Shot on location in the Congo, the action is fast-paced with all manner of shootings, stabbings, looting, raping, and pillaging, and culminates in a *mano-a-mano* fight to the death. The action is graphic and realistic, or at least it is until near the end when Curry and Ruffo make their way into the rebel-held town and escape with the diamonds. There is also a slight attempt to address issues of trust, loyalty and political idealism. Sgt. Ruffo, who is Congolese, is intent on preventing his country from reverting to tribal warfare, while Capt. Curry is involved strictly for the money. It's obvious from the beginning that their mixed loyalties and motives will test their friendship. Unfortunately, a predictable storyline and numerous cliché moments and characters undermine the action and irony. When the ex-Nazi predictably murders the idealistic Ruffo, Curry goes berserk in mad pursuit and kills him. Curry then turns himself in for killing a rogue soldier who deserved it (all you can do is groan in disbelief). The violent and cynical edge this film worked so hard to create dissolves into a naive act of contrition. While acting and special effects are good throughout, they can't completely undo the predictable story.

What the critics say Critics rate this movie 1.0 to 4.0. "Old-fashioned thriller...notable for the amount of sadistic action."[1] "Excellent cast in nerve-wracking actioner."[2] "Lots of action; routine plot."[5] "Violent and unsettling."[7] **Final Word** An entertaining, fast-paced, big-budget actioner that fills the screen with a lot of violence.

Das Boot
1981   GER   color   d. Wolfgang Peterson

WW II: Submarine Warfare   5.0

Written and directed by Wolfgang Peterson, this is quite simply
one of the greatest war films ever made. It's 1941 and German
U-boat 96 prepares to leave La Rochelle, France, heading out
into the North Atlantic. Until now, wolf-packs of U-boats had
nearly succeeded in cutting off Great Britain from resupply by the
US. However, with increased production of destroyers, and the
advent of sonar, the hunters were becoming the hunted. By the
end of the war, 30,000 of the 40,000 crewmen who had served
on U-boats had been killed in action. This movie is based on an
autobiographical book by Lothar-Günther Buchheim, who had
been a German war correspondent aboard a U-boat. What
ensues is a decent into a claustrophobic hell that will, at times,
make you grasp for breath. U-96 is depth-charged until men
become psychotic and the water pressure pops bolts that sound
like gun fire. Part of what makes this movie special is its ability to
bring you into the physical reality of men living on a submarine—
the cramped quarters, the humid environment, the moldy food,
and the alternating boredom and terror these men faced. The
special effects in this movie are superb, and there are scenes of
this sub in open water that you will never have seen before. At
the core of this story is the "Captain," wonderfully played by
Jürgen Prochnow, without the histrionics and paranoia of all the
submarine captains who preceded him (and who will inevitably
follow). Prochnow gives an incredibly understated performance
as a war-weary soldier. This is a German film that displays a high
degree of disdain for Nazism and the German high command.
But more than anything, this movie mocks a heroic vision of war,
as it explores the absolute limits of human endurance and the
will of soldiers to survive against all odds. We are taken into a
world in which survival is the ultimate act of heroism.

What the critics say Critics rate this movie 4.5 to 5.0. "Few films
convey the horror of war as powerfully."[3] "A decent into the pit of
hell with slim odds of ever returning."[4] "*Das Boot* is simply one of
the great war films. No other submarine films comes close."[5]
Final Word As a result of *Das Boot* there may not be any point in
making future WW II submarine movies.

D-Day, the Sixth of June

1956   USA   color   d. Henry Koster

| WW II: Wartime Romance | 3.0 |

Like many innocent war movie watchers, you will see the title *D-Day, the Sixth of June* and think, "Normandy invasion." Wrong! Which is why I have included this film for review. Calling this wartime romance "D-Day, the Sixth of June" would be like calling *Casablanca* "The Invasion of North Africa." There is, however, a somewhat interesting wartime romance here, set against the upcoming Allied invasion of Europe. At the very end, there's a brief combat scenario in which "Special Force Six," as part of a pre-invasion commando operation, knocks out a 14-inch German gun overlooking the Normandy beachhead. You will not want to rent this film in order to watch this rather routine 15-minute segment. Fortunately, there is a romantic triangle (no not a ménage à trois) that takes place in London, in 1944, which is slightly more interesting. The triangle stars Valerie Russell as a young and innocent English hottie, Dana, whose boyfriend, Col. John Wynter (Richard Todd) volunteers for a British commando unit in North Africa. Along comes Capt. Brad Parker (Robert Taylor), a married American army officer stationed in London. You guessed it, Dana and Capt. Parker fall madly in love, quickly dispense with any guilt, and hook up big time—if you get my drift. (Which I can buy into because she is really cute.) For Robert Taylor, an aging actor, this is probably the last chance to score a young woman like this on the screen. It's not quite perversion, and her father did die recently, so she could be searching for a father figure. Anyway, where was I? If you're the soldier in the field and your girlfriend is fooling around, you might feel some occasional rage. If you're the wife holding down the homefront, don't worry, the depression and anxiety will lift. Besides, who cares! This is wartime! Now, of course, it all comes to a dramatic showdown, with a bittersweet twist at the end that gives this movie some realism and emotional honesty.

What the critics say Critics rate this movie 2.0 to 4.0. "Extremely moving wartime love story."[4] "Slow-moving account of the Normandy invasion."[7] (They obviously didn't watch this movie.) **Final Word** If you are a sensitive war movie type of guy, you might like this movie. It's still a lot better than any of the contemporary wartime soap operas, such as *Captain Corelli's Mandolin* or *Pearl Harbor* or *Yanks*.

Dear America: Letters Home From Vietnam
1988   USA   color   tv   d. Bill Couturié

Vietnam War: Documentary   5.0

Yet another outstanding HBO film about the Vietnam War. This documentary is based on a book of the same name and edited by Bernard Edelman. In the opening moments, we are told that this is an authentic account of the Vietnam War from actual letters of the men and women who served there and that every scene, every shot in the film is real. Nothing has been reenacted. The film chronicles the Vietnam War from 1964 through 1973, showing actual news footage, with a musical score composed of popular 1960s and '70s music that adds a powerful dimension to the viewing experience. Year by year we are shown the war—with a tally of American soldiers sent to Vietnam, the number killed in action, and the number wounded. This is a view of war exclusively from the viewpoint of the soldier. We see the pictures of many of the men who wrote these letters, and who later died in combat. One soldier writes home, "We are all scared. One can easily see the emotion in the eyes of each individual. One might hide it with his mouth, while another might hide it with his actions, but there is no way around it, we are scared." A soldier writing home to the mother of a buddy who was killed writes: "I am a hollow man, Mrs. Percal. I'm a shell and when I am scared I rattle. I am no one to tell you about your son." This documentary is filled with small, poignant moments of despair, love, and the suffering of soldiers in the field. It is ultimately moving, haunting and mournful, as one looks into the faces of so many handsome young men, mostly 19 years old, sent to kill and possibly die in a war that their letters show they don't understand: "We are in desperate need of love," a soldier writes. It is hard not to make the case that this is a strong antiwar film. However, if it is antiwar, it's only because public sentiment turned against this war as did the soldier in the field. The action is real and fierce, the emotions strong and powerful.

What the critics say Critics rate this movie 3.5 to 5.0. "Extremely moving account...gut wrenching human drama."[2]
Final Word This HBO movie had an independent theatrical release. This is not strictly a combat film, but rather the best documentary of this war. No fan of war movies or student of the Vietnam War should miss this film.

Death of a Soldier

1986   AUS   color   d. Philippe Mora

WW II: GI Murder Story   2.0

This movie represents itself as a fact-based story about the trial of an American GI, Edward Leonski, who was hanged for the murder of three women. Stationed in Melbourne, Australia in 1942, Leonski was brought before a military tribunal and court-martialed for murder under Art. 92 of the Articles of War. The *cause célèbre* for which this movie was made, was that Gen. MacArthur ordered hanged a mentally ill soldier in order to prop up the US-Australian relationship during a critical period of the war. At the time, there were 48,000 American soldiers in Melbourne waiting to ship out to Guadalcanal. In an epilogue, it's noted that the Military Code of Justice was subsequently revised as a result of this case. But in reality, this movie is nothing more than a poorly made, semilurid murder and mayhem story that focuses primarily on the murders and capture of the American soldier (played by Reb Brown). Portrayed as a psychopath from an extremely disturbed family, Leonski would get extremely intoxicated and strangle women. The movie also features a rather wooden James Coburn as Maj. Dannenberg, chief of military police. Dannenberg spends most of the movie charming an Australian socialite and harassing two Australian police detectives. Throughout the movie, the Americans and Australians are at each others throats, including an incident of a brief firefight between American and Australian troops that was ordered covered up (this in itself is a hundred times more significant and worthy of a movie than the story of Pvt. Leonski). All the elements are here for an a interesting legal drama about a relatively unknown chapter of the war, that, unfortunately, was not the focus of this movie. As the movie switches from manhunt to courtroom trial, the director has Coburn move from military police chief to defense attorney in order to keep his smiling mug on the screen (this is truly a stretch even by military standards of justice). *Death of a Soldier* fails at the most basic level in telling this story, that is, in addressing the issue of whether Leonski was in fact mentally ill.

What the critics say Critics rate this movie 2.0 to 2.5. "Not as interesting as it sounds."[2] "A well-mounted recounting of a true story."[3] **Final Word** Just enough perversion to keep the voyeuristic impulse involved, but not the heart or mind.

The Deep Six

1958   USA   color   d. Rudolph Maté

| World War II: Naval Combat | 1.0 |

The title *The Deep Six* says a lot more about this film than the studio probably intended. Based on a novel by Martin Dibner, the story takes place onboard a US Navy destroyer patrolling in the South Pacific, but it doesn't engage in any action and there isn't the slightest hint that this ship is in a war. Also, it's not clear why, in 1958, a war movie is addressing the issue of a sailor's Quaker pacifism. While religious pacifism was a recurrent theme in 1940s and Korean War flagwavers, why now in 1958? Alan Ladd, a long-time matinee idol is cast, at the end of his career, as a wimpy, self-doubting graphics illustrator called to active duty as a destroyer gunnery officer (Lt. Alec Austen). The question of this officer's pacifist beliefs becomes an issue he has to resolve by demonstrating to the crew that they can depend on him in combat. I might add that nothing occurs in this movie to give the audience the slightest clue as to Lt. Austen's thinking on the subject, or how or why it resolves—but it is resolved and he gets the girl. There is quite a cast—Alan Ladd, William Bendix, Keenan Wynn, James Whitmore, Efrem Zimbalist and Joey Bishop (doing his schtick). But this movie is no better than the early Hollywood "B" movies of the 1930s and 1940s. Any war movie that opens to a Madison Avenue advertising agency and then takes the next half-hour to explore a relationship is already in trouble. By the time we get to the war side of the movie the story has played out like a light musical comedy, sans the music (I guess Alan Ladd couldn't sing). About ten minutes of unenthusiastic action occurs at the end during a commando raid. This is when Lt. Austen learns that he can fire a gun but can't hit anything. Oh, and the girl (Dianne Foster) resolves her many complex problems, quits her job, and is waiting at the docks to marry her wounded war hero as he returns.

What the critics say Critics rate this movie 1.0 to 3.5. "An aging star contends with many hazards: slipshod production, poor colour, a dull script, and an unplayable part."[1] "Good action and the magnetism of a popular Alan Ladd...who doesn't know the meaning of the word *fear*."[7] (this guy must have been whacked at the time he saw this movie). **Final Word** A studio executive probably said, "deep-six it," and was misunderstood, so someone titled it *The Deep Six*.

The Deer Hunter

1978   USA   color   d. Michael Cimino

Vietnam War: Coming Home	2.5

This "coming home" evocation opens with a long look at the lives of five working-class young men from a steel mill town in Pennsylvania. Very little is said for over forty-five minutes as we simply watch the interplay of personalities and relationships. Then the movie quickly shifts to the middle of a combat scene in Vietnam, in which three of the buddies are captured and tortured by the Vietcong. The last third of the movie focuses on what happens to each of these young men as the war ends. There are many ways to look at this film—as an examination of the impact of war on soldiers, as a character study of the quiet heroism of Mike (played by Robert Di Nero), or how a working-class community was impacted by the events of the Vietnam War. Throughout this movie there is always present a quiet blue-collar patriotism, and, as critics have noted, a harsh stereotyped portrayal of the Vietnamese. Director Michael Cimino has also laden the film with obscure metaphors about Russian roulette and hunting. Here are the problems. The first act is overly long and uninvolving, as it examines the prewar lives of these young men. The second act is intense and interesting but has no basis in reality. The sadistic torture of captured American soldiers with games of Russian roulette, in order to entertain the Vietcong, is simply way over the top. The last third of this movie, which packs an emotional wallop, is full of melodrama you would expect from a cheap exploitation-actioner, as the Christopher Walken character haunts violent games of chance in the back alleys of Saigon. And when Mike returns to rescue him, it all becomes too bizarre to make any important statement about the war. In the end, all the dramatic artifices introduced by the director detract from a powerful story of men coming home from war.

What the critics say Critics rate this movie 3.0 to 5.0. "A hollow spectacle...full of specious analogies, incoherent sentimentality."[1] "Intense, powerful and fascinating...ambitious and succeeds at a number of levels."[4] "Cannot be seen as any kind of serious comment on the war or the country of Vietnam...ludicrous at best, racist at worst."[6] **Final Word** This movie won the Academy Award for Best Picture in 1978 and is a AFI top 100 film. This movie is worth seeing but not revisiting.

The Desert Fox

1951   USA   b/w   d. Henry Hathaway

| WW II: Biopic of Field Marshal Rommel | 2.5 |

Based on a biography of FM Erwin Rommel by Desmond Young, *The Desert Fox* gets "B" movie treatment. It opens with a great action sequence as British commandos attempt to assassinate Rommel in 1941. From here on, this movie becomes progressively less interesting and jumbled, with the exception of an outstanding performance by James Mason as Rommel. With voice-over narration and documentary combat footage, this movie begins with the defeat of Rommel's Afrika Korps, at El Alamein in 1943 by Montgomery's 8th Army. It is disappointing that we are not shown his rise to prominence and what has always fascinated us about Rommel—his brilliant mastery of *Blitzkrieg* tactics in France and later in North Africa. His defeat is really without controversy. He was sent to North Africa in a token attempt by Hitler to save Germany's Axis partner, Italy, from defeat. Without air cover or gas for his tanks, Rommel was to lose a war of attrition. The focus of this movie is really on Rommel's evolution from that of a supporter of Hitler's, to believing that Germany had to be rescued from a madman. Rommel's later suicide was the result of charges of treason brought against him because of his involvement in an assassination attempt against Hitler. Ultimately, Rommel choose suicide over a show-trial, with assurances his family would remain unharmed. He committed suicide by poison in October 1944. It's highly unusual, to say the least, that an enemy general, during wartime, would attain the celebrity status Rommel achieved, and would be affectionately known as the "Desert Fox" by his enemies. Churchill offered during the war: "We have a very daring and skillful opponent against us, and, may I say across the havoc of war, a great general." Mason plays a great Rommel but, unfortunately, this film does not tell us why Rommel was a great general or why he was venerated by his enemies.

What the critics say Critics rated this movie 2.0 to 4.5. "Vivid but scrappy account of the last years of a contemporary hero."[1] "Standard early '50s fare lifted from oblivion by the remarkable Mason."[8] **Final Word** At the time of this movie's release, veteran groups protested the sympathetic portrayal of Rommel. You might prefer to read *The Trail of the Fox* by D. Irving.

The Desert Rats

1953 USA b/w d. Robert Wise

WW II: Desert War in North Africa   2.5

On January 22, 1941, British troops entered Tobruk on the North African coast of Libya, having defeated its Italian garrison. The British forces, including Australian troops, held out against furious Afrika Korps armored assaults until Tobruk fell to Rommel on June 21, 1942. By holding out for so long (242 days), the British thwarted Rommel's attempt to capture Cairo and gain control of the Suez Canal. Goebbel, the Nazi propaganda minister, referred to the Aussie troops defending the garrison as "rats," and that led the British army to proudly adopt the name "Desert Rats." This movie broadly chronicles the efforts of the Australians to defend Tobruk against Rommel's initial efforts to take back Tobruk. There's good use of documentary combat footage and decent special effects as we watch Richard Burton play a young English captain in command of Australian soldiers. Burton, ever handsome, intense, brooding, and aristocratic (and probably miscast in this movie), at first has doubts about the rebellious Australians, but their heroic efforts eventually win him over. Later, in a commando raid led by Burton to blow-up a German ammunition dump, Burton is captured and has a brief tête-à-tête with Rommel himself, reprised by James Mason from his role in *The Desert Fox*. Even though the British eventually surrender Tobruk, Burton wins the war of verbal wits with Rommel. Five months later in November 1942 the British 8th Army, under Montgomery, defeated Rommel and reentered Tobruk. There's a somewhat hokey side story to this movie when Burton encounters a former teacher, now an enlisted man in the Australian army, who is alcoholic and cowardly. Burton has a great deal of respect for this soldier who is later influential in softening Burton's approach to the Australian soldiers. *The Desert Rats* tends to run into trouble with the use of voice-over narration that gives it a documentary feel at times. It also fails to provide any substantial character development—or story for that matter. It does, however, pays tribute to the defenders of Tobruk.

What the critics say Critics rate this movie 3.0 to 4.5. "Actioner made to cash in on the success of *The Desert Fox*."[1] "Fine WW II actioner."[2] **Final Word** Serious war-buff junkies and war-gamers will enjoy this slightly above average movie. Rommel received his field marshal's baton after retaking Tobruk.

Desperate Journey

1942   USA   b/w   d. Raoul Walsh

WW II: Classic '40s Flagwaver   1.5

Desperate Journey uses a formula that is still highly popular today—lots of mindless action mixed with a large dose of humor and some drama that no one is supposed to take seriously. Having matinee idol and swashbuckling hero Errol Flynn fight the Nazis just doesn't work as well as, say, Robin Hood flustering the Norman Prince John. Flynn, and a young Ronald Reagan, are members of an Allied bomber crew who have been sent on a bombing mission over Germany. Shot down, the surviving crew attempt to make their way back to England. Along the way, they are captured and escape three different times. They also manage to lift Herman Goering's car, blow up a chemical factory and make enough close escapes to rival an old Republic movie serial. This is a low-budget movie with studio-bound heroics and lots of patriotic bombast aimed at mostly incompetent and bumbling German soldiers. The special effects are among the worst of the 1940s propaganda movies, and most of the humor is cheesy and borders on old vaudeville gags. Poor Raymond Massey, as the German officer who can't quite catch up to this gang of Allied rogues, he apparently doesn't have to put his Lugar to his head but mostly scratches it in bewilderment. There are no subplots, no romantic interests, and there isn't even the slightest tension among our stalwart crew—just wisecracks and camaraderie. Unfortunately, there is absolutely nothing clever or dramatic here. The movie portrays this adventure as good fun. I suppose, in a war in which the stakes were unbelievably high, there was a need for this style of comic relief from the war—you know, where the good-guys can't help but be smart, confident and with no chance of losing, and the bad guys are completely inept. The heroes escape in a traditionally convenient manner, by finding a hidden British bomber and flying to England.

What the critics say Critics rate this movie 2.5 to 4.0. "Exhilarating adventure for the totally uncritical."[1] "Strictly propaganda intended to keep up the morale on the homefront."[6] "Swashbuckling action-adventure *par excellence*."[8] **Final Word** The critics appear to give this below-average movie a lot of room in which to work (which is true for most 1940s flagwavers).

Destination Tokyo

1943   USA   color   d. Delmer Daves

WW II: Classic '40s Flagwaver   2.0

The submarine movie is among the most challenging of all war movies to make. Once everyone is on board, the question immediately becomes, what story can you tell in this confined and highly structured environment? *Destination Tokyo*, a rather long movie (two hours and fifteen minutes), never resolves this problem. There's no crazed commander, no conflict among the crew, and no real combat crisis. Instead, the director decides to have the crew chat among themselves for two hours. The *Copperfin*, under the command of Capt. John Cassidy (Cary Grant), has been secretly ordered to enter Tokyo Bay and put ashore a meteorologist. This weather man's mission is to radio weather conditions to the carrier *Hornet* as it prepares to launch the "Doolittle Raid" on Japan in 1942 (a daring attempt to launch B-25s from the deck of a carrier in order to bring the war home to the Japanese). Nearly all the action in this movie takes place in the last half hour. But before we get to the good part, we have to suffer a great deal of boredom along with the crew: a Christmas celebration; a sailor mistaking an albatross for an airplane; defusing a bomb; an emergency appendectomy; and a self-proclaimed "Romeo" regaling us with stories of his rejection. On and on it goes with the ennui and boring routine aboard this sub. You might be inclined to think that confinement in close quarters would produce some modicum of conflict, but not with this well-mannered crew. Grant is so wan as the ship's commander that he would have been better cast as the chaplain. Unfortunately, the "good" part here is really not that good either. There's very little action, and the special effects could have been reproduced in any 50-gallon aquarium. The action that does take place is carried out in such a routine manner that it deprives the film of dramatic tension. *Destination Tokyo* is a movie with an interesting premise that was never realized due to a weak script and predictable characters and situations.

What the critics say Critics rate this movie 2.0 to 4.0. "A film whose hero is the Stars and Stripes."[4] "Superior WW II adventure."[7] "At over two hours under water, the audience begins to get the bends."[8] **Final Word** Buy a copy of *Das Boot* and forget all other WW II submarine movies.

The Devil's Brigade

1968   USA   color   d. Andrew V. McLaglen

Today, the misfit storyline is pretty familiar. Throw together a bunch of good-hearted, amiable losers, hustlers, gold-brickers, malcontents and criminals and transform them into an elite fighting unit. Seems simple enough, right? The task here falls to William Holden (Lt. Col. Frederick) who solemnly sleepwalks his way through this role. As the officer charged with forming the First Special Services Forces, Holden simply fails to bring the required energy to this role. Add one Major Crown (Cliff Robertson), a low-keyed and uptight Canadian officer who's afraid to raise his voice, and this movie is almost completely devoid of any real energy. Now there's a slight twist since this is a fact-based movie. The misfit American soldiers, who were recruited from stockades across the country, are to be integrated into a combined battalion with a hand-picked, elite Canadian force. This all plays out predictably while the Americans razz the Canadians for being prigs and hicks, and the Canadians learn to give in return, all bonding in a barroom brawl (so far so good, not really). But then something truly peculiar happens—a serious war movie breaks out in the final thirty minutes. All of a sudden our elite combined battalion is fighting at Monte Cassino, Italy in 1943, taking prisoners, breaking the German's grip on the mountain stronghold and taking serious casualties. What we now have is a serious tribute to the heroic combat efforts of the real First Special Forces. It turns out that this is not an amusing tale of adolescent amorality (*The Dirty Dozen* or *Kelly's Heroes*) at all, but rather one about the redemptive power of camaraderie and a second chance. But, in this case, the attempt is completely fraudulent (it's probably not a good idea to overanalyze or compare bad movies). To sum up, this movie is confused, predictable, slow-moving and without interesting characters or a story to tell.

What the critics say Critics rate this movie 2.5. "Flagrant but routine imitation of *The Dirty Dozen*, quite undistinguished."[1] "Standard WW 2 fare...goes on too long."[2] "Distended and stock scripting, sluggish direction, and limp pacing."[4] **Final Word** There have been worse attempts to tell a similar story, including *Darby's Rangers* and *The Misfit Brigade*.

The D.I.

1957 USA b/w d. Jack Webb

| Military Life: Marine Boot Camp | 3.0 |

The D.I. is a bleak and oppressive character study of a Marine Corps drill instructor. Produced and directed by Jack Webb (of *Dragnet* fame), he also plays Tech Sgt. Moore, the drill instructor from hell. Webb's D.I. is an intense, obsessive and joyless individual whose only satisfaction in life comes from molding young recruits into Marines. Without friends, family or a girlfriend, Moore is pathologically tied to the Corps. Into his dysfunctional family comes new recruit Pvt. Owens (Don Dubbins), whose failure to conform provokes TSgt. Moore to try to turn him around and make a Marine of him. For one and a half hours we watch TSgt. Moore relentlessly get on the case of this recruit, until it becomes clear that something darker is at work here. The private is a bright individual whose father and two brothers, all Marines, died in combat. He's also ambivalent about being a Marine; but more to the point, he's not cut out to be one. TSgt. Moore can only do one thing and that is make new recruits real men. The darker theme here is the sadism that underlies the military. There's more going on here than simply turning recruits into Marines—but making them into "real men." This means an intense degree of humiliation, domination and control. For Webb, it appears that accepting any amount of control and humiliation is tantamount to being a man. With a Marine Corps poster on the wall behind him proclaiming, "The Marine Corps builds men," Pvt. Owens is told, "If a man is yellow, he knows he's yellow." Later there's a scene in which his cold and angry mother insists that he not be discharged. Having already lost her husband and two sons to war, she wants her youngest son to be a Marine as well. While this scene was supposes to be one of patriotism, it's a chilling picture of how society has been militarized, as even mothers are insisting their sons go to war. Over and over we watch an angry D.I. harangue a recruit until the point of it all is lost. *The D.I.* is slightly effective as a character study, but its underlying premises are disturbing.

What the critics say Critics rate this movie 3.0 to 3.5. "Today a wonderful exercise in high camp."[2] **Final Word** "You saw the light. Yes sir! The great light, the white light. Yes sir! The guiding light. Yes sir! You got the vision. Yes sir! You're going to be a good Marine."—TSgt. Moore.

Dieppe

1993 CAN color tv miniseries d. John N. Smith

WW II: Battlefield Disaster	4.0

This Canadian television miniseries (three-hour, 3-vol. set) is a
scathing indictment of British and Canadian High Commands
and the role they played in the disastrous Allied raid on the
French port of Dieppe in 1942. With this film, it also appears that
the Canadians have temporarily relieved the Australians of
publicly humiliating the British for military ineptitude. On August
19, 1942, in a military action that can only be termed a fiasco,
3,367 Canadian soldiers (out of a force of 4,963) of the 2nd
Infantry Division were killed, wounded or captured in an
amphibious assault on Dieppe. This film, based on the book
Unauthorized Action by Brian Villa, is the best film attempt yet to
portray the unseemly politics of war and the loss of life that
results when egos and power collide. The real heart and energy
of this movie is its focus on Lord Mountbatten (Victor Garber)
and Canadian General Roberts (Gary Reineke). Mountbatten,
connected to the royal family, is accurately portrayed as a
pompous, publicity seeking, overly ambitious royal lightweight
desperate to do something important. Gen. Roberts is more
sympathetic as a well-intended officer who is politically naive and
unassertive in the face of authority and political pressure. As a
result, he compromises until it's too late and his men are at risk.
Watching this battle plan unfold is one of the great lessons
presented by a war film to a public that dotes on wartime heroics.
Conceived as a public relations effort by Churchill to give the
impression of creating a second front to take the pressure off the
Russians, the final political spin suggested that this unauthorized
military action at Dieppe was a dress rehearsal for the Normandy
Invasion. The only thing that keeps *Dieppe* from being a truly
outstanding drama is its attempt to be an epic by trying to tell the
soldier's story and including two poorly developed relationships.
At the end, there's a very good small-scale portrayal of the raid
on Dieppe.

What the critics say No available reviews. **Final Word** The truth
is, war is so unappealing and unsavory that the real story can't
be told during wartime. That's why we have to wait fifty years to
be told the truth. Next to enemy fire and disease, the soldiers'
worst enemies are his own commanders. This movie is truly the
antiflagwaver.

The Dirty Dozen

1967   USA /GBR   color   d. Robert Aldrich

WW II: Misfits in Action	2.0

With near cult status, *The Dirty Dozen* remains one of the most popular war movies of all time. This amoral and ultraviolent tale of war also spawned three bad made-for-television sequels, *The Next Mission, The Deadly Mission* and *The Fatal Mission*, and many imitative movies. Starring Lee Marvin as Maj. Reisman, and a cast of second-tier TV personalities, the Army offers conditional amnesty to a bunch of rapists, murders and psychopaths in exchange for conducting a covert operation. Marvin's job is to shape up this bunch of misfits and parachute into France and assault a chateau and kill as many vacationing senior German officers as possible. The task director Robert Aldrich had set out for himself was to do this in as humorous and violent manner as possible. The twelve felons handpicked by Reisman are not redeemable characters. No, they are "bad" guys trying to escape the penalty for their offenses. The "out" the film offers is that the men are all likely to die on this mission. Unlike *The Magnificent Seven* or *The Wild Bunch*, that explored violence and justice in American society, two-thirds of this movie is nothing more than a humorous, adolescent take on a long and tedious training sequence, with a lot of gratuitous violence tacked on near the end. And that's the problem. Slapstick and violence only work if the violence isn't real. When our thugs start gleefully massacring innocent civilians, it goes too far. The fact that this film came out in 1967 at the height of the Vietnam War, and cynically mocks military commanders as arrogant and manipulative, probably accounts for its success. While this movie helped open the door to the exploration of violence in films—the most explored theme in American movies today—*The Dirty Dozen*, in retrospect, comes across as an overly simplistic, if not lame, comedy. While still alive in the memory of many "Boomers," it lacks the edgy humor and intelligence that would confer it significance.

What the critics say Critics rate this movie 4.0 to 4.5. "Professional, commercial but unlikable."[1] "Exciting, funny, and well acted."[2] "One of the most entertaining war movies ever."[6]
Final Word Every war movie guy who has been to prison knows you couldn't possibly organize these characters into an elite commando unit, no matter how amusing they are.

The Dogs of War

1980   GBR   color   d. John Irvin

Post-Colonial Africa: Mercenaries	3.0

Filled with cynicism and violent imagery, *The Dogs of War* is an entertaining but ultimately disappointing foray into the clandestine world of the professional soldier-for-hire. Based on Frederick Forsyth's novel *The Dogs of War,* Christopher Walken plays a mercenary hired by an international mining conglomerate to assassinate the brutal military dictator of a fictitious West African nation. Walken redefines "intensity" in this movie—he's humorless, belligerent and prone to violence, as he attempts to gather intelligence about the political stability of this unnamed nation. Posing as a "bird watcher," he spits out scientific names of bird species with a barely contained rage (this will make ornithologists and naturalists everywhere cheer). Nearly beaten to death, Walken returns to the US only to be rejected by his ex-girlfriend. Forlorn, he accepts an assignment to overthrow the dictatorship. Completely missing is any biographical data that would give credibility to the story. Who are Walken and his three mercenary cohorts? What motivates them? What's their background or training? For the most part, these guys wear bad leather jackets and lead boring blue collar lives in a seedy part of New Jersey. Without subplots, the film's biggest failing is not naming names. What African nation are we talking about here? What dictator? What are the economic and political interests manipulating events? What is the economic prize—gold, diamonds, uranium, oil? The ambiguity results in a movie devoid of significance, rendering it mostly an exercise in violence. But the violence is credible—these guys know how to bring down a bad guy. With 24 ex-African soldiers armed with Uzis and M-60 machine guns, they stage a graphic and realistic all-out attack. However, when the director puts the mantle of "good guys" on these mercenaries, by having them betray the corporate interests that hired them, the film's dark edge is lost in order to make the audience feel better about what has taken place.

What the critics say Critics rate this movie 2.0 to 4.0. "Tough but seemingly dated modern irony."[1] "An intelligent and occasionally forceful treatment."[4] "Graphic depiction of... professional mercenaries."[5] **Final Word** The featured weapon in this movie is the XM-18, which fires 18 high explosive rounds in five seconds. Fun to watch, this gun is completely fictional.

Dragonfly Squadron

1954 USA b/w d. Lesley Selander

Korean War: Air Command   1.5

The *Dragonfly Squadron* is a low-budget, black and white movie that meets the definition of a Hollywood "B" flick. Primarily a relationship driven film, it has very little action and too much talking. On the back of the box cover a blurb states: "starring Chuck Connors." This film really stars John Hodiak as Air Force Major Matt Brady, assigned to train South Korean pilots for the anticipated conflict between North and South Korea. What little action there is takes place in Kongju, Korea in 1951, just months before the war starts. Most aerial scenes show C-47s taking off and landing with only a few P-51s doing the same. In the last 15 minutes, there is some tank action and a few seconds of documentary footage of Lockheed P-80 "Shooting Stars," Grumman F9F "Panthers" and Douglas AD-5 "Skyraiders" strafing the ground. There's also supposed to be a romance here, but it's harder to find than an air combat scene. Donna (Barbara Britton), on a medical mission in Korea, believes her husband has been killed in Indochina, only to learn that he is indeed alive and returning to meet her in Korea. The ensuing relationship triangle between her, Maj. Brady and her husband never takes place because Donna is a "good" girl. (Guess who gets killed at the end of this film.) This is a command-oriented film rather than a combat action film, since the surprising number of secondary stories focus on the conflicts of command that almost make this movie interesting. Basically, Maj. Brady carries the unfair stigma of being responsible for the death of another pilot, and there is an antagonistic journalist who continually questions his judgment and character. Chuck Connors only gets about 10 minutes of screen time as an US Army captain attempting to escort foreign nationals out of South Korea. While this film makes very limited comment about the war itself, the constant badgering of Major Brady and his having to prove himself to just about everyone, suggests a great deal of hostility and increasing distrust for military leadership in 1954.

What the critics say Critics rate this movie 2.0. "Usual Korean War story."[2] "Never gets off the ground."[5] **Final Word** The second critic has it right. This is the dodo bird (flightless winged wonder) of air combat movies.

Dr. Strangelove or: How I Learned to Stop

1963   GBR   b/w   d. Stanley Kubrick   **Worrying and Love the Bomb**

| Cold War: Antiwar satire | 5.0 |

Any movie about an Air Force general instigating a nuclear first strike because he believes he is impotent due to a Communist conspiracy, is on its way to cult-movie immortality. This black, antiwar comedy is a savage assault on the Cold War paranoia that gripped America for most of the 1950s. Based on the book *Red Alert* by Peter George, and directed by Stanley Kubrick, the film is a comedic masterpiece. There are four outstanding performances as we watch this nuclear debacle. First, the psychotic Gen. Jack D. Ripper (Sterling Hayden) sends out B-52s armed with nuclear bombs, while his executive officer, Capt. Mandrake (Peter Sellers), confronts him about his madness. Gen. Ripper is convinced there is an international Communist conspiracy to *sap and impurify all of our precious bodily fluids* by fluoridating our water. Then there's the B-52 pilot, Maj. "King" Kong (Slim Pickens), a good ol' country boy ready to engage in "nuclear combat toe-to-toe with the Rooskies." This disaster unfolds in the President's war room, with Peter Sellers playing President Merkin Muffley and Dr. Strangelove, a former Nazi scientist who is now director of research and development. In a wheelchair with a bionic right arm that keeps trying to Sieg heil the Führer, Dr. Strangelove's arm eventually attempts to choke him. Perhaps the best performance is by George C. Scott as Gen. "Buck" Turgidson, trying to explain to his girlfriend, on the phone from the war room, that he loves her, while simultaneously trying to justify a massive first strike against the Soviets. Part of this comedy's specialness is the exhilarating tension it maintains right from the opening scene. The simulation of the B-52 cockpit and its launch sequence preparation for a nuclear strike is eerily real. But the real beauty of this films lies in its ability to deconstruct the absurdity of Cold War-era logic, as the characters all try to sort out mutually-assured destruction—until it's discovered the Soviets have secretly created a "Doomsday Machine!"

What the critics say Critics rate this movie 5.0. "Unforgettable and hilarious black comedy...an undaunting piece of mastery."[3] "Black comedy masterpiece."[7] "Message movie of the highest order."[8] **Final Word** Everyone out of the TV room and into the bomb shelter, so we can watch this movie undisturbed. Now!

Dunkirk
1958   GBR   b/w   d. Leslie Norman

WW II: Evacuation at Dunkirk   2.5

This schmaltzy flagwaver plays like a 1941 British War Ministry production to get the public onboard (17 years after the fact!). Based on the books *The Big Pick-Up* by E. Trevor and *Dunkirk* by E. Butler and J.S. Bradford, this movie does a very average job of telling an important war story. John Mills stars as a corporal who leads his squad back to the beaches of Dunkirk to be evacuated, and Richard Attenborough, a businessman and prig, is indifferent to the "phony" war and out to make a pound. However, the Attenborough character eventually sees the patriotic light and helps with the evacuation. Unfortunately, neither story as told here is as interesting as what really happened. In the summer of 1940 Britain sent an expeditionary force of 200,000 men to help the French. Anticipating a stand off war of attrition, as in WW I, the Nazis blitzkrieg easily crushed all resistance in the Low Lands and flanked France's Maginot Line, cutting off British forces supporting the French army. When the British were asked by the French to counter attack, the British commander ordered a retreat at Dunkirk. He correctly surmised that any attempt to counter attack would be defeated and lead to the capture of the British army. Of course, the evacuation is the real story here, not the embarrassing military defeat. The British gathered some 693 vessels, including passenger ferries and private motor craft, and under heavy air and artillery bombardment, evacuated 338,000 soldiers (including 120,000 French soldiers) within a week. This movie does do a credible job of showing us the harrowing circumstance of soldiers trapped along the beaches of Dunkirk. As one soldier puts it, "What a shambles we've made of this whole rotten affair." "Operation Dynamo" would have been better served if this movie had shown us less about a patrol getting to the beach and more of how the civilian population rallied around its soldiers.

What the critics say Critics rate this movie 3.0 to 3.5. "Sober, small scale approach to an epic subject."[1] "On the whole, it is an absorbing rather than an emotion-stirring film."[5] **Final Word** To say the French were upset and felt betrayed by the British would be an understatement. A French retelling of this event would certainly be entertaining, but they are still too busy sorting out who collaborated and who didn't.

The Eagle Has Landed

1976   GBR   color   d. John Sturges

WW II: Espionage	2.0

What if Hitler had secretly ordered the German military to kidnap Winston Churchill? This completely fictional story, based on a novel by Jack Higgins, contemplates this possibility. One brave or very stupid German officer who questions the practicality of such a plan asks, "Why? We have already lost the war?" The response is to use Churchill as a bargaining chip in peace negotiations. For the audience it's all very simple. We know that Churchill was never kidnapped, so the only real question is, how well do the Nazis fail in this attempt? If you can accept the sheer improbability of this plot, you will have no problem believing this turkey is an eagle. Robert Duval (Col. Radl) is ordered to conduct a feasibility study, but is soon ordered by Himmler to make it operational. Duval then requests a German commando team, headed by Michael Caine (Col. Steiner), to carry out the plan. From here on, the story becomes increasingly ridiculous (if that's possible). Col. Steiner is an outstanding German officer who hates the Nazis and assaults an SS general in order to save a Jewish woman's life. As a result, Steiner and his commando team are imprisoned. Once Col. Radl is able to extract them from prison, Col. Steiner accepts the assignment but insists that they wear their German uniforms under the Polish army fatigues when they parachute into England (yes, that seems pretty transparent). The movie also features Donald Sutherland in long and irrelevant digression as a Irish Republican army expatriate who hates the English. However, the plot really implodes once the commandos reach England. Larry Hagman, an American colonel itching for action, attempts to race in and foil the kidnap attempt in a humorous interlude that borders on the bizarre. For some unknown reason, the entire point of view of this film changes from German to American. Fortunately, Hagman is shot in the forehead, and the perspective switches back. I can assure you that the ending will leave you convinced you should be writing tales of international espionage.

What the critics say Critics rate this film 3.0 to 4.0. "Uninvolving spy melodrama, lethargically directed."[1] "Action-packed...hardly a dull moment."[2] "Fast-moving, intricately plotted and solidly entertaining."[3] "The plot is totally ludicrous."[8] **Final Word** My apologies to the turkey, a noble bird.

84 Charlie MoPic

1989   USA   Color   d. Patrick Duncan

Vietnam War: Combat Hell   5.0

Through the lens of a shaky, handheld camera, we watch a six-man Army airborne reconnaissance team patrol Vietnam's Central Highlands in August 1969. This documentary-style movie was written and produced by Patrick Duncan, a Vietnam veteran. Individual soldiers are interviewed and talk to the camera as the patrol works its way "in country," until its extraction after a bloody and costly engagement with North Vietnamese regulars. This recon team's basic mission is to identify the movement of Vietcong and North Vietnamese troops and call in artillery and air strikes. "LT" (Jonathan Emerson), an ambitious lieutenant, convinces his superior that he could film "lessons" from the field for training soldiers. (MoPic is an abbreviation for motion picture.) This introduces a basic conflict between "LT" and "OD" (Richard Brooks), a tough, angry Black sergeant who demands perfection and control in the field. This movie is unique in providing an intimate close-up of men at war. It lingers on the details of surviving minute to minute, rather than day to day. We see what it take for "boonie rats" to survive, including the heightened awareness and constant attention to small details that ensures their survival. They talk about "boonie voodoo" and their constant superstition about good luck—who has it and who doesn't. What is unusual for a Vietnam War film is the complete absence of politics. There are no debates about who the enemy is or moral ambiguities about what they are doing. These soldiers are good at what they do, and what they do best is kill and survive. You will never get closer to men in this type of combat than this movie takes you. The acting is excellent and the combat is exceedingly real. A times the pace seems slow and the dialog too cute, but this film packs a lot of tension and pulls no punches.

What the critics say Critics rate this movie 4.0 to 4.5 "Powerful and energetic." "Sheds new light on the subject of the Vietnam War."[5] "From the opening image...to the final shot...looks and feels like the real deal."[6] "Powerfully realistic...a compelling and engrossing experience."[7] **Final Word** Somewhat derivative of Schoendoerffer's great film, *317th Platoon, 84 Charlie MoPic* stands on its own as an outstanding war movie. See it right away, if you haven't already.

Empire of the Sun

1987 USA color d. Steven Spielberg

WW II: Prisoner-of-War	2.5

Steven Spielberg's rather twisted adaptation of J.G. Ballard's semiautobiographical novel has turned Ballard's childhood in a Japanese internment camp into a preadolescent fantasy that might better be dubbed "POW Land." This movie chronicles the story of an eleven-year-old English boy, Jamie (Christian Bale), whose upper-class parents reside in Shanghai just prior to the Japanese invasion of this city in 1941. Having lived an extremely sheltered and privileged life, Jamie is separated from his parents and has to learn to fend for himself amid the chaos of the streets, and later at the Sochow Creek Internment Camp from 1941-1945. Spielberg succumbs to making this a Dickensonian tale of a street urchin, frequently referred to as "Kid," who learns to hustle and take care of himself. John Malkovich, as Basie, is an American street peddler and hustler who befriends the "Kid" and teaches him the ropes (see Fagan *à la Oliver Twist*). The story turns on this young boy's transformation from snotty and spoiled to confident and obnoxious. Spielberg is later able to tell the same story, only better in *Hook*, where there is no difficulty separating fantasy and reality. Basically, this is not a story for adults, but one for kids. Told from the rather romanticized perspective of an 11-year-old, the story never really grows as a movie. There are no fully developed characters or relationships. As a result, its not possible to respond to one emotionally charged scene after another as if they really mattered. Rent this for your kids to watch, but don't waste your time since you could not possibly gain insight into the experiences of J.G. Ballard. This movie gets the full-Hollywood. Shot on location in Shanghai, the movie has some beautiful photography, but a better look at childhood wartime experiences can be gotten from the excellent movies *Au Revior, Les Enfants*, *Hope and Glory* or *When Father Was Away on Business*.

What the critics say Critics rate this movie 2.5 to 4.0. "Intelligent and thought provoking movie."[1] "Sprawling, ambitious and emotionally distant and loaded with cinematic crescendos."[7] **Final Word** This is a very hollow movie in which the dramatic experiences of the characters and the audience haven't been earned. Let's be thankful Spielberg hasn't given the Holocaust this treatment, yet.

Enemy at the Gates

2001 USA color d. Jean-Jacques Annaud

WW II: Combat Duel at Stalingrad   3.5

Hollywood's fascination with war and romance appears to be insatiable, as *Enemy at the Gates* is yet another muddled attempt to combine the two. With the end of the Cold War and a nod towards improved relationships with Russia, this movie is set in Stalingrad (Volgograd), Russia in the fall of 1942. The German army is laying siege to Stalingrad in the hopes of a quick victory and securing the oil fields near the Caspian Sea. The story is loosely based on a real hero of the battle of Stalingrad, Vassili Zaitsev, a young man from the Urals who becomes a folk hero because of his skills as a sniper. Beyond these facts, it is not possible to know any more about this soldier from the movie. Everything else is pure Hollywood. There are two related stories here. The first is a *cat and mouse* contest between Vassili (Jude Law) and famed German sniper Maj. König (Ed Harris), as each attempts to take the other out. This is a fairly interesting if not contrived story. The men know too much about one another and their relationship is made overly personal. At the end, König becomes sadistic in an attempt to prevail, which is completely at odds with his character. The second story revolves around Vassili's attraction to a young Jewish woman, Tania (Rachel Weisz), who is also being courted by his friend Danilov (Joseph Fiennes), who just happens to be a "political officer" in the Communist Party. Danilov has also created the propaganda that has elevated Vassili to national prominence. This triangle is annoying and continually diminishes the credibility of the movie. There is a happy ending, if you consider Danilov's taking one in the forehead for his friend, a good resolution to relationship problems. The opening sequences, in which Soviet soldiers are herded into Stalingrad to be shot by the Germans, or by their own soldiers if they retreated are exceptionally well-done (but not historically accurate). The sniper action is also outstanding, as are the special effects that show us a city reduced to rubble.

What the critics say Critics rate this movie 2.0 to 3.5. "Starts strong but loses its way...diminished by a silly romantic subplot."[2] "Will captivate viewers during its grim battle scenes...unfortunately everybody's dialog is lamentably corny."[7]
Final Word This movie reflects much of our current romanticized nostalgia for WW II.

The Enemy Below

1957   USA   color   d. Dick Powell

World War II: Submarine Combat Duel   4.0

What we have here is a *mano-a-mano* combat duel in the South Atlantic between the commander of an American destroyer, Robert Mitchum, and the captain of a German U-boat, Curt Jürgens. Adapted from a novel of the same name by D.A. Rayner, *The Enemy Below* was made in cooperation with the Dept. of Defense and Navy, and won an Oscar for special effects. It's obvious from the beginning that each captain is an experienced veteran and that a complex *cat-and-mouse* chase is about to begin. What elevates this film and makes it very entertaining is the excellent job by Mitchum and Jürgens in capturing each character's cynicism and tiredness of war. For a change, we get a complex and realistic set of motives that defines each commander. In the opening, Mitchum talks about war—"We have learned a hard truth...That there is no end to the misery and destruction. We can't kill it because it's something within ourselves. You can call it the enemy if you want to, but its part of us." Jürgens is not a Nazi but a professional soldier worshipped by his crew, and weary of war. He sees war as having become mechanized and as having lost its humanness. He is tired and believes he has lived to long, he is ready to die. This is a very thoughtful, well-acted and suspenseful movie. Mitchum gives one of his best and most straightforward performances. But what really stands out is the battle of wits and maneuvering by each commander, Mitchum's efforts to sink the sub are laden with many personal motives, and Jürgens, tired of war, is simply trying to complete his mission only 48 hours from port. The special effects and degree of realism are exceptionally high, adding to the drama. If this movie has any shortcomings, it is the ending. Apparently director Dick Powell shot two endings and decided to go with the "happy" ending. Even with this decision, neither captain is made out to be overly heroic and each proves vulnerable. While the ending is a copout, it does not detract from the fact that this is a very entertaining movie.

What the critics say Critics rate this movie 3.0 to 3.5. "Fine submarine chase tale."[2] "Solid WW II yarn."[3] "Suspenseful WW II sea epic."[5] "This little-seen aquatic dual is well worth viewing."[7] **Final Word** This movie has improved over time. Among the best submarine movies ever.

Enigma

2001 GBR/USA /GER/NET color d. Michael Apted

WW II: Espionage-Romance 2.0

Take a fascinating war story—the breaking of the Nazi's Enigma coding machine—and make it a gothic murder-romance mystery and you have *Enigma*. Unfortunately, this movie is style over substance. Shot in dark blue overtones with a portentous musical score, it has a barely coherent storyline that keeps everyone guessing about what is taking place on the screen. By the end you will not care why the beautiful girl was murdered. The screenplay, by Tom Stoppard, was adapted from a novel by Robert Harris, in another recent attempt to take box-office advantage of WW II nostalgia (*Charlotte Gray, Dark Blue World, Hart's War*) that does not succeed. Tom Jericho (Dougray Scott), is a brilliant English mathematician and codebreaker who suffers a breakdown. We are left to guess why? Because he's exhausted by the near impossibility of his work and the pressure to succeed or because he was dumped by the beautiful Claire (Saffron Burrows) after a brief affair. Unfortunately, the really interesting aspect of this story, the code breaking efforts by the British at Bletchley Park, is simply backdrop to an affair and a murder. For the most part, the codebreakers come across as frat nerds trying to score with a woman, any woman. There is also the plain looking Hester (Kate Winslet), brilliant in her own unrecognized way, who assists Tom in finding out why Claire has disappeared, and while they are at it—break some German Enigma code documenting the Soviet massacre of Polish soldiers (this has some obscure bearing on the plot). There is also a semi-menacing intelligence spook (Jeremy Northam) who is over-acted to the point of irrelevance. Let's sum up—highly stylized, over-acted, poorly scripted and a convoluted plot that is hard to follow. The breaking of the Enigma machine codes was a conceptually cleaner problem than the plotline of this movie.

What the critics say Critics rate this movie 2.5 to 3.0. "Peters out as it becomes unfocused and—yes—confusing."[2] "Excessive subplots make for confusion but the story is still compelling."[5] **Final Word** There are very few movies about the Enigma codebreakers. There's an obscure Polish film *Enigma Secret,* and *U-571*, in which the Americans pretend they captured the Enigma machine (which upsets the British in real life).

Enola Gay: The Men, the Mission, the Atomic Bomb
1980 USA color tv d. David Lowell Rich

WW II: Atomic Bombing of Hiroshima   2.0

This movie is basically a colorized reprise of the same identical story as told in the 1952 film *Above and Beyond*, only not quite as good. It's amazing how one of the most significant events of WW II continues to be treated so irrelevantly. This is supposedly the story of the B-29 crew that dropped the first atomic bomb on Hiroshima on August 6, 1945, which resulted in the death of eighty thousand Japanese. The movie's brief epilogue fails to note that a second bomb was dropped on Nagasaki before the Japanese agreed to an unconditional surrender that ended the war. Based on a book by Gordon Thomas and Max Morgan Witts, this movie focuses on Col. Paul Tibbets (Patrick Duffy), commander of the 509th bomber squadron that was formed to deliver the atom bomb. Tibbets also pilots the B-29 "Enola Gay" that drops the first bomb. Let's just say that Duffy is wooden and hardly packs the *gravitas* that probably better defined Col. Tibbets. The sum total of what we learn about Tibbets is that he organized the 509th and solved technical problems in dropping and delivering the bomb, which estranged him from his wife. Tibbets had a complex organizational problem and was working under a great deal of pressure, yet this movie sheds no light on that. We never find out why he was selected for this job, what he thought about the moral dimensions of his actions nor what he emotionally experienced. At no point in this film is there a single discussion among the crew as to the seriousness of what they are doing or the historical importance of the mission. In fact, there are no stories here at all. Just lots of people keeping busy (as in many jobs) until the bomb is finally dropped and the movie ends. We learn nothing about the crew beyond their actual names. However, a restored B-29 is fun to watch. There are also a few brief scenes that take place in Hiroshima in which we see a senior Japanese officer mentoring a younger officer, perhaps to humanize the Japanese and add pathos to the coming destruction. It also allows us to see the intransigence of the Japanese military toward surrendering.

What the critics say Critics rate this movie 2.5 to 3.0. "Delves into the lives and reactions of the crew members in a fairly effective manner."[7] **Final Word** Better to watch the 1995 documentary *Enola Gay and the Atomic Bombing of Japan*.

The Execution of Private Slovik

1974 USA color tv d. Lamont Johnson

WW II: Legal Drama	4.0

This thoughtful, fact-based drama is adapted from a book by William Bradford Huie. The film features a quiet but powerful performance by Martin Sheen as Eddie Slovik, the first American soldier to be executed for desertion since the Civil War. Slovik was tried by a general court-martial and convicted under the 58th Article of War—desertion to avoid hazardous duty. He was sentenced to death and executed by a military firing squad on January 31, 1945. The movie portrays Slovik as a somewhat troubled individual who is married and working when drafted. In the Army, he's not suited to military duty but completes basic training and is assigned to the 109th Infantry in France. Before he can reach his company, he deserts after being shelled by German artillery. Fearful of being killed in combat, Slovik believes he would be unable to perform his duties as an infantryman. From this point on, he purposely avoids combat and seeks a court-martial as a deserter. The Army gives Slovik every opportunity to change his mind, but in each instance he refuses. It's also clear that the sentencing officers never expected the death penalty to be up-held upon review. This movie does not suggest that politics was a factor. But, as one soldier noted, "There are lots of deserters. Nobody ever shot one before, at least not in this war." Why this execution ever took place is not satisfactorily answered here. Clearly, the Army set out to make an example of Slovik, but his own actions were so obvious and undisguised that he also received very little sympathy. Sheen's performance and the excellent performances of the entire cast elevate this movie. Its graphic attention to execution detail is also a powerful statement about the grisly nature of the death penalty. A doctor tells members of the firing squad, "Think of the heart as a circle. It's a semiround organ and it's found in the area of the lower-third of the breast bone.... Just go for a grouping in this specific area."

What the critics say Critics rate this movie 4.0 to 4.5. "Solid drama...thoughtful, literate adaptation."[2] "Quiet power-house ...ends in deifying Slovik, which many will find hard to take."[5] "Intelligent teleplay, powerful performances, and sensitive direction."[7] **Final Word** Slovik probably didn't deserve this fate, but then neither did all the other American soldiers who died.

Fail Safe

1964   USA   b/w   d. Sidney Lumet

Cold War: Nuclear War Scenario	3.5

This grim and noirish antitechnology tale plays out like a policy wonk's dream of a WW III war game exercise. Low-budget and black and white, there are minimalist backgrounds (mostly tables in small rooms) to set the stage for a talkative exploration of American nuclear weapons policy—all wrapped in paranoia and fear of technology. The rant at the core of this movie is that technology has taken over and that we are so over-dependent on our gadgetry that decision making has been taken out of our hands. Essentially, a computer glitch has sent a squadron of B-58 bombers, armed with two 20-megaton nuclear bombs each, towards the Soviet Union with the objective of bombing Moscow. The bombers cannot be recalled since they passed the fail-safe point. In order to avoid nuclear retaliation by the Soviets, the President (Henry Fonda) has offered to bomb New York City if Moscow is destroyed. Perhaps the most astonishing aspect of this film is that it appears to be a rip-off of Stanley Kubrick's *Dr. Strangelove*, which was released a year earlier, but without the satire. Apparently, Columbia pictures felt the same way and sued the writers, film maker, and distributor of *Fail Safe*. While Fonda gets most of the on-screen time as the calm and decisive President, Walter Matthau shines as the "mad scientist." Matthau portrays Dr. Groeteschele as a cynical, war-mongering scientist who advocates a first strike against the Soviets, while calmly calculating acceptable kill ratios in the tens of millions and lecturing about our culture prevailing with only 60 to 100 million casualties. As a "message" movie, *Fail Safe* has some smart and clever things to say about "massive-retaliation" and the "balance of terror" but in the end proves to be clichéd and simplistic. The film plays like a rough draft of a screen play, rather than as a polished motion picture.

What the critics say Critics rate this movie 4.5 to 5.0. "This deadly earnest drama gets across the horror of its situation better than...Dr. Strangelove."[1] "One of the most effective films yet made about the futility and horror of nuclear war."[3] **Final Word** Students of Cold War paranoia and advocates of a first-strike will enjoy. Better to watch *The Bedford Incident* or *Seven Days in May*. A TV version aired in 2000.

Farewell to the King

1989   USA   color   d. John Milius

Yes, this is a movie about the Second World War. However, there should be a disclaimer that warns the audience—"Any relationship between this film and reality is purely coincidental." Based on the novel, *L' Adieu au Roi*, by Pierre Schoendoerffer (who directed such films as *The Anderson Platoon, Diên Biên Phu and 317th Platoon*), this movie features Nick Nolte as an Army sergeant who escapes after the US defeat at Corregidor by the Japanese in 1942, and later washes ashore on the island of Borneo. Now, exactly how a white man becomes king of 22 separate indigenous rain forest tribes, on the largest island in the Malay archipelago, is open to speculation. Some suggest it's whimsical story telling, *à la* Kipling. Others feel that it's derivative of Conrad's *Heart of Darkness*, or a combination of these two. The movie bares some thematic resemblance to Coppola's *Apocalypse Now* (director John Milius worked on both scripts). One could even feel some discomfort about the movie's underlying racist assumptions, about the superiority of the white man over the black man. However, it would probably be a mistake to overthink the intentions of this movie—which comes closest to Edgar Rice Burrough's *Tarzan*. A man escapes the "so-called" civilized world, to find a sense of inner peace and meaning to his life in the more elemental world of a tribal people. The story is mostly a combination of utopian fantasy and naive anthropology. The war soon descends on these isolated people as British special forces parachute into the jungle to recruit tribesmen to fight the Japanese. King Nolte will lend his support, but only if the Allies agree to a treaty protecting the independence of these tribes. Nolte then leads the charge against the Japanese. The photography is visually rich, but the acting is very limited, especially with Nolte hunching over in a simian fashion at times. While Nolte goes native, all the native women modestly cover their breasts.

What the critics say Critics rate this movie 2.5 to 3.5. "Intriguing premise, but result sinks into cliché."[2] "Visually stunning, thematically stunted."[3] "The clichés are as thick as the foliage."[4]
Final Word Most of us could get closer to nature than the king of the headhunters if we simply learned to garden more.

146

Fat Man and Little Boy

1989   USA   color   d. Roland Joffe

WW II: Development of the Atomic Bomb   3.0

This film chronicles what was the most significant and expensive (2 billion dollars) scientific development (Manhattan Project) of WW II. On August 6, a B-29 (*Enola Gay*) dropped the first atomic bomb ("Little Boy") on Hiroshima. On August 9th, a second bomb ("Fat Man") was dropped on Nagasaki. The movie focuses on the two men perhaps most responsible for the development of these nuclear weapons, J. Robert Oppenheimer (Dwight Schultz) and Gen. Leslie Groves (Paul Newman). Oppenheimer was a brilliant scientist with many left-wing friends and associates, who was recruited to head up the scientific development of the bomb, and Groves was charged with overseeing the entire nuclear weapons program. The task before them was daunting. In 19 months, they had to make an operational weapon. To do this, nearly all the great physicists and engineers in America and Europe were recruited to Los Alamos, NM. Unfortunately, the decision to focus this story on the conflicted relationship between Oppenheimer and Goves deprives us of an opportunity to see the great scientific breakthroughs that were achieved, and the many fascinating personalities and minds who collaborated on this work. This film also fails to show us the full scope of Grove's responsibility and the bomb's development at Hanford, WA, and Oak Ridge, TN. As the bomb was nearing completion many scientists began to debate the moral issues surrounding the development and use of the bomb. While the film acknowledges this debate, it avoids the politics, particularly Truman's decision to drop the bomb. Ultimately, this movie is unsatisfying. The characters are never fully developed and we are never allowed into the this complex and fascinating world. The film's failure to weigh in on Oppenheimer's fate is disconcerting to say the least.

What the critics say Critics rate this movie 3.0 to 4.0. "Flawed but still arresting film."[2] "Script fails to give a clue to what made this man tick...few dramatic sparks."[4] **Final Word** Even though Oppenheimer was chairman of the Atomic Energy Commission, his security clearance was suspended due to right-wing politics.. Oppenheimer was haunted the remainder of his life by what he had helped create.

A Few Good Men

1992   USA   color   d. Rob Reiner

Military Life: Legal Drama	3.5

This is a slick and entertaining drama about a military cover-up revolving around the death of a Marine private. The setting is the US naval base at Guantanamo Bay, Cuba. Based on a screenplay by Aaron Sorkin, *A Few Good Men* features two outstanding performances, one by Tom Cruise as Lt. Kaffee, a cocky and smart-aleck attorney who has no respect for military life, and the other by Jack Nicholson as Col. Jessup, a crude and arrogant Marine base commander who can barely contain his rage. To quote Col. Jessup, "Walk softly and carry an armored tank division, I always say." Demi Moore (Lt. Cmdr. Galloway) also stars in this film. She doesn't take off her clothes; there is no romantic involvement with Cruise; and her character is fairly one-dimensional. Unfortunately, that doesn't leave her much to contribute. (I take that back, she's great looking.) Kevin Bacon (Capt. Ross) is excellent as the hot shot prosecuting attorney. At the core of this story is an unauthorized but apparently common Marine disciplinary procedure called "Code Red." This informal discipline (what most of us would think of as hazing) is used to correct and motivate Marines to conform to military life. Two Marines have been ordered to carry out a Code Red against a another marine in their unit. When he's accidentally killed, the two Marines who carried out this order are charged with murder. At this point, there's a cover-up, and it's up to Cruise to care enough to unravel this case and carry the day in court. This is an entertaining movie. You know where it's heading, but watching talented actors get there, with lots of twists and turns, is a lot of fun. While this movie is mostly attitude with very little substance, it moves quickly with excellent pacing and energy, and the courtroom confrontations are intense. Unfortunately, there are numerous plot holes, some big enough for an amphibious landing by entire Marine battalion. But let's not quibble. *A Few Good Men* is lightweight fare and does its job well.

What the critics say Critics rate this movie 2.0 to 4.5. "Slick, engrossing courtroom drama."[1] "Big-time, mainstream Hollywood movie par excellence."[4] **Final Word** This is a diversion from the real world. We all need it occasionally, especially the over-serious war drama geeks. Careful. Don't overdo it.

Field of Honor
1984   NET   color   d. Hans Scheepmaker

Korean War: Infantry Combat	1.5

It's probably safe to say that *Field of Honor* is among the most
bizarre war films ever made. Be careful not to confuse it with a
1987 French film of the same name about the Franco-Prussian
War. This 1984 movie was made in Holland, filmed on location in
Korea and dubbed in English. The available reviews—the back
of the box cover and the prologue—suggest that this movie is
about the 3,418 Dutch soldiers who served in the Korean War as
part of a contingent of multinational UN forces. Wrong! This is
really the director's attempt to film a Sergio Leone type spaghetti
Western under the guise of a Korean War film about Dutch
soldiers (no exaggeration here). The film focuses exclusively on
one character, Sgt. Sire (Everett McGill). With a heavy beard and
sports headband, Sire survives with a young prostitute and her
brother in the Korean hillsides. A professional soldier who fought
in WW II, Indonesia, and now in Korea, Sgt. Sire has only one
interest, besides prostitutes—killing. He's a loner and a survivor,
full of revenge and very little remorse, but he has a soft spot for
kids and dogs. Unfortunately, this film lacks the retribution and
violent catharsis of a good spaghetti Western. There is also little
combat action, and this movie has nothing to say about soldiers
or war. The fact that these soldier are Dutch is completely
irrelevant, and it is not clear why this movie was actually made.
The film does have rather graphic—if not gratuitous—violence.
The best moment comes after the Communists have bombarded
and overrun the Dutch position, and Sgt Sire is wounded in the
leg and trapped under a truck, which gradually rolls back over his
foot and traps him. While his eventual escape is not ingenious, it
is intense and fun to watch. Watching Sgt. Sire shoot at a
prostitute who is trying to kill and eats his dog is also a lot of fun.

What the critics say Critics rate this movie 2.0. to 2.5. **Final
Word** I doubt the reviewers saw the movie. Difficult to track
down, but if you like the cheap Vietnam actioners, or want an
offbeat war movie experience, give it a try.

Field of Honor

1987 FRA color d. Jean-Pierre Denis

Franco-Prussian War: War is Crazy	3.5

Even in 1869 the French army used a lottery to draft young men. However, it was legal for young men from poor families, with exempt lottery numbers, to sell or barter their numbers to well-off families whose sons had been drafted. It was also customary that neither party know who the other party was in the exchange. *Field of Honor* opens with just such an event, but in this instance the buyers know who the other person is. In a slight twist, Pierre (Cris Campion), a young man from a poor farming family, sees the exchange as an opportunity to escape his circumstances and to go out into the world, while the young man from the middle-class mercantile family, Arnaud (Eric Wapler), feels ashamed for not serving. Within months of Pierre's induction, Napoleon III declares war on Prussia. The French, who expected an easy victory, quickly retreat and Pierre's unit is badly defeated. Wounded and barely escaping, Pierre attempts to make his way back to the French lines with the assistance of a young Alsatian boy he befriends. At this point, what started out as an interesting story about how these two young men's lives were forever entwined by this exchange of fates, unravels into a series of unrelated events that slow the movie to a crawl. This film raises interesting class issues. It also contrasts the pastoral beauty of rural France (nature) against the devastation of war (man) in a subtle and profound manner. It raises questions about our fates—can we defy them by exchanging draft numbers, or is one's social class ultimately one's fortune? Unfortunately, the film does not attempt to answer or even struggle with any of the issues it raises. The sentiments of this movie are clearly antiwar, and strongly suggests that our motives for war are arcane and primitive, and that the cost is beyond all reason. However, in this film, war is ultimately only a backdrop to telling a story that too often rambles and loses focus.

What the critics say Critics rate this movie 3.0. to 4.0. "Subtle moving drama."[3] "A quiet French antiwar drama."[5] "Muddled and meandering script causes it to fall short."[7] **Final Word** For the combat action guy this is not your movie. For the serious war drama buff it's too scattered to be either coherent or profound.

Fighter Attack

1953 USA color d. Lesley Selander

WW II: Guerrilla-Romance   1.0

Why this movie is called *Fighter Attack* is completely beyond comprehension, other than that it sounds sexier than, say, "Partisan Paisans Fighting for Freedom." The movie opens in 1944 as American fighter pilot Maj. Steve Pitt (Sterling Hayden) is shot down in his P-47 over Italy. A flight commander and veteran of 200 missions, Maj. Pitt is about to be rotated back to the states, where his fiancée is waiting for him. However, fate intervenes in the form of a very attractive young woman named Nina (Joy Page), who helps him evade the Germans and, later, his engagement, by putting him in contact with the local resistance movement. Okay, so now you realize you have been tricked, and this is not about air combat but about a romance between Maj. Pitt and Nina, and all this partisan stuff is just subterfuge to get them together. As they are trekking to the hideaway of the local resistance, in what looks like the San Fernando Valley, Maj. Pitt hits on Nina for coffee and makes small talk about the beautiful view. Despite her jealous suitor, Nina is clearly attracted to the major. There's also some conflict between Maj. Pitt and resistance leader Bruno (J. Carrol Naish), who doesn't like Pitt's pushiness (does this sound as bad as it really is?). *Fighter Attack* looks and feels like a "B" Western. Hayden is stiff and uncomfortable as a romantic lead here, but Nina has the good sense to hold him at bay because he has a girlfriend back home. Eventually, Hayden leads the partisans in an attack against an antiaircraft gun that is defending a tunnel his squadron had been unable to bomb. He then escapes back to Corsica to rejoin his squadron. No, there is more. Maj. Pitt returns to Italy after the war and finds Nina waiting for him with open arms. There's also a generous use of documentary footage of P-47s that is played over and over until you realize you have seen the same footage five or six times in the first 20 minutes. Did I mention there was a song dedicated to Nina, sung by one of the local resistance fighters?!

What the critics say Critics rate this movie 2.0. to 2.5. "Routine war actioner efficiently dispensed."[1] "Familiar WW II melodrama."[7] **Final Word** This is not camp enough to be up there with John Wayne and Janet Leigh in *Jet Pilot*, but it runs a close second as one of the worst war romances ever.

The Fighting Seabees

1944   USA   b/w   d. Edward Ludwig

WW II: 40's Combat Classic   2.5

This extremely popular film features John Wayne as Wedge Donovan (you have to like the name Wedge), a larger-than-life construction company owner who single-handedly wins the war in the Pacific with a bulldozer and a bad-attitude. (You will also get to see Wayne attempt to jitterbug for the first and last time.) Wayne joins with Lt. Comdr. Yarrow (Dennis O'Keefe) in the development of a Navy construction battalion (Seabees). These men were recruited from the construction industry to island-hop and build air fields, houses, and roads throughout the Pacific. But the task didn't start out that simple. When Wayne's crews begin suffering combat casualties, he wants to arm them and take on "Tojo and his bug-eyed monkeys" (the smiling Japanese sniper is a bit much). Of course, his solution is to hand every guy a rifle. But the bureaucratic Navy has its own way—training, procedures, chain-of-command, paper work, all the things Wayne has no time for. When Wedge impulsively leads an attack that results in unnecessary casualties to his men, he comes on board and does things the Navy's way. We even get a Seabees' fight song, "Song of the Seabees," which almost makes you want to enlist. Now there's more to this movie than Wayne and O'Keefe bumping heads. There's Susan Hayward, 25-years old at the time (and truly hot!), who holds her own with Wayne on the screen. There's also lots of backlot studio action here. In the film's final grand heroics, Wayne (or is that Wedge) collapses a fuel dump with a bulldozer, that incinerates advancing Japanese soldiers and saves the air field. Now as corny as this all sounds, *The Fighting Seabees* is probably John Wayne's most entertaining WW II movie. While the combat scenes are not particularly realistic, they are done with great enthusiasm. The movie was escapist entertainment at its best in 1944.

What the critics say Critics rate this movie 2.0 to 4.0. "Routine, studio-staged war melodrama."[1] "Spirited WW 2 saga."[2] "This furious, frivolous propaganda potboiler has virtually nothing to do with the realties of the war in the Pacific."[7] **Final Word** All of Wayne's movies are about him and the audience's fascination with his larger-than-life persona on the screen. Times change, of course, and Wayne is becoming mostly a fading curiosity today.

The Fighting 69th

1940 USA b/w d. William Keighley

WW I: Classic '40s Flagwaver	1.5

Some critics maintain that this film was really Hollywood's opening shot in a WW II propaganda campaign that was to follow. Others might rightly argue that it was simply the nadir of the WW I film—wrapping ethnic American heroes in religion and the flag in a shameless manner. Either way, the movie has a lot of blarney in it. One of this film's problems is deciding what it wants to be about—the all-Irish 69th New York Regiment, or a tribute to Army priest and war hero Father Duffy, or about the heroic redemption of Pvt. Jerry Plunkett (James Cagney), a street punk who is a slacker and coward at heart. Mostly, this film seems to be about soldiers marching off to war to stirring music, interspersed with scenes of Father Duffy (Pat O'Brien) performing a variety of religious ceremonies exhorting God to protect American soldiers. What story there is, focuses on the relationship between Father Duffy and Pvt. Plunkett. Plunkett, all-attitude and mouth, is unable to cope with military life. He is insubordinate, shirks his duties and eventually puts soldiers at risk on the battlefield. He is eventually court-martialed for desertion. Because there's absolutely nothing sympathetic about Plunkett, his redemption is bothersome. Somehow he doesn't get what he deserves. The fact that Father Duffy cares and keeps trying to rehabilitate Plunkett simply becomes annoying. In reality, Plunkett would have been dishonorably discharged in basic training, put in the stockade after he arrived in France, or fragged on the battlefield. Here he's kept around as entertainment. Many notable Irish-Americans are feted here. The poetry of Sgt. Joyce Kilmer (famed poet) is recited. Major Donovan (formed the OSS during WW II) gives a speech about the 165th Infantry or "Rainbow Division"—"one nation now, one team, an all-American team pulling together." There's lots of humor and fights—and very little action.

What the critics say Critics rate this movie 2.0 to 4.0. "Recruiting poster stuff."[1] "Overripe (but tough to dislike)."[2] "Cornball but entertaining."[5] "Early piece of war propaganda means to prepare 1940 audiences for an imminent war."[6] **Final Word** Perhaps because of Ireland's strong sympathies for Germany in WW I (and later in WW II), Irish patriotism in the US had to be reaffirmed. I suspect they mostly hated the British.

The Fighting Sullivans

1944 USA b/w d. Lloyd Bacon

| WW II: Classic '40s Flagwaver | 2.0 |

The death of the five Sullivan brothers at the Battle of Guadalcanal in 1942 has probably had a greater impact on the American psyche than any other wartime casualties in our history. All five brothers were serving on the cruiser USS *Juneau*, when it was struck by Japanese torpedo bombers and sunk. As a result of this tragic incident, the War Department immediately instituted policies to ensure nothing similar could ever happen again. Out of respect for the sacrifice made by this family, a destroyer was christened the USS *The Sullivans*. Having told you this much, it's time to say that there is no reason to watch this movie. It is strictly a fictionalized Hollywood account that focuses almost exclusively on the early childhood years of the young Sullivans (George, Francis, Joseph, Madison and Albert) growing up in Waterloo, Iowa. The movie looks as if it might have been adapted from a Norman Rockwell painting—full of gee-whiz and aw-shucks moments. We get a Depression-era paean to an Irish-Catholic family with rough 'n tumble but good kids. *The Fighting Sullivans* is a charming and maudlin picture that has almost nothing to do with reality. Half-way through, the movie switches to these brothers as young adults, working and dating, then enlisting in the Navy shortly after the bombing of Pearl Harbor. The brothers insisted they serve together, and apparently the Navy agreed. Unfortunately, we learn nothing about the family or these young sailors. Only a few minutes of the movie are devoted to their enlisting and subsequent deaths at Guadalcanal. The final scene, in which the family is told of their sons' deaths, is heart wrenching, but the patriotic message attached to this movie is one of quiet stoicism. It's everyone's job to get on with their lives because there's a war on. The father goes off to work, and the mother offers the nice Navy officer coffee.

What the critics say Critics rate this movie 3.5 to 4.0. "Inspirational true story which had wide-appeal."[1] "Truly a stirring tribute to all lives lost."[5] "This curious family drama barely qualifies as a war film."[6] **Final Word** Probably the inspiration for Spielberg's *Saving Private Ryan*. Today, the Sullivan family would be overwhelmed with talk show offers and movie deals. They would be considered fools, of course, if they didn't capitalize on their misfortune and grieve publicly.

Fireball Forward

1972   USA   color   tv   d. Marvin J. Chomsky

| WW II: Pressures of Command | 3.5 |

This is a surprisingly well-made TV movie about the pressures and tension of military command, with a whodunit twist, that breaks rank with dozens of routine wartime dramas. Ben Gazarra (Gen. Barrett) gives an excellent performance as an American army general assigned to take command of a combat infantry division that has been underperforming in combat. The action takes place days after the Normandy invasion of Europe in 1944. The Allies are trying to effect a tank breakthrough of the German lines, but are meeting stiff resistance. The 14th Division is continually suffering battlefield setbacks. Gen. Barrett, who came up through the ranks, is seen as a man of the "dogface" who can take charge and turn around the division's morale and efficiency. What takes place is a tight little drama of personalities in the forward command post. As Gazarra sets about confronting the inadequacies of this division, it becomes evident that there is a security breach. Someone is reporting the division's movements as well as the locations of their forward observation posts to the Germans. This movie works as an intense drama and intriguing mystery that will keep you involved. While Gazarra is excellent as a general who cares about his men, this movie also conveys the high level of conflict that exists up and down the chain of command. With everyone's career on the line, it becomes clear, that the higher up the chain of command you go, the less they care about your problems at the front. Security breach or not, morale problem or not, these men are going to be thrown into combat. The film also manages some insightful shots at bureaucracy and rigid officers who perform only by the book. An outstanding supporting cast includes Ricardo Montalban, Eddie Albert, Dana Elcar, Edwin Binns, L.Q. Jones and Curt Lowens, all adding to the film's credibility. Even though there are numerous action scenes, this is primarily a drama of command and not about the battlefield. *Fireball Forward* will keep you guessing right up until the end.

What the critics say Critics rate this movie 3.0. **Final Word** This is a smart movie that should be considered a real sleeper among war films. Not necessarily for the action guy, but for those who enjoy excellent drama with more than a few twists and turns of plot.

Fires on the Plain

1959   JAP   b/w   subtitles   d. Kon Ichikawa

WW II: Antiwar	3.5

In the face of an American invasion of the Philippines in 1945, the Japanese army is in retreat across Leyte, desperately trying to find transport to Japan. What transpires here is a horrific and surreal journey seen through the experiences of Pvt. Tamura (Eiji Funakoshi), who has been diagnosed with TB. Food is in such short supply that he cannot receive medical treatment unless he has his own rations to feed himself. Unable to rejoin his company because he cannot carry his share of the workload, Pvt. Tamura is a burden and told that it's his "final duty" to "use your hand grenade" to kill himself. Based on the novel by Shohei Ooka, what evolves is a journey through a bleak and desperate landscape littered with bodies of dying and dead Japanese soldiers. Unable or unwilling to surrender, most of the soldiers are fighting starvation. Circumstances eventually become so desperate that many resort to cannibalism (euphemistically called "monkey meat"). At one point Tamura shoots a native woman who is screaming from fear but who doesn't represent a threat to him. Later he kills a soldier because of the soldier's act of cannibalism. While we are shown the frightening depths we can all reach, it doesn't create sympathy for this dying soldier who keeps killing people. There's all this wandering through the depths of hell, but we are not told how the soldiers arrived at this place. We see them suffering for having refused to surrender, but there is no exploration of the Japanese military code forbidding surrender. The easy-out here is to simply moralize about the horrors of war in general. Pvt. Tamura and all the other dead Japanese soldiers have been rendered abstractions in a film seeking their redemption by asking us to care. That's hard to do when there's no contrition or acts of atonement. It would be more interesting to see a film about the anguish of the victims as the Japanese rode a crest of victories in Asia from 1931 through 1942.

What the critics say Critics rate this movie 4.0 to 5.0. "Graphically realistic, disturbing, and depressing vision of damnation on earth."[2] "Visual tour de force...as he sinks into an animal void."[6] **Final Word** The events of this dark journey raise a number of important moral questions but, unfortunately, not the right ones.

First to Fight

1967   USA   color   d. Christian Nyby

WW II: Combat Fear	2.5

First to Fight is a predictable and uninspiring psychological examination of combat fear. Set on the Pacific island of Guadalcanal in 1942, where US Marines are attempting to hold a beachhead against a Japanese counter attack, Sgt. Jack Connell (Chad Everett) a Marine veteran, and the last surviving member of his platoon, manages to single handedly repel the attack. Because of his heroic actions, he's promoted to lieutenant and awarded the Congressional Medal of Honor. He's also reassigned stateside to promote the war effort. Next we get a long interlude in which Lt. Connell falls in love with the beautiful Peggy (Marilyn Devin). This hapless and predictable romance doesn't have a nanosecond of chemistry. The movie then does the unforgivable—it shows us a lengthy scene from *Casablanca,* and throughout the rest of the movie constantly plays "As Time Goes By," often to great crescendo. When Lt. Connell is reassigned as a combat training officer, he learns that a good friend has died in combat. After much personal struggle, he returns to the war. However, life is no longer simple because Connell is now married. As platoon leader, he becomes fearful during the landing on Saipan, and his veteran platoon sergeant, Sgt. Tweed (Gene Hackman) is immediately on his case to either shape up or get the "hell" out of combat. The point of this film is to show how marriage has changed the lieutenant's sense of vulnerability. The movie, unfortunately, shows neither an insightful nor interesting exploration of the fine line between heroism and cowardice. Of course, there's a happy ending as the lieutenant is "good-to-go" after Sgt. Tweed is wounded. For the most part, the combat scenes are limited and routine. They also appear to be nearly identical to scenes in a half-dozen other war movies. The bottom line—twenty-two years after the war you would have expected a more complex examination of this subject than provided by this nostalgic flagwaver.

What the critics say Critics rate this movie 2.0 to 2.5. "Competently done but...a bit shaky in period detail."[1] "Conventional WW 2 yarn."[2] **Final Word** The capture of Guadalcanal halted Japanese westward expansion and shattered the myth of their military superiority. Japanese casualties were 37,500 to 7,500 US casualties.

157

Flat Top

1952 USA color d. Lesley Selander

WW II: Naval Carrier Action	2.0

This is a terse and stripped-down film about a squadron of young carrier fighter pilots heading into combat for the first time. The basic storyline, a precursor to the two better known 1950s Korean War carrier films, *The Bridges at Toko-Ri* and *Men of the Fighting Lady*, lacks their star power and the sexiness of jet fighters and real carriers. However, these two more glamorous movies are hardly much better. An American naval task force is heading for the Philippines in 1945, and Squadron Commander Collier (Sterling Hayden), a highly decorated veteran pilot, is unwilling to tolerate any nonsense or lack of discipline as he prepares the pilots for combat. The limited story here is about the conflicts inherent in command, which has been played out in numerous earlier war movies. The story hones in on the tension between Commander Collier and his executive officer, Capt. Joe Rogers (Richard Carlson), over how best to discipline the pilots. For those who want to know, Collier eventually wins his men over once they get into combat. Hayden plays a role he has reprised nearly his entire film career as a gruff and, at times, over bearing and overly confident officer. The movie is a generic-actioner, filled with stock characters and situations. The only drama is whether Hayden's by-the-book approach will fail or succeed. There's no focus on missions or the big picture here. Story and character development are very limited. An attempt is made to show the nervous concerns of the pilots as they approach combat with both a sense of excitement and trepidation. There is, however, a good amount of action provided by excellent colorized documentary footage. This is pretty much a flagwaver that doesn't stray very far from the war movies of the 1940s.

What the critics say Critics rate this movie 1.0 to 3.0. "Well-paced WW 2 film."[2] "Fast-paced and effective.[5] "A mediocre WW II action film."[7] "Wonderful 'B' picture dialog and cheap stunts."[8] **Final Word** Since there really aren't any good carrier films, we know the best is yet to come. By the way, the film merits an average rating because it doesn't do anything really stupid.

Flight of the Intruder

1991 USA color d. John Milius

Flight of the Intruder tells a jingoistic tale of rebellious Navy carrier pilots conducting their own personal bombing raids on missile sites in North Vietnam. This movie quickly veers from the old drab formula of the early 1950s carrier films (*The Bridges at Toko-Ri and Men of the Fighting Lady*), to a more exploitive view of pilots contemptuous of authority and angry at the conduct of the war. While Korean War pilots were not enthusiastic about the war, they were portrayed as professionals who performed their duties under difficult circumstances, regardless of the politics. Here, we have a revisionist view of the Vietnam War—namely that politics was all that was keeping us from winning. Our Vietnam-era pilots are also considerably less professional. The tiresome Vietnam veteran stereotype (slightly deranged) role is played by Willem Dafoe, who appears to have a screw loose, while Danny Glover, the squadron commander, is so emotionally over the top that he appears too unstable for command. Romance is interjected as a superfluous one-night stand. (This might be the most realistic aspect of this movie.) At first, the movie appears to be about the A-6 Intruder, (a carrier-based, all-weather attack bomber, that can strike its targets at low altitude). Clearly the producers had the cooperation of the Navy, as there are great aircraft carrier shots, and many excellent sequences of the A-6 in flight. The special effects are outstanding, with several exciting combat scenes of A-6s attacking surface-to-air missiles (SAM) sites over North Vietnam. However, when our heroes hatch a plan to bomb Hanoi during the Paris Peace Talks, the plot goes seriously awry. Brad Johnson, who plays the jock pilot, wants revenge for fellow pilots who have been killed in action, as well as a chance to bomb meaningful targets. The slightly askew Dafoe appears to go along for the fun. This movie might even have been redeemable until the very end, when the predictable crash landing and rescue scenario becomes agonizingly mindless and melodramatic.

What the critics say Critics rate this movie in the 1.0 to 1.5. "Plays like a right-wing fantasy, and a boring one, at that."[3] "The most boring Vietnam War picture since the Green Berets."[4] **Final Word** A-6s flew more than 35,000 sorties over 'Nam; 65 were shot down, 2 by enemy aircraft.

Flying Leathernecks

1951 USA color d. Nicholas Ray

WW II: Command Conflict   **2.5**

The setting is the South Pacific in 1942, where Maj. Dan Kirby (John Wayne) has just been appointed commander of the VMF 247 Marine Fighter Squadron. This squadron of Hellcat fighter planes has been stationed on Guadalcanal as the battle for control of the island is still raging. An exponent of "close air support for ground troops," Maj. Kirby is looking for opportunities to demonstrate its effectiveness to higher ups. Adding to the difficulties of his command is the squadron's executive officer, Capt. Griffin (Robert Ryan). The pilots had expected and hoped that the well-liked Capt. Griffin would take command of the squadron, as they had also heard negative rumors about Maj. Kirby. As a result, there's tension right from the start between Kirby and Griffin, and that tension escalates as the war in the air intensifies. While this is not a great war movie, it does many things well. Wayne and Ryan give solid performances, and Ryan holds his own in his scenes with Wayne. There's an excellent use of colorized documentary combat footage that's well integrated into the action scenes (with many good shots of Hellcats and Corsairs). Unlike most of the flagwavers of the 1940s, this one raises questions about higher command, and their reluctance to adapt ground-air support tactics. In the spirit of *Twelve O'Clock High*, as well as many other war movies, the story focuses on the conflicts inherent in command. Maj. Kirby knows he has to establish order and discipline and, at the same time, asks the impossible of men who risk their lives daily. This eats away at him, and Capt. Griffin can barely stand being in his presence. This film has many problems, including the predictable conflict and obvious resolution. The movie also fails to give its characters much depth or to hint at a subplot that would add complexity to the story. However, the action has a gritty, realistic feel to it, and there's nothing falsely heroic about the realities of war here.

What the critics say Critics rate this movie 2.0 to 4.0. "Empty, violent war actioner full of phony heroics."[1] "Solid, if not especially original WW 2 actioner, with good aerial scenes."[2] "Memorable WW II film deals with war in human terms."[5] "Really a pretty ordinary, if brutal, war movie."[8] **Final Word** The "Duke" brings nothing special to a film that looks and feels very familiar.

Flying Tigers
1942 USA b/w d. David Miller

Unfortunately, an interesting piece of history is completely lost in this disappointing John Wayne "buddy" movie. Wayne plays Capt. Jim Gordon, a P-40 squadron commander fighting for the Nationalist Chinese against the Japanese in 1941. While the squadron is comprised primarily of mercenary American fighter pilots ($600 per month and $500 per plane shot down), this film would have us believe that the pilots are only in this out of concern for the Chinese people. As a result, we get many scenes of appreciative Chinese and orphaned children, and the ostracizing of a hot-shot pilot, played by John Carole, because he proclaims he's in it for the cash. Fortunately, Carole steals this film from Wayne. His over-the-top impersonation of Clark Gable, his charming womanizing and self-centeredness renders Wayne just another team guy. Carole even manages to take Wayne's woman (Anna Lee)—it's about time somebody did. Of course, Carole also gets killed in a heroic, suicidal mission, but then nobody said taking Wayne's woman would be easy. Strangely, there's no mention of Gen. Claire Lee Chennault, a retired American army officer who was hired by Madame Chaing Kai-shek to organize Chinese air defenses against the Japanese. Chennault established the American Volunteer Group, otherwise know as the "Flying Tigers." This movie would have been so much more interesting if we had seen the formation of this group, the recruitment of the pilots, and the politics behind it. (But these are apparently insignificant details.) Back to the movie! There's very little action, but some nice early shots of the P-40s. This is really mostly melodrama as Wayne attempts to get his best pilot to become a team player. The unintended irony, of course, is that as soon as he succeeds the pilot dies. This is essentially war as a heroic vehicle for men of action doing the right thing.

What the critics say Critics rate this movie 2.0 to 3.0. "Mock heroics with noisy but unconvincing action."[1] "Good war film...exciting dog-fight scenes."[2] "Threadbare script...slow pacing."[4] **Final Word** The Flying Tiger symbol, a shark's mouth and eye, were adapted from an Australian fighter squadron. Gen. Chennault later formed the Civil Air Transport, the forerunner of the CIA's "Air America."

Force of Arms

1951 USA b/w d. Michael Curtiz

WW II: War-Romance   2.0

This is a desperate wartime potboiler that probably played better to audiences six years after WW II than it does today. A virtual remake and update of Hemingway's *A Farewell to Arms* (also see *In Love and War* and *The English Patient*), the movie is cliché-filled, without a romantic spark between the mismatched William Holden and Nancy Olsen. The movie opens near San Pietro, Italy in 1943, with the American 5th Army bogged down against stiff German resistance. Holden plays war-weary Sgt. Joe Peterson, who meets a young and fresh-faced WAC, Lt. Eleanor Mackay (Nancy Olsen), while on leave. Lt. Mackay initially resists his angry, war-bitter charms, since she already lost a boyfriend because of the war. She's also too chaste to fool around. Sgt. Peterson, who initially is only attracted to Lt. Mackay sexually, slowly comes to realize that he's in love with her. This romance plays out straightforwardly, and the characters are rendered so simple that it becomes nothing more than an obvious and uncompelling drama. The movie's only hedge on the probable outcome is that Lt. Peterson (he has been promoted), becomes tentative in combat as a result of falling in love. His actions may have also jeopardized the life of a friend (Frank Lovejoy). After Peterson and Mackay marry, Peterson is wracked by guilt and finally decides to return to combat (Mackay dutifully understands). There's a long interlude in which she desperately searches for him after he's reported missing in action. All I am willing to reveal here is that the movie has a happy ending—she spots him hobbling around a liberated Rome, with no explanation, whatsoever, as to why he hadn't contacted her. There are several decent combat sequences with good special effects.

What the critics say Critics rate this movie 2.0 to 2.5. "Adequately but unexcitedly mounted."[1] "A Farewell to Arms...with unmemorable results."[2] "The storyline is filled out with many gripping battle scenes. The romance rings true."[4]
Final Word There's no doubt that war-romance movies must be the most difficult subgenre of war film to make, because there are so few good ones. Except for *Casablanca*, I have yet to see another one that's truly engaging.

Force 10 From Navarone
1978   GBR   color   d. Guy Hamilton

WW II: British Commando Operation   2.0

This belated sequel to the 1961 film *The Guns of Navarone*, like most sequels, is not as good as the first. Adapted from the novel by Alistair Maclean, who had quite a run of lackluster, big-budget movies (*Guns of Naravrone, Ice Station Zebra, Where Eagles Dare*), the story focuses on a group of Allied commandos who drop into Yugoslavia to take out a bridge. Apparently this operation is so secretive (or so poorly funded) that the commandos have to steal the Lancaster bomber needed to parachute into Yugoslavia. In one of this movie's many, half-baked moments, a Sgt. Weaver (Carl Weathers), a Black GI, invites himself on the secret mission as the plane is taxiing to take off. How else were they going to get a Black guy on this operation? He spends most the mission off-screen because he's Black, and when he's on screen, he's mostly complaining that he's not being let in on the mission. Weather's role appears to be an effort at political correctness in order to give the film wider box-office appeal. One critic goes so far as to say, "Carl Weathers gives a powerful performance."[4] Trust me, it's a silly role that's embarrassing to watch. Yes, Harrison Ford stars in this movie as Lt. Col. Barnsby, the Allies' youngest Lt. Col., who right from the beginning doesn't like Major Mallory (Robert Shaw), a British commando assigned to the mission. The real question is, What are these guys going to do for 1.5 hours until they blowup the bridge? There are good and bad groups (bad fascist Chetnicks, good Communist partisans); turncoats and double agents (one is an attractive woman); our stalwart commandos are again betrayed and captured by the Germans and escape. Unlike the original movie, this sequel doesn't take itself as seriously (which is good), as our commandos wander aimlessly about the country-side attempting to wind down the shot clock.

What the critics say Critics rate this movie 1.0 to 2.5. "Routine war hokum."[1] "Awful sequel...poor in all departments."[2] "Manages over the course of two hours to keep the audience on edge."[4] **Final Word** On the back of the video box the text confuses the roles played by Shaw and Ford. Not a good sign. Just as *The Guns of Navarone* is not as good as many critics would like to think, this movie's not as bad.

From Here to Eternity

1953   USA   b/w   d. Fred Zinnemann

WW II: Relationship Potboiler   3.5

Adapted from the best-selling novel by James Jones, this movie
won eight Academy Awards, including Best Picture. It is also on
the AFI's list of 100 top films. Set in Honolulu, Hawaii in 1941 just
prior to the Japanese attack on Pearl Harbor, *From Here to
Eternity* provides a tawdry look at prewar military life. It stars Burt
Lancaster (Sgt. Warden) as a career soldier who runs an army
rifle company for an incompetent captain who's obsessed with
having a winning boxing team. Sgt. Warden also has an eye on
Karen (Deborah Kerr), the captain's wife, a coldfish with a
promiscuous past. Into this mix comes Montgomery Clift (Pvt.
Prewitt), a talented bugler and boxer who refuses to box for the
company team. As a result, he's brutally and sadistically
harassed in an attempt to break him and get him to box. Through
his alcoholic buddy, Pvt. Maggio (Frank Sinatra), Prewitt meets
Lorene (Donna Reed), a hostess at a dance club, and starts a
difficult and ultimately doomed affair. That's about it. In order to
understand the success of this movie, we probably need to look
back at the 1950s—a highly repressed time. This film, ever so
subtly, lifted the barriers on sexuality in films. By today's
standards, however, the action looks fairly innocent. Much of the
novel's dark sexuality was edited out to satisfy studio censors (in
the book, the Sinatra character hustled gay men for extra cash,
and the dance club was a brothel). The movie was also made at
the end of the studio "star" system, in which a movie's success
was determined by who starred in it. The so-called "outstanding
performances" of this movie were anything but, and consisted
mostly of "stars" reprising familiar roles. Hollywood and the
nation were into myth-making, in an attempt to make movies and
actors appear larger than life. This movie was no exception (8
Academy Awards is not believable in retrospect). Then, of
course, there's the famous "beach scene," replete with splashing
waves. Regrettably, it has little to say about military life or the
men who served.

What the critics say Critics rate this movie 5.0. "Brilliantly
acted...unforgettable action scenes."[2] "Set a new standard for
cinematic sexual frankness."[6] "Smoldering drama."[8] **Final Word**
This film was misguidedly made into a television miniseries in
1979 and an unsuccessful weekly television series in 1980.

Full Fathom Five

1990   USA   color   d. Carl Franklin

| Cold War: Nuclear Sub Thriller | 1.0 |

This may be the cheapest "off-the-shelf" sub thriller ever produced. Soviet sailors and officers walk around in white long johns and without uniforms, and the interior shots of the subs—shot in a red glow—look like cardboard cutouts. The plot revolves around an attempted CIA overthrow of a Panamanian dictator in 1999 using native, left-winged revolutionaries (the CIA is in bed with the communists?!). All that appears to matter is a beautiful woman (Maria Rangel) is one of the guerrilla leaders. As a result of the attempted overthrow, Panamanian military officers plot the hijacking of a Soviet Alpha Victor 3 class nuclear submarine, the *Kirov*, with fishing boats! The hijackers threaten to target US cities with missiles, if the plot to overthrow their government isn't called-off. The problems is, once you take-over a nuclear sub you have to be able to operate it. In desperation, Cuban political prisoners, formerly trained by the Soviets, are freed to aid the Panamanians. Are you still with me? In the mean time Capt. MacKenzie (Michael Moriarty), of the nuclear attack sub USS *Aspen,* is seriously trying to hit on the beautiful Panamanian revolutionary, who looks great with her .45 and off-the-shoulder blouse. In one of the most incongruous romances in war movie history, Moriarty, who looks and acts like an accountant for a mini-mart, flirts with a hard-core Lantina gangsta chick, who is capable of killing him with her hands. By comparison, this relationship almost makes the plot look plausible. In a dramatic conclusion, the *Kirov* is torpedoed before it can launch a nuclear strike at Houston (the Cuban captain didn't like Houston and had ruled out Florida because he had family in Miami). You will have to see the movie to find out what happens between Capt. MacKenzie and the beautiful Justine (my guess is she dumped him and has already graduated from UCLA with a major in social work).

What the critics say Critics rate this movie 1.0 to 2.5. "A waterlogged mess...far too cheap for its ambition."[2] "Boring and dumb."[5] "Adequate actioner."[7] **Final Word** This movie, along with *Gray Lady Down* and *Ice Station Zebra* are among the worst submarine movies of all time.

Full Metal Jacket

1987   USA   color   d. Stanley Kubrick

Vietnam War: Combat Hell   3.5

Fifteen years after its release, this critically acclaimed and popular film by director Stanley Kubrick is no longer a compelling Vietnam War statement. It's essentially a three-act drama adapted from Gustav Hasford's novel *The Short-Timers*, with each act telling a contrived story that is ultimately unsatisfactory. The lengthy and nearly self-contained first act focuses on Marine boot camp at Parris Island as a brutal and sadistic experience meted out by Gunney Sgt. Hartman (R. Lee Ermy). Ermy later reprises this somewhat cliché role in *Boys in Company C*. The second act follows new Marine, Pvt. "Joker" Davis (Matthew Modine), a cynical and smart aleck photojournalist in Vietnam who interviews soldiers in the field. The entire atmosphere is one of angry bravado and testosterone-rage that does very little to capture the emotions or experiences of combat soldiers. In the final act, Joker gets his secret wish and is "blooded" while patrolling the burned-out city of Hue during the Tet Offensive in 1968. The movie ends In a final dramatic sequence as a Marine squad hunts down a Vietcong sniper and kills her. Joker, the once wise-cracking journalist, has been transformed from smart-ass civilian to cold blooded killer (there's suppose to be a metaphor here). Throughout, Kubrick successfully conveys a strong sense of the futility and pointlessness of American involvement in the war. The film is filled with many good small moments, such as when an American army colonel tells Joker: "We are here to help the Vietnamese, because inside every Gook there's an American trying to get out." Unfortunately, this satiric moment feels as if it were stuck in the film to make a point about American involvement in the war. While there is much to like and watch here, this movie is more compelling for its outstanding action than for great war-film making. Ultimately, this is a film that leaves the viewer feeling emotionally distant from the action and the soldiers.

What the critics say Critics rate this movie 4.0 and 5.0 "Compelling, well-acted, and supremely well-crafted."[2] "For viewers expecting a 'traditional' war film, the result is disconcerting, frustrating, and somehow unfinished."[6] **Final Word** Based on the unrealistic expectations brought to every Kubrick film—this is an entertaining movie that still falls short.

Funny Dirty Little War

1983   ARG   color   subtitles   d. Héctor Olivera

| Argentine Civil War: Antiwar Satire | 4.0 |

In 1971, Argentine dictator Perón returned after 18 years of exile to reclaim the presidency of Argentina. This dark and farcical comedy is set in the small town of Colonia Vela, in which right-wing Peronists made a power grab to oust left-wing Peronists. This resulted in escalating violence, which eventually became an all-out civil war. With both sides evoking the name of Perón for their cause, a dozen petty bureaucrats began shooting it out in the town square. Soon the town is so divided that outsiders were called in to help take over the government. With the left calling the right "Fascists," and the right calling the left "Bolsheviks," the war of words divides friends and neighbors in what is mostly local cronyism seeking political patronage and economic favors. What begins as ridiculous and inept quickly becomes deadly and violent. When the local town administrator, Fuentes (Federico Luppi), figures out that his police chief, and a party hack, Suprino (Héctor Bidonde), are agitating that he's a Marxist, he gathers a local alcoholic, a terrified clerk, a police deputy whom he promotes to corporal, and an old man he appoints as head of the parks (and hands him a .45) to hold off the fascists from his office. With everyone claiming to be ideologically pure, no one wants to admit that this is a power struggle born mostly out of personal resentments. In this case, inept does not mean less violent, and soon the action escalates to kidnapping, torturing, murdering and blowing each other up. Based on a fictional novel by Osvaldo Soriano, this movie has the ring of truth to it. The events portrayed here mirror what overtakes Argentina with the death of Perón in 1974, when a right-wing military junta finally squelches an escalating war of terrorism. Subtitled, the film is sometimes hard to follow. However, there is no doubt that director Hector Olivera has richly captured the absurdity of it all.

What the critics say Critics rate this movie 3.0 to 4.5. "A brutal black farce of civilians succumbing to military terror."[1] "Anarchic and ruthless black comedy dissects the political absurdities and petty bureaucracy of a small Argentine village."[5] **Final Word** Most your friends only know Argentina exists because pop diva Madonna played Perón's second wife in the movie *Evita* (a nostalgic musical about a nicer, friendlier fascism).

The Gallant Hours

1960 USA b/w d. Robert Montgomery

WW II: Biopic of Admiral "Bull" Halsey   2.0

The Gallant Hour is a close-up look at Admiral William F. Halsey, commander of the US South Pacific Force, from 1942 until his retirement in 1945 (after Japan's surrender). The movie focuses on pivotal events at Guadalcanal in August 1942, when Marines went ashore and seized important air fields and an adjacent harbor at Tulagi. Guadalcanal, however, wasn't captured until February 1943, after the most determined fighting of the war and five major naval engagements, including the battles of the Coral Sea and Midway. This semibiography has a voice-over narrator that gives a documentary feel to James Cagney's taciturn portrayal of Halsey. It works best, however, when the focus is off Halsey and is showing the Japanese and American "order of battle" as well as the enormous complexity of commanding forces on this scale. The movie stops dead in the water when its focuses on Halsey's personal life and relationship to the officers who served under him. Watching Halsey swim, avoid vaccinations, or quietly meditating is slow going. While the critics complained that there was too much talk and not enough action, in reality, the movie needed a better script and more complex characterization. You will have no idea who Halsey was after watching this movie. However, when we are introduced to different commanders and the strategies for upcoming conflicts *The Gallant Hour* can be very interesting. A musical score that sounds like a liturgical hymn worshipping Halsey is intrusive, if not offensive. Certainly the tone of this score doesn't reflect the real Halsey who was an unpretentious officer. This idolatry of Halsey also fails to reflect the mounting criticism that the later war years brought, particularly at Leyete Gulf in 1944. The dogged tactics of the early war years were not as effective later in the war, and resulted in many questionable losses of personnel and ships.

What the critics say Critics rate this movie 2.0 to 3.0. "Adulatory but physically restrained biopic...too talky."[1] "The film is not pro-American propaganda, its pro-military propaganda."[6] "It's all talk and no action."[8] **Final Word** I suspect the real Admiral "Bull" Halsey would have been offended by this movie at many different levels.

Gallipoli

1981 AUS color d. Peter Weir

World War I: Infantry Combat   3.5

As this picture makes abundantly clear, the defeat of Australian forces at Gallipoli has had an enduring emotional impact in Australia and New Zealand, who blame British incompetence for the loss of thousands of Australian troops. The setting is 1915 when New Zealand and Australia (ANZACS) have sent a force of 35,000 soldiers to help take control of the Dardanelles Straits from Turkey (a German ally). Due to a great deal of military bungling (British High Command), the Turks entrench themselves prior to the invasion. As a result, British and ANZAC forces are trapped on a beachhead at Gallipoli. Unfortunately, this critically acclaimed movie does very little to tell us about the battle or the men who fought it. Two-thirds of the film focuses exclusively on the preenlistment experiences of two bored young men, Archy (Mark Lee), an idealistic, athletic and an overly sensitive type from a ranching family, and Frank, a transient living by his wits, played by Mel Gibson (with his usual charm and roguishness). Both characters are underdeveloped and fairly recognizable as stereotypes. Archy finally enlists because of his idealism and Frank, who opposes the war, because he is drifting and wants to stay close to his friends. The last third of the picture takes place after their enlistment. Most of this section shows Archie and Frank fooling around in training exercises or on leave. Here's the point. Only a small portion of this movie is about men in combat, and even this is very limited. Combat scenes are short and of a limited scale. While there is no doubting the emotional impact of watching these soldiers anticipate their almost immediate death, it is not enough to lift this film to excellence. The ending is somewhat hollow, with a freeze-frame of Archy being killed. This adds a heroic significance to his actions that undermines the meaninglessness of war that this movie was seeking to portray.

What the critics say Critics rate this movie 4.5 to 5.0. "Engrossing human drama."[2] "A visually striking and emotionally jarring war drama...a stinging indictment of military leadership and war in general."[3] "A superbly filmed, gripping contemporary drama on the waste of war. Haunting score, excellent performances."[5] **Final Word** This movie fails at too many levels to live up to its high praise.

Gardens of Stone

1987   USA   color   d. Francis Ford Coppola

Vietnam War: Military Life	2.0

Eight years after *Apocalypse Now*, director Francis Coppola again tackles the subject of the Vietnam War. Based on the novel by Nicholas Proffitt, Coppola's film gives a much quieter but no less confusing interpretation of the war. The setting is Fort Myers, Virginia in 1968, as the 3rd US Infantry Old Guard performs ritual military duties, including the guarding of the Tomb of the Unknown Soldier and the burying of America's war dead. The focus is on one Sgt. Hazard (James Caan), a decorated combat soldier who served with distinction in Korea and Vietnam. Hazard is also the Army's most sincere and weepy soldier, haunted by the fact that he can't save every young soldier sent to 'Nam (this immediately grows tiresome). Sgt Hazard and his good buddy Master Sgt. Nelson (James Earl Jones) have grown cynical and weary of the war. Into this mix comes Pvt. Willow (D.B. Sweeney), who represents everything they admire in a young soldier, except for his desire to serve in Vietnam. What plot there is circles around Hazard's inability to dampen Pvt. Willow's belief in the war effort. The young private is extremely sincere—and as his girlfriend notes, "gullible." From beginning to end we know the story is going to play out tragically. It's as if Coppola couldn't see the real story right in front of him. The movie never fully explores what these men are doing, including burying America's war dead, nor how this impacts their own sense of mortality, nor the rift between ritual and reality. All this rich material is lost and, instead, we get an absurd field-training exercise in which Hazard exhibits mystical abilities. Too much of this movie is about Caan dating Anjelica Huston, a *Washington Post* correspondent who opposes the war. You might think this would lead to conflict or at least some interesting discussion, but no, she would rather hang around and help him feel sorry for himself.

What the critics say Critics rate this movie 2.0 to 4.0. "The dialogue sounds hollow, like the sentiment itself."[2] "Muddled mediation...there's a hollowness at the film's core."[4] **Final Word** It has become clear that Coppola doesn't really have much to say about the Vietnam War. The first time he tried to say too much, and the second time he forgot what he wanted to say.

A Gathering of Eagles

1963   USA   color   d. Delbert Mann

Cold War: Pressure of Air Command   2.5

A Gathering of Eagles provides a close-up examination of the pressures a wing commander is under in order to keep his men and planes operationally ready during peacetime. It's also safe to say that the basic story has been told many times (*Command Decision, Flying Leathernecks, Twelve O'Clock High*) and that this movie has very little to say that is new or elevates the discussion. Rock Hudson gives a strong performance as Col. Jim Caldwell, who has recently been assigned as wing commander of the 904th Strategic Air Wing. The 904th is a Strategic Air Command (SAC) B-52 bomber squadron, and Caldwell's job is to shape up a command that continually receives unsatisfactory "operational readiness inspections." He's also been assigned the "classic" 1950s standard issue wife, Mary Peach, who is cute, blond, perky, well built and thrives on being a really caring person. But even this model of 1950s family virtue has had enough of her husband's self-absorbed and grumpy behavior, as he begins to confront difficult personnel decisions with officers he likes and respects. As Hudson confronts his men about their job performance, it's initially difficult to assess whether the pressure has forced him to overreact, or whether the subtle issues he's addressing are key to his command's improved performance. (I'll let you guess the answer to that one.) Initially this film looks too much like an Air Force recruiting poster, without the great visual shots of the planes, as seen in *Strategic Air Command*. However, as Hudson confronts the alcoholism of the base commander (Barry Sullivan), and the risk-adverse approach to leadership of his friend and Vice Commander (Rod Taylor), some excellent dramatic moments unfold. Unfortunately, much of this is undone with an ending that ties up everything a little too neatly. Ultimately, this movie offers a conventional view of the military that is nothing more than a peacetime flagwaver.

What the critics say Critics rate this movie 3.0 to 3.5. "Tame revamp of *Twelve O'Clock High* without the justification of war; all strictly and perfectly dull."[1] "Hudson gives one of his best performances...good script."[2] **Final Word** Between 1952 and 1962, 744 B-52s were produced. They remain operational today, with a wide variety of missions, including penetration bombing runs, cruise-missile launch platforms and conventional bombing.

Gettysburg

1993 USA color tv d. Ronald F. Maxwell

Civil War: Battle of Gettysburg	4.5

Civil War buff Ted Tuner's 4.5 hour opus to the Battle of Gettysburg is impressive. Based on the Pulitzer Prize-winning novel, *The Killer Angels*, by Michael Shaara, the movie was filmed on-site at the Gettysburg National Military Park featuring over 5,000 re-enactors. Originally, the film was a three-part television miniseries. There is simply no questioning why this film received acclaim as the best reenactment of any Civil War battle. But given its length, its focus on a command view of the war, and an emphasis on strategy and the unfolding order of battle, its appeal will be limited. While the acting is strong throughout, too much of it consists of speeaches directed to the world at large, to make sure everyone understands the historical significance of the events. Without much inner drama (story or characters) this film sacrifices emotional impact. The high point of the film is the attempt by Confederate troops to take "Little Round Top," defended by the 20th Maine Regiment, commanded by Col. Joshua Chamberlain (Jeff Daniels), who has to hold the Union flank at all costs and can't retreat. This is a ferocious battle in which the quiet college professor turned soldier brilliantly commands his men to save the day. Daniels is extremely convincing in this role, as is Sam Elliott as Gen. John Buford and Richard Jordon as Gen. Lewis Armistead. The most interesting aspect of this movie is the conflict that develops between Robert E. Lee, Commander of the Confederate Army of Northern Virginia (Martin Sheen), and Gen. James Longstreet (Tom Berenger), his best general, as they quietly debate the strategy for this battle. Lee is portrayed as keeping his own counsel, often not in touch with the battlefield. It is suggested that his strategic planning may have been overly influenced by his desire to end the war quickly. Longstreet, early on, saw the flaws in Lee's plan, but was ignored by Lee. Berenger does a good job of conveying Longstreet's dejection and near abandonment of Lee. From June 30 to July 3, 1863, over 53,000 soldiers died in the pivotal battle of the Civil War. This was the largest loss of life by American soldiers in any single battle.

What the critics say Critics rate this movie 3.0 to 4.5. "A stirring and epic historical re-creation."[1] "A magnificent re-creation."[2]
Final Word A must-see movie, but bring a thermos of coffee.

G.I. Jane

1997 USA color d. Ridley Scott

| Military Life: Navy SEALs | 3.0 |

This is a slick, fast-paced, technically well-done film that asks the highly improbable question, What if a woman tried to become a Navy SEAL? The SEALs are an elite special operations force trained for clandestine underwater demolition and raids. And what if Demi Moore (Lt. Jordan O'Neil) was the naval officer chosen to prove a woman could compete with men in a training program that drives the smartest and strongest soldiers beyond the limits of endurance? This film addresses the current and politically correct notion that women should be integrated into the military. By going one step further, the film implies that women should have an active combat role as well. Lt. O'Neil, a naval intelligence officer, is one smart, tough and determined woman. It doesn't hurt that she has a buff bod either, or that she doesn't want her "test case" to be "gender normed," in order to help her compete with men. She wants an even playing field. She also has to be beautiful and feminine. As Anne Bancroft, the coldly ambitious US Senator, who manipulated this event, says about one of the women candidates—"She looks like the wife of a Russian beet farmer." This test case is opposed at every level (DOD, Dept. of Navy, Navy SEAL Command, Lt. O'Neil's husband, by most the SEAL trainees, not to mention by the Master Chief of SEAL training). The Master Chief, played by Viggo Mortensen, is a tough and calculating SOB who is ultimately fair, if not occasionally sadistic beyond what most of us would think is reasonable. He does beat the crap out of O'Neil, but she gets in a few licks of her own. As contrived as this film is—with Demi Moore being closer to Sigourney Weaver's character of Ripley in the *Alien* trilogy than a real woman—it's hard not to root for O'Neil when everything has been stacked against her. Ultimately, this film is more about overcoming the odds and prevailing than it is about feminism.

What the critics say Critics rate this movie 3.0 to 4.0. "A bracingly gung-ho film...more like *Flashdance* in fatigues."[4] "Moore is buffed, bold and bald in this modern day fable."[5] **Final Word** Ultimately this movie has nothing to say about women in combat or Navy SEAL training, but it's highly entertaining.

A Glimpse of Hell

2001 USA color tv d. Mikael Salomon

Military Life: Navy Scandal	4.0

During a training exercise in 1989, a 16-inch gun on turret II of the battleship USS *Iowa* exploded, resulting in the peacetime death of 47 sailors. This outstanding fact-based drama, directed by Mikael Salomon and based on a book by Charles Thompson, provides an insider's look at an attempted cover-up of the tragedy by the Navy. Well-acted and scripted, this movie shows how the Navy went about manufacturing a circumstantial case that shifted responsibility for the explosion to Seaman Clayton Hartwig (Dashiell Eaves). The Navy hypothesized that Hartwig had manufactured a bomb with a timing device as part of a suicide-murder attempt, when a gay relationship with another crewman ended. The story innovates slightly by focusing on Lt. Dan Meyer (Robert Leonard), a newly assigned gunnery officer, who provides his insights and doubts about the official explanation for this explosion. Captain Moosally (James Caan), commander of the *Iowa*, is a by-the-book commander who is bucking for admiral. Caan also gives one of his best performances as a commander who initially sets out to protect his career, but eventually "breaks rank" by refusing to place responsibility on his men. The case laid out here is that, unknown to the ship's officers, a Master Chief was conducting "experimental shoots" to increase the distance these big guns could fire, in an attempt to set distance records and justify funding for battleships. The experiments also meant using considerably more powder than permitted by existing safety recommendations. Lt. Meyer also suggests that there were numerous electrical and mechanical problems in these turrets; and the powder, manufactured in 1940, was unstable and not stored safely. It's still nearly impossible to believe that no officer was informed or knew about the "experimental shoots," as this film asserts. The epilogue notes that the Navy later apologized to the Hartwig family but never fully exonerated their son by recanting the charges.

What the critics say Critics rate this movie 3.0 to 4.0. "A top-notch cast, tight screen play and riveting direction make this one worth seeing."[7] **Final Word** This movie should serve as a reminder that, first and foremost, the military is a bureaucracy whose first instinct is to protect itself.

Glory

1989 USA color d. Edward Zwick

Civil War: Black Nothern Infantry   5.0

This is the first picture to tell the story of Black-Americans in war. The long-suppressed truth is that Black-Americans have fought with distinction in every major American military engagement since the Revolutionary War. This fact-based movie tells the story of the 54th Regiment of Massachusetts, the first Black regiment to fight for the North in the Civil War. *Glory* is partially based on the letters of Robert Shaw, the son of a wealthy Boston abolitionist (played by Matthew Broderick), who was appointed commander of the regiment. The movie covers the period from the 1862 formation of the regiment, which was comprised primarily of freed slaves, to the struggles of these men in clothing, equipping, training and ultimately proving themselves in combat. It is clear that Black soldiers in the Northern army continued to struggle against racism in the military as well. (All totaled 186,107 Blacks served and 37,300 died.) This is a beautifully filmed movie with a haunting musical score. But what really stands out are the many fine performances, including Denzel Washington, as a run away slave with contemporary attitudes, Morgan Freeman as an older and emotional leader, and Andre Braugher, as a freeman raised and educated in the North. Broderick manages to emphasize the youth of this regiment's commander and his personal struggles and insecurities. The film uses thousands of "living historians" as extras, while recreating this period with great historical accuracy. The battle scenes are impressive. In the first battle, with muskets firing at point-blank range, it's impossible not to flinch. The final terrifying assault on Fort Wagner, S.C., is beautiful and melancholy to watch. However, what make this movie unique is how personal this war is for the soldiers. The reasons for their dying do not seem abstract, but noble. Many critics refer to *Glory* as an *antiwar* movie, but, in truth these men's deaths make sense—something that most film's about modern war have not been able to achieve.

What the critics say Critics rate this movie 4.5 to 5.0. "Grand, moving, breathtakingly filmed. One of the finest historical dramas ever made."[2] "Startlingly good, impressive and long-overdue story."[3] **Final Word** In America's bloodiest war, there were 620,000 deaths (360,000 Union and 260,000 Confederate).

Glory at Sea

1952 GBR b/w d. Compton Bennett

WW II: British Naval Actioner   3.0

Unlike all the other British naval action movies (*Above Us the Waves, Battle Hell, The Cruel Sea, The Sea Shall Not Have Them*), this one does away with the stiff upper lip British persona by portraying people you care about. It stars Trevor Howard (Lt. Cmdr. Hugh Fraser), who gives an excellent performance as a disgraced ship's captain recalled to active duty because of the war. Eight years earlier, Cmdr. Fraser had been scapegoated for a collision at sea and court-martialed. On his return, he sought to quietly reestablish his honor as a naval officer. Given command of a Lend Lease American destroyer for escort duty in the North Atlantic, he sets about making the HMS *Ballantrae* sea-worthy, and an inexperienced crew combat-ready. There's not a lot of action, as the story focuses on the ship's officers and crew's relationship to the captain. A task master at first, the commander later comes to the defense of the ship's pilot, who had been very critical of him but now faces a court-martial for a minor collision at sea. Then, with the death of his 17-year-old son, who had recently enlisted in the Royal Navy, his relationship to the crew softens and a new mutual respect emerges. In this movie's most poignant scene, Lt. Cmdr. Fraser is asked to give a Christmas toast, having just learned of his son's death. It's a quiet and emotional scene in which everything is revealed, but only to the audience. While this film tells the clichéd story of a crew's transformation under a demanding ship's captain, it also offers a sympathetic story of redemption. Near the end there's some fairly decent action as the *Ballantrae* is sent on a final mission to land a commando-raiding party, and to ram the port gates of a French seaport. Once grounded, the *Ballantrae* is exploded with time-delayed explosive devices. Well-acted, with good special effects, this film tried something a little different and succeeded.

What the critics say Critics rate this movie 2.0 to 3.5. "Conventional, popular seafaring war adventure."[1] "Solid WW 2 drama."[2] "Typical British salute."[7] **Final Word** In 1940 President Roosevelt agreed to swap 50 obsolete destroyers for 99-year leases on a number of British bases in the western Atlantic. This movie is partly a thank you from the British to the Americans.

Gods and Generals

2003 USA color d. Ronald Maxwell

Civil War: Epic War Drama	2.5

A prequel to Ted Tuner's outstanding 1993 Civil War movie *Gettysburg*, *Gods and Generals* is a lengthy, doleful *apologia* honoring the South and its fallen war hero, Gen. Stonewall Jackson. Based on the Jeff Sharra novel, and shot on location with over 7,500 re-enactors, this slow-moving film features tedious digressions and a musical score that borders on a lament. Viewers are given the spectacle of the early war years (1861-1863), as the South achieves surprising victories at Manassas, Fredricksburg and Chancellorsville under the leadership of Jackson (Stephen Lang) and Robert E. Lee (Robert Duvall). The movie's idolatry of Jackson is embarrassing—portraying him as a sort of Old Testament prophet smiting the enemies of the South. His preoccupation with providence guiding the outcome of the war rings theologically hollow, as does the movie's assertion that, for the South, the war was all about honor. With some small concession to the North, in the character of war hero Col. Joshua Lawrence Chamberlain (Jeff Daniels), this film is strictly about the North desecrating the sacred homelands of the South. The film's failure to deal directly with the issue of slavery, while making state's rights the key issue, will create an uneasiness for many, especially when confronted with the heroic images of the South. The battle scenes are well done, but only the battle at Fredricksburg evokes the terrible and real price of war. Too often the actors are giving speeches in formal scenes that feel disconnected. It eventually becomes obvious that there really isn't a story to tell. Jackson, accidentally shot and killed by his own men at Chancellorsville, is one-dimensional and lost in preening, self-conscious scenes that reveal nothing about him or the war. However, the film's greatest downfall is its failure to put the war into perspective. While the small details of each battle are coherent, the bigger picture is lost. Ultimately, this epic piece of nostalgia doesn't justify Turner's $60 million investment.

What the critics say Critics rate this movie 2.0. to 3.0. "Telling vignettes and vivid battle scenes."[2] "Suffers when it goes to the stories of the men it portrays."[5] **Final Word** The 70-year-old women in front of me at the theater may have said it best when the "intermission" sign came on—"Holy shit, there's more?!"

Go for Broke

1951   USA   b/w   d. Robert Pirosh

WW II: Japanese-American Unit   2.5

This average combat film has one thing going for it—Hollywood
attempted to make amends for the internment of Japanese-
Americans during the Second World War by telling the story of
the 422nd Regimental Combat Team. This unit was comprised of
volunteer Asian and Japanese-Americans, many whose families
were interned. The prologue notes that the 422nd fought with
distinction in seven major campaigns in Europe and sustained
9,486 casualties and received 18,143 individual decorations and
7 presidential unit citations. Bringing this story and these facts to
the public through this film is a major accomplishment. *Go for
Broke* stars Van Johnson (Lt. Grayson), as a conflicted and
bigoted new lieutenant who is given command of a platoon in the
422nd. However, this film does not go overboard in making its
point by featuring Japanese-Americans in lead or supporting
roles. There's a lot of humor, soldiers griping, a ridiculous scene
with Johnson and a prostitute, some documentary combat
footage, and a few limited combat scenes with good production
values, but nothing out of the ordinary. These Japanese-
American soldiers, called "Buddha Heads," get very little
development except for the standard war movie stereotypes.
There are no subplots or relationships or story to be told here.
There are attempts to address bigotry associated with race and
ethnicity, and to this film's credit the men in Johnson's platoon
don't trust him and recognize he's prejudiced. In perhaps the
film's most contrived scene, Johnson dukes it out with a former
friend and sergeant from another regiment because he keeps
referring to the men of the 4-4-2 as "Japs." In the end, this
sergeant is converted by the heroic efforts of the 4-4-2 to rescue
him during combat. This film doesn't suggest or indicate that
there was any racism on the part the military, as was common
with Black-American soldiers. This is strictly a flagwaver that
could be a lot more interesting if retold today.

What the critics say Critics rate this movie 2.0. to 4.0.
"Absolutely unsurprising war film."[1] "Fine WW II drama...cram-
med with ironic touches, and uncompromising point of view."[2]
"The social angle is never overplayed."[4] **Final Word** Addresses
an important social issue that confronted America during WW II,
but not in an interesting or convincing manner.

Good Morning, Vietnam

1987   USA   color   d. Barry Levinson

Vietnam War: Comedy-Satire   4.5

Here is a truly outstanding wartime comedy that perfectly captures the tenor of the times. Based on the real-life events of Airman First Class Adrian Cronauer (Robin Williams), an Armed Forces Radio disc jockey, the film opens in Saigon in 1965. The station is playing a smattering of Lawrence Welk, Henry Mancini and Perry Como, with DJs serving up highly edited news and safety tips for soldiers in the field. Williams turns this 1950s cultural world upside down with a stream of comedic associations that are pure genius. The baby-boomer counter-culture erupts over the air waves by way of rock 'n roll music and a never-ending steam of irreverence for authority. Cronauer assaults everyone and everything he finds anally retentive. At one point he edits a tape of then V.P. Nixon talking about the "Vietnam Conflict," that has Cronauer asking Nixon, "How would you describe your testicles?" Cronauer notes, "Its difficult to find a Vietnamese man called Charlie." There's also an excellent supporting cast, including Forrest Whitaker playing a young, Black airman quietly conforming and trying to protect Cronauer, but emotionally liberated through Cronauer's attacks on authority. However, it's the two straight men who suffer the most outrageous attacks. There's young Lt. Hauk (Bruno Kirby), who thinks he's funny and hip and wants to play polka music and tell corny jokes on air, but who is unable to get the respect of his men. There's also the menacing "lifer," Sgt. Major Dickerson (J.T. Walsh), who hates Cronauer and everything he represents. Much like *M*A*S*H*, this movie is an all-out assault on authority in all its forms, but goes a step further and asks us to look at what is happening in Vietnam. The film is not an outright antiwar statement, but leaves the viewer with an uneasy quandary about what is taking place there. As General Taylor (Noble Willingham) tells young Lt. Hauk, "You don't know if you're shot, fucked, powder burned or snake bit."

What the critics say Critics rate this movie 3.5 to 4.0. "From the start the film bowls you over with excitement and for those who can latch on, its a nonstop ride."[4] "Engaging all the way with an outstanding period sound track. Williams spins great comic moments."[5] **Final Word** As Williams notes, "We're not in Kansas anymore, Toto." A must see.

Go Tell the Spartans

1978 USA b/w d. Ted Post

| Vietnam War: Military Command | 3.5 |

This terse, low budget production is slow-moving and mostly talk. It is also, thankfully, without most of the theatrics of Hollywood productions. Based on the Daniel Ford novel *Incident at Muc Wa,* the film stars Burt Lancaster as Major Asa Barker, a US Army military adviser, stationed in Penang, Vietnam, in early 1964. Lancaster gives an excellent performance as a weary Korean War veteran whose career opportunities have passed him by. He sees his job as doing as little as possible and making sure that none of his men get hurt. This movie also features a number of good performances by supporting actors. What story there is focuses on Barker's orders to send his men to garrison an abandoned French outpost at Muc Wa. This rag-tag group of inexperienced Americans soldiers and Vietnamese mercenaries, are unprepared for the upcoming Vietcong assault. Barker understands that the whole effort is pointless and dangerous. The underlying themes are the same ones that have come to dominate Vietnam War movies—the political nature of the war, trying to identify who the enemy is, and the idealism American soldiers carried into combat. The film also expresses a surprising amount of hostility and racism by Americans toward the Vietnamese, who are frequently referred to as "dinks," "slopes," "jungle buggers" and "the little workers." At one point an American soldier spouts, in the shadow of the grave markers of French soldiers, "We won't lose, we are Americans." At the end an American soldier concludes—"It's their (Vietnam's) war." This early Vietnam War movie gives us a dark view of the war from a low level of command— probably a better character study than war film.

What the critics say Critics rate this movie 3.5 to 5.0. "We have been here before...why are we invited again."[1] "Perceptive, moving Vietnam War picture."[2] "Well made and well-acted earnest effort."[4] "Blundering but politically interesting war epic."[5] "Best and most intelligent film made to date about American involvement in Vietnam."[6] **Final Word** This is a competent movie that Vietnam War "freaks" will take an interest in. If that's you— check it out.

Gray Lady Down

1978 USA color d. David Greene

Cold War: Nuclear Sub Thriller   2.0

This low-budget, special effects thriller stars Charlton Heston
(Capt. Blanchard) as commander of the nuclear submarine USS
Neptune. Forty mile out of Norfolk, Virginia the *Neptune* is struck
by a freighter. The circumstances of this incident are murky and
too unbelievable to retell here. Suffice it to say the sub plummets
1,450 feet before coming to a precarious rest on a ledge along a
two mile deep gorge. From a totally improbable start, this movie
plays out in a completely predictable manner. The Navy has 36
hours in which to rescue the crew, or their oxygen will run out.
With 4,000 pounds of pressure per square inch threatening to
collapse a bulkhead door, and with gravity- slides threatening to
plunge the sub to the ocean floor—the second half plays out as a
topside rescue drama. Stacy Keach (Capt. Bennett) leads the
Navy rescue team and its specialized deep-sea rescue vehicle
(DSRV-1), with David Carradine (Capt. Gates) operating a
second specialized deep-sea exploration vehicle. While Heston
sleepwalks his way through this movie calmly reassuring his
crew and putting up with a hysterical executive officer, rescue
efforts on the surface give us an uninspired technical exploration
of this operation. Adopted from the novel *Event 1000* by David
Lavallee, little suspense is generated here. Early on any chance
of a nuclear power plant meltdown is ruled out (the Navy
probably wouldn't have cooperated), as is an international
incident (not rammed by Russian trawler in a politically sensitive
area, etc.). It's never mentioned if this is an attack sub or carries
Polaris missiles. What we mostly have is a dull story in which it is
nearly impossible to connect with the characters or their perilous
circumstances. The subplot that's never explored is the possible
negligence of Capt. Blanchard, and the court-martial he and his
officers certainly face. By completely ignoring this key issue, the
rescue feel very hollow, neither exploring their concerns about
their careers, the politics of blame or even bothering to exonerate
them.

What the critics say Critics rate this movie 2.0 to 3.5. "A rather
boring update...with added technology."[1] "Tired drama...good
special effects."[2] "Dull, all-star suspenser."[5] "Action packed and
well-acted."[7] **Final Word** A very tired actioner without an
interesting story and with very average special effects.

The Great Escape

1963   USA   color   d. John Sturges

The Great Escape comes to us as both a box office and critically acclaimed success. Based on a novel by Paul Brickhill and a screenplay by James Clavell, the film tells the true story of a mass escape attempt by RAF pilots from a German POW camp in 1944. This attempt involved nearly 600 prisoners of war at Stalag Luft 3, who dug three long tunnels which allowed 76 prisoners to escape. Apparently Hitler, so maddened by this event, ordered thousands of soldiers and police to hunt down the escapees. In the end, only three soldiers made it back to Britain, while 50 were murdered by the Gestapo, and the remaining 23 were returned to prison camp. (The killing of these escaped prisoners was a violation of the 1929 Geneva Convention, which permitted prisoners of war the right to attempt escape without undue punishment.) So much for the facts. What we have here is basically another overly long, star-studded Hollywood action adventure movie that portrays prison camp as a variation of adult summer camp. This movie revolves around two characters— Richard Attenborough as Bartlett ("Big X") and Steve McQueen as Capt. Virgil Hilts. Bartlett is designated the British officer in charge of escape attempts. He's intense and obsessive about the escapes as a means of disrupting the German war effort. His opposite is Capt. Virgil Hilts, a somewhat goofy, go-it-alone American pilot who sees imprisonment as a game (hence his baseball and mitt all the time). There is also genius to this escape attempt—forging documents, tailoring civilian clothing, dispersing 150,000 lb. of dirt, creating bellows to pump air into the tunnel shafts, trolleys to enter the shafts, the careful planning and concealing. It's all pretty amazing. But ultimately the movie bogs down in all the detail and irrelevant subplots that emerge near the end. It quickly loses dramatic impact, and then after the escape, we follow too many stories to care about what happens. James Garner ("the Scrounger") asks at the end, if it was all worth it. A fair question for those watching this movie as well.

What the critics say Critics rate this movie 4.5 to 5.0. "A motion picture that entertains, captivates, thrills and stirs."[4] "One of the great war movies."[5] "A great piece of escapism."[8] **Final Word** A POW actioner that's average at best. Can't recommend it, despite its critical acclaim.

The Great Santini

1979 USA color d. Lewis John Carlino

| Military Life: A Warrior in Peacetime | 4.0 |

Based on the autobiographical novel, *Lords of Discipline* by Pat Conroy, this movie is a thoughtful character study of a Marine Corps fighter pilot with a warrior's heart and no war to fight. It also shows us a classic co-dependent family having to cope with the emotional tyranny of an alcoholic. Robert Duvall gives a mesmerizing performance as Lt. Col. Meechum, aka "The Great Santini," the Marine Corps' finest fighter pilot. He's also a self-absorbed bull of a man, consumed with living life only on his driven and competitive terms. When Meechum's son Ben (Michael O'Keefe) asks him, "Would you like to be killed in action, Dad?," he replies, "It's better than dying of piles." The colonel is an emotional child in an adult's body who has been passed over for promotion, and whose career is constantly at risk because of his insubordination and alcoholic antics. He's truly only at peace with himself when flying. His relationship to his wife and four children is that of an officer to the men he commands. The kids are "hogs," who stand at attention, undergo inspection, and are given orders. In 1962, after one of many family moves—this one to South Carolina—Meechum tells the kids, "Okay hogs, I've listened to your bellyaching about moving to this new town. This said, bellyaching will end at 1530 hours. It will not affect the mood of this squadron. Do I make myself clear?" In a cast full of wonderful performances, Blythe Danner plays the dutiful wife who is protective of her husband, always explaining his actions to the children. At one point she tells them, "You must learn to interpret the signals he gives off." At the heart of this story is the colonel's relationship to his 18-year-old son, Ben, who wants desperately to please, but finds himself rebelling against a controlling and coercive father. What keeps this movie from reaching greater heights is an involved subplot that diverts from the main story, and an ending that keeps this family from ever confronting its dysfunction.

What the critics say Critics rate this movie 3.0 to 4.5. "Compelling, relevant story of a super-macho peacetime warrior with nobody to fight except himself and those who love him."[4]
Final Word An intimate account of the demons that haunt the men who go to war for us, and the price their families pay.

The Green Berets

1968   USA   color   d. John Wayne/Ray Kellogg

Vietnam War: "Fighting Soldiers"   1.0

John Wayne co-directed and starred in the first film about the Vietnam War—the only one made during the war itself. Wayne plays Colonel Mike Kirby of the 5th Special Forces, who has been sent to Vietnam to relieve the commander of a basecamp along the Cambodia-Laos border. Oddly, at no time, does "the Duke" fire a weapon during combat. This has to be more than coincidental, given the number of intense firefights in which he's engaged. Many times Wayne even holds his M-16 upside-down! This film is so unabashedly hawkish that it's embarrassing to watch. Every 20 minutes the audience is hammered with pro-war propaganda to save the children, and the enemy are always brutal and sadistic. There's also an obsession with punji sticks that is almost comical, along with a melodramatic musical score right out of a 1940s movie serial. This film should be retitled "John Wayne Attempt's to Retake Bataan Because He Couldn't Find Vietnam." Every cliché ever contrived for a WW II movie is used here, and it looks and feels as if it were shot on a studio backlot. Attempts at humor are high camp, with the frequent interjection of an annoying child whose missionary parents were murdered by the Vietcong. The VC later kill the child's dog in a scene that is nearly beyond belief, and that would do homage to *The Yearling* for sheer emotional hokum. There is also Wayne being shot down in a plastic helicopter, the fake model gun-tower falling over, and a beautiful woman being used to seduce a North Vietnamese general. Later Wayne picks the lock to the general's bedroom, carries the woman to safety, and escapes in a Citron! (the "Duke" in a French car). I suspect even the Pentagon was concerned that this film could harm public support for the war.

What the critics say Critics rate this movie 1.0 to 3.0. "Overlong actioner...violent, exhausting and dull."[1] "Incredibly clichéd ...absurd situations and unfunny comedy relief."[2] "Amazing in its stupidity."[3] "Painfully insipid pro-war propaganda."[5] "Better than its reputation...turned out to be exciting and enjoyable."[7] **Final Word** I suggest you checkout the worst war film of the past 50 years for yourself, if only for comic relief.

Guadalcanal Diary

1943   USA   b/w   d. Lewis Seiler

WW II: Classic '40s Flagwaver   2.0

At a time when the American public needed a morale boost, this was the first picture to show a decisive American victory in the ground war against Japan. An American invasion force surprised the Japanese at Guadalcanal, in the Solomon Islands, which led to the immediate capture of a nearly completed airfield and a bitter, all-out air, land and sea battle that lasted for nearly six months. American casualties were 7,500, and the Japanese suffered 37,500 casualties. Japanese expansion in the Pacific had been halted. Based on a popular book by war correspondent Richard Tregaskis, the film follows a Marine squad onboard a troop transport days before disembarking, all the way through to the final mopping up six months later. There is also an unseen war correspondent narrating the film, whose purple prose comes across as portentous and pompous—"Most of us know the awful feeling of being pitifully small. Know for a moment that we are only tiny particles caught up in a gigantic whirlpool of war." We are given soldiers whose only expression of feeling is to make jokes, with the story coming to a screeching halt every time William Bendix's big mug comes on the screen. For the most part, each soldier in this platoon is a stereotype that was cliché long before the film was made. In between scenes of guys joking around there are some intense combat sequences. At other times, the film comes across more like a documentary than a drama. As the movie progresses it become increasingly sentimental—not just in the narration, but also in the frequent, small speeches given by the soldiers. A classic 1940s flagwaver designed to boast the morale of everyone back home, *Guadalcanal Diary* continues to remains a sentimental favorite for many.

What the critics say Critics rate this movie 3.0 to 4.5. "Standard war propaganda, with good acting scenes."[1] "A painstaking, dignified and...eloquent expression of a heroic theme."[4] "One of the best propaganda pieces emanating from Hollywood."[8] **Final Word** The story and structure is surprisingly similar to James Jones' later novel *The Thin Red Line,* which was made into an even better movie in 1964. In 1998, Terrence Malick transformed Jones' novel into one of the great war films.

Gung Ho!
1943 USA b/w d. Ray Enright

WW II: Classic '40s Flagwaver   1.5

A popular film at the time of its release, today *Gung Ho!* is primarily a war movie footnote because its name has entered into the American lexicon, meaning "zealous" or "enthusiastic." Lt. Col. Evans F. Carlson (Randolph Scott), commander of the 2nd Marine Raider Battalion, adopted this Chinese term to inspire his men. Its literal translation means "to work in harmony." Based on a factual account by Lt. S. Le Francois, this movie shows the formation of "Carlson's Raiders" five weeks after Japan bombed Pearl Harbor through their first commando operation. We watch as Marines are hand picked for this specialized unit. One man qualifies because he says, "I don't like Japs." That's good enough for the Marines. The training is probably the best element of this film, as we get to see just how demanding and well trained these men are. At one point, they are required to march 45 miles in 8 hours with full packs. (That's humping it!) The emphasis was not only on team work but on individual initiative that allowed commandos to operate in a highly autonomous manner. There's also an extraneous romantic pursuit by two brothers in love with the same woman. And then there's Randolph Scott. He's all business and prone to break out into inspiring patriotic speeches at any moment. On their first mission to Makin in the Solomon Islands, the film captures the claustrophobic confines of a submarine and the stress many of the soldiers experienced. The combat is standard for the times, and is the least interesting aspect of this movie. While attacking a Japanese force twice its size, the Marines lost only 30 men and destroyed a communications center on the island. No aspect of this movie really stands out. These 1940s war movies were fairly routine—familiar characters from different parts of the country, a romantic interlude, some joking around, and an emphasis on team work and the heroic sacrifices made in combat.

What the critics say Critics rate this movie 2.0 to 3.0. "Trite flagwaver, popular at the time."[1] "Outrageous jingoism, celebrating the bloodthirsty misfits of the gung ho squadron...a jaw dropping experience."[2] "This ultrapatriotic war film has its truly outrageous moments...today its almost embarrassing."[7] **Final Word** A movie that's not very good, made for a good cause. That's always troubling for audiences and critics alike.

The Guns of August

1964   USA   b/w   d. Nathan Kroll

| WW I: Documentary | 2.0 |

Based on the Pulitzer Prize-winning book by Barbara Tuchman, this documentary is a slow-moving attempt to tell the story of WW I with grainy documentary film and tiresome narration. Perhaps most disappointing is that it provides few clues as to why this war took place, except to blame the elite classes of Europe. A prologue notes—"Millions of peaceful and industrious people were hounded into a war by the folly of a few all-powerful leaders." Much of this film is devoted to discerning the tangled roots of European royalty as the major cause of this conflict, showing how the crown heads of England, Germany, Russia and Austria-Hungary were all related. The film opens with the death of King Edward VII of England in 1910, and proceeds to portray the royals as rivalous and incompetent, as well as political and institutional anachronisms. However, scant attention is paid to the other major causes of this conflict, such as nationalistic militarism and numerous unresolved enmities between peoples and regions. The war is presented in a limited manner, noting the advent of modern weapons (machine guns, airplanes, grenades, tanks) and some details about major battles (Marne, Verdun, Somme). What's missing is a serious commentary on how modern technology, transportation and communications completely transformed warfare, and resulted in 37.5 million casualties. While it appears to have been a war without political goals or strategic objectives, there is some mention of incompetent military commanders. These generals apparently were able to mobilize entire nations to fight a war, but remained clueless and indifferent to the consequences. While the film notes the end of the "old order" in 1918, whereby the monarchies were swept from power, it makes little mention of how Communism, Socialism and Fascism filled the vacuum amid new animosities. What the French Revolution and Napoleonic Wars had set in motion came to fruition two world wars later with the end of the Cold War—democratic liberalism prevailing in Europe.

What the critics say The critics rate this movie 3.5 to 4.0. "Straightforward documentary...highly competent, if not exceptional...well worth a look."[2] "An adequate introduction to WW I, but that's all."[6] **Final Word** Unless you like your facts dry and in chronological order, this film may not interest you.

The Guns of Navarone

1961   GBR/USA   color   d. J. Lee Thompson

| WW II: Commando Adventure | 2.0 |

If you are interested in seeing a completely fictionalized account of a British commando raid on a Greek island in 1943, then watch this movie. Adapted from the novel by Alistair Maclean, this big-budget, big-name epic starring Gregory Peck, Anthony Quinn, David Niven, Richard Harris and Anthony Quayle, is a slow-moving, overly-talkative, big-time bore that comes in at 2 hours, 39 minutes (45 minutes too long). Basically, the Germans have two powerful radar-guided guns embedded in the face of an island cliff. These guns command a narrow strait that provides the only access to 2,000 British troops trapped on a nearby island. The daring commandos, if they choose to accept this mission, have less than a week to scale a nearly impregnable side of the island and disable the guns before British ships attempt a rescue. The movie has the classic "mission" structure: impossible circumstances, time pressures, highly trained specialists, conflicted protagonists (Quinn wants to kill Peck), and narrow escapes. For two hours and thirty-five minutes the director has to find a way to fill the time before the guns are disabled. He does this in the most unimaginative ways possible. For 15 minutes we watch the fishing vessel transporting the commandos sink. The commando team takes all night to scale the cliffs, and one of the commandos is wounded and has to be carted around. Later they are joined by two partisan Greek women (one of them a saboteur); they get chased all over this island by the Germans who finally capture them, but they manage to escape, again. Between these scenes the actors give bad performances comprised mostly of mindless arguing. In one scene, Niven, much like a British inspector in a drawing room murder mystery, deduces who the saboteur is (it's completely ridiculous). A movie that is full of silly drama and bad lines, it was highly thought of at the time of its release. It spawned an even worse sequel 17 years later, *Force 10 From Navarone*.

What the critics say Critics rate this movie 4.0 to 4.5. "Explosive action film...high powered adventure throughout this first-rate production."[2] "One of the best World War II adventure yarns."[7] **Final Word** Despite all the star power, this one is agonizingly tedious and just plain silly.

Halls of Montezuma

1950   USA   color   d. Lewis Milestone

| WW II: Infantry Combat | 2.5 |

This rather formulistic WW II movie is directed by Lewis Milestone, of *All Quiet on the Western Front* and *Pork Chop Hill* acclaim. The action in this movie takes place among the Solomon and Gilbert Islands in 1943, which marked the limits of Japanese expansion in the southwest Pacific. A battle-hardened platoon of Marines attempts to take control of a heavily fortified Japanese-held island, following six months of ferocious fighting at Guadalcanal. Having established a beachhead, efforts to take control of the island are seriously hampered by rocket barrages launched from a hidden location. Lt. Anderson (Richard Widmark) is ordered to take prisoners in an attempt to find out where the rockets are being launched from. Prior to this, we are introduced to an assortment of characters with their own fears and personal struggles, which unfortunately involves flashbacks and voice-overs that distract from a somewhat interesting story. However, the movie quickly refocuses on the mission. Widmark does an excellent job as the migraine-prone lieutenant, supported by Karl Malden (medic) and Reginald Gardiner, a humorous, eccentric interpreter. For the most part, this movie is effective, but too often becomes melodramatic as conflicts emerge between soldiers responding to combat situations. During the last twenty minutes, the melodrama increases as a variety of stereotypical Japanese prisoners are interrogated. The movie does, however, combine effective use of documentary footage and realistic combat scenes of a limited scale. It appears that Milestone wanted to tell a story about the fears and anxiety induced by combat, and how soldiers cared for one another. But by the end, the script mostly lapses into patriotic platitudes.

What the critics say Critics rate this movie 2.5 to 3.5. "Well-mounted, single-minded actioner."[1] "Grim WW 2 actioner...good cast makes stereotypes acceptable."[2] **Final Word** *Halls of Montezuma* is clearly a second generation WW II film, with the focus on the plight of individual soldiers. This formula reached its apogee by the 1970s when soldiers spent more time fighting each other than the enemy—see *Attack!*, *The Battle of Blood Island*, *Fireball Forward*, *Hell in the Pacific*, *The Long and the Short and the Tall*, *The Naked and the Dead* and *Too Late the Hero*.

Hamburger Hill

1987   USA   color   d. John Irvin

Vietnam War: Combat Hell	5.0

Directed by John Irvin, *Hamburger Hill* is one of the best war combat movies ever made. Based on actual events, this film gives a graphic and violent, close-up look at soldiers in combat that has rarely been depicted on the screen. The "new-realism" of 1980s filmmaking shows war unsanitized by earlier screen sensibilities. The action in this movie revolves around the 3rd Squad, 1st Platoon of the 101st Airborne Division, and their assault on Hill 937, in the Ashau Valley, in 1969. During a ten-day period, the squad stages eleven assaults on Hill 937 before taking it. Complete with blunt language and irreverent attitudes, the men piss and moan about the ennui of military life—and joke, argue and dream of getting "back in the world." In this movie's most poignant moment, a tape from home, expresses in a few simple words what's in the heart of every family with a soldier at war. The battle scenes are brutal, harrowing and among the most intense ever filmed. The acting is outstanding throughout, with a strong cast of characters that transcend the usual stereotypes. While we primarily see the war from the perspectives of Sgt. Frantz (Dylan McDermott) and Lt. Murphy (Michael Dolan), the emotional epicenter of the squad is "Doc" (Courtney Vance), an uneducated Black medic who speaks his mind and passionately takes care of these men. The film's willingness to portray real Black soldiers and to air their fears and concerns adds to its credibility. The movie pulls no punches in telling us about the lack of honor these men receive for their sacrifices. It continually reflects on what it means to die in an unpopular war, to take a hill of no strategic importance, and to have their heroism go unacknowledged. The only answer that made sense, for these soldiers, was to be found in the depth of their feelings for one another.

What the critics say Critics rate this movie 2.5. to a 4.0. "Well-produced and directed...documentary-like realism and authenticity."[1] "Authentic, with expertly staged battle scenes—but limited in its emotional power."[2] "A film so brutally real that watching it is an endurance test."[4] "Possibly the most realistic and bloodiest of the Vietnam War films."[5] **Final Word** John Irvin has now directed two of the best war movies ever—*Hamburger Hill* and *When Trumpets Fade*.

The Hanoi Hilton

1987 USA color d. Lionel Chetwynd

Vietnam War: Prisoner-of-War	4.5

This critically panned film is one of only a very few movies that has ever attempted to accurately portray the experience of prisoners of war. Movie critics have been content to praise fictional stories that run the gamut from comedy, boxing and soccer matches, to improbable escape attempts. *Hanoi Hilton*, by director Lionel Chetwynd, tells an emotionally shattering and graphic story that comes close to the truth, and the critics don't like it. Part of what they don't like is what they perceive to be the "right wing" politics of this film and its willingness to take pot shots at the media and at Jane Fonda (who subsequently apologized for her contact with North Vietnam during the war). Watching the film 25 years after the Vietnam War makes one wonder about the objectivity of the critics. This film reveals the brutality perpetrated by the North Vietnamese against many of the 250 American POWs housed at the Hoa Lo Prison in Hanoi, North Vietnam, from 1964 to 1973. At the center of this story is Commander Michael Williamson, thoughtfully portrayed by Michael Moriarty. Williamson was shot down over North Vietnam in his F-4 Phantom in 1964, and this film chronicles his experiences during his ten years of captivity. The movie makes clear that the prisoners were psychologically abused, beaten, tortured, and even murdered in an attempt to break them and use them as propaganda show-pieces to influence the media and public opinion. Ultimately it's a story of survival with dignity. The prisoners realized they could be broken by torture, but few ever gave up their identities as soldiers or their loyalty to one another. Their efforts at supporting one another and gaining psychological superiority over their captors makes for a powerful story. Their quiet and determined heroism makes them real American war heroes, something that was difficult to acknowledge for many years after the war.

What the critics say Critics rate this movie 1.0 to 1.5. "Unbearably dull, impossibly overlong, and embarrassingly clichéd."[2] "Non-stop torture, filth and degradation."[3] "Lame attempt...a slanted view of traditional prison camp sagas."[4] **Final Word** The Critics appear more enamored with fairy-tales than reality. Ignore them. This movie tells an important chapter of the Vietnam War that every war film buff should watch.

Hart's War

2002 USA color d. Gregory Hoblit

| WW II: Prisoner-of-War | 2.5 |

With the long history of prisoner-of-war films as a guide, you would think Hollywood would finally be ready to take this genre to the next level. Unfortunately, that's not the case with *Hart's War*, adapted from a novel by John Katzenbach. It's December 1944 and Lt. Hart (Colin Farrell), stationed at US Army headquarters in Belgium, volunteers to drive an officer to the front. Hart is immediately captured by German soldiers when he gets lost. Consider this the first plot contrivance in a story built on a house of cards. Lt. Hart is then sent to Stalag 6A in Germany where the American officer in command is Col. McNamara (Bruce Willis), a intense, no-nonsense officer who has very little to say. Hart is ordered to billet in the enlisted men's barracks (obviously foreshadowing events to come). Soon two Black-American fighter pilots, Lt. Archer and Lt. Scott, join Hart, which marks a shift from slight plot contrivances to outright melodrama. There's immediate racial animosity between a racist sergeant and the pilots. When German soldiers discover a planted weapon in the bunk of Lt. Archer, he's taken outside and shot. Later, the racist sergeant is found dead, and Lt. Scott (Terrence Howard) is accused of his murder (yes, you've heard me right). Now we have a murder mystery and POW court-martial drama in which the camp commandant is more than willing to assist. He has taken crime scene photos, allowed guards to testify, and even takes the stand himself (I am sure this was all taken into consideration at his war crimes trial). In order to stack the house of cards even higher, Lt. Hart is appointed defense attorney. *Hart's War* then morphs into a quasi-morality play about sacrifice, when, in reality, Col. McNamara is engaged in an elaborate escape attempt and is using the court-martial as subterfuge. Shot in a wintry dark blue, with everyone whispering or darting about in the shadows, the movie attempts a moody atmosphere fraught with tension.

What the critics say Critics rate this movie 2.5 to 3.0. "Entertaining...though its message about honor is a bit muddy."[2] "Beautiful cinematography helps off-set occasional heavy-handed direction and, at times, overwrought plot."[5] **Final Word** Prisoner-of-war movies have become the theater of the absurd among war film subgenres, and this one is no exception.

Heartbreak Ridge

1986 USA color d. Clint Eastwood

Invasion of Grenada: Humor-Action   2.5

Clint Eastwood directs, produces, and stars as a hard-drinking, insubordinate Marine gunnery sergeant who is nearing mandatory retirement. Sgt. Thomas Highway is a Medal of Honor winner from the Korean War, and a gung-ho, Semper Fi badass, with a quip for just about everything. His job is to whip a bunch of misfit, cream-puff-generation X-ers into a hardcore Marine recon company. Highway's opinion of this company is that—"These retards couldn't fight their way out of a shithouse." His men see him as a—"big leatherneck, jarhead, motherfucker." It's hard to classify this film, which works primarily as a comedy, similar to one of those movies about an out-of-control high school where a substitute teacher comes in and has all the students reading poetry by the end. You know what's coming, but getting there is the best part. Sgt. Highway also spends a lot of time trying to reconnect with his ex-wife, Aggie (Marsha Mason), while trying to discover his sensitive side by reading women's magazines (and beating the crap out of a half-dozen people at the same time). If this film has one theme, it's about aging and fear of retirement. Highway still wants to prove that old dudes can still kick-ass, and in this movie they do. The focus of Sgt. Highway's midlife crisis is Major Powers (Everett McGill), a hardass, by-the-book Marine, with no combat experience (and, yes, they go after one another in a mud pit). The movie ends with a tacked on jingoistic bit about the invasion of Grenada that is very hard to stomach. Director Eastwood portrays this invasion as some sort of post-Vietnam War redemption for American soldiers. For those who don't remember, the biggest controversy about Grenada was how to pronounce it. President Reagan ordered the invasion on Oct. 25, 1983, on the pretext of rescuing American medical students; but the real objective was to unseat a hard-line pro-Castro communist government. What the epilogue doesn't note is that US forces suffered 19 killed and 152 wounded, while communist forces suffered 74 dead and 209 wounded.

What the critics say Critics rate this movie 2.0 to 4.0. "Dismayingly predictable potboiler."[1] "Eastwood is enjoyable to watch."[2] "Vigorous war adventure."[3] **Final Word** This is entertaining, escapist fluff that's unlikely to make your day.

Hellcats of the Navy

1957 USA b/w d. Nathan Juran

WW II: Submarine Actioner   2.0

The only reason this film will ever be remembered is that it stars Ronald Reagan and Nancy Davis in their only film together. Strictly a "B" actioner based on the book by Hans Christian, this movie ranks among the bottom dwellers of submarine war movies. The introduction features Admiral Chester W. Nimitz, Commander and Chief of the Pacific Fleet, retired (who has a cameo role as well), while Reagan plays Commander Casey Abbott, skipper of the USS *Starfish*. Besides torpedoing Japanese ships in the Sea of Japan, the main drama is a predictable conflict between Cmdr. Abbott and his executive officer, Lt. Cmdr. Landon (Arthur Franz). The conflict centers on Abbott's decision to dive quickly because of a fast approaching Japanese destroyer, while a diver is still in the water. This leads to a series of confrontations between the commander and his executive officer, and culminates in the executive officer being faced with an identical decision, in having to leave Cmdr. Abbott (Reagan) in the water while the sub dives. To say this plot resolution is contrived would hardly do justice to its lameness. But the executive officer now, of course, fully appreciates the complexity and pressures of command. There is enough action here to keep the viewers from *nitrogen narcosis*, with a commando raid, frogmen diving to disarm mines, and an enormous amount of Japanese tonnage sunk. Of course, what is really interesting here is watching Ronald and Nancy in a dour and tepid romance without the slightest chemistry. Davis comes across as a cold and controlling nurse and Reagan as stiff and uncomfortable in a physical role. Together, on the screen, they have a hard time physically embracing and Reagan often turns away when talking to Davis. You might want to note that they never laugh or smile in each other's presence. This movie is strictly for channel-surfing insomniacs and Reagan biographers.

What the critics say Critics rate this movie 1.0 to 3.0. "Flimsy jingoistic potboiler."[1] "Satisfying actioner."[2] "None too exciting drama"[7] "This cliché-riddled submarine drama...is pretty dire fare."[8] **Final Word** There is nothing in Reagan's performance here, in 1957, to even remotely indicate he would go on to star as President of the United States.

Hell in Korea

1956   GBR   b/w   d. Julian Amyes

Korean War: Infantry Combat	2.0

This is one of many post-WW II movies that touches on a dark and, for the most part, unrealized fear that the average soldier is likely to turn on his own—a Hobbesian creature with a base and brutish nature. Based on a book by Max Catto, *Hell in Korea* supposedly chronicles real-life events as a British army patrol is cut off and surrounded by Communist Chinese soldiers. While attempting to escape entrapment over a three day period, the ensuing "unit" drama revolves around conflicted personalities and how soldiers respond to life-threatening circumstances. There is the inexperienced lieutenant (George Baker), the battle-hardened sergeant (Harry Andrews) and a variety of dysfunctional personalities that clash, joke around and complain an awful lot. The soldiers eventually make their way to a hilltop Buddhist temple, where they are surrounded by Red Chinese troops, while receiving friendly fire from American jets and getting picked off by snipers. In one of many incomprehensible moments, they begin playing soccer. There is also the melodrama of a soldier accused of cowardice who goes berserk and gets killed as he runs toward the enemy's position (how many times have we seen this?). Then, inexplicably, after what seems like an interminable group therapy session, the patrol wipes out a machine gun emplacement and simply walks to safety. The fact that the young lieutenant proves himself in combat is not irrelevant, given the class nature of British society. There's also a vaguely racist blue collar polemic with frequent references to "gooks," "chinks" and "slant-eyes," and a limited discussion of the "Yellow Peril" and the battle between the "whiteman" and the "yellowman." This low-budget production, shot mostly at night or in dark interior settings, appears to have started with modest goals and achieved them.

What the critics say The critics rate this movie 1.0. to 4.0. "Minor war talk-piece, shot in Surrey and looking it."[1] "Standard war drama."[2] "Low-budget...apology by the British film industry for its general non-participation in the Korean War film genre."[8] **Final Word** While this is not a bad movie, there's simply not enough here to justify the time, cost and energy it would take you to find it.

Hell in the Pacific
1968   USA   color   d. John Boorman

WW II: Antiwar-Survival Drama   1.5

Take your pick. Is this John Boorman film a WW II Robinson
Crusoe survival update or an antiwar allegory, or both? It really
doesn't matter because it's too silly and inane to matter. Shot on
location in the Palau Islands, the movie opens with an American
pilot (Lee Marvin) and a Japanese naval officer (Toshirô Mifune)
stranded on a small, remote South Pacific island. What ensues is
a dull effort to infuse humor into a predictable story about two
closed-head trauma victims having to cooperate in order to
survive. We have scenes of Marvin urinating on Mifune from a
tree, and telling him that if he doesn't share his water—"You
know they got rescue boats out looking for me, and if I tell them
that you wouldn't give me any water, boy they're sure going to
give it to you!" (Now there's a serious threat!) In later scenes, an
aging Lee Marvin runs about the beach in a loin cloth (not a
postcard moment). Then in a reversal of who has captured
whom, Marvin tries to get the tied-up Mifune to fetch a stick as if
he were a dog. (This movie looks and feels like it was
conceptualized while "taking a lunch," with "my people" getting
together with "your people" for a weekend island shoot—
improvising the entire script.) No one could have purposely
labored over the scenes and dialogue in this movie. The Mifune
character, while not an outright stereotype of an Asian male,
certainly creates a grunting, running-about angry character that
borders on racist. But given Marvin's portrayal of an American
officer who appears psychotic at times, why can't Mifune's
character be an Asian idiot as well? Not knowing how to end this
movie, director Boorman simply lets the characters get drunk
together and blows them up (a metaphor for an atomic bomb I
suppose). Because nothing in this film is realistic or probable,
and all attempts at humor are about men having tantrums and
acting immaturely, it must be a serio-comic allegory about our
survival—or a really bad film.

What the critics say Critics rate this movie 3.0 to 4.5. "Highly
artificial and pretentious allegory."[1] "Microcosm of WW II and
extrapolates a parable on the insanity of war."[3] "Psycho/macho
allegory." "Overly obvious anti-war statement."[6] **Final Word**
Forget this allegory-parable nonsense. The film doesn't work at
level one.

Hell is for Heroes

1962 USA b/w d. Don Siegel

WW II: Infantry Combat	2.5

Directed by Don Siegel and starring Steve McQueen and Harry Guardino, this confused—but sometimes entertaining—low-budget picture opens in France, in the autumn of 1944, as a squad of American soldiers is anticipating being shipped back to the states. Into this mix comes a sullen Pvt. John Reese (Steve McQueen), a recently busted NCO, who is a hardened loner but outstanding combat leader. After being notified that they're immediately "going back on line," the squad takes up a position near the "dragon's teeth" along the German's Siegfried Line. Ordered to reinforce a nearby position, they leave a squad behind to cover their exposed flank. (You should never leave a squad alone is the moral here.) In order to deceive the Germans about their limited strength, this squad begins to act squirrely and turns this movie into a comedy with the Germans playing the straight men. Up until this point, this movie plays more like *Kelly's Heroes* than a serious combat film, which is confusing. The wisecracks and jokes are nonstop, and by the time the story turns to serious combat, Steve McQueen is wound so tight that he looks like he's in the wrong movie and needs to lighten-up. When the squad realizes that the Germans have nearby listening posts, James Coburn (Cpl. Henshaw) rigs up a jeep to sound like a tank. When it's discovered that the Germans have a microphone hidden nearby, Bob Newhart (Pfc. Driscoll) performs a telephone skit right out of his standup act. In addition, Nick Adams (Pvt. "Homer" Janeczek) and Bobby Darin (Pvt. Corby) also have humorous roles that appear to mock the angry and sullen McQueen character. It's only near the end that this movie becomes realistic, with graphic combat scenes and soldiers dying. In a strange scene, the ever calm and reassuring McQueen character goes off the deep end to salvage his pride, and this completely undermines his character's development from the beginning of the film. While there are some entertaining moments here, the redeeming end is too little, too late.

What the critics say Critics rate this movie 4.0 to 4.5. "Tough, taut WW 2 film."[2] "A gripping, fast-paced, hard-hitting dramatic portrait."[4] **Final Word** Trust me when I tell you that the critics are deluded. This is a confused film that undermines its characters by not being able to decide if war is funny or serious.

Hell to Eternity

1960   USA   b/w   d. Phil Karlson

WW II: Biopic of Guy Gabaldon   3.0

While this fact-based movie about a real American war hero can still be found on the shelves of few video outlets, it deserves to be re-released. Guy Gabaldon grew up in east Los Angeles in the thirties. Chicano, he was orphaned at an early age and was raised by a Japanese-American family (Nisei) where he learned to speak fluent Japanese. An interpreter in the Marine Corps in 1944 during the invasion of Saipan, he was awarded the Silver Star for capturing over 1,500 Japanese civilians and combatants. Unfortunately, this movie pretty much gets the full-Hollywood, with Jeffrey Hunter cast as Gabaldon (not much sense of his Hispanic heritage here). There's a long and overly sentimental introduction to his Japanese family and his relationship with them, and then a ridiculous interlude that interjects prostitutes and hard drinking while on leave. The movie finally begins with the battle for Saipan, in which American soldiers faced their first "banzai" charge by 4,000 Japanese soldier. In a 15-hour battle, nearly every Japanese soldier was killed. Before the end of this three week struggle nearly 7,000 Japanese soldiers and civilians committed suicide by jumping off cliffs. The actual portrayal of Pvt. Gabaldon conducting "solo raids" from cave to cave and threatening and coaxing soldiers to surrender, appears to correspond to the record. His capture of the Japanese commander appears to greatly embellish an already interesting story. He did, in fact, single-handedly convince 800 soldiers and civilians to surrender all at one time. An astonishing accomplishment! There are several well-staged and intense battle scenes. However, this movie's attempt to be a little of everything is too much. Filled with sentimentality about family, a morality tale about the mistreatment of Japanese-Americans, titillating sex scenes, and over inflating a hero's story, robs this movie from being so much more.

What the critics say Critics rate this movie 2.5 to 3.0. "Battle-strewn biopic which after two hours seems to lose its point."[1] "Antiprejudice, antiwar drama...lots of battle scenes."[7] "Good action scenes...rescue this true-story morality drama."[8] **Final Word** Efforts are currently under way to upgrade Gabaldon's Silver Star to the Medal of Honor, for which he was originally recommended.

The Heroes of Desert Storm

1991   USA   color   tv   d. Don Ohlmeyer

Gulf War: DOD Public-Relations Effort   1.0

There's a fine line between making a movie that shows the sacrifice and heroism of soldiers, and one that is nothing more than propaganda. Made for TV shortly after the Gulf War in 1991, the film mostly utilizes television news footage and bad actors to give viewers a window into how everyday Americans were making the ultimate sacrifice for their country. The prologue states that this movie was based on "true stories," and provides an introductory message from former President Bush on the sacrifice made by these "real" American heroes. What is hard to notice are the very brief credits flashed across the screen after the movie is over, indicating the cooperation of the DOD, Navy, Army, Air Force and Marine Corps, as well as nine military project officers consulting on this film (1-DOD, 2-Navy, 3-Army, 1-Air Force, 1 Marine, 1-Coast Guard). Now the question arises, why did ABC television need so many military consultants for a low-budget made-for-TV movie? The answer is, this movie was primarily a propaganda effort to help maintain volunteer enlistment rates. As a young female reservist is called up, she says, "I made a deal. I'll stick to it." Placing soldiers in harm's way is justified by lines such as, "every effort is important," "we all pay a price." (And every Patriot missile hit a SCUD, too.) The movie consists mainly of sanitized news footage and one incredibly cheap shot at Vietnam War veterans. A Marine sergeant and Vietnam vet tells a private, "Nothing like 'Nam...no conscripts in this war, all volunteers, better trained, and some even say better educated." (Holy moly, what is this all about?) Volunteers are somehow more virtuous than draftees who fought and died. Better trained and educated? What the hell is the message here? We lost 'Nam based on the quality of the soldier and not from political and military ineptitude? There are many levels of bad movies in hell—this one has found its own.

What the critics say Critics rate this movie 2.0 to 2.5. "The human spirit of the people who fought...is captured in this film."[5] "Flag-waving pedestrian effort shows how quick it was made to cash in on patriotism."[7] **Final Word** A lame propaganda effort by the DOD to maintain recruitment levels for the volunteer army, following a major military engagement.

The Heroes of Telemark

1965 GBR   color   d. Anthony Mann

WW II: Espionage-Actioner	2.0

This fictional account of a real-life attempt to sabotage a German heavy water factory during WW II simply has too many scenes of whistling Norwegians to be truly entertaining. In 1942 the Germans and the Allies were in a race to develop an atom bomb. Heavy water was an important moderator to slow down neutrons so that they could be more easily captured by the fissionable atoms (plutonium or uranium) in a nuclear reaction. The Allies, convinced that the Germans were ahead, sent in British commandos to work with the Norwegian resistance movement. Their mission was to sabotage the Norsk Hydro heavy water plant near Telemark. (It turned out, of course, that the Germans weren't even close to producing the bomb.) While Richard Harris (Knut Straud) plays the resistance leader, Kirk Douglas (Dr. Rolf Pedersen) is the real star, who gets nearly all the close-ups and the girl. After the British commando unit is wiped-out attempting to land in Norway, the nine-man resistance team attempts to take the factory out on their own. Failing at this, they attempt to destroy a shipment of heavy water to Germany. Oh yes! Kirk Douglas is briefly reunited with his ex-wife (Ulla Jacobsson), who is initially cold to his advances but soon thaws. Unfortunately there's not much action, very little intrigue or plot twist, and no surprises except for the singing-whistling Norwegian resistance fighters. The movie's primary focus is on lots of snow and soldiers skiing down beautiful Alpine slopes. There's one predictable moment when the stalwart resistance-guys allow a complete stranger to join them (he's dressed in black when they are all in white!), and guess what, he betrays them. Built into the mountainside of a fjord, the Norsk Hydro plant was finally destroyed by some extraordinary bombing raids by British Mosquito fighter-bombers (see *633 Squadron*).

What the critics say Critics rate this movie 2.5 to 3.5. "Ambling narrative with big action sequences which often seem irrelevant"[1] "Douglas and Harris spend more time battling each other than the Nazis."[2] **Final Word** A leaden actioner that must have thought that "Heavy Water" was a Norwegian bottled water. The 1947 movie *The Battle for Heavy Water* is a superior telling of the same story.

The Hill

1965   GBR   b/w   d. Sidney Lumet

WW II: Military Prison Camp   4.5

The British are at it again, this time in a tense and powerful drama about the abuse of authority at a British military stockade. As Lord Acton (another Britisher) put it so well, "Power tends to corrupt; absolute power corrupts absolutely." Based on the novel by R.S. Allen, the prison camp is set in North Africa during WW II and is run, *de facto*, by Sgt. Major Wilson, played by Harry Andrews. Andrews gives a brilliant performance as a tough and, at times, cruel soldier who wants to break every prisoner in order to make him a better soldier. In the opening scene Sgt. Wilson tells a group of prisoners who are being discharged, "You know why I make you suffer? To find out if there's any good in you." Wilson is old-school and will go to any length to prove the superiority of his personal military code. Into his prison comes Sgt. Major Joe Roberts (Sean Connery) and four other new prisoners (Ossie Davis, Alfred Lynch, Roy Kinnear, Jack Watson). Sgt. Major Roberts is immediately targeted to be broken because of his rank and because he was believed to have acted cowardly in combat. Part of Sgt. Major Wilson's code is to back his sergeants unquestionably, in a show of solidarity that the prisoners cannot penetrate. However, a new sergeant, Sgt. Williams (Ian Hendry), is a sadistic and brutal individual whose sole goal is to break prisoners. What follows is a close-up look at how power corrupts, and the battle of wills between the prisoners and the guards. This is an intelligent script and the acting is outstanding throughout. Many excellent small details make the setting exceptionally real, particularly the camp itself and the manner in which prisoners have to double-time everywhere, even in the chow line. And, of course, there is the "hill," an artificial rock and sand hill at the center of the camp that prisoners are forced to double-time up and down, in full gear, as punishment. We can also thank director Sidney Lumet for a realistic and uncompromising ending.

What the critics say Critics rate this movie 4.0 to 4.5. "Powerful drama...with superb performances by all."[2] "It is a harsh, sadistic and brutal entertainment, superbly crafted."[4] "Sadistic guards and a rough, tough, unlovable bunch of inmates."[8] **Final Word** While *The Hill* is not a true prisoner-of-war drama, it's the next best thing. It's at the top of its class.

Home of the Brave

1949 USA b/w d. Mark Robson

WW II: Racism in the Army   3.5

Hollywood for the first time, in 1949, seriously addresses the issue of racism in the military and features a Black male lead in a war movie. *Home of the Brave* is a stark psychological drama about a Black GI (James Edwards) who suffers an emotional breakdown during combat. Originally a play by Arthur Laurents about being Jewish, not Black, this creates problems with the script. This may also be the first movie to introduce modern psychological concepts as an explanation for racism, for understanding war neurosis, and offering a talking-treatment as a cure. Pvt. Moss (James Edward) has volunteered for a dangerous intelligence mission to survey a Japanese-held island. It turns out that one of the other three volunteers, Pvt. Finch (Lloyd Bridges), was Moss's best friend in high school. Their squad is also comprised of openly-racist Cpl. T.J. (Steve Bodie), and Sgt. Mingo (Frank Lovejoy) and Maj. Robinson (Douglas Dick) who are sympathetic to Moss. At the conclusion of an intelligence operation, Moss suffers amnesia and paralysis. The treating psychiatrist (Jeff Corey) works with him to recount events leading to his breakdown. Told in flashbacks, a tense drama reveals the racial conflict between Moss and T.J., and that Moss is ambivalent and always has been about his friendship with Finch. When Finch is shot and captured by the Japanese, Moss is confronted by a host of conflicting emotions, which lead to his breakdown. Many of this film's problems result from its having been a play. All the issues are wrapped up a little too neatly, with Moss's treatment too condensed and preachy. The sentimentality portrayed in the relationship between Moss and Finch feels contrived, and the breakdown itself appears to work more at the level of plot device than believability. While this is a flawed film, it represents a step forward from the safe formulas characteristic of most war dramas of the time.

What the critics say Critics rate this movie 2.0 to 4.5. "More daring when made than now, but still hard-hitting."[2] "Hollywood's first outstanding statement against racial prejudice."[5] **Final Word** James Edwards, a fine actor, has had many war film roles, including *Battle Hymn, Men in War, Patton, Pork Chop Hill* and *The Steel Helmet*.

The Horse Soldiers

1959 USA color d. John Ford

Civil War: Cavalry Action   1.5

Director John Ford's treatment of this fact-based Civil War story—an embarrassment of clichés, romance and western-movie nostalgia—will disappoint most war movie fans. Adapted from the novel by Harold Sinclair, *The Horse Soldiers* is based on the true story of Col. Benjamin Grierson. In April 1863 Grierson led 1,700 Union cavalry on a successful 300-mile raid behind Confederate lines to destroy southern rail lines at Newton Station, Mississippi, and cut off vital supplies to Vicksburg. John Wayne plays hard-nosed Union cavalry officer Col. John Marlowe, hand-picked to lead this desperate raid. Blustery and in command, Marlowe, immediately begins quarreling with Maj. Kendall (William Holden), an overly-sincere physician assigned to his command (predictably, a mutual respect develops). The film then degenerates into nonsense when Marlowe encounters Miss Hannah Hunter (Constance Towers), a southern belle who hates the North, but when overhearing their plan to attack Newton Station, is forced to accompany Marlowe and his men. Beautiful and angry, Miss Hunter conflicts with the gruff and no-nonsense Marlowe. Ultimately, the cute, quarreling banter between Marlowe and Miss Hunter becomes insufferable (leaving most serious war movie fans hoping he shoots her for spying). Ford's overly romantic notions about the West don't translate into a film about the Civil War. Given the opportunity to address slavery, he completely ignores it. This film's final incompetence occurs near the end when young cadets from a nearby military academy attempt to engage Col. Marlowe and his troops. The colonel, of course, honorably retreats rather than risk killing young boys. It's too much (especially, in real life, when cadets from the Virginia Military Institute acquitted themselves well at the Battle of New Market in 1864). Long and tedious, with many irrelevant digressions, the film lacks action or a compelling story.

What the critics say Critics rate this movie 2.0 to 4.0. "Typically sprawling John Ford cavalry Western with not too many high spots."[1] "Saddled with one ludicrous moment after another."[6] **Final Word** Wayne does not fire a weapon in this movie. What is going on here? Nearly ten years later he pulls the same stunt in *The Green Berets*.

The Human Condition

1959   JAP   b/w   subtitles   (parts 1, 2 and 3)   d. Masaki Kobayashi

WW II: Antiwar Epic	4.5

This monumental wartime trilogy by director Masaki Kobayashi is without doubt a great war epic. Based on a set of six novels by Junpei Gomikawa, the film runs 9.5 hours. Part 1: *No Greater Love* was released in 1959; Part 2: *Road to Eternity* in 1960; and Part 3: *A Soldier's Prayer* in 1961. Set in Manchuria, 1943, the film tells the story of a pacifist's decent into wartime hell. Kaji (Tatsuya Nakadai), a young Japanese manager, accepts assignment in a remote location in Manchuria to oversee the labor force at a iron ore mine. In return, his military active duty is deferred. Kaji is not only a pacifist but a humanist who has very modern theories about labor, which he brings to the mines. In the process, Kaji makes a Faustian bargain when he attempts to get the Chinese laborers to stop resisting and escaping, with the promise he will improve their conditions. He's blind to his role in exploiting them, for which he pays a high price. What truly elevates *The Human Condition* is its unflinching look at the brutal manner in which Chinese POWs were treated as slave labor. This may be the only Japanese film to address this issue. In Part 2 Kaji is conscripted into the army where he attempts to improve the condition of young recruits. A natural leader, he again steps forward and is beaten and humiliated. This portrayal of the Japanese army as sadistic, brutal and unthinking is unparalleled in movie-making. Part 3 is a shattering look at a defeated and desperate army trying to survive. In the end, Kaji surrenders to the Soviets rather than risk the lives of others. Irony comes full circle—he's now a slave laborer in a Soviet work camp. In one of the great modern documents about man's inhumanity to man, Kobayashi examines how all the competing forces loosed by war and the oppressive forces in Japanese society robbed them of their humanity and destroyed men of conscience.

What the critics say Critics rate this movie 3.5 to 4.0 . "An epic chronicle of one man's struggle to retain his humanity."[3] "Acting, cinematography, and editing are all first rate in this heart wrenching tale."[7] **Final Word** Very long, dense, and tries to say so very much. The focus is on the repetition of desperate images and scenes in a world without hope. This is not an American war story; however, you will carry the images with you for a long time, even if they are without catharsis.

The Hunley

1999   USA   color   tv   d. John Gray

Civil War: Submarine Warfare	1.0

Is it possible to make a movie about the first operational combat submarine, the CSS *Hunley* of the Confederate navy, and not tell the audience a thing about the man who invented the submarine? What inspired the invention; what technical difficulties did he struggle with and overcome? What financial problems and politics did he encounter? Somehow, this movie manages to overlook all this and more. The movie opens with the second sinking of the *Hunley*, apparently due to an operational failure that resulted in the deaths of its crew and its inventor, Capt. Hunley. What we get to watch is one Lt. Dixon, played by a completely miscast Armand Assante, salvage the sub, assemble a crew and, in the last ten minutes of the movie, torpedo a Union ship blockading the Confederate port of Charleston. The concussion from the explosion also sinks the *Hunley*, drowning its entire crew. The time is 1864 and the Union is blockading and laying siege to Charleston. In an attempt to break the blockade, the Confederacy financed the development of a "diving torpedo boat." The movie doesn't explicitly show this, but it seems logical given the little information provided. The sub itself is all metal and propelled by eight men turning a hand crank. The interior is very claustrophobic and difficult to enter or exit. No information is provided about design or performance specifications (length, weight, length of time it could submerge, depth it could reach, speed, construction materials). Instead, the movie focuses on dreamy flashbacks of Lt. Dixon's relationship with his wife and scenes of his half-madness over their separation and her death. In other irrelevant scenes the crew got drunk and fought with each other. What's missing is the submarine and the development of the its torpedo. (Obviously, this is not a very good movie.) Oh yes, Donald Sutherland stars as Gen. Beauregard, commander of the Confederate army in Charleston.

What the critics say Critics rate this movie 2.0 to 2.5. **Final Word** This is not just a bad movie you can easily dismiss. Its total incompetence leaves you angry and disappointed. You could learn more about submarines by holding the producer of this movie underwater for an extended length of time than by watching it.

The Hunters

1958 USA color d. Dick Powell

| Korean War: Air Combat | 2.0 |

Primarily a wartime romance, *The Hunters* stars Robert Mitchum as Maj. Cleve Saville, a decorated WW II fighter ace who requested assignment to Korea in 1952. The other stars of this film are the beautiful F-86 jet fighter plane and the outstanding aerial photography in this movie. This movie typifies many of the big-budget war movies of the early 1950s, particularly those about the Korean War. The audience needed its war movies softened by a strong emphasis on relationships, with the war in the background. Maj. Saville, when queried about whether this war has a "bigger meaning," responds, "It came along too soon after the real big one." Another pilot comments, "It's a war you can't feel, there is nothing simple about it like the last one," and a third pilot adds, "Sometimes I forget what this one is all about." These comments probably represent much of the American public's ambivalence about the Korean War. However, there's no doubt about the sentiments of this movie towards war films—a vehicle for heroic action by larger-than-life men who dominate events. In short order, Maj. Saville seduces the beautiful woman (May Britt) (rejecting her in the end out of noble intent), is quickly the lead dog in the new squadron, shoots down the Chinese ace, crashes his plane to rescue a pilot (the husband of the woman he is romancing), and leads his men back to safety from behind enemy lines. He also avenges the death of a Korean family. The movie, based on the novel by James Salter, is so preposterous that it was embarrassing to watch at times. However, if you truly enjoy watching vintage 1950s jet fighters, there are scenes that will bring tears to your eyes. Where else will you see thirty F-86s flying in information and engaged in long, eye-popping aerial combat scenes?

What the critics say Critics rate this movie 3.0 to 3.5. "A standard war thriller, good to look at when airborne but pretty boring on the ground."[1] "Melodrama set during the Korean War...incredible aerial photography sets this apart from other films of the genre."[5] "Lumbering soap opera is probably the F-86's finest hour."[6] **Final Word** I liked the romance better than the war story. That's a bad sign. If you get off on 1950s jet fighters, don't miss this movie.

The Hunt for Red October

1990 USA color d. John McTiernan

Cold War: Submarine Thriller 4.0

Based on Tom Clancy's best-selling novel, this movie is one of the best of the Cold War thrillers. It has a lot going for it—great special effects and close-up looks at nuclear submarines in dry dock, on the ocean's surface, beneath the sea and inside the high-tech environment that constitutes a nuclear sub. An outstanding cast includes Sean Connery (Capt. Marko Ramius) as an elite Soviet sub commander; Alec Baldwin (Jack Ryan) as a CIA intelligence analyst; Sam Neill (Vassili Borodin) as executive officer to Capt. Ramius; Glen Scott (Bart Mancuso) as commander of the USS *Dallas*, a Los Angeles Class nuclear attack sub; and James Earl Jones as a CIA intelligence chief. The basic story is fairly simple but becomes complicated. Capt. Ramius plots with a handful of trusted officers to defect with a new Soviet submarine, *Red October*, whose silent jet water propulsion system can evade sonar detection. However, the system has been detected by Jack Ryan, submarine warfare expert for the CIA. Capt. Ramius' motives are mixed but based primarily on the fact that *Red October* is a first strike weapon that he doesn't trust the Communists with. Clearly, what we have here is a major thaw in Cold War relationships—sympathetic views of a Soviet officers, and Ryan trying to convince "hawkish" American military officers to back off. Of course, all hell breaks loose when the entire Soviet fleet tries to hunt down the *Red October* and enlists the aid of the US. The action never slows down, and there are enough plot twists for several movies. In a nice touch, the Soviet characters have accents or speak Russian. There's lots of high tech detail—Russian bombers, carriers, helicopters and air dropped torpedoes—wow, this is a heck of a ride. While the plot does muddle at the end—too *mano-a-mano* for a submarine thriller—Connery is outstanding as Capt. Ramius, who is calculating, in control and, when necessary, will matter-of-factly murder the ship's political officer.

What the critics say Critics rate this movie 4.0 to 4.5. "Exciting complex thriller."[2] "Well-paced and gripping Cold War drama filled with intrigue and exciting action."[3] "Complicated, ill-plotted potboiler that succeeds breathlessly."[5] **Final Word** This is not a great war movie but rather pure escapist entertainment at its best.

Ice Station Zebra

1968 USA color d. John Sturges

| Cold War: Submarine Adventure | 2.0 |

Based on a novel by Alistair Maclean (*The Guns of Navarone* and *Where Eagles Dare*), this is one of those overly-long (2.5 hours), big-budget Hollywood adventures with a well-known cast with limited acting ability. A Soviet spy satellite has set down near an American weather station (Ice Station Zebra) at the North Pole. Under the guise that the weather station is experiencing problems, the Americans and the Soviets send military teams to recover a satellite that contains photographs of American ICBM sites. Because of poor weather, the American nuclear sub *Tigerfish* is dispatched in the hope of reaching the station before the Soviets. The cast includes Rock Hudson as the submarine commander who has not been told what his motivation is for this character; Ernest Borgnine, a blustering expatriate communist, whose presence, in any war movie, should be a warning not to watch it; Jim Brown, a Marine commando captain who likes to eat bullets; and Patrick McGoohan, a British intelligence "spook" who is all unconvincing intensity. To put it bluntly, this is a static action movie that has everyone standing around talking, with absolutely nothing to say or do. Fully half of this movie is comprised of "bearing 2-8-0," "range 90 double 00," "all ahead flank," "rudder midship." "port ahead 1/3," "shut the vents," "take her down, dive." The plot itself is not fully revealed until two hours into this waterlogged turkey. In the meantime, each character does his thing with as little imagination and character development as possible. This movie is without suspense or drama and grows increasingly tedious the longer it goes on, until the final showdown, when "nothing" really happens. However, in a spirit of détente, the Soviet colonel is a reasonable guy who is ready to, you guessed it—"talk." There's no shoot-out at the end; Borgnine is a double agent who gets what he deserves, and the satellite photos are destroyed.

What the critics say Critics rate this movie 2.5 to 3.0. "Talky and unconvincingly staged spy adventure with a disappointing lack of action."[1] "Standard Cold War nail-biter."[2] **Final Word** If a movie is based on a book by Alistair Maclean, stars Ernest Borgnine or has a cast of Hollywood extras and is over 2.5+ hours, don't rent it. Better to rent *Crimson Tide* or *The Hunt for Red October*.

Immortal Battalion

1944 GBR b/w d. Carol Reed

WW II: Classic '40s Flagwaver **3.0**

Popular at the box-office and well reviewed, this sentimental and entertaining British tribute to the citizen-soldier has almost nothing to say about being a soldier or fighting a war. What we get is a nostalgic vision of the average guy befuddled by finding himself in the rigid structure of the military and resenting being told what to do. The gentle complaining of this odd lot of characters and their good natures make them endearing as they try to find their way. The popular image of the class-ridden and snobbish British officer, reviled throughout the empire, is transformed. Instead, David Niven (Lt. Perry) portrays a soft-spoken and avuncular officer who ends up taking tea with his men. There's also the hard-as-nails Sgt. Fletcher (William Hartnell), who cajoles his men into being soldiers. There is really no American equivalent of this movie, at least in giving us a squad of men for whom you eventually feel genuine affection. Their transformation to proud soldier is gradual, and is not completed until they face combat in North Africa. While David Niven is ostensibly the star of this movie, his role is only one of a strong cast that shares the lead. The best scenes are not battles but watching these men get taken in by an aging widower every Sunday for tea and biscuits—not to mention a hot bath. The characters are like eight little boys complaining while their mother takes care of them. It's all very charming. Following these men from the train station as they leave to join the army, through basic training and eventually into combat, this story is fully told before they reach North Africa. The action is real enough and there is no patronizing heroism, but most of what precedes North Africa is amiable whimsy. While reviewers keep referring to this movie as semidocumentary in style, forget it, it's not.

What the critics say Critics rate this movie 3.5 to 5.0. "Memorable semi-documentary originally intended as a training film."[1] "Exhilarating wartime British film...full of spirit and charm."[2] "This gem of propaganda...a heartfelt appreciation of the men who do the hard work of war."[6] **Final Word** Sentimental and reassuring to audiences in 1944, the film offers little for the contemporary war movie fan.

The Immortal Sergeant

1943   USA   b/w   d. John M. Stahl

WW II: Classic '40s Flagwaver   1.5

Choking on Depression-era, Capraesque sincerity and humility, this movie is not even about the immortal sergeant in the title. Rather it's about Cpl. Colin Spence (Henry Fonda), an insecure and self-effacing newspaper reporter and writer who just can't muster up the courage to express his feelings for his girlfriend Valentine (Maureen O'Hara). There's some token action in the Libyan desert in 1941, with Fonda as a Canadian soldier fighting in the British Eighth Army. And there's Sgt. Kelly (Thomas Mitchell), a cheery Irishman who defines stereotype. While Sgt. Kelly leads a patrol to scout for German and Italian forces in the area, the real action comes in a series of flashbacks by Spence, as his obnoxious and successful friend, Benedict (Reginald Gardiner), makes a play for his girlfriend. There are, in fact, two separate and unrelated stories here. One is a low-budget, studio-bound war movie with little realistic action and bad special effects, that focuses on the relationship between Sgt. Kelly and Cpl. Spence. Kelly sees Spence's potential as a leader and attempts to nurture it. In an opening scene Sgt. Kelly is conferred sainthood—"If you asked me, there goes the whole bloom'n British army rolled up into one." (Trust me, the movie only goes down hill from here.) The second story features parties and nightclubs, with Spence tripping over his being a nice guy in jeopardy of losing his girl. Ultimately, Spence finds his courage in battle (becomes a war hero), as he's guided by the voice of Sgt. Kelly (this is truly a bad moment in war movie history). Spence then tells his girlfriend-stealing friend to get lost, and let's his woman know he's in charge now (which she goes for big time). The only wartime lesson I could discern is that a military uniform will help a guy get the girl (which was probably true).

What the critics say Critics rate this movie 3.0 to 4.0. "Quite neatly done but a shade embarrassed by its poetic leanings."[1] "This early effort leaves much to be desired, both as entertainment and as motivation."[6] "Thankfully, decent battle scenes break up the psychological over-indulgence."[8] **Final Word** This movie uses a formula that's prevalent in many war films—war scenes interspersed with flashbacks of a relationship back home. A formula that has <u>never</u> been successful, to my knowledge.

The Imperial Japanese Empire
1985 JAP color dubbed

WW II: Epic War-Romance   2.0

This epic war-romancer is the Japanese equivalent of *In Harm's Way* or *Winds of War*. It's a sprawling, disjointed story that's as much soap opera as war movie. However, what's really interesting is the Japanese view of the war. By paying just a little attention, you will immediately notice some minor differences in how the Japanese view WW II as opposed to, say—Americans! As the Japanese were minding their own business conquering China and the rest of Southeast Asia, they practically became forlorn when the US and its allies instituted an oil embargo against them. They believed that President Roosevelt had bated them into war by putting one over on the US military. Roosevelt, they felt, used the "old rules of the Western gunfighter" to get the opponent to draw first, so that the Japanese become responsible for the war. There is more loss of face because the US refused to negotiate with Japan as long as it was occupying China and Manchuria. The Japanese believed this was tantamount to a declaration of war. So there you have it—Pearl Harbor was completely justified as an act of self-defense and national self-preservation. Also, contrary to popular American opinion, Gen. Hideki Togo, was not a militarist and war monger, but a peaceful family man forced into this conflict against his conscience. (Gen. Togo was later hanged as a war criminal when his suicide attempt failed.) What we have in this film, for the most part, is a documentary chronicling the war from 1940-1945, replete with terrible narration and poor quality archival film footage interspersed with average special effects. In between war scenes we are shown the impact of the war on two couples. For American audiences the film shows a more human side to the Japanese soldier and suggests that most Japanese had wanted an end to this war long before its government surrendered.

What the critics say No available reviews. **Final Word** No mention here of the enslavement of Korean women as "Comfort Girls" or of the 731 Biological Warfare Research Unit that conducted biological experimentation on Chinese prisoners and then murdered them so they wouldn't talk. As a Japanese perspective on the war, this is truly an interesting, if not eye-opening, movie experience.

In Harm's Way
1965   USA   b/w   d. Otto Preminger

WW II: Naval Operation in South Pacific   3.0

As wartime melodrama, director Otto Preminger's adaptation of the James Bassett novel works better than expected. Critics did not like this movie for many good reasons, but at least it's not one of those sappy, nostalgic films about WW II that seem to abound. Starring John Wayne (Admiral "Rock" Torrey), Kirk Douglas and Patricia Neal, this film breaks with the nostalgic tradition and has moments of gritty realism. It also has bad special effects ("The ships are models and the battles are conducted in a bathtub."[7]). Unfortunately, *In Harm's Way* is too long and cops out in too many instances when it comes to storyline. The movie opens on December 6, 1941, the night before Pearl Harbor is bombed by the Japanese, and follows the first year of the war in the Pacific. This is not an action film in the slightest, but more of a behind-the-scenes look at naval operations and at the romantic relationships of officers. The story focuses on Admiral Torrey, who is assigned to take over a battle group stalled in occupying a Japanese-held island group. Before this battle is over, Admiral Torrey's son is killed, the admiral loses a leg, his son's girlfriend commits suicide, and his executive officer, Commander Eddington (Kirk Douglas), rapes a young nurse and then takes-off on a suicidal mission. There aren't any war heroics, and the romances are fairly jaded affairs. And if you don't believe war is hell, there's Wayne's romantic interest, Patricia Neal, a woman whose voice is more gravely than his own (however she does a fine acting job). This film also examines the politics of command and political influence in obtaining rank and assignments, and it's not above making admirals grandstand for influence and promotion. The sprawling WW II nostalgic-epic would reach its zenith with Herman Wouk's outstanding 1980s television miniseries *Winds of War* and its sequel *War and Remembrance*.

What the critics say Critics rate this movie 2.0 to 3.5. "Overlong, melodramatic account of warfare in the South Pacific."[2] "It's a full, lusty slice of life."[4] "Long, lumbering naval epic...mixture of soap-opera action...and cheap looking special effects."[6] **Final Word** Wayne and Neal do a good job in a surprisingly entertaining relationship-oriented war movie.

In love and War

1987   USA   color   tv   d. Paul Aaron

Vietnam War: Prisoner-of-War   4.0

Based on the book *In Love and War* by Navy pilot Jim Stockdale and his wife Sybil Stockdale, this true story is a close-up and emotional look at the plight of American POWs. Cmdr. Stockdale (James Woods), stationed aboard the carrier USS *Ticonderoga* in the Gulf of Tonkin in August 1964, was in the air searching for the North Vietnamese torpedo boats that had allegedly fired on the destroyer USS *Maddox*. He makes it clear that no such attack took place and that the subsequent "Gulf of Tonkin Resolution" was a fraudulent pretext to attack North Vietnam. A year later, in 1965, Stockdale is shot down on a bombing run over the North and captured. For the next eight years he is held at Hoa Lo Prison ("Hanoi Hilton") until his release in 1974. Probably to the detriment of this movie, it also attempts to tell the story of Sybil Stockdale's (Jane Alexander) efforts to bring the plight of prisoners of war to the American public. This was at a time when our government did not want to acknowledge POWs were being tortured. Her efforts are laudable and played an important role in pressuring our government to act. But the important story is Cmdr. Stockdale. The fact is, the North Vietnamese routinely tortured and in some instances killed American POWs in an effort to utilize them for propaganda purposes. Stockdale, as the senior officer, attempts to organize resistance. He concludes that, to survive, the POWs have to "refuse to be reasonable" and develop their own code of conduct as to what is right or wrong. It is understood that prisoners could be broken by torture but that they had to make their captors hurt them before giving anything up. In solitary confinement for nearly eight years, Stockdale was constantly threatened, subjected to unending physical beatings and torture on a daily basis. His resistance and survival is truly a profile in courage. Though this movie is not structured in a satisfying manner, it is well-acted and an important Vietnam War movie.

What the critics say Critics rate this movie 3.0 to 3.5. "Graphic but strangely uninvolving dramatization."[1] "Both stars offer compelling performances, though the absorbing story isn't quite as powerful as it could have been."[3] **Final Word** The critics generally seem more enamored of silly fictional POW dramas and have a harder time involving themselves in the bloody truth.

In Pursuit of Honor

1995 USA color tv d. Ken Olin

| Military Life: End of American Cavalry | 3.5 |

This well-done action movie, based on true events, tells the story of mutiny and desertion by five American cavalry soldiers in 1935. Gen. Douglas MacArthur, in trying to cut costs and speed up the mechanization of the American army during the Depression, ordered all excess cavalry horses destroyed. Cavalry officer Lt. Buxton (Craig Sheffer) and four enlisted horse soldiers, led by Master Sgt. Jack Libbey (Don Johnson), are ordered to herd 500 horses to Mexico. Here they are to shoot the horses. To cavalry soldiers this was nothing short of murder. Lt. Buxton said it well, "They fight beside us and they die beside us. They deserve the same respect, the same honor." In a grizzly and gut-wrenching scene, a hundred horses are killed. The soldiers, sickened by what they are witnessing, gather the remaining four hundred horses and begin herding them north towards Arizona. Beautifully filmed in Australia and New Zealand, a long chase ensues between the Army and these deserters. With no plan and uncertain that they even want to be in this situation, the deserters have the opportunity to turn back or surrender, but choose instead to head 2,000 miles north towards Canada. There's something of a subplot here between a retired cavalry officer (Rod Steiger) and his young daughter (Gabrielle Anwar) that adds little or nothing to this movie. There's also a villainous officer, Col. Hardesty (Robert Gunton), who leads the pursuit. Mostly a functionary, the colonel gets no personal rise from these events, but it's clear that he will carry out his order to the bloody end if necessary. While MacArthur is correctly portrayed as an unsympathetic, President Roosevelt issues the deserters a full-pardon. A tale of honor among men who want to do what is right, watching these men confront the realization of what they had done and what lies before them makes this movie well worth watching.

What the critics say Critics rate this movie 3.0 to 4.0. "Invigorating retelling of a little-known episode in American history."[2] "Rugged performances."[5] "Thoughtful Depression-era drama."[8] **Final Word** Thirty-four years earlier, in the Boar War (1899-1902), the British lost 347,000 out of 518,000 horses. The end had come for "the horse" that had transformed war and dominated the battlefield for 2,000 years.

In Which We Serve

1942   GBR   b/w   d. Noel Coward/David Lean

WW II: Classic '40s Flagwaver   **2.5**

This fictionalized account of the sinking of Lord Mountbatten's destroyer, the HMS *Kelly*, off the island of Crete in 1941, was a hugely popular film on both sides of the Atlantic. Produced, directed, scored, scripted and acted in by Noel Coward, he received a special Oscar for his many contributions. As sailors flounder in the water holding on to a life-raft, flashbacks of the homefront show their wives and families, as well events leading up to the building, commissioning and eventual sinking of the fictional HMS *Torrin*. The hyperbole for this movie was excessive even for the time—"One of the screens proudest achievements at any time and in any country." (*Newsweek*); "Never at any time has there been a reconstruction of human experience which could touch the savage grandeur and compassion of this production." (Howard Barnes, *NY Herald Tribune*). All I can say is that, today, there's nothing about this picture that makes it standout from dozens of other rather ordinary propaganda films of the 1940s. During a war in which a small island nation was struggling for its very survival, this paean to the sailors and ships that guaranteed its existence is laudable. The sacrifices by family and sailors is honored here in a touching manner. But this is not compelling moviemaking, awash in sentimentality and lacking a coherent story. Coward says in the opening, "This is the story of a ship...." But it really isn't. It isn't even the story of the men on this ship, but rather a series of limited flashbacks of family, each touching in a Norman Rockwell way. Coward, ever class-conscious, lends a rather paternalistic if not condescending footnote. As Capt. Kinross, he makes a heartfelt speech about duty and sacrifice as he attempts to make personal contact with the men who survived the sinking.

What the critics say Critics rate this movie 4.0 to 5.0. "The flashback memories of stricken survivors is now so dated, it is difficult to take it all seriously today."[8] **Final Word** Mountbatten, a royal hanger-on and military lightweight, was suspect after the HMS *Kelly* sank. He went on to even greater incompetence, and was responsible for the disastrous raid at Dieppe in 1942 (see the excellent movie *Dieppe*).

Ironclads
1991   USA   color   tv   d. Delbert Mann

Civil War: Naval Warfare	2.5

This Turner Home Network Civil War movie is not up to the standards it set by *Andersonville* and *Gettysburg.* The film purports to tell about events leading up to the historic battle of the first iron ships (ironclads) on March 9, 1862, in Hamptom Roads, Virginia. While *Ironclads* does tell this story in vague detail, it seems far more interested in one Miss Betty (Virginia Madsen), a Virginia socialite whose sympathies are with the North but whose heart is with a Confederate naval officer. Miss Betty gets all confused about her loyalties, spying for one side then trying to protect her lover, when, frankly, no one gives a damn. The story that isn't told here is how two ships, the Union's USS *Monitor* and the Confederate's CSS *Merrimack*, revolutionized naval warfare. Build in only a few months time with very different designs, the ships dueled for nearly five hours to a standoff, never to engage in battle again. The *Merrimack* was subsequently scuttled and destroyed by the Confederacy two months after the battle, to keep it from falling into the hands of the Union. The *Monitor* later sank at sea during a storm in December 1862. One day prior to their battle the *Merrimack* had sunk two steam-driven battleships, the *Cumberland* and the *Congress* before the *Monitor* arrived on the scene. The South had hoped that by breaking the North's blockade at sea they could entice France and Britain to support their war effort. There is a good opening battle sequence as the South captures Portsmouth, Virginia, as well as the sunken USS *Virginia*, which provided the hull for the future *Merrimack*. Near the end of the movie there are two outstanding naval engagements as these ships battle it out at close quarters. Unfortunately, the film skipped over politics and strategies and almost no effort was devoted to giving insight into the men who built these ships. To say that these omissions are disappointing is a gross understatement.

What the critics say Critics rate this movie 2.0 to 2.5. "Memorable dramatization...the special effects are the only thing worth watching."[5] "History lesson is almost ruined by silly subplots."[6] **Final Word** Civil War geeks will want to check out the action—and find out what happens to a women who separates her heart from her head.

The Iron Triangle

1989 USA color d. Eric Weston

Vietnam War: Combat Duel   2.5

Twelve years after the Vietnam War the inevitable attempt to retell the war from both sides is produced (reunion plans will take longer). The opening scenes reveal that this movie is based on the wartime diary of an unknown Vietcong soldier. It's also a completely fictionalized and preposterous account of the bond formed between a 17-year-old Vietcong soldier, Ho (Liem Whatley), and an American army officer, Captain Keene (Beau Bridges). The film also features Haing S. Ngor, Oscar winner for *The Killing Fields* (1984), as a Vietcong "partyline" officer, Col. Tuong, in a limited role that appears to mostly capitalize on his name recognition. The events supposedly take place in 1969 along the Ho Chi Minh Trail in an area known as the "Iron Triangle" (a Communist stronghold 20 cliks north of Siagon). The protagonists paths cross on two occasions, as each is captured by the other side, with each intervening and saving the other's life. What makes the story confusing is that the audience is watching this movie primarily from the viewpoint of a VC soldier, while the entire story is told by the American army captain (Bridges) who discovered the lost diary. If this sounds confusing, it is. While the director attempts to weave the stories of these two soldiers, the American officer is mostly a one-dimensional character whose primary role is storyteller. Despite the director's good intentions at humanizing the Vietcong, by showing us their daily struggles and local Communist party politics, the characters and stories are undeveloped. While the basic premise and story telling are interesting, the plot is contrived to the limits of good fiction. And with too many poorly staged combat scenes and a barely present Capt. Keene, this is pretty much an average war actioner. However, the producer correctly surmised that the American movie-going pubic was not ready for a story about a Vietcong soldier. I suspect interest in the plight of the VC is probably not very high in the US, even thirty years after the war.

What the critics say Critics rate this movie 2.5 to 3.0. "Effective in its small way."[1] "Intriguing as a look at the war from the enemy side but the result is confused and slight."[2] "Solid blood-and-guts war drama."[7] **Final Word** On a very slow war movie night you might want to consider renting this one. There's a political assassination with a knife that will certainly keep you awake.

Is Paris Burning?

1966   FRA/USA   b/w   d. René Clément

WW II: The Liberation of Paris   3.0

Is Paris Burning? is a sprawling, big-budget, all-star war epic about the liberation of Paris, based on a bestselling book by L. Collins and D. LaPierre. The confusing screenplay was written by Francis Coppola and Gore Vidal, among others. Following the Allied invasion of Europe on June 6, 1944, Paris was liberated on August 25, 1944. However, as the film makes clear, this wasn't a done deal. The Allied plan had been to bypass Paris and to press the attack against the retreating German army. Ultimately, the Free French forces, under Gen. de Gaulle in Algiers and the Resistance in Paris, convinced the Allies to take Paris in order to prevent German reprisals and atrocities. This black and white, pseudo-documentary-style film initially focuses on the disorganized Resistance movement in Paris, who are unable to agree on when to initiate armed resistance against occupying German forces. The first half of the movie rambles and is confusing. However, the best part of the movie focuses on the German commander of Paris, Gen. von Choltitz (Gert Fröbe). The commander had direct orders from Hitler to destroy Paris if the Germans weren't able to defend the city against Allied forces. In a convincing performance by Fröbe, Gen. von Choltitz first obeys orders and plans the demolition of Paris. But as the Allied invasion quickly progresses, he sees little military value in destroying the city and, in the end, refuses to give the order. There are many outstanding combat scenes as fighting takes place in the streets, along with well-integrated documentary film footage. However, this three-hour film fails to deal with the conflict between de Gaulle's Committee of National Liberation (Forces Francaises de l'Intérieur) and Marshal Pétain's Vichy government in Paris and the difficult issue of reprisals against German collaborators.

What the critics say Critics rate this movie 2.0 to 4.0. "Muddled...confusing attempt at a thinking man's all-star war epic."[1] "The street fighting is done with fervor and dynamism and the little cameos give an ironic, tender, dramatic, pathetic feel to the overall happening."[4] **Final Word** This film is an attempt to welcome the French back into the war effort with a measure of dignity after a stunningly quick defeat in 1940.

Jet Pilot

1957   USA   color   d. Josef von Sternberg

Military Life: Cold War Romance   1.0

Starring John Wayne (Col. Jim Shannon) as an Air Force pilot
and squadron commander stationed in Alaska, and Janet Leigh
(Lt. Anna Marladovna), as a Soviet fighter pilot who has defected
and is seeking asylum, this has to be among the silliest movies
ever concocted. Originally produced by Howard Hughes in 1950,
this film was not released until 1957. Why it was ever released is
not clear; however, it's a black mark on the "Duke's" film legend.
As Lt. Marladovna strips off her flight suit (Wayne has to strip-
search her), she is wearing a turtleneck sweater and tight skirt
underneath. And each time she removes an article of clothing a
jet fighter zooms-bye. Within minutes she is showering and as
she is searching for a towel, Wayne tells her, "Now put your
hand on the knob." (Let's just get it out of the way. Janet Leigh is
truly beautiful and build like a brick igloo. I only finished watching
this movie because of the way her uniforms fit.) The Duke looks
like he is about to trip over his tongue throughout the movie. The
plot—Col. Jim Shannon is assigned to seduce Lt. Marladovna
and find out if she is spying. He protests, "I'm a jet man, not a
gigolo." A lot of cute and coy moments between them are done
to the aerobatics of F-86s piloted by Chuck Yeager. "The
temperature is beginning to rise in my tailpipe," Leigh tells
Wayne. Later Wayne calls her a "silly Siberian cupcake." (Who
would have ever believed the day would come that the "Duke"
would whisper a line like that to a Commie!) Let's continue. After
they marry Col. Shannon discovers his wife really is a spy and
tips her that she is about to be arrested. Acting as a double
agent Col. Shannon helps his wife escape and defects with her
to the Soviet Union. There they reconcile the relationship and
escape by jet fighter back to the good ol' US of A. The final
scene shows them having a cozy dinner at an upscale restaurant
in Palm Springs (final proof of the economic superiority of
capitalism over Communism). The state of American and Soviet
relationships, seen in this movie, would not be this good again
for many years to come.

What the critics say Critics rate this movie 2.0 to 2.5.
"Lamentably dull and stupid romantic actioner."[1] "Ridiculous."[2]
Final Word Check out Janet Leigh and some great shots of F-
86s, or vice versa.

Judgment at Nuremberg

1961   USA   b/w   d. Stanley Kramer

| Post WW II: Legal Drama | 5.0 |

This film is an extremely thought provoking and important fictionalized reenactment of the "Nuremberg Trials" following WW II. Adapted for the screen from a *Playhouse 90* television production, written by Abby Mann, and produced and directed by Stanley Kramer, the film won Academy Awards for Best Screenplay and Best Actor (Maximilian Schell). In 1948 the latter stages of the trial of Third Reich politicians, military officers and high-ranking officials for "crimes against humanity" were being carried out. This film focuses on the trial of four Nazi judges who implemented the law as dictated to them by the Nazi government of Germany. However, this film has a more ambitious goal than simply indicting these jurists. The trial examines how educated and influential Germans took part in these crimes. It asks, what did they know about the Holocaust? And, most importantly, who was ultimately responsible? There are many pointedly ironic moments as Schell, the Judge Advocate for the jurists, makes clear that the lines of responsibility for the rise of Nazism, and those who went along with it, were worldwide. Now that the Cold War had heated up, there was enormous pressure to make this a show trial and get it over with as quickly as possible. Spencer Tracy gives an ennobling performance as an American judge who oversees this tribunal. Schell is intense as he seeks to exonerate the German people as well as the Nazi judges. Burt Lancaster is outstanding as an eminent German judge and legal scholar who is shamed by his actions but continues to rationalize his conduct. Richard Widmark plays an impassioned prosecutor who ultimately yields to political pressure to bring the trials to a close. Other excellent performances include those of Montgomery Clift, Judy Garland and Marlene Dietrich. If this film has any flaw, it's when the story wanders from the court room. These trials set controversial legal precedents in international law for bringing heads of state and other war criminals to trial.

What the critics say Critics rate this movie 4.5 to 5.0. "Heavy-going dramatic documentary."[1] "Deeply moving and powerful."[5] "The film boasts some terrific performances."[8] **Final Word** Lost Best Picture Oscar to *West Side Story*. Only in Hollywood. Perhaps there should be a category for Most Important Picture!

Kelly's Heroes

1970   USA /YUG   color   d. Brian G. Hutton

| WW II: War Comedy | 2.5 |

A wartime comedy full of amiable characters, this movie attempts to combine the misfits-behind-enemy-lines subgenre with the larceny-in-their-hearts caper film. Starring Clint Eastwood (Lt. Kelly), Telly Savalas, Donald Sutherland, Carroll O'Connor and Don Rickles, this collection of eccentric soldiers attempt to rob a bank holding 16 million dollars in gold. The bank happens to be 30 miles behind German lines (Yes, this movie was probably the genesis for one of the great war-action films ever, *Three Kings.*) *Kelly's Heroes* is also filled with humor and sensibilities that characterized the 1970s. Donald Sutherland is off the wall as a hippie, flower-child tank commander who's stoned throughout the action and prone to spouting phrases such as—"Why don't you knock it off with those negative waves!" Eastwood, who says and does very little besides scowl (which he does very well), is the instigator of the robbery. The driving force for these men appears to be greed and, as this film makes clear, every soldier can be bought, including the entire army if necessary. In the film's funniest moment the robbers pay off the German tank commander guarding the bank with a Tiger tank. While this movie does have a few funny moments, too often it's slow and predictable. Rather than having a funny script, the movie hired funny actors. And even though it's a caper film, it doesn't have any of the plot twists and surprises a true caper film turns on. Rather than action, it's filled with lots of noise and explosions. *Kellly's Heroes* is not a film one should look too deeply at, as it never challenges the assumption that money (gold) is king—not war, conscience, love, life or death—nothing challenges this possibility or interrupts the efforts to attain the gold. In fact, no other possibility is even raised, which puts this somewhat cynical, if not amoral, tale that attempts to tweak the establishment of the 1960-1970s, in bed with the "Man." Odd indeed.

What the critics say Critics rate this movie 2.5 to 3.5. "An entertaining romp."[3] "Nearly satirical in its overall effect."[4] "An amiable rip-off of the The Dirty Dozen...funnier at the time of its original release."[7] **Final Word** Provides a mostly playful and nostalgic memory for all the adolescent war movie guys of the late 1960s (many probably stoned at the time).

King of Hearts

1966   FRA/ITA   color   subtitles   d. Philippe de Broca

WW I: Antiwar Satire   4.5

King of Hearts, by director Philippe de Broca, is a grand carnival that will parade through your consciousness, telling you that we "live only for the moment." Near the end of the WW I in 1918, a Scottish soldier is sent on a mission to a French town to discover where the retreating Germans have hidden a munitions dump rigged to explode. What he discovers is a celebration of life. When Pvt. Plumpick (Alan Bates) arrives, the town is inhabited by inmates of a nearby "lunatic asylum." The audience understands that this is all a parable meant to teach a lesson, and that the events that take place aren't real. For those who have difficulty suspending disbelief, when it comes to the whimsical, this film may not be your cup of tea. As the inmates escape from the asylum, they each take on a role and dress in bright costumes. There is the General, the Cleric, the Prostitute, the Duke and Duchess, and so on. Plumpick is later crowned the King of Hearts, as the inmates parade joyfully throughout the town where wild circus animals roam freely through the streets. This movie is filled with many wonderful Chaplinesque moments and the theater of the absurd. In a surprisingly touching scene, the hero is near to falling from a roof, and all the characters pull up chairs and make his fears and anxieties their theater. This all contrasts with the insanity of the war waging around the town and its intrusion into this alternative reality we have briefly entered. This film asks—of all the crazy possibilities, what could be crazier than the murderous realities of war? Inside, "the world is simple...just men and women." Outside, we are told by the Cleric "to love the world...you have to get away from it." How far we have come as individuals and as a culture from our own lost innocence appears to be at the center of this movie's concerns— and it is very far indeed. In a touching way this movie lets those open to this possibility experience their innocence over again, if just briefly.

What the critics say Critics rate this movie 3.0 to 4.5. "A moving celebration of the triumph of innocence."[3] "Light-hearted comedy with a serious message, definitely worthwhile."[5] "Wartime fantasy provides delightful insight into human behavior."[7] **Final Word** A poignant antiwar statement of magical realism that is deserving of its cult status.

King Rat
1965   USA   b/w   d. Bryan Forbes

| WW II: Prisoner-of-War | 4.0 |

For a prisoner-of-war movie, *King Rat* is surprisingly well made and entertaining. Starring George Segal, as Cpl. King ("King Rat"), the film is based on the novel by James Clavell, himself a POW during WW II. The action takes place in a Japanese POW camp (the Changi Jail) in Singapore, Malaysia, in 1945. Comprised of British, Australian and American prisoners who are living a subsistence existence under great hardship, this camp is fairly open, but extremely difficult to escape because of the surrounding ocean and jungle. This story centers on a character who has become a staple of most POW films, the "hustler" or "scrounger." Cpl. King is an ambitious small-time loser who runs a black market operation, exchanging goods and services between inmates and guards. The scrounger also takes a percentage and lives better than anyone else in the camp—his uniform is laundered, his shoes are shined, and he is the only prisoner of normal weight. Despite all the resentment this creates, Cpl. King has bought off all the senior officers in the camp with weekly protection money. He also dispenses cigarettes like a king throwing baubles to his subjects while a pack of losers do his bidding. Finally, a POW film that's not about escape but about what it takes to survive a treacherous environment. It's a nice change of pace to see that the British officers are not only on the take, but are skimming food from their own men. In an absolutely hilarious scheme, Cpl. King raises rats and sells the meat to British officers as Malaysian mouse deer. At the center of all this is a friendship between King and a young British officer, Lt. Marlowe (James Fox), who is fluent in Malay and helps him hustle deals. Of upper-class background, Marlowe rejects his British peers because of his complete fascination with King's ambition and amorality (not to mention all the perks). The performances are outstanding, and despite the humor, the film provides a stark portrait of a punishing existence in which survival is the driving force.

What the critics say Critics rate this movie 4.0 to 4.5. "Thoughtful presentation rises above clichés; many exciting scenes."[2] "Grim, downbeat and often raw prison camp drama."[4] **Final Word** One of my favorite POW films, original, funny, touching and, at times, realistic.

K-19: The Widowmaker

2002 USA /GBR/GER color d. Kathryn Bigelow

Cold War: Nuclear Submarine Disaster   3.5

Yet another obsessed submarine captain! Where do navies find these rare breed of men? The legacy of Melville's great work (*Moby Dick*) is destined to haunt us forever. Harrison Ford stars in this special effects thriller as Captain Vostrikov, recently appointed commander of the Soviet nuclear sub K-19. It's 1961 and the Soviets are desperately trying to catch up with the US who has deployed nuclear powered Polaris submarines. As a result, the Soviets are rushing through sea-trials in order to make the K-19 immediately operational. But it's not going to be that easy. "Inspired by real events" in 1961, a Soviet nuclear sub did experience a coolant leak in its reactor core, and many sailors suffered life-threatening radiation poisoning attempting to repair it. However, the similarity between the facts and this movie end here. There was no chance of a nuclear explosion setting off WW III, nor was there an attempted mutiny. Undeterred by the facts, this movie portends doom from the opening credits. We get somber classical music, hurried, claustrophobic shots and a Soviet sub that better resembles a Filipino jitney ferry, than a sleek edifice of modern technology. The real underlying drama here is about Capt. Vostrikov abuse of authority, frequently putting his crew and ship needlessly at risk with drills that exceed the design limits of the ship. He appears to be taking these risks in order to please Politburo cronies, and to live down the shame of his father being sent to the gulags for treason. When his executive officer, Capt. Polenin (Liam Neeson), a reasoned and respected officer, confronts him in a tense showdown, you can only groan that it took so long. By this time you have stopped caring about the outcome. The concluding scenes are a hollow and manipulative attempt to forgive and forget. Well-acted, great special effects, entertaining, but over-wrought and too predictable from beginning to end.

What the critics say Critics rate this movie 2.5 to 3.0. "Much Sturm und Drang...but not enough meaning."[2] "Cold War tensions abound."[5] **Final Word** The director's gives us a dysfunctional family and asks us to honor and feel nostalgia for the abusive alcoholic in the family, in a co-dependent conclusion—I don't thinks so! Melville got it right the first time. Ahab gets what he has coming.

Korea: The Forgotten War

1987   USA   b/w

Korean War: Documentary	2.0

This is a dry, fact-laden wartime documentary that is stuck on fast forward. The images and facts flash by so quickly that, at times, it's impossible to follow what is happening. Narrated by Robert Stack, with an occasional map thrown in, the images on the screen appear to accurately reflect what we are being told, though the quality of the film is poor and the cuts so frequent that it's difficult to follow. The director treats all events equally—rather than focusing on key events, he rushes past them all. The last year of the war, which stalemated along the 38th parallel into modern trench warfare, is skipped over. The political complexity of this war, and the later peace negotiations are not fully explored either. However, this film does present a balanced picture of Gen. MacArthur's role in the early success of the war, particularly the landing at Inchon, and of his later refusal to accept that the Chinese would enter the war. MacArthur's open conflict with President Truman and the Joint Chiefs of Staff is acknowledged, and the film duly notes that he deserved to be sacked for attempting to widen the conflict with China, including the use of nuclear weapons. The film makes mention of a few interesting historical facts—US planes used napalm for the first time and helicopters were first used to evacuate the wounded to MASH units. Surprisingly, there is no mention of the air superiority American fighters and pilots established. This war, begun on June 25, 1950, with 95,000 N. Korean soldiers invading the South, ended on July 27, 1953, with 35,000 American dead and 100,000 wounded. The end came because it was too expensive for the proxy nations (China and the Soviet Union) to continue. This documentary does note that thousands of American deaths and casualties suffered in the last year were incurred primarily because American negotiators were unwilling to return Chinese prisoners of war who did not want to repatriate.

What the critics say No available reviews. **Final Word** For those who like their MacArthur on a pedestal, try the biopic *MacArthur* or *Inchon,* financed by the Korean Unification Church (Moonies).

Lafayette Escadrille

1958   USA   b/w   d. William A. Wellman

WW I: Aerial Romance   1.5

Directed by William A. Wellman, whose earlier credits include *Battleground*, *The Story of G.I. Joe* and *Wings*, this movie might have been better titled "Lafayette Escargot." Wellman, who served in the Lafayette Escadrille, had intended this film to be a salute to the squadron as well as a summing up of his war experiences. Due to studio interference Wellman left the set prior to finishing the film. Now for the reason. The movie stars Tab Hunter (there's reason enough right there) as Thad Walker, a young man from a wealthy family who gets into trouble with the law and runs off to France to join the Lafayette Escadrille. During training he strikes an officer, and while awaiting court-martial goes AWOL, and nearly beats a French soldier to death in order to steal the soldier's uniform. Hiding out at his French girlfriend's (Etchika Choureau) apartment (she's a prostitute), he starts working for a pimp. While escorting an American general to a house of ill repute, he tells a sob story and the general intervenes by getting him a commission in the newly formed US Air Corps. (Right!) Poorly acted and filled with melodrama having little to do with the famed unit, we are asked to give a damn about a character without a single redeeming quality. The movie simply fails to create any credible circumstances to explain this character's behavior. Near the end, there's two-minutes of aerial combat that's average at best. The movie also has a happy ending for Thad and Renée. If you believe this, it's unlikely you are a war movie type of guy. A Hollywood studio has once again turned a fascinating war story into a truly dismal movie.

What the critics say Critics rate this movie 2.0 to 3.0. "The director's valedictory film, on a subject close to his heart, is a curious disappointment, flat and disjointed affair."[1] "Part actioner with typical romantic lead."[2] "Hunter is banal in the lead."[5] **Final Word** The Escadrille de Casse Nieuport 124 was formed in 1916 as war propaganda by a group of wealthy Americans headed by William Vanderbilt. Their goal was to push the American public towards the Allied cause with newspaper accounts of these pilots. They financed the training, paid for uniforms and mess accounts and gave the pilots $250 for every German plane shot down. All total, 180 American pilots, mostly well-to-do sportsmen and soldiers of fortune, served in this famed unit.

The Last Castle
2001 USA color d. Rod Lurie

| Military Justice: Prison Takeover | 2.0 |

Be warned! This slick and mildly entertaining film will require a serious suspension of disbelief at many levels. *The Last Castle* features Robert Redford as Lt. General Irwin, a highly respected officer and former Vietnam POW who has been court-martialed and given a 10-year prison sentence. Apparently Gen. Irwin, while conducing an overseas commando operation, ignored available intelligence and directly disobeyed an order. This resulted in the death of 8 soldiers. (Anyone who has been in the service knows that some major who has been passed over for promotion several times would have been blamed.) There's a US military prison that had previously been a castle (I don't think so!) This movie appears to borrow the castle notion from *The Colditz Story*, a true story about British POW who were housed in a German castle. There's a bureaucratic psychopath, or what most of us have come to think of as "the warden," Col. Winter (James Gandolfini). He's strictly out of a "B" prison movie somewhere on the Mississippi delta in the 1930s. Somehow the quiet and unassuming Gen. Irwin, who is completely lacking in military bearing and with an emotional range somewhere between a wan smile and a slight frown, manages to instill in every prisoner a sense of self-respect and duty as a soldier. And even though Irwin lacks charisma, he manages to galvanize Hispanic, Black and white gangs, at war with one another, to take over the prison. (Watching Reford take off his shirt and lift rocks is not an inspiring sight, trust me.) And, of course, all the prisoners are redeemable because, you guessed it—they are patriotic. (This move is so insipid that it makes inmates look more redeemable than reformers and do-gooders.) While the cat-and-mouse games leading to the take over of the prison are fun to watch, the actual takeover is strictly comic book—homemade bazookas, catapults, flaming slingshots and water cannon grappling hook. But what's most disappointing is the film's complete predictability from beginning to end, without subplots, surprising twists, or actual drama about the real threats that exist in prison.

What the critics say Critics rate this movie 1.0 to 2.5. "Stale drama of redemption...miscasts Redford as an action hero."[1] "The script is swimming in movie clichés."[2] **Final Word** The best movie on this subject is *The Hill*, starring Sean Connery.

The Last Detail

1973   USA   color   d. Hal Ashby

Military Life: Comedy-Drama	3.5

This military slice-of-life film, adapted from a novel by Darryl Ponicsan, is a story of two incorrigible down-and-out Navy petty officers assigned to escort a young seaman to the naval prison at Portsmith, New Hampshire. Before they arrive at the prison, five days later, petty officers "Bad Ass" Buddusky (Jack Nicholson) and "mule" (Otis Young) give the sincere and naive 18-year-old kleptomaniac Meadows (Randy Quaid), the best time of his young life. The petty officers are two "lifers" whose only ambitions are to stay in the Navy and drink beer. The master-at-arms commandeers them from transit housing to act as "chasers," that is, basically military security who escort Meadows to prison. He has just received an eight-year prison term for the theft of a polio contribution box (about $40) from the base PX. Meadows, a sad-sack loser who couldn't get mad if he tried, is a conforming, chronically nice guy that Bad Ass refers to as a "classic pussy." As this buddy journey unwinds, the escorts begin to feel sorry for their prisoner, figuring he got a raw deal. Along the way, they try to do something for him. Inhabiting low-end bus stops, cheap bars and hotels, the three begin a week-long binge of beer drinking, porno shop hopping, fighting, ice skating and barbecuing in the middle of winter. Finally, they get Meadows laid by a cute young prostitute (Carol Kane), or as "Bad Ass" tells him—"welcome to the wonderful world of pussy, kid." In places the movie is touching and funny, and ultimately sad. Nicholson and Quaid give very solid performances, but this movie, shot in faded light with a hollow sound track, never quite takes off—at times it's quiet and slow-moving and feels improvised. The script itself was never fleshed out to reveal enough about the characters or the side of life they were exposing us to.

What the critics say Critics rate this movie 4.0 to 5.0. "Foul-mouthed weekend odyssey, with a few well-observed moments for non- "Superior comedy- "A salty, bawdy, hilarious and very touching story."[6] **Final Word** It's fun to see the real Nicholson, before he became "Jack." While often too cute and predictable, this movie does has some real fun along the way.

The Lighthorsemen

1987 AUS color d. Simon Wincer

World War I: Cavalry Combat	5.0

This movie chronicles the true-life events of the Australian Light Horse at the battle of Beesheba, where British and Australian forces confronted Turkish and German forces in Palestine in 1917. This was a victory seized from near disaster by the Light Horse, after 60,000 infantry troops were unable to take Beesheba. With water supplies running out, the Light Horse broke through entrenched infantry and captured the city. This movie has three things going for it: Some of the most spectacular cinematography of any war film you will ever see; outstanding performances by the entire cast; and the highest degree of military realism—particularly with cavalry—you will ever encounter. The story is straightforward. A young man, played with wonderful innocence by Peter Phelps, joins the Light Horse and is immediately shipped with the 4th Brigade to Palestine. This brigade is combat-hardened from numerous battles, including Gallipoli. He struggles to earn the respect of the three other men (Jon Blake, John Walton and Tim McKenzie) in his unit and to prove himself. Ultimately, he is unable to kill but remains accepted by his Light Horse mates and transfers to the field ambulance. With no stereotypes and few clichés, the movie is a series of skirmishes and several subplots leading to a cavalry charge that exceeds that seen in the *Charge of the Light Brigade*. As in many Australian war movies, there is no lack of potshots at British military command and its general incompetence and misuse of Australian soldiers. As one Light Horseman comments on the arrival of a new British general, "Look at the bastard! Typical bloody idiot Tommy brass—wouldn't know a horse from a camel."

What the critics say Critics rate this movie 3.0 to 3.5. "Sweeping wide-screen adventure, stunningly filmed...genuinely exciting."[2] "The thrilling true story...sweeping saga."[3] "Compelling WW I drama...superbly filmed...fine performances."[5] "Entertaining film marked by absolutely spectacular riding sequence."[6] **Final Word** The critics are unusually harsh on this outstanding war movie (see low ratings), and disparaging of the character development. Ignore them—they are bloody idiots. This is a must-see war movie—go and rent or buy it immediately.

The Long and the Short and the Tall
1960   GBR   b/w   d. Leslie Norman

WW II: Jungle Patrol	1.5

Directed by Leslie Norman, this overwrought drama is about a British patrol that turns on itself in the Malayan jungle—to quote the cartoon character Pogo, "We have met the enemy and he is us." A seven-man patrol, led by a Sgt. Mitchum (Richard Todd), is involved in a special operations mission using "sonic deception," (tape-recorded sounds to mislead Japanese intelligence about the movement of British troops). From the start, the patrol bickers and complains. This quickly devolves into a lack of discipline and ultimately into intense personal animosities (did I say they don't like each other). What makes this all unappealing is that there doesn't appear to be any obvious reason for it. The leader of these vitriolic outbursts is Pvt. Bamforth (Laurence Harvey), who's aggressive, critical and emotionally histrionic (making you hope that a sniper puts a bullet in his head to shut him up). Because this movie is based on a play by writer Willis Hall, one is forced to contemplate the possibility that there might be a serious message. Without an officer to lead the patrol, the simplest understanding of this movie would be that it's an elitist statement about the uncouth and undisciplined lower-class rabble that constitutes enlisted men. Lacking discipline and authority, they are as likely to fall on their own bayonets as the enemies. And in fact, their lack of leadership does eventually result in their demise. Near the end, the worst of the lot, Pvt. Bamforth, is all for saving their Japanese prisoner when everyone else wants to off him. Perhaps this is an attempt at irony—the real idiot of the group is the most humanitarian. However, in the big scheme of this war the death of this prisoner appears inconsequential as a statement about the morality of these men (particularly when they are all killed by Japanese soldiers). This rancor filled low-budget, low-action, stage-bound movie eventually wears you down.

What the critics say Critics rate this movie 2.5 to 3.0. "Stark war drama with the emphasis on character. Vivid at the time, it now seems very routine."[1] "Well-delineated account...focusing on their conflicting personalities."[2] **Final Word** An attempt at a cynical, edgy war drama that fails on every level. The British produced a film very similar to this one, *Too Late the Hero*. In both films the real battle is class warfare.

The Longest Day

1962   USA   b/w   d. Ken Annakin/ Andrew Marton et al.

World War II: Big Battle	2.0

This is a three-hour epic Hollywood, big-budget, all-star (43 named stars) extravaganza and flagwaving tribute to the Allied soldiers who participated in the D-Day invasion at Normandy. The invasion, on June 6, 1944, involved 3 million men, 11,000 planes and 4,000 ships. There is also John Wayne, Robert Mitchum, Henry Fonda, Richard Burton, and too many others to bother naming. (The Allies couldn't possibly lose with this cast.) Covering the 24-hour period that constituted the invasion, the film touches on all aspects of the invasion—from the Allied and the German perspective, to the grunts and generals. Get the picture? This is a really bad movie. Where to begin? With interminable introductions and stars reiterating what a really important moment this is the film is an hour too long. A dozen addled moments border on the bizarre in an attempt to show the small events. For example, the scene of a priest who keeps diving under water to find his confirmation kit. Or perhaps it's Richard Burton as a wounded RAF pilot, giving a Shakespearean soliloquy on war, claiming he is on morphine when to all the world it looks like bourbon. Now, consider Peter Lawford in a fashionable turtleneck sweater leading British commandos with a soldier playing bagpipes! (There are just too many of these preposterous moments to share them all.) Because the story is told from so many points of view, no coherent story unfolds. More importantly, no attempt is made to question any of the strategic or tactical military decisions being made. Unless, of course, you are in the German army, which the movie portrays as the most inept army of all time. On the positive side, there are some terrific battle scenes and superior special effects. But with three directors, five writers, and too many egos, *The Longest Day* was out of control.

What the critics say Critics rate this movie 4.0 to 5.0. "A triumphant marriage between cinema and one of the greatest days in all of history."[5] "Owes as much to Hollywood's bloated biblical pictures as it does the war films of the 1940s and 1950s."[6] "Magnificent re-creation...this epic film succeeds where others may fail."[7] **Final Word** Thank goodness it was Ike and not producer Darryl F. Zanuck who planned the Normandy Invasion.

The Lost Battalion

2001 USA color tv d. Russell Mulcahy

WW I: Meuse-Argonne Offensive   3.5

Just five weeks before the Armistice was signed, 600,000 American troops advanced north across the Argonne Forest in the opening attack of a 47-day campaign known as the Meuse-Argonne Offensive. This fact-based story shows the Army's 77th Division, 308th Battalion advancing ahead of the main body and becoming isolated and surrounded by German troops. Led by Maj. Whittlesey (Rick Schroder), the division held out four days against a larger counter-attacking German force without resupply of food or ammunition. Shelled by American artillery, the 77th suffered heavy casualties, with only 200 of the nearly 500 men surviving. For this, Maj. Whittlesey, Capt. Holderman and Capt. McMurtry all receive the Congressional Medal of Honor. (American troops suffered 115,000 casualties, with 15,000 deaths, in the offensive that ended the war.) While focusing on the heroism of American soldiers, this very good movie makes no bones about how they became isolated. This film clearly blames the American commander, Gen. Alexander, for ordering the advance with an unprotected flank. Though not specifically stated, perhaps having three Congressional Medals of Honor winners helped deflect the ineptness of high command. The battle scenes are intense and realistic, but this movie becomes static when there's no fighting. There's much playing up of the fact that these soldiers are from New York and are an ethnic mix, so much so that it begins to feel too politically correct. And, unfortunately, the only thing not sanitized here is the combat. The soldiers are all sympathetic characters who don't swear or get mad, and all their officers are competent and caring. Whittlesey, portrayed as an idealist, is opposed to the war in principle but chose to be a soldier out of a sense of duty. Even when he verbally protests his commander's orders, he's clearly a team player. Perhaps the most disappointing aspect of this movie is Schroder's understated performance, which brings a good movie to a standstill at times.

What the critics say Critics rate this movie 2.5 to 3.0. **Final Word** This is a good movie with outstanding combat action. While it attempts to tell an important story, it never quite decided what that story is was.

The Manchurian Candidate

1962   USA   b/w   d. John Frankenheimer

Cold War: Political Thriller	3.0

This critically acclaimed amalgam of Cold War and 1950s-era paranoia is an AFI top 100 and is considered a film classic. A political thriller, adapted from the best selling novel by Richard Condon, *The Manchurian Candidate* is about a conspiracy to assassinate the President of the United States. (It was also withdrawn from release after Kennedy's assassination and not rereleased for many years.) How well does it hold up forty years later? The short answer is, not very well. It's a noirish and preposterous concoction of political paranoia that is completely foolish. Let's sum up. A haranguing, publicity-seeking, red-baiting, Joseph McCarthy-style Republican Senator (James Gregory) is seeking the presidency. His coldly ambitious and calculating wife (Angela Lansbury) enters into a conspiracy with Russian and Chinese Communists to have a brainwashed American soldier assassinate the President. Coincidentally, this soldier turns out to be the ambitious wife's son Raymond (Laurence Harvey), which is just fine with her. Are you still with me here? Raymond was captured while on patrol during the Korean Conflict, along with Frank Sinatra and other members of their company. They were then brainwashed, and Raymond singled out to be the assassin. For a political thriller the movie is slow-moving and talkative, with numerous irrelevant digressions. There's even a treacherous Chinese scientist who conducts the brainwashing. As the smartest and funniest character in the film, he tells a colleague—"His brain is not only washed, as they say, it has been dry cleaned." Feminists might have problems with the manipulating mother as the source of all the machination, which borders on evil itself. In many ways, this film is Hollywood's political left responding to "McCarthism." It's hard to know what part politics played in the film's acclaim, but the hysteria it resonates with continues to provide a minor level of interest.

What the critics say Critics rate this movie 4.5 to 5.0. "Insanely plotted but brilliantly handled."[1] "One of the wildest fabrications any author has ever tried to palm off on a gullible public."[4] "Darker level of paranoia where all the fears and hatreds of the Cold War coalesce."[6] **Final Word** I suspected all along that the Communists and Republicans had secretly gotten together, long before Reagan's "Evil Empire" and the fall of the Berlin Wall.

A Man Escaped
1956 FRA b/w subtitles d. Robert Bresson

WW II: Prisoner-of-War	4.5

This is one of the best prisoner-of-war movies ever made. Written and directed by French "New Wave" director Robert Bresson, who spent a year in a German prison during the war, he tells a minimalist story of one man's determined efforts to escape. With images infused with a dark realism and a sparse dialog, utilizing voice-over narration by the imprisoned Lt. Fontaine (Francois Leterrier), we watch Fontaine set about escaping a German prison in Lyon, France in 1943. Bresson sticks close to the fact-based story of André Devigny, who consulted on this film. We learn very little about Fontaine other than he's a member of the French resistance who has been sentenced to be executed for espionage and a bombing. The only other thing we come to know about him is his determination to escape his circumstances. Filmed mostly in his cell or immediate confines, Fontaine begins to make contact with other prisoners and devise escape plans. If the details of this film were not factual, the director would probably be considered indulgent. Here we see day-by-day, week after week, a plan emerge and get carried out. The one constant is Fontaine's ambivalence about action. He has made a plan, but taking the leap from the safe denial that doing nothing will work out, to the certainty of being killed if caught escaping is what this movie is ultimately about. It's also what separates Fontaine from most the prisoners around him—he confronts his ambivalence with action. A remarkable aspect of this escape is how many chances he takes in trusting prisoners. In each instance his acts of trust (faith) guide his escape, which would not have been possible without them. Bresson alludes to a spiritual aspect to this with Mozart's Great Mass in C Minor. This movie manages to capture the constant tension and fear that inhabits this world. Bresson gives us an austere and isolated environment in which each prisoner is ultimately alone with himself and his reality.

What the critics say Critics rate this movie 4.0 to 5.0. "A riveting drama set almost entirely within a prison cell.[3] "There's an excruciating realism about Bresson's account."[5] "A cold, unsentimental examination of isolation."[7] **Final Word** This movie is the antithesis of the highly stylized and often empty POW dramas we are familiar with.

Marine Raiders

1944   USA   b/w   d. Harold Schuster

WW II: Classic '40s Flagwaver   2.5

This 1940s wartime melodrama uses a formula seldom deviated from for the past sixty years. A soap opera is sandwiched between two battle sequences, which leads war movie guys to think it's going to be a serious war movie. Here, the battles are being fought by the 1st Marine Raider Battalion at Guadalcanal and on the islands of Torokina and Puruata. With the generous use of documentary footage and reasonably good special effects, the combat scenes are intense and well staged. The movie also includes a handful of stock characters who mostly joke around when not fighting. While this movie is short on real people, it does accomplish something rarely seen in war films, which is develop a friendship between Lt. Col. Lockhard (Pat O'Brien) and Capt. Dan Craig (Robert Ryan) that seems genuine and goes beyond camaraderie (no it's not the romantic interest in this film, for those of you experiencing gender panic). While war movies often refer to the intense relationships created by war, they seldom create one on screen. Later, after being stationed in Australia, Capt. Craig falls in love with a young Australian nurse, Lt. Ellen Foster (Ruth Hussey), and they impulsively decide to get married. As a result, there's very little romance and a lot of tame desperation without the slightest chemistry. However, marital bliss is interrupted when Capt. Craig is wounded by Japanese bombers and is immediately shipped to the States. Unable to say good-bye, he mopes around a lot before he's reassigned to the Marine Corps Training Center in San Diego. At this point a great deal of wartime propaganda is inserted which features a lot of marching Marines. Craig also blames his friend Lt.Col. Lockhard for busting up his romance—don't worry they work it out. At the end, Hussey gives a speech about the price women pay during wartime, a theme raised earlier in the movie. This low-budget romantic actioner, with the emphasis on romance, actually manages to break out of the mold in several small ways.

What the critics say Critics rate this movie 1.0 to 3.0. "Standard romantic flagwaver."[1] "Typical RKO WW 2 film."[2] "One of the lessor contributions to the story of the US Marines at Guadalcanal."[8] **Final Word** This movie is interchangeable with dozens of similar films, many of them made fairly recently.

M*A*S*H

1970   USA   color   d. Robert Altman

| Korean War: Comedy | 4.0 |

A popular box-office hit in the 1970s and cult classic today, *M*A*S*H*, written under the pseudonym Richard Hooker, is a movie of unrelenting irreverence and anarchic impulses. Set during the Korean War, three young surgeons, Captains "Hawkeye" (Donald Sutherland), "Trapper John" (Elliott Gould) and "Duke" (Tom Skerritt) have been drafted into the Army. We watch as they battle it out with the military chain of command at a Mobile Army Surgical Hospital unit (4077th MASH) three miles from the front. Contrary to what many critics have suggested, this is not an antiwar film but rather an anti-establishment film. While it makes limited comment about war, there's no limit to ridiculing military authority; and these young doctors make the perfect foil with their "surgeons-as-gods" status exempting them from conforming to military conduct. (Yes, the war is the Korean War, but this movie is really about the Vietnam War.) In this movie the anal retentives (lifers) are Maj. Frank Burns (Robert Duvall) and Maj. "Hot Lips" Houlihan (Sally Kellerman), who see the draftee surgeons as godless, immoral misfits. The film is not a "black" comedy." It's not about the gory surgery and the death all about the MASH unit, rather it strives for something simpler and easier to attack—authority in all its forms. Whatever form authority takes these three surgeons are against it. There are simply too many funny scenes, asides and characters to describe in full—from the microphone in the tent of Majors Burns and Houlihan broadcasting their sexual tryst, to the frequent insertion of comic PA announcements. However, where this film misses is in not going for something more poignant or darker. The director cops out with a lengthy football game at the end, rather than focusing on the departure of Hawkeye and Duke, the two characters at the center of all the mayhem. In retrospect, *M*A*S*H* could have been so much more. Most people will know this movie today from the long-running TV series, a less rebellious and acerbic adaptation, starring Alan Alda.

What the critics say Critics rate this movie 4.5. to 5.0. "Gave meaning to the word irreverence."[2] "One of the most devastating black comedies and potent antiwar films to hit the screen."[3] "An all out antiwar festival."[5] **Final Word** Very funny and well worth renting for the irreverent at heart.

236

The McConnell Story

1955 USA color d. Gordon Douglas

Korean War: Comedy-Romance Biopic   1.5

This films opens with a US Air Force general offering a salute to Capt. McConnell and the men who served our country. Captain Joe McConnell was a true American war hero. He served both as a B-17 navigator, flying missions over Europe during WW II, and later as an Air Force jet fighter pilot (F-80s and F-86s) during the Korean War. He was America's first "triple jet ace," and credited with shooting down sixteen Mig-15 jet fighters over "Mig Alley." After the war, he was killed while testing jet fighters at Edwards AFB in Southern California. Unfortunately, that's about all you're going to learn about him from this movie. Capt. McConnell gets the full-Hollywood, including June Allyson playing his wife, the same exact silly character she played for Jimmy Stewart in *Strategic Air Command* and for Humphrey Bogart in *Battle Circus*. Alan Ladd, starring as McConnell, is stiff and lifeless in this role. For the most part this movie is nothing more than a tepid romantic comedy, with too many overly cute and charming moments between Ladd and Allyson. There is not the slightest insight into what motivated McConnell to want to fly or excel and take risks as a fighter pilot or later as a test pilot. There is some interesting footage of a German Me-163 rocket plane shot from B-17s over Germany, and there are many excellent shots of F-80s and F-86s. However, the movie refuses to focus on the lives of pilots and the difficulties they were up against during the Korean War. In fact, there is no discussion of the war at all. I suspect if McConnell had seen this film first he would have refused to have anything to do with it.

What the critics say Critics rate this movie 1.0 to 3.0. "Crude, obvious and saccharine biopic."[1] "Weepy yet effective fictional biography."[2] "Run-of-the-mill romanticized biopic."[7] "Limp biopic."[8] **Final Word** I suspect the real McConnell was neither as funny nor romantic as portrayed here. What an embarrassing portrayal of a true war hero. Watch *Reach for the Sky* to see a superior story of British fighter pilot hero Douglas Bader.

The McKenzie Break

1970 IRE/GBR color d. Lamont Johnson

World War II: Prisoner-of-War   3.5

This is an exciting *cat and mouse* prisoner-of-war drama with a twist, *The McKenzie Break* is about an escape attempt by 600 German officers who are being held at a British POW camp. Directed by Lamont Johnson and adapted from the novel "The Bowmanville Break" by Sidney Shelley, there may well be some historical basis for this movie, as German POWs actually attempted to rendezvous with a submarine in an escape attempt. The film has many clever twists and turns and few lulls in the action. At the center of the story are Capt. Connors (Brian Keith), a hard-drinking Irish captain in an intelligence unit in the British army, and Capt. Schluetter (Helmut Griem), a cunning Nazi U-boat commander who is plotting an escape from the camp. Conners has been brought in to help the commander of Camp McKenzie, in Scotland, regain some semblance of control over the German officers. What ensues is a fascinating battle of wits as well as a clash of personalities. Capt. Schluetter, arrogant and ruthless, has cleverly manipulated a series of confrontations in order to disguise the escape. However, Capt. Connors, a suspicious and skillful officer, driven by his own personal demons and a serious drinking problem, tries to make this an important intelligence coup in an effort to salvage a career near ruin. Connors also appears willing to risk letting the Germans escape in order to raise the intelligence stakes. The excellent acting and the tight, well-paced script makes this an exciting movie to watch, and the ending is not a cop-out. If this movie has any major flaws it is the over-elaborate escape plan, and perhaps the fact that it reveals too soon what the British know about the plan. This movie would have been more interesting if the German captain had not been of the "evil" Nazi variety, willing to sacrifice his men for his own personal ambitions (German POWs did hold "courts of honor" and executed guilty prisoners.)

What the critics say Critics rate this movie 3.0 to 4.0. "Engrossing movie fare."[2] "A taut...drama with an original twist. An imaginative, intelligent script...crackling direction."[4] "Taut, suspenseful drama."[5] **Final Word** An entertaining movie that is well worth renting—sauerkraut and meat pies all around!

Mediterraneo

1991 ITA color subtitles d. Gabriele Salvatores

WW II: Comedy   4.5

The epilogue to this charming and nostalgic comedy states—this movie is "dedicated to all those who are running away." In 1941 eight Italian soldiers are sent to garrison a small remote Greek island in the Aegean. Although the island had been previously occupied by the Germans, all the men on the island have been deported and the Germans have left—so begins a three-year idyll in which the Italian soldiers are stranded and forgotten in paradise. This group of "misfits" is led by a young lieutenant (Claudio Bigagli), a teacher and painter who immediately abdicates command and takes to painting frescoes. Vassilissa (Vanna Barba), a young and beautiful prostitute, introduces herself to the men and a schedule is worked out for them to visit her. Each man finds his own way. One reads poetry and eventually falls in love with Vassilissa; two brothers fall in love with a shepherdess and have a sexual-spiritual relationship. The demanding and tough-minded sergeant (Diego Abatantuono), who needs order, eventually becomes introspective and free-spirited. The soldiers dance, drink, play soccer, and allow their lives to drift in a way that we have all dreamed about. The essence of this film is simplicity. As a result of being trapped on the island, each soldier lets go of his ambitions for the real world and learns to live in the moment. Initially relieved about being saved from the war, as the years pass their thoughts eventually return to the idea of going home. Ambition is rekindled. They must return to help rebuild their nation, find careers and most importantly, find their way in life. Filled with many fun and touching moments, the photography is beautiful as only a Greek isle can be, and the wonderful score is a siren's song. Having won an Academy Award for Best Foreign Film, *Mediterraneo* strangely enough engendered considerable hostility from the critics. This movie is for those who don't have to hold on so tightly that they cannot dream about and laugh at what is lost.

What the critics say Critics rate this movie 2.0 to 4.0. "Based on a true story...this picture is a pleasant, bitter-sweet, nostalgic comedy."[1] "Catering unashamedly to the saccharin-loving movie-goer."[3] "Languid, charming comedy."[5] "A pleasant, bittersweet fable."[7] **Final Word** Yes, you will want to run away to an Aegean island, for a brief moment, but it will pass in time.

Mein Krieg

1993   GER   b/w   d. Harriet Eder/Thomas Kufus

World War II: Documentary	2.0

The basic premise of this film is interesting; six German soldiers, all amateur photographers, have filmed their participation in Germany's invasion of the Soviet Union in 1941. As their 8-mm record is being shown, the soldiers are interviewed by the filmmakers about the events they experienced. The filmmakers appear to have two objectives—to show a unique firsthand account of the war, and to indict these soldiers. Unfortunately, there is nothing unique or even interesting about these amateur attempts, which are like bad home movies with no coherent picture of the war. There are no action or combat scenes and nearly all the film footage is comprised of bombed-out buildings and damaged tanks. The level of comment is mundane, and for the most part these men have very little to say about what is transpiring on the screen (because nothing is happening). However, the real objective of this movie is to suggest that these men are unrepentant as soldiers. While there is no explicit effort to incriminate them for Nazi war atrocities, when one former soldier is asked about the shooting of Russian peasants, he responded, "Do I have to answer that? Spare me the answer." One of the men recorded the capture of 90,000 Russian soldiers, mostly wounded and starving. When asked what happened to them, he responded, "I don't know, and better we don't know." Mostly, we see old men trying to explain their actions when they were 18 years old. They were simply obeying orders, fighting for their lives and the lives of their fellow soldiers. They were not Nazis, had no political agenda, and were the same as soldiers in almost any army. Most seemed proud of their service, and one noted—"A German soldier fights to the final victory," (or in this case defeat). They all seemed emotionally detached from the destruction they had caused, and why not, as it had occurred nearly fifty years earlier. This film is an attempted indictment of the "good German" mentality that was responsible for so much destruction in Europe. It doesn't succeed.

What the critics say No available reviews. **Final Word** Of the 5.7 million Red Army soldiers taken prisoner, over 3 million died of starvation, disease and maltreatment. Forty-five percent of German prisoners died. This film is good for graduate students seeking war crime tribunal candidates.

Memphis Belle

1990 GBR color d. Michael Caton-Jones

WW II: Air War over Europe   3.0

Filled with nostalgic memory of World War II, *Memphis Belle* tells the fact-based story of a B-17 aircrew as it prepares for its final mission. Stationed in England in 1943, the Memphis Belle (8th Air Force, 324th Squadron, 91st Heavy Bombardment Group) survived 24 missions without casualty, and will be rotated back to the states after completing its 25th mission. The film focuses exclusively on the final and extremely dangerous mission over Germany. Part of what makes the film interesting is that it's derived from a 1944 documentary film, *Memphis Belle: A Story of a Flying Fortress*, by William Wyler, which tells the same story. (In fact, some of the original documentary footage is included in this movie, and the co-producer, Catherine Wyler, is the daughter of William Wyler.) Unfortunately, the newer film never gets into the controversial politics of daylight bombing, which proved to have limited effectiveness but resulted in enormous losses of planes and crews. (The epilogue noted that over 200,000 Allied air crews lost their lives over Europe.) The story centers on a young aircrew having to cope with their upcoming last mission and the tension that emerges among them. There are several desperate and melancholy romances, and the lush score speaks volumes about this film's commercial intent. Unfortunately, there are too many predictable circumstances and familiar characters. The special effects are well done and the final mission is tense and bloody, but with too many shattering moments taking place all at once. What this film does best is explore the real fears and dreams of an aircrew preparing for its last mission.

What the critics say Critics rate this movie 3.0 to 4.0. "It's still hard to believe that such a cornball script could be concocted in 1990".[2] "Satisfying Hollywood version of the documentary of the same name."[5] **Final Word** Disappointing in that it never gets below the surface of the characters or the issues involved in daylight bombing. I highly recommend *Command Decision* and *Twelve O'Clock High* for the serious war geeks. All the rest should enjoy this movie.

Men in War

1957 USA b/w d. Anthony Mann

Korean War: Infantry Combat   2.5

Directed by Anthony Mann and based on the novel *Day Without End (Combat)* by Van Van Praag, the action takes place in Korea in September, 1950. A battered platoon (2nd Platoon, D Company, 34th Infantry) is surrounded by North Korean and Communist Chinese soldiers as UN forces are retreating all around them. Led by Lt. Benson (Robert Ryan), these soldiers are attempting to reach and secure Hill 465 in an effort to reunite with their battalion and escape entrapment. As all this transpires, the infantrymen encounter Sgt. Montana (Aldo Ray), who is racing in a jeep with a mute, combat-shocked colonel strapped in, trying to get to safety. The story that ultimately unfolds is about the confrontation between Lt. Benson and Sgt. Montana— two hard-nosed and experienced veterans who dislike one another. Like nearly all Korean War movies *Men in War* ignores politics and the big picture. There is no examination of war beyond soldiers trying to survive moment-to-moment. Soldiers confront artillery shelling, mines, snipers, North Koreans dressed as Americans and, at the end, attack two machine gun emplacements. Like nearly every low-budget Korean War movie, this one manages to get at least one thing right, in this case it portrays the anxieties and fear soldiers face in combat. However, the focus on the conflict between Benson and Montana, and Sgt. Montana's obsessive concern for the colonel, is not only contrived but ultimately degenerates into a soap opera. Though slow moving and tedious, to its credit the movie offers an uncompromising view of men in war.

What the critics say Critics rate this movie 2.5. to 4.5. "Stereotyped small-scale war heroics; film makes its point but fails to entertain."[1] "Good action scenes distinguishing usual story."[2] "A two-fisted account...told with a general air of excitement, tension and action."[4] "A worthwhile effort with some good action sequences."[5] "Low-keyed Korean War effort...still quietly effective."[8] **Final Word** Well-acted, this film has a contrived plot to distract viewers from its low-budget, low-action formula.

Men of Honor

2000 USA color d. George Tillman, Jr.

Whether you like this movie or not will depend on your tolerance for inspiring stories. Yes, such stories are generally predictable and usually exaggerated for dramatic effect, but they also help keep alive the myth that everyone can realize their dreams. This movie tells the story of Carl Brashear, the first Black-American to qualify as a Navy master diver, and the first amputee in the history of the Navy to return to full active duty. This is one of those feel-good movies that used to be reserved for television, but now gets the full-Hollywood. The film stars Cuba Gooding, Jr. as Carl Brashear, in what is probably his best performance to date. It opens with a tired film cliché, and shows Brashear as a child who loved to swim in the ponds of rural Kentucky. It then skips forward to his leaving home to enlist in the Navy during World War II, with only a seventh grade education and his father's last words haunting him, "Don't quit on me, ever!" What follows is a series of emotional events right through to the climatic hearing in which Brashear is reinstated in the Navy as an amputee. There was a strong institutional prejudice in the Navy towards Black seamen holding skilled jobs in the 1940s and 1950s. Another obstacle that confronts Brashear is Master Chief Billy Sunday (Robert DeNiro), a crude, fowl-mouthed, alcoholic, southern racist, who is intent on making Brashear quit the US Navy Dive and Salvage School. (You have probably guessed it by now.) DeNiro ultimately does the right thing and reforms his bigoted and alcoholic ways. Brashear has a romantic interest (Aunjanue Ellis) that is undeveloped. There's also an eccentric based commander (Hal Holbrook), who attempts to have Brashear killed rather than graduate as a Navy diver. (I suspect that this is the part of the movie where we have to accept that the life of Carl Brashear inspired the movie, and that the story might not be totally factual.)

What the critics say Critics rate this movie 2.5 to 3.5. "Old fashion but rock-solid biopic."[2] "Performances are grimly earnest but the lengthy film has too many climaxes to far apart."[7] **Final Word** I suspect the real-life story of Carl Brashear might have been very interesting—the drive to realize his dream against many, many difficult obstacles in life—a story played out quietly by millions of Americans everyday.

Men of the Fighting Lady

1954   USA   color   d. Andrew Marton

| Korean War: Naval Air Combat | 2.5 |

This big-budget and popular war movie is based on two articles written for the *Saturday Evening Post*, James Michener's, "The Forgotten Heroes of Korea," and Navy Commander Harry A. Burns' "The Case of the Blind Pilot." It tells the story of disillusioned naval fighter pilots stationed aboard an aircraft carrier off the coast of Korea in 1953. Two thirds of this movie plays out like a public relations film for the Navy. What plot there is revolves around a conflict between the squadron commander (Frank Lovejoy), who flies recklessly and expects his men to do likewise, and a decorated WW II veteran (Van Johnson) who disdains the commander's tactics and believes pilots shouldn't take unnecessary risks. In addition, the movie showcases jets, a carrier, strafing railroads, a sea rescue and a blind pilot (Dewey Martin) guided back to the carrier. There is also a syrupy voice-over narration filled with wise and annoying observations—"a man has to do what he has to do." It's the voice of the ship's doctor (Walter Pidgeon) whose main duty is to dispense brandy to pilots. On the positive side, this movie does not glorify combat and takes a hard look at the risks these pilots faced. For those who can't get enough of vintage 1950s jets, there are many very good scenes of F9F "Panthers." Among the pilots there is a definite antiwar sentiment—"there are no heroes in Korea" and the war is a "nut house chess game." The pilots see their involvement in the war and the risks they take as having limited strategic value. The movie's answer was to emphasize the pilots' altruism and willingness to risk their lives in order to protect one another. Primarily because of its production values (carrier, jet fighters, excellent aerial footage), this movie is a cut above the routine Korean War actioner. Compared to the more acclaimed and bigger budgeted Korean War carrier movie *Bridges at Toko-Ri*, this is the better of the two.

What the critics say Critics rate this movie 2.5 to 4.0. "Above par Korean War actioner."[2] "Offers plenty of exciting battle footage."[5] "Korean War exploitation...with routine plot and borrowed footage."[8] **Final Word** This is a slightly above average Korean War movie. Watch it primarily to see the old jets, which are a lot of fun to watch.

Merrill's Marauders

1962 USA color d. Samuel Fuller

WW II: Burma Campaign   3.0

This is Samuel Fuller's best war film. It has a tight storyline, good
action, is based on actual people and events, and is not given to
the histrionics and bizarre meanderings his movies typically
exhibit. Loosely based on a book by Charlton Ogburn, this movie
chronicles the exploits of Gen. Frank D. Merrill (Jeff Chandler),
as he led the only American ground forces to fight in Burma
during WW II. This force consisted of 3,000 volunteers who were
known as the 5307th Provisional Composite Unit, popularly
called "Merrill's Marauders." In a three-month span, the unit
crossed 200 miles of jungle undetected, where they wiped out a
Japanese supply depot at Walawbum. They then headed for a
railway depot at Shaduzup and finally pushed to Myitkyina to
meet up with British forces, The unit was then demobilized. In
retrospect, it now seems crazy to have braved the jungle, heat,
humidity and disease (not to mention the Japanese army) for
limited objectives in Burma. This movie is primarily a tribute to
the limits to which men can be pushed and survive as effective
combatants. Jeff Chandler stands out as a determined Gen.
Merrill, who knows he is pushing his men to the limits. The film
focuses on a platoon led by Lt. Stockton (Ty Hardin), who has a
father-son-like relationship with Merrill. Thankfully, Fuller doesn't
resort to his usual cast of crazed and rebellious characters at
each other's throats. These are soldiers simply wanting to
survive under the harshest of conditions. Shot on location in the
Philippines, the action is realistic, as are the simple conflicts of
command that arise from difficult circumstances. Just as
MacArthur's decision to liberate the Philippines was more
political than strategic, the British decision to fight in Burma was
more face saving than important military objective. Unfortunately,
the issue is not explored here. Be aware, that because this fight
was primarily a British effort, the British tend to resent it when it
appears the Americans won it in Burma.

What the critics say Critics rate this movie 2.4 to 4.0.
"Physically exhausting war adventure with emphasis on hand-to-
hand combat and much bloodshed."[1] "This is not a film about
victory, heroism, or the adrenaline rush of action."[6] **Final Word**
Gen. Merrill died from a heart condition during this action, as did
Jeff Chandler before the release of this movie.

Merry Christmas, Mr. Lawrence

1983   GBR/JAP   color   d. Nagisa Oshima

WW II: Prisoner-of-War	2.0

Based on a semiautobiographical novel, *The Seed and the Sower*, by Laurens van der Post, this movie was beautifully filmed in New Zealand and Cook Island, and features a haunting New Age score. The screenplay, co-written by Japanese director Nagisa Oshima, also features rock star David Bowie. Set in a Japanese prisoner-of-war camp on the island of Java in 1943, this movie is one of the most astonishing POW films ever made. At the center of this story is a homoerotic attraction between Maj. Jacques Celliers (David Bowie) and the camp commander Capt. Yonoi (Ryuichi Sakamoto). Billed as an examination of the cultural clash between the Japanese and British soldiers, the story reeks of historical revisionism and ideas of "cultural relativism" that would probably make the upper lip of any living British POW quiver. The film also features Tom Conti as Col. Lawrence and Takeshi Kitano as Sgt. Hara, a brutal guard, who was simply doing a soldier's duty (as explanation for why he was being executed for war crimes). While many critics describe the story as a clash of wills between two officers, Bowie comes across as some sort of "prettyboy" weirdo who is strange even to British officers. His odd behavior seems more related to personal pathology than cultural differences. Equally strange is Col. Lawrence, who suffers many random beatings and nearly dies, then meets with Sgt. Hara in 1946 prior to the sergeant's execution, and tells him—"The truth is, of course, nobody's right." Col. Lawrence appears to be suffering from "Stockholm Syndrome," in which captives identify and become emotionally close to their captors. They then reminisce about the time at Christmas that a drunken Sgt. Hara didn't have Col. Lawrence beaten and killed, and act as if this somehow made Hara a good person. (Unbelievable!) The movie is mostly a lot of nonsense and tension with the pretense of being something more significant.

What the critics say Critics rate this movie 3.0 to 4.5. "It seems to head straight for every cliché perpetuated by the *Bridge of the River Kwai*."[1] "Strange, haunting drama...rewarding for those willing to stick with it."[2] **Final Word** In the conflict between Bushido and the Geneva Convention, this movie wants to split the difference.

A Midnight Clear

1992 USA color d. Keith Gordon

World War II: Antiwar Satire	4.5

This surreal-satire is full of quirky moments and irreverent humor that border on fable. The action takes place in the Ardennes Forest near the French-German border in December 1944, during the Battle of the Bulge. Directed by Keith Gordon and based on a novel by William Wharton, perhaps action is not quite the right word for what is about to transpire. A Lt. Ware (Larry Joshua) has decided that his intelligence recon squad should have smart people if it's truly to be an "intelligence" squad. As a result, he has combed the records of the entire regiment to find the smartest men. (By today's standards we would have to conclude this squad is comprised almost entirely of "nerds" and "geeks.") At half-strength, this six-man squad, fearful and anxiously aware of their own incompetence, is sent to occupy a chateau and monitor German movement in the sector. Then a series of truly strange events begins to transpire, or as Sgt. Will Knott (Ethan Hawke) describes it, "I am not exactly sure what country we are in...I don't know what day it is. I have no watch, so I don't know what time it is. I am not sure of my name. The next thing you know they will be making me a general." Before long the squad is making snowmen mocking Hitler, and nearby German soldiers are responding with a scarecrow and snowball fight. Into this strangely innocent moment reality intrudes when the only member of the squad who truly is crazy ("Mother" played by Gary Sinise) commits an apparently rational act resulting in a tragic event. This film has a very contemporary viewpoint, as one squad member notes—"This particular brand of the German army seems to believe in turning off the war every once in a while." The struggle between the men's innocence and the reality of the war all around them makes a powerful statement about the irrationality of war. This movie is well acted and well directed and will keep you continually off balance and surprised.

What the critics say Critics rate this movie 4.0 to 4.5. "Quietly ironic tale of the idiocies of war."[1] "Top-notch antiwar drama ...filled with insight, irony, and eloquence."[2] "One of the most impressive sleepers in video stores."[6] **Final Word** Up there with *Catch-22* and *King of Hearts*. Watch this movie and be surprised.

247

Midway
1976 USA color d. Jack Smight

WW II: Big Naval Battle   3.5

This Hollywood war epic is a surprisingly adept re-creation of the Battle of Midway. Directed by Jack Smight, *Midway* was conceived as a tribute to the American bicentennial. In the tradition of the 1970s blockbusters (*A Bridge Too Far* and *Tora! Tora! Tora!*), it was released in Sensurround with an all-star cast, including Henry Fonda, Glenn Ford, Robert Mitchum, James Coburn, Hal Holbrook, Cliff Robertson and Robert Wagner. Fortunately, these actors have very little to do. Charlton Heston has the only significant role, which includes a completely out-of-place melodramatic subplot. If you can ignore the story of his pilot son wanting to marry a young Japanese-American girl, you'll see a big battle unfold. The movie opens with scenes from *Thirty-Seconds Over Tokyo* and the "Doolittle Raid" on Japan. It then proceeds to show a command view of the most significant naval battle of the Pacific war. Combining excellent documentary film footage with outstanding special effects, the battle order evolves from both the American and Japanese perspectives. The initial attack plan, by Admiral Yamamoto (Toshiro Mifune), had anticipated a major victory over a crippled American fleet. The full force of the Japanese navy would then strike at the island of Midway, hoping to gain control air lanes throughout the Pacific. This would, hopefully, bring America to the peace table. On the American side was Admiral Nimitz (Henry Fonda), who was able to set up the Japanese for a surprise strike near Midway. As a result, the US won the war's most significant naval battle, crippling the Japanese navy with the loss of four carriers. The movie makes clear that many factors accounted for this victory, including superior intelligence gathering as well as a certain amount of luck. Where this movie really comes alive is showing the carrier planes striking across the open seas, braving enormous losses as this battle hung in the balance. This movie proves to be more than just another flagwaver.

What the critics say Critics rate this move 2.0 to 3.0. "Some of the drama and impact of the great naval battle comes through."[6] "This film is accurate and maintains interest."[7] "An opportunity missed."[8] **Final Word** Check out the documentary *The Battle of Midway* and two less entertaining movies about this battle, *Task Force* and *Wing and a Prayer*.

Mission of the Shark

1991   USA   color   tv   d. Robert Iscove

WW II: Sinking of American Cruiser   4.0

This is a true WW II naval saga about the worst naval disaster in US military history. Well-acted, and with excellent special effects, director Robert Iscove tells the story of the last voyage of the USS *Indianapolis*. In July 1945, the cruiser *Indianapolis* is dispatched on a top-secret mission to the island of Tinian in the Marianas. Its mission is to deliver the uranium core and other components of the atomic bomb that would soon be used to devastate Hiroshima. Under the command of Capt. Charles McVay (Stacy Keach), a highly respected and decorated officer, the order is to proceed with all due haste. After delivering the bomb, Capt. McVay proceeds to Leyte in the Philippines, where the *Indianapolis* is torpedoed by a Japanese sub and immediately sinks. Out of a crew of 1,196 men, 880 are killed during the sinking or exposure in the ocean for five days before being rescued. The core of this film revolves around the sinking of this ship and the sailors' attempts to survive in the ocean. The Navy doesn't find out about the sinking until a seaplane accidentally discovers hundreds of men floating in the ocean 72 hours later. The ocean survival scenes are truly harrowing, with a vicious and gory feeding frenzy by sharks and callous and murderous behavior by fearful and hysterical sailors. Six months after the rescue, Capt. McVay is court-martialed by the Navy for failure to execute zig-zagging maneuvers to evade torpedoes. Even though testimony at the trial doesn't support the effectiveness of this procedure, the captain is court-martialed and accepts being scapegoated "for the good of the service." The epilogue notes that, shortly after the court-martial, the Navy set aside its verdict and reinstated Capt. McVay, who retired in 1949. McVay took his life in 1968. In 2000 Congress fully exonerated him, as did the Navy a year later.

What the critics say Critics rate this movie 3.0 to 4.0. "True WW 2 drama about a long-hushed-up naval scandal."[2] "Terrifying scenes of the men's struggle to survive five days without food or water in the shark-infested ocean."[7] **Final Word** The Japanese had reconfigured torpedoes to carry a sailor (Kaiten or human torpedoe) to replot their course after having been fired (not a good job!). They were available but not used against the *Indianapolis*.

Mister Roberts

1955   USA   color   d. John Ford/Mervyn LeRoy

WW II: Comedy in the Pacific   2.0

Here is another example of a highly acclaimed movie that is very average. With an all-star cast, and adapted from an award-winning Broadway play (novel by Thomas Heggen), the film offers mostly tepid humor and maudlin sentimentality. The setting is a Navy cargo ship in the backwaters of the Pacific near the end of the WW II. The cast includes a crazed captain (James Cagney) who is willing to sacrifice his crew for a promotion; cargo officer Lt. Roberts (Henry Fonda), who is desperate for combat duty; and one Ensign Pulver (Jack Lemmon), a good-hearted slacker in charge of laundry and morale. There's also Doc (William Powell), an old-timer who focuses the story emotionally. This entire movie revolves around the crew's complaints and boredom at sea, while Lt. Roberts intervenes on their behalf with the captain, who is an irascible curmudgeon unsympathetic to their plight. That's it! There's almost nothing else to say about this movie, except that it's not funny. The comic high point is Lt. Roberts throwing the captain's potted palm overboard, with all the seaman crowding around and bowing to the empty pot (I'm telling you the truth here). There are no romances or subplots, only a movie that is overly cute and coy in it's belief that it's funny. Every crewman is a Broadway actor who has been polished until he shines, and the dialogue is just as stilted. Full of set-pieces that are completely predictable, this movie makes *Francis in the Navy* look dark and edgy. Jack Lemmon (Oscar for Best Supporting Actor), is both affable and annoying, but he fortunately disappears for most of the movie. It's really Fonda and Cagney who shine. However, the most unforgivable aspect of this film is an attempt to add emotional *gravitas* to a lightweight piece of fluff by having the highly sympathetic Mister Roberts, who gets his transfer for combat, killed in action.

What the critics say Critics rate this movie 4.5 to 5.0. "Superb comedy-drama."[2] "Gets bogged down; and the whole shebang only works thanks to the all-around performances."[8] **Final Word** This film's success may well have spawned many similarly cute and tepid movies, including *Don't Go Near the Water, Ensign Pulver, Father Goose, Heaven Knows, Mr. Allison, The Horizontal Lieutenant* and *Operation Petticoat.*

Mosquito Squadron

1969 GBR color d. Boris Sagal

WW II: Secret Bombing Mission	2.0

This very average actioner tells the fictional story of British Mosquito fighter pilots who train to drop a "skipping" bomb into a tunnel that leads to a German rocket Skunk Works. This facility houses Germany's next generation V3 and V4 rockets. Training for this mission, in reality, would be like golfers practicing hole-in-ones! *Mosquito Squadron* is a marriage of two earlier but not much better British war films *The Dam Busters* and *633 Squadron*. The convoluted plot requires that the dastardly Germans house RAF prisoners of war near the research facility, where one of the prisoners is the husband of the woman (Suzanne Neve) Flight Leader Quint Munroe (David McCallan) is in pursuit of (everyone thinks her husband is dead). Ultimately, the plot requires that the POWs somehow escape before the bombing takes place. In *The Dam Busters*, based on real events, a skipping bomb was designed to take out dams providing hydroelectric power to German industry. In *633 Squadron*, Mosquitoes were used to bomb a German rocket fuel plant. Clever how this movie combined the two and threw in a tepid romance as well. Unfortunately, too much of this film requires David McCallan to be the principle lead. Watching this milquetoast cringe when an attractive woman chases him is almost too much to bear. McCallan, with all the charm and charisma of a warm pint of English ale, is badly miscast as the heroic fighter pilot who gets the girl, or in this case she gets him. If you are going to make an uninspired, poorly scripted and badly acted actioner, at least have the dignity to cast a rogue hero. Watching McCallan trying to rescue the husband of his girlfriend, without having the guts to tell her that her husband is still alive, and later not telling her the truth after his real death, is as gutless at it gets. This invertebrate may get the girl, but he's surely clueless as to what to do next. For the most part, the special effects are decent, and for the action guys this movie holds a modicum of escapist entertainment value.

What the critics say Critics rate this movie 2.5 to 3.0. "Very minor and belated heroics for double-billing."[1] "Good ensemble performance in a tired story."[2] **Final Word** Unforgivably, this movie never does show the bomb skipping into the tunnel and blowing up the rocket works.

Mutiny

1999 USA color tv d. Kevin Hooks

WW II: Port Chicago Disaster   3.0

As a straightforward fictional telling of a real incident during World War II, *Mutiny* places an ugly mark on US Navy race relations. On July 17, 1944, at Port Chicago in the San Francisco-Bay Area, a Liberty ship that was being loaded with war munitions exploded, and resulted in the death of 320 sailors and injury to 390 more. This was the worst homefront disaster of the war. What makes this incident compelling, beyond the obvious tragedy, is that nearly all the sailors were Black. When 200 of them were forced to return to loading munitions three weeks later, without compassionate leave, they refused. When confronted with court-martial, 150 returned to work. The remaining 50 were court-martialed and found guilty of conspiracy to make a mutiny, and received 15-year prison sentences. A inquiry into the explosion determined that its cause was due to rough handling; however, the story is more complicated. Relevant facts regarding the case never came up at trial, including that the men hadn't received the training or equipment required to safely perform their jobs. In addition, unrealistic loading quotas had been set, almost assuring a serious accident. In 1948 President Truman ordered an end to segregation in the armed forces and commuted the sentences. It's interesting to note the active role Thurgood Marshall, attorney to the NAACP and future Supreme Court Justice, played in attempting to bring to light the unfair trial these men received. Unfortunately, this movie is not up to telling this story in a compelling way. While the performances are generally good, none of the characters or their stories are developed. Equally unexplored are the dramatic focal points of this film—the explosion and subsequent trial. Both are quickly disposed of as if to get to something more important, such as the end of the movie. While *Mutiny* does a good job in showing the racism in the Navy, it never makes the case that these Black sailors were more at risk than white sailors performing similar duties.

What the critics say Critics rate this movie 2.5 to 3.0. **Final Word** A solid job about a wartime tragedy few people today have ever heard about. It's also a reminder how far the military has come—now a model of race relations for our entire society.

The Naked and the Dead

1958   USA   color   d. Raoul Walsh

WW II: Combat in South Pacific	2.0

Directed by Raoul Walsh, this film fails to capture almost any element of Norman Mailer's best selling novel, including its profanity. Which is why Mailer called it—"One of the worst movies ever made." While Mailer is harsh, he is closer to being right than wrong. Set in the South Pacific in 1943, the film opens with an American invasion force establishing a beachhead on a Japanese-held island. The rest of this movie concerns itself with a platoon of soldiers who have been ordered to occupy a mountain pass and report on enemy activity. The platoon treks up and down hills and across streams, and there are irrelevant flashbacks about relationships and numerous scenes of soldiers engaging in antics and sitting around complaining. The story itself revolves around three characters who, unfortunately, are never fully developed: Sgt. Croft (Aldo Ray), a psychopath who is an instinctive leader in the field; Lt. Hearn (Cliff Robertson), an uninvolved rich kid who is ambivalent about exercising authority as an officer; and Gen. Cummings (Raymond Massey), an aloof and incompetent career officer who remains detached from the war and the men he sends into combat. Despite the setting, there are limited action scenes, making the film mostly an examination of command conflict. In a failed attempt to adapt some of the central ideas from the novel, there is a limited examination of power in the conflict between Lt. Hearn and Gen. Cummings. This is really the best part of this movie. Lt. Hearn, who closely identifies with the combat soldier, is dismayed and disdainful of Gen. Cummings, who sees the war as a "chess game" and declares, "The only morality of the future is a power morality...that can only flow from the top down." The test of wills between these two officers hinges on this idea, and the film should have focused on it. Instead, it jumps around, and constantly changes points of view until it simply devolves into clichés. While there is a glimmer of a more intelligent film here, it somehow gets lost in war movie conventions.

What the critics say Critics rate this movie 2.0 to 3.5. "Its familiar, disparate characters have surfaced in just about every 'platoon' film."[3] "It catches neither the spirit nor the intent of the original yarn."[4] **Final Word** Probably one of the most disappointing war films ever made.

Never So Few

1959 USA color d. John Sturges

WW II: Romance and Action in Burma   2.0

The real strategic military issue raised by this film is whether Carla (Gina Lollobrigida), a beautiful and sophisticated young woman with a wealthy and handsome but older benefactor, will give up everything to marry Capt. Tom Reynolds (Frank Sinatra). The answer is an emphatic yes! In fact, Carla makes clear that she craves getting pregnant and living in a house with a white picket fence in the suburbs while Tom manages a hardware dealership in Indianapolis (I kid you not). If your movies require the slightest reality check, then this one may not be for you. Reynolds, an American officer in the British O.S.S., is leading Kachin warriors (a native people of Northern Burma) in covert operations against the Japanese army in the early 1940s. He constantly complains that his Kachin troops don't get enough support, despite the heavy losses they are suffering. After taking a Japanese airfield near the Burma-China border, his troops discover evidence that the Chinese government has authorized Chinese warlords to attack across the border in order to loot. These attacks have resulted in the death of American soldiers. Outraged, Capt. Reynolds crosses the border against orders in an attempt to engage the Chinese bandits. This entire debacle leads to a diplomatic snafu at the highest levels. Facing a possible court-martial if he doesn't officially apologize, Reynolds produces evidence that American soldiers were killed. Right wins out this time. This is a movie of limited action that takes place in bad studiobound jungles sets that are distressingly cheap. Here's what bothers me. Initially, Carla can't stand Capt. Reynolds, but in the next scene she is all over him. How can Frank, I mean Capt. Reynolds, tell her—"You're on the green side of 25, and you're put together like a Christmas package."—and she falls for it! Maybe it's the wartime uniform thing. Don't be fooled by the video cover notes, Charles Bronson and Steve McQueen have small irrelevant parts in this movie.

What the critics say Critics rate this movie 2.0 to 3.5. "Well enough made but not very interesting."[1] "Salty performances...made one forget the clichés and improbabilities."[2] "Marred at times by the philosophizing of...Frank Sinatra."[7] **Final Word** Gina was a hot babe, that's all I can say.

No Man is an Island

1962   USA   color   d. John Monk, Jr.

WW II: Biopic Survival Story   2.5

This is the Hollywood version of the real-life story of naval radio-operator George Tweed (Jeffrey Hunter). Stationed on Guam when Japan bombed Pearl Harbor on December 7, 1941, Guam came under immediate attack, and Japanese forces quickly overwhelmed the island's 500 American defenders. This movie, shot on location in the Philippines, purports to tell the story of five sailors who escaped into the mountains and their lone survivor, Seaman Tweed. Unfortunately, the movie was written, directed and produced by J. Monks and R. Goldstone, resulting in a poorly scripted, badly acted and slow-moving story that doesn't give us a clue about the real George Tweed or his survival experience. If we are to believe the movie, Tweed's four other companions are bumbling, erratic nitwits who basically deserved to be killed. Initially, Tweed is hidden in a Catholic hospital that treats lepers. While there, he helps the priest start a newsletter that provides islanders factual war information based on radio broadcasts. However, the Japanese eventually track down the source of this information. They burn down the hospital and torture the priest, but Tweed escapes and is hidden on a secluded hill top. Here he's provided food, shelter and water by a nearby farmer, who just happens to have a cute sister (Barbara Perez) he sends to visit Tweed a little too often. Eventually, the resourceful Tweed rigs a signaling device and contacts a US destroyer, that relays information about Japanese troop strength and movement on the island. The device ultimately helps him escape the island. (Just in case you were worried, he comes back for the girl.) The real heroes of this movie are the people of Guam who made every effort to protect these sailors, frequently at the risk of their own lives.

What the critics say Critics rate this movie 2.0 to 3.0. "Unexceptional war adventure in the jungle."[1] "Spotty production values mar true story."[2] **Final Word** Read *Robinson Crusoe, U.S.N.* which better chronicles Tweed's war time exploits, for which he received the Legion of Merit. He died in a car crash in 1989. In an ironic twist on this survival story, the last Japanese defenders of this island, having hidden out in the mountains as well, surrendered in 1972. (Probably hoping to get retirement benefits.)

No Man's Land

2001   BOS-HRZ/SLO/ITA/FRA/UK/BEL   color   subtitles   d. Danis Tanovic

Balkan's Conflict: Antiwar Satire	4.5

Set during the fratricidal Bosnian conflict in the early 1990s, this antiwar satire about the human condition could be about any of the ancient conflicts that abound in the world today. With wit and insight, writer-director Danis Tanovic mocks the sheer stupidity by which these animosities are kept alive. The only hope he offers is in our becoming outraged by the absurdity of it all. The action takes place in a trench between Serbian and Croatian lines. Three soldiers are trapped there, including Serbian Nino (Rene Bitorajac), a somewhat naive young man who has suffered a wound to the abdomen; Tchiki (Branko Djuric), an older but not wiser Croat veteran wounded in the shoulder; and Cera (Filip Sovagovic), who is lying on top of a "bouncing" mine. Into this complicated setting come inept and politically-minded UN peacekeepers, a German mine expert, and international war correspondents looking for a story. Meanwhile Cera, when asked by Tchiki, "How do you feel?" responds, "Great. Couldn't be better. First, they shoot at me, then I wake up on a mine...the whole world's watching me, I need to shit...and you piss me off with your stupid stories." But for Nino and Tchiki the conflict escalates, as each angrily blames the other side for the conflict. As an AK-47 changes hands several times, their personal conflict becomes about the perception of power and justice—"Because I have a gun and you don't," is the answer to every absurd request. Nino and Tchiki argue, shoot, stab and, in the end, kill one another even after they are free to return to their own lines. Almost more frightening than the violence is the sheer indolence and stupidity that abounds everywhere. Soldiers shoot because it's the simplest thing to do; ineffectual peacekeepers do nothing because it's safer than risking bad publicity; and the press are like jackals tearing at a carcass. Well-acted and well-directed, this film will leave you wondering if you are like the idealist UN French Sgt. trying to do the right thing, but to no avail, or like Cera lying on a mine, a sane realist with no way out.

What the critics say Critics rate this movie 2.5 to 4.0. "Riveting seriocomic war parable...in this terrific film."[2] "Absurdity and grim reality are joined at the hip in this bracing, dourly satiric war is hell story."[7] **Final Word** This intimate look at war is a must-see for every war movie guy.

None But the Brave

1965   USA /JAP color   d. Frank Sinatra

WW II: War in the Pacific Actioner   1.0

Just when you think you have seen the worst war film of all time, along comes another one. In *None But the Brave*—the first film co-produced by American and Japanese film companies—Frank Signature directs the only movie of his career. Set somewhere in the Solomon Islands, there is a small garrison of Japanese troops who have lost radio contact and appear to have been forgotten. Their isolation is broken when an American navy C-47 is shot down and crash-lands on the island. (I might add the special effects are truly bad.) Out jumps Frank Signature as a boozing medical corpsman with a cigarette butt dangling from his lip, a chip on his shoulder, and a quip for everything. He also has a heart of gold and sense of justice regarding the Japanese. This movie co-stars Clint Walker as a Navy captain, and he is the only character who appears to be taking this movie seriously. (Someone should have clued him in to lighten up.) Of course, in any antiwar film, there are attempts to kill the enemy, as one Japanese soldier observes—"Those slippery Yankee snakes." If there's anything completely incongruous about this movie, it's that the characters keep killing each other, no matter how farcical the film becomes. Eventually, a tenuous spirit of cooperation prevails, but only after more mindless killing. The truce lasts until the very end, when there's a tearful separation and the Americans are about to be picked up by a Navy ship. In order to protect the Japanese, they fail to report enemy soldiers on the island. But, in a final harebrained sequence, the Japanese soldiers ambush the Americans as they are leaving. If it weren't for the green plastic leaves everyone is wearing to camouflage their helmets, there would be nothing realistic about this film. It may well be that this film was trying to make an ironic point (how similar enemies are), but I am completely unable to discern it. The best I could come up with is, the Americans are good and the Japanese are treacherous—but then, why would the Japanese want to co-produce this film?

What the critics say Critics rate this movie 2.0 to 3.0. "Taut war drama."[1] "Sinatra gives an especially appealing performance."[3] **Final Word** I suspect many critics were worried about getting whacked by the "Chairmen of the Board."

North and South

1985   USA   color   tv miniseries   d. Richard Heffron/Kevin Connor

Civil War: Epic Melodrama   2.0

North and South is a television miniseries that combines all the romantic melodrama of *Gone With the Wind* with all the juicy plantation sexual-exploitation of *Mandingo*. Adapted from two novels by John Jake, *North and South* and *Love and War*, this production comprises two six-volume video sets, with a subtext of how slavery morally impacted our nation. Unfortunately, most war movie fans will be disappointed with the series' focus on costume spectacle, as it provides a limited view of the war. Book I is an epic chronicling two families. One is a northern indus- trialist family from Pennsylvania whose son, George Hazard (James Read), meets and befriends Orry Main (Patrick Swayze) when they are cadets at West Point. The other is Orry's family, wealthy cotton plantation owners from South Carolina. While the first six episodes follow the friendship and families from 1842 through 1861, until the bombardment of Fort Sumter, the primary focus of Book I is the desperately forlorn relationship between Orry and Madeline (Lesley-Ann Down). Madeline is an aging southern belle who marries a well-bred southern gentleman out of practical concerns (she is also beaten and raped by her husband on their wedding night). Orry is later wounded at the Battle of Churubusco in 1847 during the Mexican War (causing him to limp for the rest of the series). In Book II the series shifts from George and Orry to their now grown-up younger brothers and sisters, with the Civil War years (1861-1865) as a backdrop. Of course, the families and their friendship are tested by the issues of slavery and secession by the South, as evident from all the illicit affairs and desperate romances. Despite several well- staged battle scenes, the war is not the real focus of this story. Long and tedious, this bodice-ripper has a voyeuristic pulse that will keep you involved long after you should have gone to bed.

What the critics say Critics rate this movie 3.5 to 4.0. "Lavish spectacle...lots of intrigue and excitement."[5] "Epic, all-star TV miniseries...the human drama unfolds on both sides of the conflict, inside the war rooms and bedrooms."[7] **Final Word** In 1994 John Jake's third novel, *Heaven and Hell*, was made into a miniseries about the postwar period of Reconstruction. While not produced on the same grand scale, this final chapter was a critical disappointment.

Objective, Burma!

1945 USA b/w d. Raoul Walsh

WW II: Classic '40s Flagwaver   2.0

The first American film about The Burma Campaign (1941-1945),
a British theater of operations during the World War II,
unfortunately upset the British. *Objective Burma!*, directed by
Raoul Walsh, was pulled from distribution in Great Britain after its
first week of release and not re-released until 1952. This time,
there was a prologue noting the British sacrifices in Burma. This
movie is a fictional account of an American infantry platoon that
parachutes behind enemy lines in order to take out a communications center, just prior to the British invasion in May 1943. Led
by Capt. Nelson (Errol Flynn), the men successfully complete
their mission but are unable to be airlifted out due to close
pursuit by Japanese soldiers. What ensues is a long and tedious
film that features numerous skirmishes with the Japanese, and
ends with the Americans being rescued by British troops. Despite
critical acclaim, this 2.5-hour movie (an hour too long) is poorly
shot in the jungles of Southern California, with an intrusive
musical score and incredibly bad jungle sound effects. But
perhaps most distressing is the casting of Errol Flynn in the lead.
Flynn never speaks above a whisper, and projects the charm
and charisma of a limp biscuit. (His swashbuckling days were
clearly over.) This movie, without characters or a story, leaves
the audience with no sense of who these men are. Yes, the
jungle is hot and miserable, and the men are dying, but that's
basically all that happens. Many action movies can overlook plot
and characters because of the great action. But there is very little
action here, and when it does occur, it's very routine. The 1962
film *Merrill's Marauders*—a considerably better movie, tells a
fact-based story of the only American troops to fight in Burma.

What the critics say Critics rate this movie 2.5 to 5.0. "Deemed
by many to be the greatest and most moving WW II production
released during the war."[5] "Remains one of the best 'suicide
mission behind enemy lines' tales put on film."[6] "Overlong action
film."[7] **Final Word** British soldiers displayed great courage in
Burma, a theater of war that had no strategic significance on the
outcome of the war. This may partially explain the limited
American involvement. We weren't into colonial honor, except in
the Philippines, of course.

The Odd Angry Shot

1979   AUS   color   d. Tom Jeffrey

| Vietnam War: Infantry Combat | 1.5 |

Written and directed by Tom Jeffrey, this movie is the lone
Australian entry among Vietnam War films. Based on a novel by
William Nagle, this low-budget film (Vietnam looks suspiciously
like Australia) appears to be well intented and is not an
exploitation-actioner. However, if you don't like to see Australian
soldiers drinking enormous quantities of Fosters and carrying on
endlessly about bad cooking, the rain, or how their feet smell,
this may not be the movie for you. The plot revolves around a
group of Australian "Special Air Services" (what we would call
special forces), departing from Australia and deploying at a base
camp in Vietnam for a one year tour of duty. There is much light-
hearted camaraderie, drinking, card playing, horsing around, but
not much action. The men's humor is neither angry nor insightful,
but of a variety that establishes their adolescent spirit and good
hearts. Basically, this is a slow moving war movie with several
combat scenes that are not particularly well staged. Near the end
of the film, "Bung" (John Hargreaves), the older bloke in the
group, talks about how unappreciated they will be when they get
back home. We don't really learn anything about these soldier.
There are no moments of personal crisis, conflict between
soldiers, no hint of subplots and, most disconcertingly, no
comment about the Vietnamese people or the war itself—
nothing. (They arrive, get drunk, find the prostitutes, almost as an
after thought go on patrol, return and get even more sodden,
whoops!, tour of duty is up—time to go home.) The high-point of
this film is a betting contest between American soldiers, who
have a scorpion, and the Australians soldiers, who have a
tarantula (I don't want to spoil all the excitement, but the scorpion
wins). The contest ends in a good-natured drunken brawl
between these mates.

What the critics say Critics rate this movie 2.5 to 3.0. "Personal
drama emphasized more than combat in poignant, sometimes
broad comic work."[2] "Ironic perspective of men struggling with
their feelings about war."[5] **Final Word** If I were to later find out
that these critics had only read the back of the box cover, I
wouldn't be surprised. (Fosters is Australian for "drunken.")

An Officer and a Gentleman

1982   USA   color   d. Taylor Hackford

| Military Life: Naval Aviation School | 3.0 |

This Hollywood soap opera and box office success manipulates just about every emotion possible. In a series of contrived and improbable situations at the Naval Aviation Flight Candidate School, Zak Mayo (Richard Gere) breaks through the blue-collar ceiling he confronts, and grasps success (the American Dream). Zak is a street-wise young man from a broken home, with an alcoholic father and a mother who committed suicide. He wants to earn respect and turn his life around by becoming a jet fighter pilot. His romantic interest is Paula (Debra Winger), who's in a going no where factory job and trying to escape the dead-end life by marrying a naval aviator. Apparently, Paula and her girlfriend Lynette (Lisa Blount) have slept their way through quite a few graduating classes in their efforts to break free. To achieve his goal, Zak has to undergo a transformation from loner and hustler, to someone who fits the image of a proper naval officer (despite the badboy tattoo on his arm). An obstacle to respectability looms in the menacing figure of Sgt. Foley (Lou Gossett, Jr.), a way over-the-top drill instructor intent on washing Zak out of the program. But, don't worry, Sgt. Foley comes on board (it is the American Dream we are talking about here!). There's also a subplot involving Zak's friend Sid (Robert Loggia), who commits suicide when he is dumped by another ambitious factory slut. Zak overcomes this emotional hurdle to find success. The performances are excellent and the characters have more depth to them than one has any right to expect, except for Gossett. Unfortunately, the worst is saved for last. A newly commissioned Lt. Mayo, in dress whites, carries Paula away from her low-paying job to the applause of factory workers—to the perfect life as a naval aviator's wife (they will have broken up before Zak completes six weeks of flight training at Pensacola. But that's for another movie.)

What the critics say Critics rate this movie 3.0 to 4.5. "A well-worn Hollywood formula script."[2] "Soap opera has never been art...right balance between the ridiculous and the sublime."[7]
Final Word Unfortunately, there's almost nothing here seriously related to the military or military life. Zak could just as well have been to be a stockbroker, attorney, or doctor—and probably should have been.

One Man's Hero

1999 USA/SPA/MEX color d. Lance Hool

Mexican War: Irish Deserters   2.5

For starters this wartime action melodrama, based on real events, suggests the US Army was the reincarnation of the Spanish Inquisition. The film focuses on a handful of Irish-American soldiers who desert the Army during the Mexican War (1846-1848), because of their persecution as Catholics ("Papists") and Irishmen ("potato famine clods"). An Irishman and career soldier, Sgt. John Riley (Tom Berenger), starts out assisting the deserter's escape, and eventually joins them. This small group, along with hundreds of other Irish deserters, form the "San Patricio" brigade and fights alongside the Mexican army against the United States. The movie highlights these events against the millions of Irish who had immigrated to the US in the 1840s due to the potato famine in Ireland. It also suggests that many immigrant soldiers had very little identification with their new country, and when faced with hardships and discrimination, they deserted. At the same time, President Polk was looking for any excuse to seize the western territories from Mexico. Mexico, still not accepting the loss of Texas, attacked the US Army in 1846, and gave Polk the excuse he needed. The history books note that the US Army, under General Taylor, incurred as many as 9,000 desertions, with 10,000 more soldiers refusing to reenlist or being discharged as disciplinary problems. Despite these problems, the Mexican War is considered a brilliant military campaign in which a much smaller American army consistently defeated a larger Mexican army on its own territory. Unfortunately, this movie provides a limited historical perspective on this war, with almost no insight into why these soldiers deserted or why they were mistreated. Ten minutes into the movie they are deserting—and that's all you get to know about them. The film offers honorable bandits and a romantic love interest (Berenger gets the girl), but more importantly, numerous well-staged battles with great period detail, featuring artillery duels and musket volleys at point-blank range.

What the critics say Critics rate this movie 2.0 to 3.0. "Based on a true story, but more earnest than exciting."[2] "Heavy-handed ...the action stops for romantic interludes."[5] **Final Word** This look at a little known chapter in American military history is ultimately disappointing, but worth a look for the action.

The One That Got Away

1957   GBR   b/w   d. Roy Ward Baker

| WW II: Escaped German Pilot | 3.5 |

This intriguing and well-made movie tells the true story of German Lufftwaffe pilot Lt. Franze von Werra, who was shot down over England in 1940, captured, and made a prisoner-of-war. Based on a book by K. Burt and J. Leasor, the film stars Hardy Krüger as a young pilot who speaks good English and is a confident, if not arrogant, mixture of cleverness and nerve. Lt. von Werra immediately attempts to escape but does not succeed until the third attempt. However, the second attempt, in which he nearly succeeded, is quite remarkable. Von Werra tunnels out of a POW camp, dons a makeshift flight uniform, and passes himself off as a Dutch pilot in the RAF who has crashed nearby. With this ruse, he is able to get into the cockpit of a Hurricane fighter and start the engine before he's recaptured. The lieutenant's successful third escape is epic. While being transported to a POW camp in Canada, he jumps a train near Montreal in the dead of winter, crosses into the US, and claims asylum in a neutral country. Before Canadian and British authorities are able to legally extradite him, he escapes to Mexico and makes his way to Peru, Bolivia, Brazil, Spain and finally to Berlin in April 1941. The epilogue notes that Lt. von Werra was shot down in October 1941 and was last seen crashing into the sea. The only motive alluded to for his persistent escape attempts is his determination to return to his girlfriend. The movie also makes the interesting point that Lt. von Werra was something of a fraud, given a hero's status in Germany, as a fighter ace, for trumped-up victories. This is a well-acted movie, and Krüger does an excellent job of showing von Werra improvising the escapes, as he is enormously persistent, resourceful and lucky. This movie has limited dialogue, as the focus is on the sheer physicality of the escapes. While Lt. von Werra is not portrayed as a likable hero, wartime politics are kept to a minimum.

What the critics say Critics rate this movie 3.0 to 4.0. "Fast paced and exciting."[5] "Well-directed and performed, this adventure is highly recommended."[7] **Final Word** Well-done and an exciting true story. While the movie doesn't make the point, clearly the excitement and grandiosity of these escapes suggest this young pilot got-off on showing up his captors.

On the Beach
1959 USA b/w d. Stanley Kramer

| Cold War: Nuclear Holocaust | 3.0 |

On the Beach stands out as the first major motion picture to deal with the subject of nuclear holocaust. Directed by Stanley Kramer, the film is a low-budget, low-tech affair based on a popular novel by Nevil Shute. The opening scene takes place aboard the *Sawfish*, an American nuclear submarine, in a post-apocalyptic world in which only the inhabitants of Australia have survived a nuclear exchange between the US and Soviet Union. The *Sawfish*, commanded by Capt. Towers (Gregory Peck), is heading for Australia, which is about be engulfed in a cloud of radiation. In Australia, life appears to be going on in a bizarrely normal fashion. A drunken Eva Gardner hits on Gregory Peck at a party, while Anthony Perkins and Donna Anderson are concerned Peck will cry, due to the recent loss of his wife and children—and spoil the mood of the party. Fred Astaire is a party-pooping scientist who insists, "We're all doomed you know. The whole, silly drunk pathetic lot of us. We haven't got a chance." Everyone else, however, is going to work, spending weekends at the beach, racing cars, fishing, and carrying on as usual (no looting, no rioting, no desperate acts of nihilistic hedonism). In fact, hardly any one even talks about the impending doom. Then in the last few days, everyone quietly queues for pills to end their lives. In order to fill up the last remaining boring days of life on earth, this movie provides long irrelevant interludes lacking imagination. No one is talking about the end of civilization and the movie refuses to explore what people are feeling. No. The film hangs on a romance between two aging stars and a musical score that consists solely of *Waltzing Matilda*. To this film's credit, it doesn't leave the door open for survival—Capt. Towers dumps the relationship to take his men back to their homes, where everyone is dead and the men will die alone in an empty place by themselves. This downbeat ending is even less realistic than the romance.

What the critics say Critics rate this movie 4.5 to 5.0. "Gloomy prophecy...content to chat rather than imagine."[1] "A solid film of considerable emotional, as well as cerebral content."[4] **Final Word** The film's determined grimness elevates it above the average. A TV version came out in 2000 and is also available on tape.

Operation Crossbow

1965   GBR   color   d. Michael Anderson

WW II: Take Out German Rockets	2.5

By today's standards this big-budget, special effects, star-driven production can only be described as ordinary. Starring George Peppard and Sophia Loren, as well as a long list of British war movie veterans (Mills, Howard, Quayle, Todd), *Operation Crossbow* is a confusing movie that doesn't know what it wants to be about. Alternately, it's about German rocket development, the bombing of London by V-1 and V-2s, an espionage-sabotage thriller, and a special effects actioner *a la* James Bond. To add to the movie's incongruity, a long and irrelevant sexual tryst takes place between Peppard and Loren, that has nothing to do with the story's development, except to slow the tepid pace to a crawl (however, Loren looks very good). This fictional story is fairly strait forward. British intelligence has unconfirmed reports of the development of long-range rockets by the Germans at Peenemünde, Holland. After the initial bombing of the site, the rocket works are moved underground. The highly improbable plot requires the British to assemble a team of scientists to parachute into Holland and, with the assistance of the Dutch resistance, gain entrance to the rocket research center as workers. The team initially gathers data, but as the rocket prototypes are made operational, they are asked to help sabotage the facility. To the film's credit, there are many good special effects, particularly those showing the development of the V-1 (buzz bomb). Initially, the story is told from both the British and German viewpoints but this quickly stops. Then it is shown from the viewpoint of British military and intelligence, but then this disappears, and finally the viewpoint is that of the agents who parachute in—but who they are and what they do proves to be irrelevant to the dramatic bombing of the rocket plant. The only twist in this incoherent storyline is that both Peppard and Loren are killed.

What the critics say Critics rate this movie 3.0 to 4.0. "Sometimes suspenseful war melodrama."[4] "Action-packed espionage tale."[3] "Exciting, if shallow and glossy."[6] **Final Word** This is a case where the truth is more interesting than fiction. Werner Von Braun, technical director of Peenemünde, became director of NASA's Marshall Space Flight Center and was instrumental in the development of American's missile and space programs.

Operation Pacific

1951   USA   b/w   d. George Waggner

WW II: Submarine Action   2.5

While this isn't the worst John Wayne WW II actioner, it comes close at times. The movie opens onboard the *Thunderfish*, a submarine commanded by John T. "Pops" Perry (Ward Bond), with Wayne as executive officer Lt. Cmdr. Duke Gifford. You guessed it! They are rescuing nuns and orphans from a South Pacific island. For his part, Wayne carries a small baby onto the sub and, later, boils a rubber glove to act as a nipple to feed him. For the next twenty minutes cute kids run around the sub as crewmen attend to them, and even a few of these cute urchins have to be shooed away because Wayne is trying to torpedo a Japanese destroyer. You have to ask yourself—how desperate does a director have to be? Apparently it's not enough that good men are fighting and dying thousands of miles from home, but they are cast as saints as well (doesn't quite blasphemy their patriotism, but comes close). Now this movie only gets stupider. Being around these children leads Wayne to mope like a real sorry puss about his divorce from nurse Lt. Mary Stuart (Patricia Neal). (It must have been that time of the month for the "Duke.") The rest of the movie is consumed with Wayne trying to win back the affections of his ex-wife. There is also some minor competition from Lt. Larry (Scott Forbes), (an officer so in awe of Cmdr. Gifford's brass balls that he has no chance). Some action is interjected as Wayne dives off the sub to rescue a downed pilot, torpedoes a half-dozen Japanese ships, rams and sinks a freighter, and assists in redesigning torpedoes that had been misfiring (in reality, the Navy's Mark XIV torpedoes ran too deep and the detonators were often crushed on impact. It took the Navy nearly two years to admit this was a problem). Produced six years after the war, this movie is pretty much a generic 1940s flagwaver, with Wayne winning the war in the Pacific.

What the critics say Critics rate this movie 1.0 to 4.0. "Routine war heroics, tolerably done."[1] "Action, suspense, comedy, and romance are nicely mixed."[7] "Gung-ho Wayne vehicle... eminently forgettable."[8] **Final Word** While Wayne was still fun to watch, by 1951 Hollywood had transformed him into a big screen icon and a caricature of his former self. His serious acting days were over.

Paradise Road

1997   USA /AUS   color   d. Bruce Beresford

WW II: Women POWs	3.5

Directed and written by Bruce Beresford, this fact-based (loosely, I suspect) film is mostly about upper-class colonial women in the Far East (American, Dutch, British and Australian). After the fall of Singapore to the Japanese army in early 1942, the women were incarcerated in prisoner-of-war camps in Sumatra until the end of the war in 1945. This story focuses on the forming of a "vocal orchestra," that performs thirty different compositions from 1943-1944. The epilogue notes that the choir ceased performing due to the deaths and ill health of its members. The leader of this effort, Adrienne (Glen Close), uses the music to distract the women from the everyday deprivation and brutality they face. There's an ensemble cast (Frances McDormand, Pauline Collins, Cate Blanchett, Jennifer Ehle, and Julianna Margulies) in which no one character takes center stage. As a result, we never learn anything about these women or their relationship to one another. There is little more to this picture, with a few exceptions. For one, there's something annoying about these well-bred, manor ladies living their sheltered and privileged lives with an arrogant disdain for everyone and everything around them. This creates little sympathy for them. In one scene, a sadistic officer takes Adrienne into the jungle at gun point and, get this, sings to her. We are supposed to believe that music is a universal language that helps the two to transcend their circumstances. Right! (Note: this scene may have been taken from an actual event, based on the book *Three Came Home* by Agnes Newton Keith. The book, made into a movie in 1950, tells the author's experiences as a POW in Borneo.) But the director could have picked a more sympathetic officer in order to make this scene palatable. Earlier in the movie he douses a woman with gasoline and sets her on fire. It's obvious that the music is bridging a gap of sorts, but who really gives a damn at this point?

What the critics say Critics rate this movie 2.0 to 4.5. "Too often shallow and manipulative to be moving."[1] "Heartfelt (though cliché-ridden)."[2] "Affecting, hard-hitting story...though sometimes approaches sappy and clichéd waters."[3] **Final Word** A sincere effort that avoids most the POW clichés by finding new ones.

Paths of Glory

1957   USA   b/w   d. Stanley Kubrick

WW I: Antiwar	4.0

Paths of Glory is another example of a "classic" war movie that has begun to dim with age. Adapted from Humphrey Cobb's 1935 novel and based on real events, director Stanley Kubrick stages an all out assault on the arrogance and incompetence of the French army command. The time is 1916, and 500 miles of trenches separate French and German troops. The stalemate in this struggle has been maintained without significant change for over two years. Gen. Mireau (George Macready) is offered another star as a promotion if he will order the 701st Regiment to assault highly fortified German positions. The general knows fully-well that his troops are unlikely to succeed. When the attack, led by Col. Dax (Kirk Douglas), fails, Gen. Mireau orders his artillery to shell his own troops. When this order is refused, he decides to execute 100 soldiers as an example to his troops. Negotiations later reduce the number to 3. During the soldiers' court-martial it's revealed that in the French army it is acceptable practice to pick examples by lot. These men didn't fail to obey orders and were not cowards, they were simply selected by lot. Col. Dax defends his men in a "show trial" in which he is not allowed to present a defense. However outrageous these events are, they are compounded by the arrogance and self-servingness of Gen. Mireau, who tells Col. Dax before the trial that the men of the 701st "are scum, Colonel, the whole rotten regiment, a pack of sneaking, whining, tail-dragging curds." Obviously, Gen. Mireau is not a nice man, and this is the major flaw of this movie. The case being made is so one-sided, so morally self-righteous, and the bad guys so vile and contemptible that the story-telling gets in the way of the brutal facts. This movie works best when Kirk Douglas is on the screen. The trench warfare scenes are outstanding. This is not a Kubrick masterpiece, but rather the early work of a soon-to-be master.

What the critics say Critics rate this movie 4.5 to 5.0. "An overpowering piece of cinema."[1] "Shattering study of the insanity of war."[2] "Scathing attack on the hypocrisy of war...Kubrick's first true masterpiece."[3] "It's a brilliant, flawed work."[6] **Final Word** A compelling movie (it wasn't allowed to be shown in France until 1975).

Patton

1970   USA   color   d. Franklin Schaffner

WW II: Epic Biopic of "Blood 'n Guts"   5.0

Directed by Franklin Schaffner, *Patton* won seven Academy Awards, including Best Picture and Best Actor and is an AFI top 100 film. Adapted from Gen. Omar N. Bradley's *A Soldier's Story* and Ladislas Farago's *Patton: Ordeal and Triumph*, the film is a screen triumph for the sheer scope of the story it tells and for the intelligence with which it tells it. Standing above all this is the performance of George C. Scott as General "Blood and Guts" Patton. Scott gives one of the great screen characterizations. In an opening six-minute monologue, standing in front of an enormous American flag, in gaudy military splendor, Scott sets the messianic tone for this wartime biography: *We are not just going to shoot the bastards (Germans), we are going to cut out their living guts and use them to grease the treads of our tanks.* Flamboyant and controversial, Patton maintained a deeply held belief that he was the reincarnation of a warrior and was destined for greatness. Counterpoint to Patton's grandiosity was his assistant, Gen. Omar Bradley (Karl Malden), unassuming, cautious, reasoned, and ever concerned about the loss of life. Malden gives a solid performance. This movie show us war on a grand scale and with great battlefield scenes. It opens with GIs landing in North Africa and suffering a bloody defeat at the Kasserine Pass. Finally, we see a chastised Patton commanding the Third Army in its breakout at Normandy and sweep across France. The movie concludes with Patton's miraculous rescue of the 101st at Bastogne in December 1944. Portrayed as ever rivalous for victories and fame, Patton takes on Rommel as well as England's Field Marshal Montgomery in an exercise of egos and wits. This is a complex picture about a great American demi-hero, flaws and all. (Patton did not go out the way he envisioned the perfect soldier's death—the last bullet, in the last battle, of the last war. Instead, he died in a car accident in 1945 at the age of 60.)

What the critics say Critics rate this movie 5.0. "Brilliantly handled wartime character study which is also a spectacle."[1] "Milestone in screen biographies: Scott is unforgettable."[2] "One hell of a war movie...amazingly brilliant depiction of men in war."[4] **Final Word** One of the best war films ever! You should have two copies of this movie in separate locations—just in case.

Pearl Harbor

2001 USA color d. Michael Bay

WW II: Romance and War   2.5

Thanks to *Pearl Harbor* the movie, an entire generation of Americans, hoping to get nothing more than a big budget special effects fix, were suddenly confronted with World War II—Pear Harbor, the "Doolittle Raid," Franklin Delano Roosevelt and Japan. While the revelation there had been a WW II was probably disconcerting to many in the audience, you can be sure that after the movie more than a few had the epiphany that there must have been a World War I. *Pearl Harbor* is a gimmicky attempt at a lush and nostalgic romance filled with vacuous and beautiful people. Superimposed on the Imperial Japanese navy's surprise attack on the American Pacific fleet stationed at Oahu in the Hawaiian Islands, is a farfetched romantic wartime melodrama. Evelyn (Kate Beckinsale) is the girlfriend of Rafe (Ben Affleck), an American fighter pilot who is believed to have been shot down over the English Channel and killed. Evelyn is now pregnant by her new boyfriend Danny (Josh Hartnett), who is Rafe's life-long best friend (yes, this is all too close to reality TV). However, when Rafe suddenly shows up without warning (obviously he hadn't been killed and has a serious problem communicating) the resulting conflict has numerous predictable twists right up until the cop out ending. Using war as a backdrop to romance simply doesn't need to be done on this scale. While the special effects showing the bombing of Pearl Harbor are outstanding, they are uninvolving and after a few minutes even boring. In order to broaden the box office appeal of this movie, it appears that Cuba Gooding, Jr. was tossed in at the last moment with very little to do. This movie's distortion of facts becomes serious when it focuses on the "Doolittle Raid" on Tokyo. I suspect the success of this movie is due more to the hype of a great public relations campaign than to compelling moviemaking.

What the critics say Critics rate this movie 2.5 to 3.0. "Spectacular to look at but rather empty inside."[3] "At times laughably melodramatic...a masterpiece of Hollywood pyrotechnics."[7] **Final Word** Yet, another war romance that is mostly false sentiment and nostalgia packaged for the mass entertainment market. The best contemporary war romances are the Masterpiece Theater productions *We'll Meet Again* and *And a Nightingale Sang.*

The Pentagon Wars

1998   USA   color   tv   d. Richard Benjamin

Military Life: Fact-Based Satire   4.5

This priceless send-up of military bureaucracy and malfeasance, based on a book by Col. James G. Burton, provides an insider's look at the Army's procurement of the Bradley Fighting Vehicle (troop transport). Developed by defense contractor FMC, this weapons system cost 14 billion dollars and took 17 years before it went into production. Anyone who has ever been in the military or worked for a large corporation will immediately understand the type of program inertia and careerism that drove the Bradley's development. Kelsey Grammer plays Gen. Partridge, who heads up weapons development for the Dept. of Defense. Grammer is absolutely right on as the greatest bureaucratic spinmeister and double-talker who ever walked the hallways of the Pentagon. When Gen. Partridge is asked by a House Armed Services Committee about a rigged test, he responds, "There was a verifiable deviation from the standard test data accumulation." He then claims some "spectacular successes," and when asked about them, explains, "That's classified." This truly inspired script rings true throughout. Into this boondoggle comes Col. Burton (Cary Elwes), appointed by Congress as an independent analyst. Gen. Partridge tells Colonel Burton, "Now we got the Army, Navy, Air Force and Marines doing a circle-jerk over weapons testing, and you get to hold the big dick." Unfortunately for Col. Burton, his primary concern is for the soldiers' safety. He simply wants to test the Bradley to determine if it performs to its design specs. The amount of deception and phony testing that plagued this system are beyond belief. Wanting to put sheep in the vehicle to see what happens when hit by a TOW missile, an office of "Ruminant Procurement" is set up to run tests specs on sheep before they can be used. Burton's job is defunded by the Army to get rid of him. Later reinstated, due to political pressure, he's transferred to Alaska, and in the end forced to retire. The ultimate "white elephant" went into production in 1986.

What the critics say Critics rate this movie 3.0 to 4.0. "A wonderful adaptation...a fascinating story."[7] **Final Word** Not many available reviews. Let's sum up. This is *Catch-22* come true. An absolute must-see movie. Burton puts it all into perspective. The Pentagon is all about "cash flows and egos" and not about the soldier in the field.

Piece of Cake

1988   GBR   color   tv miniseries   d. Ian Toynton

WW II: Fighter Combat	4.5

This excellent six-part British television miniseries, based on a Derek Robinson novel, follows the exploits of the fictional RAF Hornet Squadron during the first year of Britain's entry into WW II. An irreverent tone is immediately established in the opening scene when the squadron leader accidentally falls off the wing of his plane and dies, after having just survived running his plane into a ditch. The Hornet Squadron is then transferred to France in late 1939. The new squadron leader, "Rex" (Tim Woodard), is an incompetent flight leader whose dated combat tactics put his men at risk. He's also an arrogant aristocrat who turns the squadron into his own genteel country club. Over the course of the six episodes, viewers watch the transformation of these pilots as the Defense of France quickly turns into the Battle of Britain. By nine months, the British pilots are suffering astonishing losses that take an enormous emotional and physical toll on the survivors. An outstanding cast of characters includes "Moggy" (Neil Dudgeon), who aggressively dominates the squadron; "Chris" (Boyd Gaine), a wealthy American who quickly tires of British manners and snobbery; "Uncle," (David Horovitch) the understanding squadron commander; "Mother" (Patrick Bailey) the erudite and witty intelligence officer, and many more. *Piece of Cake* is a rich mixture of well-drawn characters thrown together by war, as they interact against a backdrop of British social class and manners. But slowly the realities of war begin to strip away all personal and class pretenses. The truest moment is when Moggy ditches his plane into a village, killing civilians. His response is complete indifference. If it meant staying in the plane longer to avoid them and risking his life, they could die. Besides, he reasons, "They can't fly Spitfires." The movie's aerial photography is simply outstanding and shows a love for Spitfires. Though not an action movie, there is plenty of good action. It's the best depiction of "men" in airplanes yet.

What the critics say No available reviews. **Final Word** Churchill put it best, "Never in the field of human conflict was so much owed by so many to so few." (and Moggy adds, "does that mean we can go home now.") British television has created an intelligent series that requires you to sit back, relax, and take it all in.

Platoon

1986 USA color d. Oliver Stone

Vietnam War: Unit Conflict   4.0

This highly acclaimed war film, which won the Academy Award for Best Picture in 1986, has a brilliant opening scene. Twenty-one year old Private Chris Taylor (Charlie Sheen) is a college drop out and idealist—"Maybe from down here I can start up again and be something I can be proud of...see something I don't yet see...learn something I don' yet know." He is shown landing in Vietnam and disembarking from the bays of C-141, as stacks of body bags pass by him on their way home. The time is 1967-68, with Bravo Company, 125th Infantry near the Cambodian border. The first two thirds of this movie involves an intense and intelligent film about life as a grunt during the Vietnam War. The setting is highly realistic, and the combat action is intense and real. In addition, *Platoon* is ambitious in portraying the many levels of personal conflict experienced by American soldiers in this war. Unfortunately, director Oliver Stone would have us believe that the primary conflict was really among American soldiers, touching on issues of rank, class, race, education, drug abuse, age, and all manner of dualisms. For Stone the ultimate conflict is between good and evil and lost innocence. Much, if not most, of these issues are well handled and contribute to the intensity and complexity of the film. However, the last third of the movie devolves into a jumble of mixed-up messages and metaphors about the Vietnam War, trying, too hard to make a larger statement about the war. It's at this level that this film fails. All this complexity is ultimately distilled into a conflict between two sergeants, Barnes (Willem Dafoe), the good one, and Elias (Tom Berenger), the bad one, that takes on tragic and metaphorical overtones regarding the war. At this point a good war movie stops and plot takes over, leaving viewers at an emotional distance from the film and the soldiers in the field.

What the critics say Critics rate this movie 4.5 to 5.0. "Harrowing, realistic and completely convincing."[2] "A great cinematic work that stands high among the finest films ever made."[4] "Considered by many to be the most realistic portrayal of war on film."[5] **Final Word** The American Film Institute named *Platoon* among its top 100 films. I would suggest you disregard the hype. This is a solid war film effort that's doesn't rank among the very best Vietnam War movies.

Platoon Leader

1988   USA   color   d. Aaron Norris

Vietnam War: Combat Hell	1.5

This Vietnam War movie walks a fine line between legitimate war movie and "exploitation-actioner." No date or location is provided for the events detailed in this story. The setting is a firebase camp occupied by a battle weary company of Army airborne troops (Bravo Company, 2nd Platoon) near a small hamlet in the Vietnamese countryside. *Platoon Leader* tells the simplest of all combat stories. A young and inexperienced West Point second lieutenant, Jeff Knight (Michael Dudikoff), receives his first combat command and struggles to earn the respect of his men. There's a bearded Chuck Norris (martial arts TV star) as a M-60 toting extra (you'd think there would be no way America could lose now). And, perhaps not coincidentally, this movie is directed by Aaron Norris, brother of Chuckie. It doesn't take long for Lt. Knight to go from idealistic and eager cherry to hardened combat veteran. Wounded, he returns to his company and commands their respect by becoming more cunning and ruthless, as he embraces the unwritten code of survival in the field. A difficult movie to watch without falling asleep, it is saved only by sporadic gunfire. This movie lacks clearly defined characters or roles. In fact, everyone is really an extra, some of them on the screen longer, so they have starring roles. (No names will be mentioned in order to protect their Screen Actor Guild cards.) Seriously, besides the bad acting, the painful dialog and an uninteresting story, there is never any sense of who these soldiers are, including the lieutenant, the main character. As a result, you stop caring about what happens once you have figured out the outcome of the war. Although there are several intense battle scenes, too much of this movie feels contrived or borrowed from other bad war movies. Nothing is surprising or new. Perhaps worst of all, there is a false sense of heroism throughout the film and a musical score that would make most of us welcome the Vietnamese top 10.

What the critics say Critics rate this movie 1.0 to 2.5. "Obnoxious, bloody PLATOON rip-off."[2] "Battle drenched portrait."[5] "Leaden bore."[7] **Final Word** Obviously this was not a well-liked film. I rated it 1.5 because no Vietnam War movie can be as bad as *The Green Berets*.

Pork Chop Hill

1959   USA   b/w   d. Lewis Milestone

Korean War: Combat Command	3.0

Directed by Lewis Milestone (*All Quiet on the Western Front*), this noirish production is the undisputed king of Korean War "B" movies. A fact-based story adapted from the book by Brigadier General S.L.A. Marshall, the movie stars Gregory Peck as Lt. Joe Clemons, commander of King Company. The story takes place in 1953 as the Chinese Communists take Pork Chop Hill shortly before a final peace accord is signed. Lt. Clemons is ordered to retake the hill and hold it against a counterattack. The soldiers, their commanders, and the American negotiators (at Panmunjon seventy miles away) all understand that this is a political face-saving strategy that will not influence the outcome of the war. It is essentially a test of American resolve by the Chinese. While this low-budget, black and white movie has a gritty and realistic feel, the combat scenes are limited due to the static nature of the directing and the narrow focus of the camera. A typical scene might involve only three or four soldier in a shot. And too much of this movie is devoted to Peck standing or sitting around talking strategy and pointing to people to go here, do that. The key is that the soldiers know they are being sacrificed for political rather than military objectives. Lt. Clemons comes to symbolize their dilemma. His response, however, is stoic and self-sacrificing. A company of 135 men, reduced to 25, mostly due to the incompetence of their own headquarters, are prepared to make a last stand when the division commander decides it's not worth the loss of life to reinforce them. Even though military command is portrayed as incompetent and callous, the epilogue concludes that taking the hill was the right decision: "Millions live in freedom today because of what they did." While the conclusion rings hollow, this critical look at military command was virtually unprecedented at the time (and still is).

What the critics say Critics rate this movie 3.0 to 4.0. "Ironic war film with vivid spectacle separated by much talk."[1] "A gritty, utterly realistic story that drives home the irony of war."[4] "A powerful, hard-hitting account...of a no-win situation."[5] **Final Word** This movie could have been a contender, except Milestone was unable to embrace the ironic film about the futility of war he had created.

Pretty Village, Pretty Flame

1996 GRE/YUG color subtitles d. Srdjan Dragojevic

Balkans Conflict: Urban Combat   5.0

This movie is a terrifying decent into a new vision of war, a modern urban war waged with deadly weapons and incredible ferocity. What adds to its impact is its contemporary realism—the cell phones, video cameras and frequent references to modern life. The juxtaposition of past, present and future also brings home powerfully the craziness of this war in contrast to the normalcy that precedes and follows it. Told in a series of flashbacks from a hospital bed, this film relates the story of two young boys who grew up together as best friends, and end up on opposite sides of the civil war in Bosnia. After the breakup of Yugoslavia in 1991, a centuries-old conflict between Muslims and Serbs was renewed under the guise of a national independence movement. One Muslim, Halil (Nikola Pejakovic) and the other Serb, Milan (Dragan Bjelogrlic), ultimately come to a brutal confrontation in the casual genocide of the never ending revenge that occurred in this region of the world. The film plunges into a surreal world of violent madness where neighbor kills neighbor, friends kill friends, and rape, murder, torture and looting are everywhere. It's as if every man were an army unto himself, and his only objective were to destroy the world. This is a well-acted, well-directed movie that maintains a high level of tension throughout, culminates in a claustrophobic confrontation as a small group of armed Serbs are trapped in a car tunnel by Muslim forces. Inside this tunnel begins a grim and dark self-examination of the personal and political pathologies that engulf them. Pervading this extremely violent and realistic movie is an ironic and cynical humor that holds out little hope for the future.

What the critics say Critics rate this movie 3.0 to 4.0. "An angry, bitter film about the madness of the conflict that overwhelmed Yugoslavia."[1] "Wry, sarcastic and lyrical in expression—frames this often powerful...antiwar film."[3] "Powerful story of the Bosnian conflict that is loosely based on a true incident."[5] **Final Word** The critics' ratings don't match their words. A mesmerizing decent into hell. You won't have time for popcorn.

Prisoner of the Mountain

1996 RUS color d. Sergei Bodrov

Chechen Revolt : Antiwar Drama   4.5

Don't let the fact that this film is loosely based on a novella by
Leo Tolstoy keep you from renting it. This is an outstanding war
movie. Yes, the movie is literate and has somber truths.
However, it's also filled with humor and wonderful characters.
With the breakup of the Soviet Union, Chechen rebels in the
Caucasus region of southern Russia (a mountainous region that
runs between the Caspian and the Black Sea) made a bid for
independence beginning in 1994. This is the story of two Russian
soldiers, Sacha (Oleg Menshikov) and Vanya (Sergei Bodrov),
who are captured in an ambush by Muslim rebels. They are then
turned over to Abdul-Mourant (D. Sikharulidze), patriarch of a
mountaintop village, who hopes to exchange the captives for his
son who is being held prisoner by the Russians. Many things
begin to happen. The other villagers want the captives executed
and begin to pressure Abdul. Slowly, the two prisoners form
relationships with Abdul's young daughter and her mute uncle.
Vanya, a young naive recruit who knows little of life, and Sacha,
a sergeant who fancies himself an actor and enjoys being top
dog in this relationship, are constantly on each other's nerves,
since they have been chained together. This movie also provides
an insightful glimpse into rural life in a region of the world few of
us have ever seen. For a movie revolving around the sobering
realities of these prisoners' dire circumstances, it's surprisingly
humorous. Ultimately, relationships form, and while they cannot
undo the violence of the past or what is about to take place, the
world is changed for the better as a result. Behind this story is
the centuries-old story of retribution and recriminations, in which
all the characters are now caught up. The acting is outstanding
throughout, and the photography vividly presents this vast,
desolate and beautiful region of the world. Rather simple and
slowly paced, the movie is able to scale this conflict down to its
human dimension.

What the critics say Critics rate this movie 3.0 to 4.5. "An
engaging and tragic account of growing respect and affection
across ethnic divides."[1] "Heart-rendering message on the
insanity of war."[3] "A rare theater of war for cinema."[8] **Final Word**
It's all pretty simple. The best films about war are coming from
Eastern Europe, not from Hollywood.

Prisoners of the Sun

1990   AUS   color   d. Stephen Wallace

WW II: POW/Legal Drama	4.5

This outstanding Australian war film raises serious questions about attempts to impose justice after a war. In 1945, just months after Japan formally surrendered, the Australians have set up a war crimes tribunal to try Japanese officers charged with mistreating and murdering Australian prisoners of war. The prologue notes that on the island of Ambon, Indonesia, 650 miles north of Australia, the Japanese Imperial Navy had established a POW camp (Tan Toey) that, at one time, held 1,100 Australian soldiers. At the war's end only 300 prisoners survived. Investigation uncovers a mass grave with 300 bayoneted or decapitated Australian soldiers. What ensues is a legal attempt to establish the criminal responsibility of Vice Admiral Takahashi (George Takei) and of the camp commander Capt. Ikeuchi (Tetsu Watanabe). The attempt is complicated by the fact that the US is uncooperative in providing military records, because it hopes to utilize senior Japanese officers to further its post-war political agenda in Japan. There are many excellent performances, particularly one by Bryan Brown as Capt. Cooper, the prosecuting attorney for the Australian army. Adding to the richness of this film are several compelling stories that emerge as the trial proceeds—the key one being the prosecution of Lt. Tanaka (Toshi Shioya) for following orders and executing a captured Australian pilot. The interesting legal/moral issue is, how realistic is it to expect a low-ranking Japanese officer to question the legality of an order given by a Vice Admiral? There are many difficult-to-watch scenes as Australian soldiers are beaten, tortured and murdered. However, this film is reaching for a much more subtle message about justice and who is responsible for carrying out orders, as it becomes increasingly clear that the Australian's search for justice is unjust in many ways. A strongly ironic and sad ending to this complex film does justice to a very difficult subject.

What the critics say Critics rate this movie 3.0 to 4.0. "Gritty, gripping...incisive, well acted tale."[2] "Complex look at justice ...especially when it's clouded by political corruption."[7] **Final Word** A thoughtful and compelling post-war legal drama that is well worth renting.

PT109

1963 USA color d. Leslie H. Martinson

WW II: Naval Combat	2.0

This Hollywood salute to President John Fitzgerald Kennedy, based on the book by Robert J. Donovan, chronicles his exploits as a PT torpedo boat commander in the South Pacific in 1943. (It should be pointed out that the film was released just months before Kennedy was assassinated.) This fact-based movie, starring Cliff Robertson as Lt. John Kennedy, shows us the sinking of Kennedy's PT boat, which was rammed at night by the Japanese destroyer *Amagiri*, while patrolling in straits around the Solomon Islands. Kennedy and ten other crew members swam three and a half hours to a nearby island where they were rescued six days later by islanders and an Australian coastal watcher (the record shows that Kennedy acted selflessly and heroically over and over again). The movie portrays Kennedy as a straightforward and unpretentious individual, respected by the men who served with him. It also emphasizes that he sought out combat duty. Unfortunately, the movie fails to tell this compelling story. The first half plays out like a 1950s comedy in which you half expect cast members to break out into song and dance. The second half, in which all the anticipated action occurs, is tedious and overly-long, bringing this barge to a standstill. The Kennedy character is simply not complex enough to be interesting. For example, it would have been nice to know more about his drive to seek out combat, and getting his father to pull strings. And what about his bitter and rivalous relationship with his older brother Joe, the star of the family who was being groomed to become president? (Joe died in a reckless act of heroism in 1944). With a shallow script about such an important American figure, the movie becomes disrespectful in its own way. However, there is no doubt that Kennedy was a true war hero.

What the critics say Critics rate this movie 2.0 to 2.5. "Extraordinarily protracted and very dull action story which seems to have been overawed by its subject."[1] "Standard (but overlong) action film."[2] **Final Word** Hopefully, someday, Hollywood will tell the real story of Kennedy in the Pacific. It would make a terrific movie. In the meantime, checkout *Thirteen Days*, a terrific movie which give a much more nuanced Kennedy during the "Cuban Missile Crisis."

The Purple Heart

1944   USA   b/w   d. Lewis Milestone

WW II: Classic '40s Flagwaver   2.5

This grim fictionalized story is a sort of "what if" account of the aftermath of the "Doolittle Raid." On April 18, 1942 sixteen B-25 bombers launched from the carrier *Hornet* and struck Japan in a surprise attack. Director Lewis Milestone (*All Quiet on the Western Front*), based on a script by Darryl Zanuck, offers a political show trial of eight American crewmen who were shot down on the raid and captured by the Japanese (in reality three American fliers were executed by the Japanese). The issue is not about accidentally bombing civilians, but about trumped up charges of machine-gunning women and children and bombing hospitals and schools. In order to circumvent the Geneva Convention the crew is charged with murder and tried in civil court. So far, so good—there's even a nice plot advance. A Japanese army intelligence officer is in a political struggle with a naval officer who insists that the Americans couldn't possibly have gotten a carrier close enough to launch. If the crew will tell where they've launched from, the charges would be dismissed (Roosevelt simply told the world they launched from Shangri-la). At this point, the movie take a turn for the worse. The scenes of confinement and torture become uninteresting, and slow the movie to a standstill. Perhaps it's the sentimental poetry, the flashback of Capt. Ross (Dana Andrews) with his wife and child, the predictability of the crews refusal to break, or their constant defiance and patriotic gestures in the courtroom. But, mostly, the film's problem is its predictability. The crew is going to choose execution over providing information. While the "Doolittle Raid" was a great morale booster, it was hardly the secret it's being treated as here. When the prisoners exit the courtroom with the *Battle Hymn of the Republic* playing, viewers are left with a queasy feeling that what has transpired is more a collective act of suicide than patriotism.

What the critics say Critics rate this movie 2.0 to 4.0. "Relentlessly somber flagwaver...persuasively presented."[1] "This fascinating film is a minor classic."[6] "Vitriolic Jap-basher."[8] **Final Word** Interestingly, today, the US is trying al-Qaida terrorists in military tribunals for war crimes against civilians as a means of circumventing civil trials, while acknowledging the use of torture.

Pursuit of the Graf Spee

1956   GBR   color   d. Michael Powell/Emeric Pressburger

WW II: Naval Warfare   **3.5**

It was no accident that Britannia ruled the waves for nearly 400 years. However, WW II marked the beginning of the decline of Britain's remarkable history of seafaring dominance (but not quite yet). This movie, written and directed by Michael Powell and Emeric Pressburger, documents the first major naval engagement of World War II as the British hunt down the German pocket battleship KMS *Admiral Graf Spee*. The battleship was highly modernized and faster than the traditional battleship, but more heavily armed than a cruiser. It was mobile and deadly. The action takes place in late 1939, just months after the start of WW II. The commander of a force of three British cruisers, Commodore Harwood (Anthony Quayle), is confronted with trying to track down the *Graf Spee*, which he likens to finding a needle in a haystack. With limited intelligence and with some good guesses, the commodore successfully predicts where the *Graf Spee* will show up next (one of the last major naval battles without radar). In a dramatic battle, the German ship is damaged and forced to seek refuge in the neutral port of Montevideo, Uruguay. International law limits the ship's stay; as a result Capt. Langsdorff (Peter Finch), unable to escape, must fight it out or turn his ship over to a neutral nation. He opts to scuttle the ship at sea. Most of the footage at sea is of real ships, while the battle scenes look studio bound. Where this potentially very good movie falters is in telling the story. There are too many shifting points of view, as well as a lack of interesting characters. Initially, the story is told from Langsdorff's perspective, then from that of the captured British officers on the *Graf Spee*, then from the view of British commanders at sea, and finally as a diplomatic and intelligence effort from Montevideo. The portrayal of Langsdorff as an honorable war hero (chivalrous Prussian) has some basis in fact.

What the critics say Critics rate this movie 2.0. to 3.5 "Disappointingly patchy and studio bound."[1] "Taut documentary-style account."[2] "Highly enjoyable...featuring a solid cast."[8] **Final Word** The film omitted that Admiral Langsdorff committed suicide after scuttling his ship. Slow and lightly armored, "surface raiders" such as the *Graf Spee* and *Bismarck* were obsolete before they ever left drydock.

Raid on Entebbe

1977   USA   color   tv   d. Irvin Kershner

ISR-PAL Conflict : Commando Operation   2.0

Three very average movies were made about this successful
Israeli commando operation, including *Raid on Entebbe*. Both
this movie and *Victory at Entebbe* were made for TV, while the
motion picture *Operation Thunderbolt* was made in Israel. All
three were rushed into production almost immediately after the
event. The two TV movies have surprisingly star-studded casts.
Raid on Entebbe features Peter Finch, in his last role, as Prime
Minister Rabin, as well as Martin Balsam, Jack Warden, John
Saxon, and Charles Bronson. (The cast of *Victory at Entebbe*
includes Kirt Douglas, Burt Lancaster, Anthony Hopkins and
Richard Dreyfus, among others.) For those not familiar with the
raid on June 27, 1976, the Popular Front for the Liberation of
Palestine hijacked Air France flight 139 on its way from Tel Aviv
to Paris by way of Athens. The plane was then forcibly landed at
Entebbe, Uganda. With the cooperation of Ugandan President
and Field Marshal for Life, Idi Amin Dada (in an outstanding
performance by Yaphet Kotto as the insouciant "Big Daddy"), the
hijackers demanded the release of 53 "revolutionary heroes" who
were being held for acts of terrorism in Germany, Switzerland,
France and Israel. They also demanded 5 million dollars. Eight
days later, on July 4, 1976, an Israeli commando team, headed
by Gen. Shomron (Charles Bronson in this film), flew two C-130s
2,500 miles undetected, and successfully landed at the Entebbe
airport under cover of night. In a firefight with the terrorists and
Ugandan soldiers, the commando team extracted the hostages
and returned safely to Israel. This sounds exciting and was no
doubt terrifying for the hostages. Unfortunately, every aspect of
this movie feels as if it were rushed, and not a single character is
developed. It plays more like a corporate training film for
workplace violence than an exciting real-life action drama.

What the critics say Critics rate this movie 2.0 to 3.5.
"Intelligent drama."[2] "A gripping actioner all the more compelling
because true."[5] **Final Word** Amin was driven into exile in 1979,
after having murdered 100-300,000 of his countrymen. He died
in 2003 at the age of 75, having lived a comfortable retirement in
Saudi Arabia. *Amin: The Rise and Fall* is a very average 1981
movie chronicling his reign of terror.

Raid on Rommel

1971   USA   color   d. Henry Hathaway

It's hard to understand why *Raid on Rommel* was ever made. The movie has the same exact fictional storyline as *Tobruk*, which was made four years earlier (one critic suggested it might originally have been intended for television). It opens in Libya in 1942 with a team of British commandos attempting to infiltrate the city of Tobruk. They want to knock out a coastal gun emplacement overlooking the harbor to allow the Royal Navy to land a larger commando force. This force would then destroy large underground fuel depots supplying Rommel's panzer divisions heading for the Suez Canal. From the British standpoint, there is urgency here—they do not want Rommel to gain access to the Suez Canal and to the oil fields of the Middle East. This version of the story stars Richard Burton as Capt. Alex Foster, while the older one featured George Peppard (neither actor has a very good German accent). *Raid on Rommel* not only has many of the same exact scenes as *Tobruk*, it actually uses a great deal of the action footage from Tobruk. The only significant difference is that *Tobruk* utilized German Jews to impersonate German soldiers, while *Raid on Rommel* used British commandos impersonating German soldiers. The characters also include a beautiful Italian woman, the consort of an Italian general and a seductive hysteric (Danielle De Metz), who has to be medicated occasionally to be kept quiet. (There is some suggestion of impropriety by one British soldier.) There's also one of those typically incongruous scenes that must have been improvised during shooting, when a British doctor swaps stamp collecting stories with Rommel (Wolfgang Preiss). Richard Burton's presence in this movie is a complete mystery. In fact, his performance suggests that George Peppard might be able to act. Burton looks as if he had been tranquilized, and doesn't brings the slightest flair to a German tank commander.

What the critics say Critics rate this movie 1.0. to 2.0 "Dispirited low-budget actioner."[1] "Worn-out WW 2 actioner."[2] "Predictable drivel."[5] **Final Word** Many historians have suggested that the North African theater of war had no strategic relevance to either side and that Tobruk, which changed hands three times, was only important for propaganda purposes on the homefronts. This might explain why there are so many irrelevant movies about it.

Reach for the Sky

1956   CAN/GBR   b/w   d. Lewis Gilbert

WW II: Biopic of RAF Fighter Pilot   4.0

If this story wasn't basically true, most audiences would groan that it's all too improbable to be believed. This inspiring story is based on the biography, *The Story of Douglas Bader* by Paul Brickhill, about the highly decorated RAF pilot Douglas Bader. Bader overcame a disabling injury from a plane crash and the surgical amputation of both of his legs in 1931 to became a fighter ace during the Battle of Britain. When Britain declared war on Germany in 1939, Bader was allowed to rejoin the RAF. A natural leader, he innovated fighter tactics and was soon made a Wing Commander. Shot down over France in 1941, Bader was taken prisoner by the Germans. He made three escape attempts until he was freed by Allied troops from Colditz Castle in 1945. As with almost all attempts at war hero biographies, it's extremely difficult to know where entertaining drama and characters leave off and the real people begin. Of this much we can be certain—Bader was an individual of great personal courage and an indomitable spirit. Nearly dying in the plane crash in which he was showing-off, Bader recovered and immediately began wearing tin prosthetic legs, refusing to ever use a cane. Kenneth More portrays Bader as smart, competitive, athletic, prone to disobeying the rules, and possessing an extremely engaging personally. The movie reveals nothing about Bader's early life or his life after the war, and there's little insight into his inner-character or what drove him to such achievements. If he was possessed by demons, this movie does not reveal them. The acting is excellent, and the special effects, along with documentary war footage, are well-integrated. For modern war film sensibilities, *Reach for the Sky* probably plays somewhat naive and sentimental, but enough of the truth shines through to make this an inspiring and entertaining film.

What the critics say Critics rate this movie 2.5 to 3.5 "Kenneth More (Bader) depicts with unerring skill the humor, friendliness and supreme fortitude of one of the war's most honored heroes."[4] "In hindsight, actually, it is a preening, sentimental and outmoded film. It's not very palatable."[8] **Final Word** Most war biopics make it nearly impossible to get close to a real war hero, but this story is so compelling it's worth watching.

The Red Badge of Courage

1951 USA b/w d. John Huston

Civil War: Heroism and Cowardice   3.5

This was a highly unusual movie for its time, as was the book by Stephen Crane for its time (1895). The story is a psychological study of an introspective and anxious young soldier heading into battle. Directed by John Huston, the film stars Audie Murphy (America's most decorated WW II soldier). Crane, twenty-one at the time he wrote this classic, had never served in the military and took many of the details for his book from newspaper accounts of the battle at Chancellorsville in 1863. The main character, "the youth," is an 18-year-old enlistee in the Union army. Fearful that he will act cowardly and flee from battle, "the youth" deals with his anxiety by constantly talking with others soldiers, but never lets on that he's afraid. Later, in order to cope with his fears, "the youth" isolates himself from the other soldiers or puts on an act of false bravado. There is also a pompous narration that tell us—"He felt alone in space. No one else seemed to be wrestling with such a terrific personal problem. He was a mental outcast." In his regiment's first engagement with Confederate troops, "the youth" watches as many of the men around him flee. Fearful, he also runs. Later, too ashamed to return to his unit, he finds out that they had held the line. Disconsolate and wondering aimlessly, "the youth" is struck by the rifle butt of a fleeing Union soldier. In effect, "the youth" receives his "red badge of courage." As the battle is reengaged, he charges ahead time and again, impervious to any danger to himself. He's now seen by his comrades as a brave and heroic soldier. There's still much debate about exactly what Crane had wanted to say in his book. It's clear that "the youth" was motivated by fear each time—the first time by fear of death and the second time by fear of what his comrades would think of him. Crane appears to make the case that there is no simple heroic motive in soldiers. There are several well-staged battle scenes and the acting throughout is very good.

What the critics say Critics rate this movie 3.0 to 4.5. "Fresh, poetic but dramatically unsatisfactory."[1] "Curiously moody, arty study of the psychological birth of a fighting man."[4] "Sweeping battle scenes."[5] **Final Word** *The Thin Red Line* and *When Trumpets Fade* are two recent films that explore the psychology of combat. This is an area ripe for exploration by war movies.

Red Ball Express
1952 USA b/w d. Budd Boetticher

| WW II: Action-Complainer | 2.5 |

This movie raises the serious question, if soldiers didn't complain would there be armies? The soldiers of the army transportation company in question are self-described "gold-brickers, trouble-makers and misfits." However, when it really counted, they learned to pull together. In this sense the film does not vary significantly from the earlier 1940s flagwavers. It tells the story of Patton's 3rd Army breakout at Normandy and of the US Army's efforts to organize 6,000 trucks to supply him with fuel, ammunition and food. (The term "red ball express" was a railroad term for "high priority freight.") Just about everyone in this outfit has a bone to pick. None of the commanders believes this mission can be accomplished. The entire operations is a hodge-podge of men and equipment from different commands. In charge of the company of "bus drivers and traveling gas station attendants" is Lt. Campbell (Jeff Chandler), a tough but fair-minded officer who is hated by his first sergeant, Sgt. Kallek (Alex Nicol). Kallek blames Campbell for the death of his brother in civilian life. Pvt. Wilson (Hugh O'Brien) is resident cynic and chronic malcontent and Cpl. Robertson (Sidney Poitier) believes that the lieutenant is treating him in a prejudicial manner. Attempts at levity are supplied by the bumbling and romantically inclined Pvt. Partridge (Charles Drake). Unfortunately, it's all very formulaic and familiar, and the action consists of watching lots of trucks being driven from here to there and unloaded between complaints. Given that the American army was not integrated until after WW II, it's nice that Hollywood choose to have three Black soldiers in this company (Sidney Poitier, Bubber Johnson and Davis Roberts), who actually had lines and relevant role, and introduces racism as an issue in the film. With voice-over narration and documentary war footage, this low-budget affair fails to derive any dramatic tension from the events, the characters, or the quarrels between them.

What the critics say Critics rate this movie 2.0 to 3.0. "Standard war adventure, not too convincingly mounted."[1] "Pretty good WW 2 story."[2] "Fast-paced action highlights this WW II story."[5] **Final Word** This is a pretty straightforward attempt to look at the stressors of command and the difficulty of getting soldiers to work as a team.

Red Dawn
1984 USA color d. John Milius

Cold War: WW III Survivalist Fantasy   2.5

It is probably safe to say that nearly every American male has secretly fantasized about the United States being invaded by a foreign army. As the world's most heavily armed civilian population, we would be on the beaches waiting, hoping the enemy would show up. But writer Kevin Reynolds and director John Milius have a different scenario—one that's closer to paranoid, survivalist fantasy than reality. The Soviet Union launches selected nuclear strikes against command and control centers in the US (Washington, D.C., SAC bomber and missile bases, and so forth), and then unleashes the Cuban army to invade the midwest while Soviet troops invade through Alaska. If you can stop laughing long enough to suspend disbelief, you will find a slow-moving, plotless and violent film that, at times, comes closer to an wilderness adventure than serious resistance movie. The story has Cuban paratroopers invade a town in Colorado and shoot school children, while a handful of teenagers (Patrick Swayze and Charlie Sheen, among others) hightail it to the mountains to form a resistance movement. The Commies burn books, ruthlessly execute civilians, and imprison people in re-education camps. In the meantime, Soviet and Cuban troops are successfully holding zones of occupation throughout the US. That's it for this story. While the action scenes and special effects are well done, there are no real characters or subplots, no romances, no attempts to aid the town people, no efforts to hookup with other resistance movements or the military. The plot ends in a silly *mano-a-mano* shoot-out between the "bad" Russian colonel and Swayze. Not surprisingly, the best line is a bumper sticker proclaiming—"They can have my gun when they pry it from my cold dead fingers," which actually happens here a lot.

What the critics say Critics rate this movie 2.0 to 3.5. "Ludicrous...Cold War throwback with little entertainment value."[1] "Good premise gunned down by purple prose and posturing—not to mention violence."[2] "Contrived (and often ridiculous) political action-adventure film."[3] "Nothing more than Reaganesque paranoia."[8] **Final Word** The true survivalist fantasy is being hunted down by your own government (Ruby Ridge, Waco)—but in 1984 the Commies were the next best thing .

Reluctant Heroes

1971   USA   color   tv   d. Robert Day

Korean War: Misfits Become Heroes   1.5

This low-budget television production is an embarrassing mix of low-brow humor, politically correct sentiments and ridiculous wartime heroics. Set during the Korean War, a group of "misfits"—Pvt. Rivera (Trini Lopez), Cpl. Sprague (Warren Oates), Cpl. Lukens (Jim Hutton), Sgt. Bryce (Cameron Mitchell) and Lt. Murphy (Ken Berry), among others, have been ordered to establish an observation post on Hill 656. They soon come under heavy fire by North Korean soldiers and have no way of getting off the hill. (As a result a lots of witless events take place.) What we have here is a generic attempt at a "misfits" picture (*The Devil's Brigade, The Dirty Dozen, Kelly's Heroes*) that frequently lapses into a confused, stupid, TV war-humor episode of *Hogan's Heroes* or *McHale's Navy*. (The success of these movies no doubt encouraged the producer to find the lowest common denominator for a stupid-humor war movie.) Lt. Murphy, the reluctant leader of this squad, happens to be a Army historian who eschews all trappings of rank, and prefers to be addressed on a first name basis. In fact, this entire movie is about the lieutenant's transformation from *idiot savant* to heroic leader, as he uses his knowledge as a military historian to prevent his men from being killed. In the process, the squad blows up a bridge and saves its regiment from certain annihilation. Oddly, there are several intense scenes of racial conflict. In one, a white soldier racially insults a Black medic (Warren Oates). Then in keeping with the "happy" face of war presented by this movie, this conflict is resolved by having the racist soldier invite the medic to get together after the war. Let's just say that it's truly difficult to reconcile this movie's theme song of "Old MacDonald Had a Farm," with a soldier taking a bullet in the head. At the end, the "reluctant hero," Lt. Murphy—who still does not know how to salute—goes off to play with the children at a nearby Buddhist orphanage. Somehow, the squad manages to take only one serious casualty, which raises the question: Why did anyone have to die in this movie?

What the critics say No available reviews. **Final Word** This movie was reviewed because it was a "rare" Korean War movie. And, in the tradition of every Korean War movie ever made, it's not very good.

Retreat, Hell!

1952   USA   b/w   d. Joseph H. Lewis

Korean War: Infantry Combat   3.0

The title of this film refers to a statement made by Gen. O.P. Smith regarding the Marines' retreat from North Korea in 1950. His full statement was, "Retreat?! Hell, we're just attacking in another direction." This is a "standard" war movie that was well done and had the potential to be outstanding. The story follows the Marine Corps 1st Reserve Battalion as it is called up to active duty—"Retreads from the last war, kids without combat experience, untried men."—and deployed as part of the landing force during the invasion of North Korea at Inchon. Meeting with very little resistance, the battalion penetrates to within 60 miles of the Yalu River and Communist China. The Chinese then mount a surprise counteroffensive and drive UN forces from the Pusan Reservoir area to the 38th Parallel. *Retreat Hell!* shows this episode of the Korean War in graphic detail, with many excellent combat scenes and well-integrated documentary footage. This movie is also without much politics, which is one of its significant failings. It does not touch on the "big picture" behind the invasion or the politics of pursuing the North Koreans to the Chinese border. At a personal level, the stories are interesting but still too stock and too "Marine to the core" to be truly three-dimensional. There's tough, no-nonsense Lt. Col. Corbet (Frank Lovejoy); Capt. Hansen (Richard Carlson), a married WW II vet with a family, who resents his call-up to active duty; and the young, naive private (Russ Tamblyn). Unfortunately, the characters fall all over each other in trying to prove they are good Marines. However, this movie achieves a high level of combat realism and portrays the heroic efforts of Marines fighting and surviving under extremely difficult circumstances. At one point, they are cut off from ground resupply and run out of ammunition as the Chinese are attacking. Their order to "fix bayonets," is one of many tense and well-done scenes.

What the critics say Critics rate this movie 2.5 to 3.0. "Grim drama."[2] "Topnotch war drama...with tense action."[4] "Standard gun-ho military orientation with dismal results."[5] "Predictable war film."[7] "Pays little more than lip service to the context of the US Marine's retreat from Chosin."[8] **Final Word**. A very good but flawed war film. One of the better Korean War films. Check it out.

Rough Riders

1997 USA color tv d. John Milius

Spanish-American War: San Juan Hill   3.0

The so-called "Splendid Little War" (four months in 1898), as portrayed here, makes America's 19th century imperialistic expansionism and military jingoism look like a *National Lampoon* vacation movie. The characters are so cliché and over-the-top that they border on parody. Tom Berenger, as Teddy Roosevelt, looks and acts like an *idiot savant*. Sam Elliott continues in the very tired role as a larger-than-life man's man, and Gary Busey plays a renegade, alcoholic general (Gen. "Fighting Joe" Wheeler) spoofing his many roles as a psychotic. If waging war is truly as idiotic as unintentionally suggested here, and it may well be, then this is one of the strongest arguments yet against it. While this movie attempts to highlight the adventurism this war engendered in the men who volunteered, it comes too close to making them look like weekend paintball warriors. The story focuses on the 1st US Volunteer Cavalry that was formed to help spearhead an attack on the Spanish in Cuba. Admittedly, the Cubans had implemented some draconian measures (concentration camps) that resulted in an insurgency movement. In seeking naval bases and booty in the Pacific and Caribbean, the US found a perfect opportunity to justify its actions when the USS *Maine* exploded in Havana harbor. (The explosion was blamed on a Spanish mine—sounds like the Tonkin Gulf Incident.) The Spanish, knowing they could never defeat the US, did the honorable thing, skirmished and surrendered. This movie does have one redeeming feature; it reenacts for nearly an hour one hell of an intense, large-scale battle between American and Cuban soldiers, and culminates in the charge up San Juan Hill. Outstanding period detail and plenty of artillery and machine gun fire (Maxims and Colts) enliven the conflict. Total US combat casualties were 385 dead and 1,662 wounded. Post-war investigation determined that the *Maine* blew up due to an internal explosion.

What the critics say Critics rate this movie 3.0 to 4.0. "High production values...epic battle scenes blend grit with glory."[7] **Final Word** Action war-guys will find this movie highly entertaining. For everyone else, it will all seem too pumped up with a lot of questionable gallantry.

Rules of Engagement

2000   USA   color   d. William Friedkin

This movie opens as a quasi-Vietnam War "buddy" film with an intense, well-done combat scene, and then fast forwards to post-Desert Storm. The Vietnam War buddies are now Marine colonels, with Tommy Lee Jones portraying Col. Hodges, a Marine JAQ officer, and Samuel L. Jackson as Col. Childers, commander of a Marine special operations battalion. Childers is ordered in to rescue the US ambassador to Yemen and his family who are under siege from a radical Muslim terrorist group. Two squads of Marines are choppered in and immediately come under heavy fire and take casualties. After completing the rescue, Childers orders his men to open fire on a crowd in front of the embassy, in which there are many unarmed men, women and children. Eighty-three people are killed and 100 wounded. This is all shown with a high degree of authenticity and great intensity. However, what follows is an empty legal drama replete with a drunken buddy fight scene and a rogue National Security Advisor who destroys video evidence that would exculpate Childers. Childers claims he saw terrorists in the crowd shooting at him and his men, and ordered his men to return fire. However, after the event, there is no evidence that the crowd was armed. Childers is charged with murder and violation of the "rules of engagement." It also appears that he's being made a scapegoat in order to appease moderate Arabs. Based on a novel by former Secretary of the Navy, James Webb, this movie has too many plot holes to be anything more than what it is—glib entertainment pandering to its two stars Jones and Jackson. The fact is, Childers didn't really have to fire into the crowd in order to escape the embassy rooftop. A more interesting take would have been for Childers to have tried to cover up his actions and later be acquitted, and have to live with the guilt of this personal knowledge. Instead, there is a predictable story and ending.

What the critics say Critics rate this movie 3.5 to 4.0. "Watchable but sometimes silly melodrama."[1] "Merely grazes the complex issues of military decision-making due to its skeletal script."[5] **Final Word** James Webb was obviously more prescient of events to come in the Middle East than most State Department undersecretaries and CIA analysts.

A Rumor of War

1980   USA   color   tv   d. Richard T. Heffron

Vietnam War: Combat Hell	5.0

This outstanding film was adapted from the Pulitzer Prize-winning novel by Philip Caputo about his Vietnam War experiences. Originally a TV movie, it was given a video release with nearly 1.5 hours edited from the original. Brad Davis plays a young man seeking to prove himself and to "be a somebody." Having just graduated from college in 1964, Caputo enters Marine Officer Candidate School. Upon graduation he is immediately shipped to Vietnam as an inexperienced second lieutenant. The film then chronicles a series of "in country" patrols seeking to make contact with the Vietcong. In a brief interlude from combat, Lt. Caputo is assigned to the 3rd Marine Headquarters to tally "body counts" and "calculate kill-ratios." Here, he sardonically dissects the pathology of commanders out of contact with the realities of the battlefield. Dismayed and angry at what he sees Caputo volunteers to return to his company. In an emotionally moving and believable manner, this film succeeds in slowly showing Lt. Caputo's transformation—as a result of his combat experiences—from naive and idealistic soldier to a killer and survivor. Intelligent and realistic, this film has a strong supporting cast (Brian Dennehy, Stacy Keach, Keith Carradine and Michael O'Keefe). *A Rumor of War* ultimately seeks to explore how soldiers can no longer separate good killing from bad killing. Lt. Caputo tells us—"We relieved our own pain and fear by inflicting it on others." As they routinely face death from an enemy that is undetectable from the civilian population, and those closest to them are being killed, they close ranks. Later, when Caputo is tried and acquitted for the murder of civilians, he simply acknowledges, "I had survived, that was my only victory." This film offers a scathing indictment of military command, yet remains fairly neutral about American involvement in the Vietnam War.

What the critics say Critics rate this movie 4.5 to 5.0. "Outstanding made-for-TV Vietnam War drama...compelling and rich performance by Brad Davis."[3] "The first big Vietnam drama for TV is a triumph."[5] "Solidly realistic atmosphere and a deeper understanding of the mistakes that were made in the early stages of the Vietnam War...that acting is superb."[6] **Final Word** Definitely check this movie out if you haven't seen it. It's one of the best Vietnam War movies.

Run Silent, Run Deep

1958 USA b/w d. Robert Wise

WW II: Command Conflict on a Sub　　　　4.0

With overtones of the maniacal Captain Ahab hunting down
Moby Dick (the white whale), Commander Richardson (Clark
Gable) of the USS *Nerka* is hell bent on sinking the Japanese
destroyer that sunk his sub off the coast of Japan a year earlier.
The only problem is that Lt. Bledsoe (Burt Lancaster) was in line
to take command of the *Nerka* and is resentful that Capt.
Richardson pulled strings to get the command. What transpires
from here is an intense and well-paced drama in the claustrophobic confines of a submarine. The loyalties of the crew and
officers are split, and even suggest the possibility of a mutiny.
Lancaster excels as Executive Officer Bledsoe, trying to contain
his personal resentment, but openly questioning Commander
Richardson's decision making when he violates their basic order.
Demanding and obsessive, Commander Richardson senses the
crew's hostility towards him and relies on his authority to make
the ship operate by his standards. This movie is a gripping
examination of command conflict, particularly since the commander's judgment is questionable, if not impaired. If this film
has a major flaw, it was in not pursuing the conflict between
these two officers to its inevitable conclusion. Instead, the
director gives us a happy ending, when Executive Officer Bledsoe begins to identify with Commander Richardson, providing
Richardson the redemption he had been seeking. While
Lancaster shines in his role, Gable appears tired and dissipated
as the commanding officer. Because the filmmakers had the
cooperation of the Navy, there is a high degree of realism with
excellent special effects. Adapted from a novel by Commander
Edward L. Beach, this story may have been too Navy—the whale
is killed and everyone lives happily ever after. (I don't think so!).

What the critics say Critics rate this movie 2.0 to 4.5.
"Competent, unsurprising war actioner trading on its stars."[1]
"One of the great WW 2 'sub' pictures."[2] "A taut, exciting drama
of submarine warfare."[4] "Pity the script and plot are not strong-
enough for the above average cast."[8] **Final Word** This move is
well worth watching, with great sub action and human drama
below the high seas.

Sahara

1943   USA   b/w   d. Zoltan Korda

WW II: Classic '40s Flagwaver   **2.5**

A classic 1940s Hollywood war movie directed by Zoltan Korda,, *Sahara* is a mildly entertaining actioner trapped by the propaganda demands of its era. Humphrey Bogart plays Sgt. Joe Gunn, an American tank commander attached to the British 8th Army. The British have been driven back by Rommel's Afrika Korps, and Sgt. Gunn and his crew (Dan Duryea and Bruce Bennett) have been ordered to retreat toward the British lines. Along the way, they encounter six British soldiers (South African, Scottish, Welsh, Irish and English), and then a British Sudanese soldier, Sgt Tambul (played by Rex Ingram, a Black-American in a surprisingly prominent supporting role for the times). Sgt. Tambul also has an Italian prisoner (J. Carrol Naish). Later a German pilot is added as they make their way to an abandoned settlement with a well that barely drips water (and, yes, we now have a microcosm of the world at war here). Up until now, this has been a fairly interesting movie with strong characters and thoughtful interaction. But when Sgt. Gunn steps forward to suggest making a stand to fend off a German mechanized battalion of 500 soldiers in order to slow their advancement, you can only groan in disbelief. While Gunn doesn't mention the Alamo, he does toss in Bataan and Corregidor in a lengthy speech about sacrifice which everyone buys into—when they could have easily escaped and informed the British of the German position. (Holy moley!) While Bogart was in the process of becoming a star, his role here is one-dimensional. Humorless and unfriendly, he issues orders, takes command and robs the film of any tension about who is in charge or what they are going to do next. The action is lackluster and unrealistic as ten guys and an aging M-3 tank hold off 500 German soldiers—they even get the Germans to surrender at the end. (Right!) A popular film at the box-office, British audiences were not as enthusiastic about a lone American leading them to victory.

What the critics say Critics rate this movie 3.0 to 4.5. "Pithy dialog, lusty action and suspense...avoiding ultra-theatrics throughout."[4] "Yes, the plot is ludicrous and the symbolism sledgehammer-subtle, but some of the action is top-notch."[8]
Final Word This reprise of John Ford's *The Lost Patrol* is done in by plot flaws and patriotic speeches.

Sands of Iwo Jima

1949 USA color d. Allan Dwan

WW II: Classic '40s Flagwaver	3.0

This is probably John Wayne's most complex and sympathetic character among his WW II films. As Sgt. John M. Stryker, he instills fear and discipline in his men. One Marine complains— "Sometimes I don't know which I hate worst, him or the Nips." On a personal level Stryker is deeply conflicted, drinks too much and is estranged from his ex-wife and young son. He's as much at war with himself as with the enemy. While this hugely popular film is probably Wayne's best war movie, it's still not a great war film, mostly because these movies were designed as star vehicles for him and, as a result, too much is often missing. When Wayne has a brief interlude with a young prostitute, and stops getting drunk after helping her out, his complex character softens and his heroic screen image is protected by the studio once again. (The extensive colorized documentary film showing US Marines taking Tarawa and Iwo Jima is the real star of the movie.) The film opens with Stryker and his squad redeployed to New Zealand after having fought on Guadalcanal. Most of the drama revolves around two members of his rifle squad who can't stand his tough, give-no-quarters attitude—"Before I am through with you, you're going to move like one man and think like one man. If you don't you'll be dead." In the end, despite much melodrama, the squad predictably comes to appreciate what Stryker had forced them to learn. Because the conflicts between Stryker and his men have no real plausible cause, their happy resolution feels hollow. When Stryker catches a sniper bullet, and a letter to his son is read, it's all a bit too much. Structurally, this films suffers from repeating itself, and by the time the Marines invade Iwo Jima, it's one island too many. While this is an entertaining movie, it doesn't wander far enough from the other safe flagwaving efforts of the 1940s to be a great film.

What the critics say Critics rate this movie 3.5 to 4.5. "Story and character are pretty two-dimensional and a bit worn."[2] "Falls short of greatness because of its sentimental core and its superficial commentary on war."[4] "The portrayal seems the definitive Wayne."[8] **Final Word** The final scene of Marines raising the flag on Mt. Suribachi, on February 23, 1945, included three Marines who staged the actual event.

Saving Private Ryan

1998   USA   color   d. Steven Spielberg

WW II: Infantry Combat   4.0

This movie opens with one of the most intense and visceral portraits of combat ever put on film. Director Steven Spielberg provides a harrowing grunt's eye-view of the Allied invasion at Normandy. From here the story focuses on the days immediately following, as a squad of eight soldiers, led by Capt. John Miller (Tom Hanks), is sent on a mission to find a Pvt. Ryan (Matt Damon) who parachuted into France on D-Day. Because Ryan's three brothers have been recently killed in combat, he is to be relieved of combat duty. The movie's central question—how many lives do you risk to save the life of one man? is unfortunately not a particularly important question in the middle of the Normandy Invasion. In a lethal environment with a high mortality rate, Capt. Miller seems somewhat oblivious as he and his squad proceed on a philosophical quest to justify their possible deaths—while thousands of men are dying all around them! The circumstances feel contrived and the impact of this is only amplified by its unoriginal exploration and the stringing together of too many war movie clichés. Too often Spielberg's instincts reach for the emotional jugular. As an example, there's an overly emotional scene in which a German soldier pleads for his life, and later Sgt. Horvath (Tom Sizemore) pulls a gun on one of his own squad members. The story itself is framed with two sets of bookends, one overly sentimental in which an elderly Pvt. Ryan returns to France to visit the grave sites of those he fought alongside. However, the second set of book ends truly distinguishes this film as a superior war movie. The reenactment of the invasion at Omaha Beach is astounding in its ferocity and brutality. Near the end of the movie, a lengthy and gripping combat sequence shows us a handful of American soldiers holding a bridge against German armor. In some ways the intensity even exceeds the opening combat scenes. The acting is excellent throughout the film and the use of handheld cameras gives a documentary effect that adds considerable realism.

What the critics say Critics rate this move 4.5 to 5.0. "Crafted with...realism, raw emotion and technical superiority."[3] "A vivid, realistic and bloody portrait of armed conflict."[4] **Final Word** The craftsmanship is impeccable but the story-telling is too simple to put this in the pantheon among the best ever.

Savior

1998   USA   color   d. Pedrag Antonijevic

Balkans Conflict: Antiwar	5.0

This powerful antiwar film explores the atrocity-ridden civil war in Bosnia as seen through the experiences of an American army officer turned Serbian mercenary. Produced by Oliver Stone and filmed in the Republic of Montenegro, the story descends into this war torn country with Joshua Rose (Dennis Quaid) as he begins a long and bitter journey of redemption. In 1987 Rose is an American army officer stationed in Paris when a bombing by Muslim terrorists kills his wife and son. In a murderous rage, he walks into a nearby mosque and shoots everyone praying there. For the next six years he serves in the French Foreign Legion— his means of hiding and starting his life over. In 1993, at the end of his enlistment, he becomes a mercenary soldier and sniper for the Serbian army in Bosnia. He has become a cold-blooded assassin, killing whoever comes into his sights. In one chilling scene he shoots a young boy to death as he casually extinguishes a cigarette with his boot. Later, while at a prisoner exchange, Rose meets Vera (Natasa Ninkovic), a young Serbian woman who is pregnant having been raped by Muslims. The remainder of this movie is a tense and emotional drama as Rose attempts to rescue Vera, the baby, and himself from the craziness and killing surrounding them. This woman and child ignite feelings in Rose that he had buried about his own family, as he slowly begins to care about something more than killing. Dennis Quaid and Natasa Ninkovic give outstanding and emotionally compelling performances in a film that is chillingly real in its depiction of the torture and murder of civilians. In a brutal and haunting scene near the end, a busload of civilians is commandeered by Croatian soldiers and bludgeoned with a sledge hammer for the soldiers' bemusement. *Savior* brings an intense realism that works at many levels, including allegorical, to what has transpired in the Balkans.

What the critics say Critics rate this movie 3.0 to 4.5. "Gut-wrenching film inspired by a true story."[5] "Dennis Quaid's performance is stellar."[7] **Final Word** Surprisingly not many critics reviewed this movie. This is compelling war movie making that will be hard for many to watch .

The Sea Shall Not Have Them

1954   GBR   b/w   d. Lewis Gilbert

WW II: Air-Sea Rescue	1.5

This movie is an earnest effort to tell the story of British air and sea rescue efforts during World War II. In retrospect, a 15-minute documentary would have done the job better. Slow moving, this movie defines generic British WW II film. Released in 1954 and based on a novel by John Harris, it's a 1940s style flagwaving effort to show the valiant efforts of unsung war heroes. The action is shown from four points of view—the command operations center; a downed bomber crew in a lifeboat; the crew of a rescue patrol boat; and briefly, an air rescue crew (in a very interesting biwinged seaplane called the "Sea Otter.") Unfortunately, no story or drama evolves from any of these points of view. The film just switches back and forth from these multiple perspectives and fills the screen with idle chatter, personal gossip, and the sailors' abiding interest in coffee and hot chocolate. Most of the dialog is comprised of British stoicisms and sailors carrying on with complaints about everyday life. There is some attempt at a plot, as one of the soldiers among the downed bomber crew is carrying copies of the German designs for V-1 and V-2 rockets, making his rescue an important intelligence coup. But there isn't even an incoming storm to add drama. The rescue crews finds the lifeboat without much problem, though their boat does break down and they have to wait for repairs. Viewers also get an opportunity to develop an appreciation for the fog and drizzle in the English Channel. In the last few minutes, there is a dramatic rescue run while they evade German shore batteries. (The boat doesn't suffer any serious damage.) The film credits indicate that Michael Redgrave and Dirk Bogarde have starring roles, but they weren't required to act in their brief appearances on screen. No-action, no-drama, low-budget effort that has become a "classic" of sort.

What the critics say Critics rate this movie 2.0 to 3.5. "Decent drama/adventure."[5] "Nicely done WW II film."[7] "Glum tale...seen it all before somewhere."[8] **Final Word** The British War Ministry must have continued churning out these films without realizing the war was over.

Sergeant Rutledge

1960 USA color d. John Ford

Indian Wars: Race-Based Legal Drama 2.5

Only the subject matter distinguishes this movie from a hundred other routine Westerns. Sgt. Rutledge, played by Woody Strode, is a Black sergeant in the 9th US Cavalry, the first all-Black unit (known as "Buffalo Soldiers") formed during the American-Indian wars. Based on a book titled *Captain Buffalo* by James Bellah, and directed by John Ford, this movie centers on the trial of Sgt. Rutledge for rape and murder. The story is told in flashbacks by witnesses testifying at the court-martial. Sgt. Rutledge is portrayed as a man of honor who has acted in a heroic fashion, but is unlikely to receive a fair trial due to racism. Badly scripted, poorly acted and with clumsy storytelling, the movie focuses on a white officer, Lt. Cantrell (Jeffrey Hunter), Rutledge's defense attorney. The court-martial board, comprised of cronies and alcoholics, is a misguided attempt to add levity to a serious subject. However, when the camera is on Sgt. Rutledge an important movie is at work. Strode does an excellent job of portraying a man of dignity, who is faced with events beyond his control. In a poignant moment, the sergeant tells the court that he came back to stand trial because he didn't want to be on the run like some "nigger." "Do you hear me, I am a man." However, this movie is surprisingly unliberated in many other ways; for example, women are routinely ordered about, spoken down to and made to look silly and frivolous (obviously another liberation to come). "Indians" are mostly bloodthirsty savages (yet, another liberation issue to be dealt with). The courtroom drama is stilted and plays out like an episode of *Bonanza*, replete with a *Captain Buffalo* theme song. Ford, an icon of the Western genre, is attempting something important—to confer on a Black man the mantle of western hero, thirty years before Hollywood is ready to embrace this idea. Unfortunately, this is a case of a truly bad movie trying to do something important.

What the critics say Critics rate this movie 3.0 to 4.5. "Strode is commanding in the central role."[2] "A muddled mix of the Old West and contemporary politics."[3] "A detailed look at overt and covert racism handled by master director Ford."[5] **Final Word** Strode, whose presence dominates this movie and who plays the title character, gets second billing in the credits, and is listed with the rest of the cast (still a long way to go here, too).

Sergeant Ryker

1968 USA   color   d. Buzz Kulik

Korean War: Legal Drama 1.5

As a legal drama this movie is just below an average television episode of *Perry Mason* or *Matlock*. In fact, in 1963, *Sergeant Ryker* aired on television as a movie before it received a theatrical release in 1968. What keeps this movie from being even average is the presence of Lee Marvin as Sgt. Ryker. Marvin does his usual impersonation of an angry, defiant soldier who's his own worst enemy (basically, the only role he's ever played). Then again, maybe the problem is the most implausible plot ever concocted for a war movie. Ryker's good friend from his college days is now a Communist Chinese general. As a result, Ryker is sent on a secret mission as a defector to infiltrate the Chinese military command. Upon his return, he's arrested and charged with treason. When the colonel who ordered the mission is killed and Ryker is unable to produce any record authorizing the mission, he's court-martialed and sentenced to be hanged. Wait a minute! The prosecuting attorney for the Army, Capt. Young (Bradford Dillman), doesn't believe Ryker received a fair trial, and with the assistance of Ryker's wife, Ann (Vera Miles), goes on a rampage to get a stay of execution and new trial. In a bizarre sequence, the general in charge of American forces retreating in the face of advancing Communist Chinese forces (this is Korea 1951), takes the time to follow Capt. Young in the middle of the night. Guess what? He discoverers Capt. Young in the arms of Ryker's wife. Now, even though the general ordered Capt. Young's court-martial, he will let the captain represent Ryker in the retrial in order to ensure its impartiality and fairness. (If I were the presiding judge, I would rule the scriptwriter in contempt of court and order the movie held as evidence.) The romantic intrigue here is as tepid as Perry Mason and Della (his reliable secretary) going to lunch. The video cover states, "Lee Marvin explodes into action as Sergeant Ryker. The battlefield is his home...he will protect it...at all costs!" and shows him with an automatic weapon in a combat scene. You might find it misleading.

What the critics say Critics rate this movie 3.0 to 3.5. "Blah courtroom drama."[1] **Final Word** Several other military legal dramas are just as bad, including, *Death of a Soldier, The General's Daughter* and *Serving in Silence*.

300

Sergeant York

1941   USA   b/w   d. Howard Hawks

WW I: War Biopic	3.0

This movie was released twenty-three years after Sergeant Alvin York was awarded the Congressional Medal of Honor. On Oct. 8, 1918, at the battle of Meuse-Argonne, Sgt. York single-handedly killed 25 German soldiers and captured 132 others. When this young Tennessee farm boy returned home from the war, he was greeted as America's greatest wartime hero. York refused to capitalize on his fame and for many years resisted all efforts to make this movie. Eventually he agreed to consult on the movie and provided director Howard Hawks access to his personal diary. Gary Cooper, who played the role of Alvin York, won the Academy Award for Best Actor in 1941. Many critics have made the point that this film was, to a large extent, flagwaving propaganda. It has been described as "Hollywood's most honored piece of propaganda" and as "part of a larger effort by the entertainment industry to prepare the country for WW II."[6] Most of the movie shows us York in the year preceding the US entry into the war, and follows his transformation from trouble maker to religious convert, to conscientious objector. Now to cut to the chase. After watching this movie you will have no idea where the truth ends and Hollywood begins. The movie is one of the greatest heepings of corn pone ever served, and it is also funny, moving, and even sweet, but it's not a serious war movie. Far too many scenes are nothing more than homilies to the noble innocence of the rural poor, or recruitment speeches to justify the war effort. Near the end, the film deteriorates into a patronizing sermon about heroism. And, of course, there is a happy ending. Sixty years after this movie was made, it works better as an American pastoral fable. It pays homage to the values and spirit of America's rural poor, as one man wrestles with his conscience and decides to go to war. Sgt. York becomes the humble icon of America's virtues (or as Alvin himself puts it, the "corn is thicker than fur on a squirrel.").

What the critics say Critics rate this movie 4.5. to 5.0. "In the end Sergeant York is unabashed, unembarrassed hero worship."[6] "It was military propaganda for those Americans with pacifist leanings."[7] **Final Word** Whatever its flaws, this is an entertaining movie and should be seen by all war movie fans, preferably with your kids.

301

Serving in Silence

1995 USA color tv d. Jeff Bleckner

Special Issues: Sexual Orientation   2.5

This movie makes a strong case that preventing gays and lesbians from serving in the military is a prejudice based primarily on fear and ignorance (which is pretty much true). It also purports to tell the story of Col. Margarethe Cammermeyer (Glenn Close), an Army nurse for twenty-five years, who was a decorated Vietnam veteran and Chief of Nursing for the Washington State National Guard. During a security clearance interview, the colonel volunteered that she was a lesbian. A subsequent Army board of inquiry resulted in her "honorable discharge" from the service. The epilogue states that in 1994 the US Supreme Court ruled that the government had violated Col. Cammermeyer's constitutional rights to due process and equal protection and ordered her reinstated. (The military's do no ask, do not tell policy was not addressed.) Beyond this, it's hard to know anything more about Col. Cammermeyer from this feel-good message-film that is mostly feminist polemic. Important aspects of military life and nearly all the legal issues involved are pretty much ignored. The movie also avoids examining the conflicting details of the colonel's life, such as her marriage of 15 years and her four sons, who were apparently more aware of her sexual orientation than she was. However, the most disingenu-ous aspect of this film is its failure to explore any darker motivations Cammermeyer might have had for "outing" herself and challenging the military. Her reason is reduced to the safe message that she is simply a truth-teller at heart and a good person doing what she believes is right. (By the end of the movie Cammermeyer is a nominee for a military accommodation.) Unfortunately, the focus of this film is her uninspiring relationship with a woman artist (Judy Davis), which ultimately leads her to her public acknowledgment that she was a lesbian (I guess she did it for love is the real message here). This movie is right on the issues but wrong on the story.

What the critics say Critics rate this movie 2.5 to 3.5. "This feminist response to the military's "don't ask, don't tell policy was co-produced by Close and Barbara Streisand."[2] "TV film won 3 Emmy awards."[5] **Final Word** Works better as a 20 minute seg-ment on a TV news magazine show. Cammermeyer's father put it best when he stated: "Where is your sense of privacy?"

Seven Days in May

1964   USA   b/w   d. John Frankenheimer

Cold War: Military Coup	5.0

Seven Days in May is a suspenseful, absorbing and highly realistic political thriller. Taken from the novel by Fletcher Knebel and Charles Bailey, and adapted for the screen by Rod Sterling, the movie contemplates the possibility of a US military takeover of the American government. In the plot, Gen. James Scott (Burt Lancaster), Chairman of the Joint Chiefs of Staff and right-wing demagogue, organizes a military coup in the event the President (Fredric March) signs a nuclear non-proliferation treaty with the Soviet Union. Gen. Scott is convinced that the very survival of the United States is at risk if the US disarms in the face of an aggressive and untrustworthy enemy. On the streets, public opinion runs strongly against the treaty, and the President's ratings in the polls plummet to a no-confidence level. Gen. Scott sees himself stepping in and taking control with strong public support and the backing of the entire Joint-Chiefs-of-Staff. Col. Casey (Kirt Douglas), the General's aid, however, is considered too liberal and not quite trustworthy enough to be in the conspiratorial loop. Slowly, the Colonel begins to assemble disparate pieces of information that eventually lead him to believe a coup might be taking place. He then secretly goes to the President with his fears. The second half of the story builds suspense as both sides race to prevail. This drama is truly a companion piece to the 1964 movie *Fail-Safe* (about an accidental nuclear war), as both get to the heart of the underlying hysteria and paranoia that gripped America during the Cold War years. With fears of a worldwide Communist conspiracy, a recent legacy of McCarthyism; the "Cuban Missile Crisis" in 1962; and President Kennedy's assassination in 1963, film makers could plausibly give serious consideration to this possibility. Director John Frankenheimer has created a tense, noirish, well-paced film that is believable and contains outstanding performances throughout.

What the critics say Critics rate this movie 4.0 to 5.0. "This flawless political thriller is so frightening because it is so possible."[3] "A strikingly dramatic, realistic and provocative topical film."[4] **Final Word** We are a people and government founded on distrust of authority and, therefore, I recommend everyone—both "hawks" and "doves"—see this movie to confirm your suspicions.

Shot Through the Heart

1998   USA /CAN   color   tv   d. David Attwood

Balkans Conflict: Antiwar	4.5

This is yet another powerful antiwar movie about the breakup of Yugoslavia and the ensuing civil conflict between centuries-old antagonists (Serbs, Croats and Muslims). Seen through the eyes of the Croatian people of Sarajevo, director David Attwood provides a close-up look at the civil war that beset Bosnia. Based on the article "Anti-Sniper" by John Falk, the story revolves around boyhood friends, Vlado (Linus Roache), a Croat, and Slavko (Vincent Perez), a Serb, who are now competing as adults on the Yugoslavian Olympic competitive-shooting team. With the outbreak of hostilities in 1992, Slavko becomes a sniper instructor for the Serbian army, which has surrounded Sarajevo with tanks and artillery. Vlado, who has a home and business in Sarajevo, stays with his family, and never believes that educated Europeans in a modern city would ever wage war against their friends and neighbors of many decades. Quickly, the streets of Sarajevo become a "killing zone" in which Serbian snipers attempt to terrorize the inhabitants into surrendering, and even randomly shoot women and children. The violence is gut-wrenching, and slowly Vlado begins to realize not only the serious error in judgment he has made, but that his life-long friend is instrumental in the killing. This film is not about Rambo being turned loose, but rather about a man who realizes he has the shooting skills to take out these snipers and to confront his friend. The acting is outstanding. Filmed in Sarajevo and Budapest, this movie is exceptionally realistic and has a visceral impact as the lives of these families and this community disintegrate. What elevates this film above so many other war movies is its ability to intimately involve viewers in the lives of these two soldiers, as their folly unfold in different ways. The sheer authenticity of what is transpiring on film brings you close to the insanity that is occurring— and it is hard to forget.

What the critics say Critics rate this movie 4.0 to 4.5. "Searing tale based loosely on actual events and set during the atrocious, inhuman siege of Sarajevo."[7] **Final Word** A handful of recent movies about the breakup of Yugoslavia are among the best war films ever—*No Man's Land, Pretty Village, Pretty Flame, Savior, Vukovar* and *Welcome to Sarajevo.*

The Siege of Firebase Gloria

1989 USA color d. Brian Trenchard-Smith

| Vietnam War: Combat Hell | 2.5 |

Although this movie opens with the following statement, "This is the story of a group of Marines and how they defended Firebase Gloria against overwhelming odds during the grisly Tet Offensive," there is no indication that it's based on real events. *The Siege of Firebase Gloria* stars Wings Hauser (Cpl. DiNardo) and R. Lee Ermey (Sgt. Major Hafner). Ermey, a former Marine sergeant, also starred in *Boys in Company C* and *Full Metal Jacket*. However, his performance in this movie is so over-the-top that it nearly pushes it into the action-exploitation category— "I'd like to know where those needle-dicked Dinks are getting new AKfortyfucking sevens at." This is a sort of Vietnam War tribute to a long-line of similarly structured war films where the enemy has the good guys surrounded. However, in a bizarre and confusing plot twist halfway through the movie, there is a heroic view of the Vietcong fighting for their country against the American invaders, or as the Sgt. Major puts it, "We were killing Charlie wholesale, but he didn't seem to care. Guess we'd do the same if Charlie occupied South Carolina." In this sense, the movie offers a somewhat neutral view of the war, as both sides are shown committing atrocities. Soldiers on both sides are sacrificed for larger strategic goals and political interests. And they are all dying and killing at a furious pace. But the movie concludes, in its own way, that the Vietcong are dying for something more important. Unfortunately, this film is comprised primarily of war film clichés such as the spaced-out basecamp commander; an orphan child; a naive nurse; and even an old fashioned *mano-a-mano* scene between the VC commander and the Sgt. Major—and just too many similar tired scenes and characters to mention. While there is some great combat action, this is an all out leaden bore because the great action has no dramatic focus.

What the critics say Critics rate this movie 1.5 to 5.0. "Hopelessly hackneyed."[5] "This is the film that John Wayne's *The Green Berets* might have been."[6] "Grisly scenes of death and destruction bring the Vietnam War close to home."[7] **Final Word** This is a low-budget affair that got a limited release and will be hard to find on the video store shelves. Strictly for the hardcore action junkies.

Sink the Bismarck!

1960   GBR   b/w   d. Lewis Gilbert

World War II: Naval Combat	3.0

Directed by Gilbert Lewis and based on a book by C.S. Forester, this popular and entertaining movie details British efforts to sink the newly commissioned German "pocket" battleship KMS *Bismarck*. Shot in documentary style, this movie provides a command view of the British struggle to keep the *Bismarck* from breaking through their blockade into the North Atlantic. In 1941, U-boats were inflicting heavy damage on shipping lanes between Britain and the Unites States. The Germans were anticipating that the *Bismarck*, one of the most powerful battleships of the Second World War, would further help disrupt supply convoys and cripple the British war effort. On the British side, this *cat and mouse* game plays out from inside the Admiralty war room as the new Director of Naval Operations, Capt. Shepard (Kenneth More), takes charge. Capt. Shepard is a "by-the-book" officer who is adverse to letting emotions get in the way of his command. Of course, young, single and very fetching Lt. Anne Davis (Dana Wynter) may have something to say about this. (Its all very sweet and proper of course.) On the other side, the German fleet commander Admiral Lutjens (Karel Stepanek), on board the *Bismarck*, carries on as a fanatical Nazi and Hitler sycophant. With good use of models and documentary footage, this is an exciting real life, high stakes drama. In an initial encounter with the *Bismarck,* the HMS *Hood*, Britain's largest battleship, is sunk with only three survivors out of a crew of 1,500 men. For the British, this is a life or death drama that's played out in the press as the pursuit and evasion takes place over the course of several days. Many factors weighed into the sinking of the *Bismarck* including the weather, British naval air power, and nearly all the breaks going to the British. By today's special effects standards this movie is unsophisticated, but the twists of plot and a few good broadsides all serve to make it entertaining.

What the critics say Critics rate this movie 3.0 to 4.0. "Excellent special effects help make this well-made WW II action-drama."[3] "Stirring naval battles and stylish documentary-style direction."[5] "Topflight war adventure."[7] "More interesting than enjoyable."[6] **Final Word** This story is well told and fun to watch, but first you need to listen to the Johnny Horton song "Sink the Bismarck."

633 Squadron
1964 GBR b/w d. Walter Grauman

WW II: Secret Bombing Mission 1.5

This fact-based movie, adapted from the novel by Frederick E. Smith, can best be described as a generic war movie (and not in the best sense of the word). Its primary redeeming value is providing a close-up look at an interesting fighter plane, the Mosquito (an all plywood fighter and one of the fastest planes of the war, used primarily for high altitude reconnaissance). There is plenty of footage of the planes taking off, landing and flying by. Oh yes, the story! In 1944 Germany had begun installing V2 rocket launch pads along the French coast. RAF Wing Commander Roy Grant (Cliff Robertson) and the 633 Squadron have been assigned a secret mission. They are to bomb a German rocket fuel plant in Norway in order to stop Germany from making its rockets operational. However, the plant can't be bombed directly, so the plan is to use specially designed munitions to tumble a mountainside down onto the plant—a dangerous mission that the ever cynical but one hundred percent can-do Wing Commander takes on. George Chakiris plays Lt. Erik Bergman, a Norwegian naval intelligence officer working with the underground in Norway. His sister, Hilde (Maria Perschy), is the romantic interest. (Please note that there's one oddly camp, if not lurid, moment in this movie.) Lt. Bergman, who is captured by the Germans, is tortured by a woman Nazi officer, who rips of his clothes and appears to be torturing his genitals. This scene has absolutely nothing to do with the plot but must have titillated 1960s audiences. The acting is as wooden as the planes they are flying and Robertson, too American, is completely miscast as a British air officer. For the most part, the special effects are decent except for the frequent use of bad plane models. All of this probably could have been overlooked if the characters had been developed or the story told in an interesting manner.

What the critics say Critics rate this movie 3.0 to 3.5. "Standard war heroics with enough noise and disorder to keep most audiences hypnotized."[1] "Pretentious WW 2 aviation film."[2] "Cinematically...a spectacular achievement, a technically explosive depiction of an RAF unit."[4] **Final Word** Skip the equally bad rip-off of this movie, *Mosquito Squadron*, and just go directly to *The Dam Busters*.

Soldier of Orange

1977 NET color subtitles d. Paul Verhoeven

WW II: Dutch Resistance Movement   4.0

Based on the autobiographical novel by Dutch resistance leader
Erik Hazelhoff Roelfzema, and directed by Paul Verhoeven, this
is a tense and dramatic wartime story of the Dutch resistance
movement. The lives of six self-absorbed, upper-class university
students are changed forever when the Nazis invade Holland in
1938. Each of these six friends deals with the German
occupation in his own way—one becomes a member of the
Dutch-German SS, and yet another is turned by the Gestapo to
inform on his friends and the resistance movement. But the focus
of the story is on Erik Lanshof (Rutger Hauer), who is initially
reluctant to join the resistance, but is slowly drawn in by events
and his friendship with resistance leader Guus LeJeune (Jeroen
Krabbé). The first half of this movie is outstanding film-making,
filled with well-realized characters in a time and place that's
recreated with wonderful detail. Intrigue and dramatic tension
arise from the dangerousness situations these men are in. The
scenes of interrogation and torture and of the secret police tailing
resistance members and planting disinformation, keep viewers
closely involved. This film is also not interested in covering up
the truth. It show us many Dutch citizens with anti-Semitic and
anti-democratic sentiments and collaborating with the Germans.
The second half of the movie is decidedly different, almost as if
there had been a change in directors, and plays more like a
conventional action-adventure-thriller. Lanshof morphs from
insecure and passive student into an action hero, commando,
RAF bomber pilot, and romantic lead. Despite this abrupt change
in storyline, this movie is vastly superior to most attempts to tell
similar stories of espionage. The ending is somewhat anticlimactic as Queen Wilhelmina returns from exile and resistance
hero Lanshof accepts a high level civil service position.

What the critics say Critics rate this movie 4.0 to 5.0.
"Intelligent and engrossing adventure."[3] "Exciting and
suspenseful; cerebral; carefully made and well-acted."[5] "This is
an exceptional work; an exciting, suspenseful, and intelligent war
adventure."[7] **Final Word** "Orange" refers to the House of
Orange, the royal government of the Netherlands. This film made
Hauer an international star. Highly recommended!

A Soldier's Story

1984 USA color d. Norman Jewison

WW II: Racial Drama   4.5

This near-brilliant movie examines racism during the investigation of the murder of a Black Army sergeant in 1944. Based on the Pulitzer Prize-winning play by Charles Fuller, and directed by Norman Jewison, this whodunit is an intense character study and compelling examination of racism. The acting is outstanding, and most of the original cast members from the Negro Ensemble Company are featured—Denzel Washington, Robert Townsend, David Alan Grier, John Hancock. The story is told through interviews by Capt. Davenport (Howard Rollins), an attorney and rare Black officer in the Army who has been assigned to investigate this murder. At this Black army base in Louisiana, there's pervasive racism in the white community and the white officer core. As the base commander tells Capt. Davenport, "The worst thing you can do, in this part of the country, is to pay too much attention to the death of a negro under mysterious circumstances." What elevates this movie is the realization that the victim, Sgt. Waters, was himself openly racist against many Black soldiers. Memorably portrayed by Adolph Caesar, Sergeant Waters had served honorably in WW I and had made the military his life. His intense hatred of racism not only created a rejection of his own Black identity, but led him to openly scorn and despise any characteristics of Black soldiers that he perceived as fitting white stereotypes. As he puts it, we have to "close our ranks on the chitlin, collard green, cornbread types." Sgt. Waters self-hatred provides a searing look into the hidden elements of racism in American society. On the downside, this highly provocative film wraps up a little too neatly, and has a certain smug satisfaction in its political correctness that detracts from its edge.

What the critics say Critics rate this movie 4.0 to 5.0. "Electrifying drama...a riveting film."[2] "Crackling with racial tension...brilliantly acted with power and grace."[3] **Final Word** One of a handful of films that examines racism in the military and one of the best films reviewed for this book. Also checkout *Glory*, *Mutiny* and *The Tuskegee Airmen*.

Stalag 17
1953   USA   b/w   d. Billy Wilder

WW II: Prisoner-of-War   3.0

Many will recognize *Stalag 17* as the basis for the popular TV show *Hogan's Heroes*. Produced and directed by Billy Wilder and adapted from the successful play by Donald Bevan and Edmund Trzcinski (both former POWs), this movie has received a great deal of critical acclaim. In 1953 William Holden won the Academy Award for Best Actor in his role as Sgt. Sefton. Stalag 17 is a German prisoner of war camp with over 40,000 POWs, of whom 630 are American air crewmen housed in a separate compound. This movie is alternately a comedy and a "whodunit," as it becomes apparent that one of the men in Barracks 4 is a "stoolie" and supplying information to the Germans. The focus is on Sgt. Sefton, a part-time grifter and hustler in the barracks, who is always willing to bet that an escapee won't make it. Even if one tries hard, it's truly difficult to understand why audiences in the 1950s liked this movie. Seven years after WW II, the ability to find some humor in those grim events may have provided some cathartic relief. The film also gives expression to Cold War paranoia, and addresses issues of trust, loyalty and the coercive power of the group over the individual. Viewed today this movie appears clumsy and farcical, and without the required irony or satire. (It's simply a bad mixture of silly humor and serious circumstances.) One major problem with this film is that Sgt. Sefton, while unfairly accused, is hardly a sympathetic character. The Germans are so benign and bumbling that they almost make the Americans look smart. Somehow, mixing all this with pranks, high jinks, and humorous song and dance is incomprehensible. More to the point, *Stalag 17* is no longer funny, and its attempts at humor appear to merely get in the way of a potentially interesting story.

What the critics say Critics rate this movie 3.0 to 5.0. "Granddaddy of all WW 2 POW films...Wilder brilliantly blends drama with comedy."[2] "One of the very best American movies of the 1950s."[5] "Really does not live up to its reputation...worse yet, the moments of comic relief are appalling."[6] "This film still holds up brilliantly today."[7] **Final Word** If you think you may have seen even one episode of *Hogan's Heroes*, there is no need to watch this movie.

Stalingrad

1958 GER b/w subtitles d. Frank Wisbar

WW II: German Disaster on the Volga   4.5

No American film is the equivalent of this German movie, and perhaps the reason is simple—America has never endured the death of so many soldiers, in a battle on this scale, and lost. Imagine a film trying to show American audiences how nearly 250,000 soldiers died as a result of an ill-conceived battle plan, in which they attacked a city of no strategic importance. While this movie was remade in 1993, this 1958 version stands on its own and is nearly as good as the remake, if not better in many aspects. Grainy black and white filming that is integrated with documentary footage, gives the movie an exceptional degree of realism. It also provides an outstanding overview of the war, from the viewpoint of the German high command all the way down to the soldiers fighting in the streets. This film pulls no punches as it tries to show German audiences how such a military disaster could have occurred. Hitler had ordered the German 6th Army, under Gen. Paulus, to take Stalingrad, despite its lack of strategic importance. Stalin was determined, for similar political reasons, to hold the city at all costs, and thus began the single most important and legendary battle of the Second World War. What inner-story there is revolves around a conflict between a young German artillery officer, Lt. Wisse (Joachim Hansen), and his commanding officer, who has absolute faith in Hitler and the German army. Even as the Red army encircles and entraps a German army that does not have winter gear and is short on ammunition and near starvation, the German commanders in the field refuse to "break rank." They are unwilling to disobey Hitler in order to save the army. *Stalingrad* is about the disintegration of this army and the desperation of the individual soldier. In one brilliant scene, hundreds of wounded and dying soldiers are listening to a radio broadcast as Goebbels gives a 10th Reich Anniversary speech dismissing the loss of Stalingrad as treasonable and unimportant. Estimates are that 60,000 German soldiers died at Stalingrad and 110,000 surrendered, of which only 6,000 returned home.

What the critics say No available reviews. **Final Word** A great war film, well-worth the effort to track down and watch. In 1958 this may well have been the best war film ever made, and is alternately titled—*Dogs, Do You Want to Live Forever?*

Stalingrad

1993   GER   color   subtitles   d. Joseph Vilsmaier

WW II: Infantry Genocide on the Steppe   5.0

This truly outstanding war movie takes the viewer into the streets of Stalingrad, in what would become the largest and most costly battle of the Second World War. In the summer of 1942 Hitler ordered the German army to take Stalingrad. Of the 260,000 soldiers of the German Sixth Army, only 91,000 survived to surrender and of these only 6,000 ever returned to Germany. Ultimately this battle produced over a million casualties. This conflict is shown through the eyes of Lt. Hans von Witzland (Thomas Kretschmann) and five other soldiers in his platoon. Directed by Joseph Vilsmaier, the movie opens with the soldiers on leave in Italy. Within months they are fighting in Stalingrad, and their battalion of 600 men is down to 62. While there are several outstanding large-scale combat scenes, this movie is most memorable for the intensity of many small dramatic moments—the truce with Russian soldiers so that both sides could gather their wounded, German soldiers ordered to execute Russian civilians or be shot themselves, and their arrest and imprisonment for seeking medical aid. Slowly, these soldiers come to question authority, and ultimately desert to no avail. This is a surprisingly introspective film about Germany's responsibility for the war. A soldier confronts his commanding officer—"We don't have a chance. Why not surrender?" The officer responds, "You know what would happen if we did." The soldier replies, "Do we deserve better?" The officer adds, "I am not a Nazi Otto." The soldier tells him in disgust, "No, you are worse. You lousy officers, you went along, even though you knew who was in charge." This film examines and challenges military command, and portrays officers as obsessed with discipline and who often encourage brutal acts against civilians and even shooting their own wounded. This movie is a gut-check, graphically depicting the horrors of war and, ultimately, the soldiers' bleak fate on the snows of the Russian steppe.

What the critics say Critics rate this movie 4.0 to 5.0. "Stunning German production."[3] "Realistic depiction of war is not for the fainthearted."[5] "Spectacularly well made."[7] "Realistic and harrowing account of men in combat as you are likely to find."[8] **Final Word** This is the real deal. Confront your wife or girlfriend now about not interrupting you while you're watching this movie.

The Steel Helmet

1951 USA b/w d. Samuel Fuller

Korean War: Infantry Combat   1.5

Rumor is that this low-budget actioner, written, directed and produced by Samuel Fuller, was filmed in just twelve days with a budget of $165,000 (It looks and feels like it was shot in a week for $50,000). The story takes place during the opening months of the Korean War, as American forces are in retreat. The story centers on Sgt. Zack (Gene Evans), a larger than life caricature of the mythic WW II "grunt." Zack is crude, opinionated and domineering, and an experienced veteran among a small, inexperienced and makeshift group of GIs (Black medic, Nisei vet, inept lieutenant, and young boy, among others) who have come together in the confusion of war. Let's be up front, this movie has less realism than a *G.I. Joe* comic book. Any war film in which the primary relationship is between an overly cute 12-year-old boy and the grumpy main character is in trouble. Sgt. Zack is played so over-the-top as to be buffoonish. Attempts at humor play like slapstick; for example, while an observation post is being set up in a Buddhist temple, there's a *cat and mouse* encounter that is right out of a 1940s whodunit. This movie is mostly talk, except at the end where there are a few minutes of documentary combat footage and ten minutes of the good guys shooting it out with the "Reds." In the film's most interesting moment, a captured North Korean officer confronts the Black medic and Japanese-American soldier as to why they are fighting the white man's war. Their answer is, that they are Americans first—while the North Koreans are "gooks" and "little rats" who use deception to kill Americans. Near the end, when the small boy is killed by a sniper, Zack finally loses it and shoots the unarmed prisoner (Zack thought he deserved it). This grim look at the "good guys" and the "bad guys" makes the case that a good war movie can't be made in two weeks.

What the critics say Critics rate this movie 4.0 to 4.5. "Grim, fatalistic, completely without patriotic fervor."[6] "Actually improves with age...packed with irony...and vivid action."[7] "Magical Fuller moving making...brutal, its honest, it's very, very exciting."[8] **Final Word** Over the years Fuller's movies have achieved a "cult" status. While he often manages to bring an interesting contemporary angle to his films, collectively they are among the worst war films ever made.

The Story of G.I. Joe
1945　USA　b/w　d. William A. Wellman

WW II: Infantry Combat Unit　　　　2.5

Critics have consistently praised this William A. Wellman film as the best war movie of the World War II years, and General Eisenhower called it—"The greatest war picture I've ever seen." Adapted from the book *Here is Your War*, by the Pulitzer Prize-winning war correspondent Ernie Pyle, this movie is, at best, an average attempt to tell the story of the grunt in the field. During the war, Pyle was a respected and popular journalist who accompanied soldiers to the front lines in order to tell the American public the soldier's story (Pyle was killed by a sniper on the Pacific island of Ie Jima just before the film's release). Sporadically narrated by Pyle (Burgess Meredith), the movie opens in 1942 with the American invasion of North Africa, and follows Company C, 18th Infantry through the invasion of Sicily and Italy. A low-budget, low-action movie, it appears to have been made without the benefit of a script or story to tell. In short, it's a somewhat sappy and oversentimental look at the hardships GIs faced, or as Pyle put it, "The GI, he lives so miserably, and he dies so miserably." (He even goes so far as to suggest that they don't die clean shaven and well-fed like pilots do!?) Oddly, this movie is not about Pyle, who comes and goes throughout and says very little. What motivated Pyle to take risks and, even more, what he wrote, is unfortunately not part of the movie. The GIs joke around and complain a lot but do their job no matter what the cost. There are lots of close up mug shots, as they trudge through the mud and rain and eat bad food. At the end, the GIs head out for another battle, paying respects to their fallen commander (Robert Mitchum). There's one good combat sequence with no war heroics—a movie primarily about the daily grind and hardship soldiers face.

What the critics say Critics rate this 4.5 to 5.0. "The authentic story of GI Joe...a production that's superb, casting and direction that's perfect and a...flawless group of artists."[4] "Registering genuine emotion and realism."[5] "A story that's been told many times, but seldom with such grace and poetry."[6] **Final Word** An early attempt to get away from wartime propaganda, with the focus on rain and mud. I would have personally preferred to know more about Ernie Pyle, who lived and died a soldier.

Strategic Air Command

1955 USA color d. Anthony Mann

Cold War: "The Big Birds"   2.5

It's 1955 and American school children are hunkering down under their desks during air raid drills in the event of a nuclear war. And the Strategic Air Command (SAC) is America's first line of deterrence against a possible nuclear attack by the Soviet Union. This movie, directed by Anthony Mann and starring Jimmy Stewart, and June Allyson as his wife, is a patriotic, flagwaving tribute to the men and women who served in SAC. Basically, it's an Air Force public relations effort to sell their mission and increase enlistment rates. The slight plot revolves around Lt. Col 'Dutch' Holland (Stewart) who is called up from active reserve status to fly B-36s. Currently an all-star third baseman with the St. Louis Cardinals, Holland has recently married. As a former WW II B-29 pilot who flew missions over Japan, he is resentful of a peacetime call-up to active duty. However, his resentment wanes as he finds himself enthralled while flying sophisticated planes on important missions. His eventual allegiance to the mission and abandonment of his wife and baseball career is the central conflict of the movie. Okay! Let's put all this unimportant stuff aside for a moment. The real stars of this movie are the B-36s and B-47s. There are incredible shots of these planes on the ground, in the air, and in vast numbers. You have a chance to climb inside and look around and, most importantly, a chance to watch them take off and fly. An aviation buff's dream, the film has the most beautiful aerial photography of military planes ever put on film. For those fascinated with the "big birds," the contrail shots of these B-36s will be reverie. This is an entertaining peacetime military movie that fortunately had the complete cooperation of the US Air Force.

What the critics say Critics rate this movie 2.5. to 3.0. "Sentimental flagwaver featuring the newest jets of the fifties."[1] "Only gets off the ground when Stewart does."[2] "Sweeping view of a B-36 with its jet engines skywriting long hyphens in blue smoke—this is visually stirring stuff."[4] "A classic post-WW II chunk of Air Force patriotism."[5] **Final Word** The critics are right, of course, but this lightweight entertainment is well worth enduring for the planes.

The Tanks are Coming

1951   USA   b/w   d. Lewis Seiler

WW II: Tank Action in Europe	1.5

Forty days after the Normandy invasion in July 1944, the 3rd Armored Division helped spearhead Patton's 3rd Army breakout at St Lô across France. Six months later, they entered Germany. This movie is a comic book version of these events. Directed by Lewis Seiler, the story was provided by Samuel Fuller (who can be credited with many of the worst war movies ever). The movie features Steve Cochran as Sgt. Sullivan, a larger-than-life tank commander who personally believes he can win the war. Sgt. Sullivan is your standard SOB who can do no wrong, but has a caring side that he tries to hide. He drives his men mercilessly to be better soldiers, and most of them hate him for it. Eventually all the conflicts around his character and tactics are justified by the results. Like "Sgt. Rock" in the comics, Sgt. Sullivan always leads the charge and emerges unscathed by war. There's also a narrator cheerleading events just in case you can't tell that the good guys are winning. For the most part, this movie is comprised of soldiers complaining, joking around and complaining some more (all of it is just a little too humorous to be taken seriously). In one scene, a fearful private who's a little goofy, seeks out an American general to complain about how the shells from the 75-mm guns on their Sherman tanks just bounce off the German Panzers, while the German's 88-mm guns rip the American tanks apart. The rather avuncular general then promises the private a better tank soon. There's some energy in this movie, which includes two credible battle scenes and a whole host of Sherman tanks and Army vehicles. However, this is all undone at the end, when Sgt. Sullivan transforms from cliché grunt to amor-plated caricature in the film's final combat scenes. As for the complaining private, he receives a new Mark IV tank.

What the critics say Critics rate this movie 1.0 to 3.0. "Tedious war drama which ties in vain to interest us in non-characters."[1] "A hard-line war movie...it has since become a cult favorite."[7] "Flag-waving nonentity."[8] **Final Word** Produced nearly six years after the war, this movie exceeds the most egregious flagwaving war movies of the 1940s. It suggests that our victory was inevitable and that some combat soldiers were bulletproof.

Task Force

1949   USA   b/w   d. Delmer Daves

This movie purports to be about the development of naval aviation and the aircraft carrier when, in fact, it's mostly about the battle of Midway. It's basically another low-budget, flagwaving affair that is poorly written, directed and acted. Perhaps its most egregious flaw is casting Gary Cooper in the lead role. Cooper, who was nearly fifty at the time, is cast as a young naval aviator and romantic lead in his twenties. The first half plays like a romantic comedy, with Cooper wooing a young Jane Wyatt (he looks like her grandfather). It's all perfectly incongruous. In reality, Cooper is reprising his role in *The Court-Martial of Billy Mitchell*. All the same political and military issues about the role of the airplane in future wars are addressed here, including the lack of funding, the backwards and bureaucratic thinking in the Navy and Congress, and an over-emphasis on battleships, etc. While this movie is overly dependent on newsreel and documentary footage, there are some interesting shots of early planes and carriers (but the first half of this movie is mostly *Pirates of Penzance*—filled with costumed soldiers and ballroom dancing). The second half is almost exclusively newsreel footage, and culminates in the air and sea battle for Midway. The movie then skips three years ahead, without warning, to the battle for Okinawa. The fact that Cooper and Walter Brennan are even in it is irrelevant at this point. There are a few scenes with them sitting around smoking, waiting for news, as well as a few comments about Cooper being too old to fly. Then the combat just stops and we see Cooper collapsing in the arms of Wyatt. There are numerous wartime propaganda speeches (too many for 1949) and very little examination of any aspect of this war. The one exception is the film's willingness to criticize the one person in the entire Congress without the foresight to build aircraft carriers (the US was planning to deploy 90 aircraft carriers in the invasion of Japan).

What the critics say Critics rate this movie 2.5 to 3.0. "Stilted and long-drawn-out flagwaver.[1] "Standard military soap opera...predictable script."[7] "Heavily-propagandized fare in 1949."[8] **Final Word** At Okinawa the Japanese lost 4,000 airplanes in attempting Kamikaze attacks, while they sank only 36 Allied ships.

Tears of the Sun

2003 USA color d. Antoine Fuqua

| Post-Cold War: Navy SEAL Operation | 3.0 |

A violent actioner, *Tears of the Sun* is filled with just enough patriotic hubris and plot holes to cancel any serious emotional edge, despite its focus on genocide. Set in contemporary Nigeria, the film involves rebel militia forces engaged in the ethnic cleansing of a rival tribe. Lt. Waters (Bruce Willis) and his Navy SEAL team are ordered to help evacuate American embassy personnel. After a successful operation, Waters is immediately sent back in to extract Dr. Kendricks (Monica Bellucci), a physician at a humanitarian-aid mission. Once Lt. Waters makes contact with the doctor, she refuses to leave unless he will escort her 70 patients to safety. (Obviously this movie is in serious trouble when the Lt. doesn't leave the doctor to be raped and murdered.) But because the doctor is dedicated and beautiful, Lt. Waters tricks her into going to the extraction site by pretending to evacuate her patients. As the rescue helicopters pass over a nearby village that is being massacred (you guessed it) Waters orders their return to assist the stranded patients (you can only groan out loud). Yes, the soldiers are American, and Americans always contravene their orders to do the right thing—but just so Lt. Waters can get a date? Derivative of Kurosawa's *Seven Samurai* and its American counterpart, *The Magnificent Seven*—and more recently the outstanding *Three Kings* (1999)—this movie doesn't provide a satisfactory explanation for veteran soldiers to make this sacrifice. Waters is a hardcore guy whose violent life has left him jaded and empty—its hard to believe that this doctor has given him something to believe in. Equally important, the movie fails to develop characters or relationships which could explain Water's actions. Instead, we get an enigmatic and unemotional Willis tied to a formulaic plot. On the plus side, many well-staged action sequences focus on the plight of the African people, and shows the horrific violence taking place on this continent. Predictable from beginning to end, this movie is primarily an enthusiastic action-ride.

What the critics say No available reviews. **Final Word** The movie is focused strictly on a personal epiphany. *Tears of the Sun* fails to address what price American soldiers should pay in order to police the world.

Thanks of a Grateful Nation

1998   USA   color   tv   d. Rod Holcomb

Persian Gulf War: Gulf War Syndrome   3.0

This movie is a long and compelling effort to highlight the government's attempted cover-up of "Gulf War Syndrome." Unfortunately, director Rod Holcumb didn't know how to tell this important story. Shot in a semi-documentary style, replete with real-life interviews, the facts about this illness are shown from three perspectives. A special forces soldier (Matt Keeslar) contracts the illness as a result of participating in the conflict. Also a member of a post-war clean-up crew (Steven Webber) becomes ill. Lastly, we watch Jim Tuite (Ted Danson), a legislative analyst for Senator Riegle (Brian Dennehy) from Michigan, spend years trying to get the DOD, VA and FDA to stop stonewalling treatment for veterans. While the acting is excellent the story telling is digressive and unfocused. This film simply tries to tell too much from too many points of view. The real story is about the politics of money and bureaucracies that do not want to take responsibility, and a government that didn't want to sully the image of a military victory and its redemption for Vietnam. The causes of this illness were variously attributed to posttraumatic stress disorder, psychosomatic illness and even malingering. Because no cause and effect could be established, it was easier to believe it didn't exist. From one Congressional hearing to another Gulf War Syndrome was alternately attributed to depleted uranium from spent shells, petro-chemical fires, the bombing of Iraqi chemical and biological sites and the multiple untested vaccines soldiers received. The movie implicates American companies for selling the Iraqis the biological and chemical agents that may have resulted in this illness. Ultimately, the movie concludes there is no "smoking gun." Parallels are drawn with the government's denial of exposing troops to radiation poisoning in the 1950s and Agent Orange and dioxide contamination during the Vietnam War. The epilogue notes that between 1996 and 1997 the government revised its estimates of soldier exposed to biological and chemical contaminates from 300-400, to 5,000, then to 20,8676 and finally to 100,000.

What the critics say No available reviews. **Final Word** A stinging indictment. GWS is now euphemistically termed Multisymptom Undiagnosed Illness!?

The Thin Red Line

1964   USA   b/w   d. Andrew Marton

| WW II: Infantry Combat | 4.5 |

This is director Andrew Marton's original film adaptation of
James Jones' novel. In its own way this 1964 war movie is
exceptional and probably represents the final and best statement
of the classic WW II combat movie. By 1965 the Vietnam War,
along with a new moving-making realism, changed war films.
The opening scenes portray an anxious infantry company on a
troop transport prior to the invasion of Guadalcanal. The story
eventually comes to center on the company's attempt to take a
well-entrenched group of caves on a mountainside held by
Japanese. The focus of this story is on Pvt. Doll (Keir Dullea) and
Sgt. Welsh (Jack Warden). Both Dullea and Warden give outstanding performances. Welsh, is the chorus of war in the deaf
ear of Pvt. Doll. A hardened combat veteran, Welsh understands
the liability for soldiers who think too much and who are not
hardened by the killing and dying. The Sgt. has one primary
message —when your number is up, there is nothing you can do
about it. Don't get sentimental about the killing and dying. Doll,
on the other hand, is obsessed with surviving and believes his
destiny is in his hands and that he cannot trust anyone else.
Their difference in viewpoints quickly escalates to a personal
conflict. But this movie is about more than just their conflict. The
sergeant is in conflict with the company commander, and the
company commander is in conflict with the battalion commander.
In fact, everyone has conflicts with the realities of war but can't
change the fact that they are in a war and men are dying. This
movie is better than any before it in confronting the realities
faced by the combat soldier. How do you survive war? Doll and
Warden represent two extremes to this dilemma. There are many
excellent combat scenes that have a high degree of realism. This
is a hard-edged and unsentimental movie without heroes or propaganda. It also asks hard questions about how many lives
should be sacrificed for a military objective.

What the critics say The critics rate this movie 3.0 to 4.0. "Gritty
adaptation...about personal conflicts during the bloody attack on
Guadalcanal."[2] "Crackling, combat-centered...and explosive
melodramatization."[4] **Final Word** There were a lot of combat
films from 1940 to 1964 about WW II. This may be the best.

The Thin Red Line

1998   USA /CAN   color   d. Terrence Malick

WW II: Infantry Combat	5.0

This controversial film, adapted by director Terrence Malick from the James Jones novel, chronicles the attempt by a company of American soldiers, in 1942, to take a heavily defended hill on Guadalcanal. However, what this film is really about, is the very real fears of men in combat. In many ways this 1998 version may be the best film yet about this experience. From the opening scenes it creates a mood of pervasive anxiety and never lets up. The experience is magnified by the serenity and beauty of the natural world that surrounds these soldiers. Also, a voice-over narration quiets the film and contrasts the mystical experiences of a country boy, Pvt. Witt (James Caviezel), who has found peace with the killing around him, with the quiet rage of Sgt. Welsh (Sean Penn), a pessimistic realist, who is the opposite of the enigmatic Witt. Many will find this film hard to follow and even harder to understand. It's different from any war film that has preceded it, in that it's about death, rather than killing. As he sees the destruction all around him, Witt speaks to death—*Who are you to live with these many forms? You're death that captures all. You too are the source of all that is going to be born. You're the glory, mercy, peace, truth, you give calm to the spirit.* If director Malick has failed in any way, it's for trying to reach for too much in an attempt to break away from war movie clichés and find something more meaningful. The many outstanding performances include Nick Nolte as Lt. Col. Tall, stopping at nothing to attain promotion; Elias Koteas as the sincere and protective Capt. Staros; and James Caviezel in a wonderfully quiet performance as a soldier questing for the salvation of all men at war. The photography is rich in its use of light, shadows and movement, and the lush tropical beauty will provoke questions about paradise lost. The battle scenes are among the most realistic you will ever encounter. For those who have tired of the usual, this movie is up to the challenge.

What the critics say Critics rate this move 2.0 to 5.0. "Gorgeous looking...poetic, ethereal though slightly flawed epic."[3] "Visually stunning...the combat scenes are naturally, beautifully shot and effective."[5]" "Will hold its own with the best of the genre."[8] **Final Word** Pvt. Witt asks, "What is this war at the heart of nature." One of the very best war movies ever.

They Were Expendable

1945   USA   b/w   d. John Ford

WW II: Naval Combat   2.5

They Were Expendable is director John Ford's patriotic tribute to American sailors who served and fought in the South Pacific. Adapted from the book by William L. White, the movie stars John Wayne (Lt. "Rusty" Ryan) and Robert Montgomery (Lt. John Brickley) as PT boat commanders stationed in the Philippines shortly after the bombing of Pearl Harbor. The Navy has asked them to demonstrate the combat worthiness of the experimental motor torpedo boat. The only subplot involves a short-lived and awkward relationship between Lt. Ryan (Wayne) and nurse Lt. Davys (Donna Reed) that doesn't work on the big screen. The dramatic high point is the evacuation of Gen. Douglas MacArthur from Corregidor. With no plot and very little action, the real stars of the film are the six motor torpedo boats, which are exciting to watch. Unfortunately, too much of this movie involves bantering servicemen who work on the boats. Ford is trying to make the points that good men are dying tragic deaths in war. Unfortunately, this point is made in too many scenes of sailors dying and later being honored. While Ford wants the audience to be aware of the selflessness of sailors who died without complaint, he also becomes carried away with this theme. There's also a bizarre scene in which an aging American national sits on the steps of his shack with his rifle across his lap and moonshine at his side. With the "Red River Valley" playing in the background, he refuses to leave, and insists on fighting it out with the "Japs." You begin to wonder if this American was preparing to fight the Japanese or government revenuers (it's a surrealistic moment). This was, no doubt, Ford's homage to America's Depression Era "everyman." To ensure the movie's patriotic intent, the "Battle Hymn of the Republic" is trotted out twice for emotional effect.

What the critics say Critics rate this movie 4.5 to 5.0. "Long drawn out flagwaver."[1] "One of the finest (and most underrated) WW 2 films."[2] "Rousing WW II drama."[3] "First-rate action-drama...no phony heroics or glory."[7] **Final Word** Wayne was sued for damaging the reputation of the real Commander Kelly he portrayed. The plywood PT boats, while useful, never proved to be an effective weapon. Despite this movie's popularity and critical clamor, it is average at best.

Thirteen Days

2001 USA color d. Roger Donaldson

Cold War: Cuban Missile Crisis   4.0

For six terrifying days in October 1962 the world's two major superpowers stood on the brink of nuclear war. With an intelligent script and crisp pace, director Roger Donaldson carefully chronicles these events from inside the White House. In early October a U-2 spy plane photographed Soviet SS-4 and SS-5 ballistic missiles in Cuba. Carrying one megaton nuclear warheads these missiles had a range up to 1,000 miles. The response by the US and the internal politics that shaped it are intriguing and chilling. It is also clear that the final negotiation was fragile and unsupported by hawkish elements on both sides. Based on a book by Ernest May and Philip Zelikow, we watch this crisis play out through the character of Kenny O'Donnell (Kevin Costner), a personal friend and special assistant to President Kennedy (Bruce Greenwood). (Costner is annoying in this role and detracts from the film focusing on the Kennedys and other major players in this drama). All the other performances are first rate and the dialogue sparkles with realism and thoughtfulness. Also impressive are the settings and special effects. One feels absolutely present during these events. The story that evolves here is complex. There is a great deal of mistrust between the American military establishment and the Kennedy administration. From the beginning the Joint Chiefs assert an aggressive response that would stalemate a negotiated settlement and ensure an escalating crisis. Kennedy doesn't have an answer but distrusts the solutions he has been presented with. The pressure is on. In a few days these missiles will be operational and a strike to take them out would probably fail. A negotiated way out is finally offered by Khrushchev and Adlai Stevenson, US Ambassador to the UN. This is an important movie, not just for documenting this event, but for showing us the strength of character it took for Kennedy to seek a settlement and resist the over-whelming consensus of a military solution.

What the critics say Critics rate this movie 3.5 to 5.0. "Exhilarating entertainment...complex, articulate and often nerve-racking."[3] "Costner's overwrought theatrics overshadow much finer work."[7] **Final Word** A first-rate television movie also tells this story—*Missiles of October*.

Thirty Seconds Over Tokyo

1944 USA b/w d. Mervyn LeRoy

WW II: Doolittle Bombing Raid   2.0

One hundred and thirty-one days after Japan bombed Peal Harbor, Lt. Col. "Jimmy" Doolittle led a bombing raid on Japan with sixteen B-25 bombers launched from the aircraft carrier *Hornet*. Using a *Collier's* magazine story by Capt. Ted Lawson and Robert Considine as a basis, Hollywood created a box-office success that won an Academy Award for special effects. The cast starred Spencer Tracy as a no-nonsense Doolittle, and Van Johnson (Lt. Ted Lawson) and Robert Mitchum (Lt. Bob Gray) as B-25 pilots. While this raid is without doubt one of the most interesting stories of the Pacific war, it is only a small part of this movie. Unfortunately, the only times this movie deserves attention is when Spencer Tracy is on the screen and during a fifteen-minute segment in which the raid takes place. The well-staged raid is sandwiched between two stories that will seriously raise your blood-sugar levels and can only be described as "flagwaving" sentiment for a wartime audience. The early part of this movie focuses on a vapid (dull, boring, lifeless) romance and the last third is preoccupied with Capt. Lawson, who is being nursed back to health after crash landing his B-25 in China. The latter is wholly anticlimactic. Too much of the movie is tedious, with most of the pilots singing and carrying on as if they were in a frat house and the war was an upcoming football game. A problem the movie never addresses is a series of poor decisions by Capt. Lawson. He continually suspects engine trouble with his B-25 and is aware that the gun turret is malfunctioning, but refuses to bring attention to them out of concern the plane will be scrubbed from the mission. While the movie makes this out to be patriotic zeal, in reality it was poor judgment. Director Mervyn LeRoy's movie should have been about the American hero Doolittle, and not the prettyboy Van Johnson.

What the critics say Critics rate this movie 3.0 to 4.5. "Sturdy WW II action flagwaver."[1] "Dated but still interesting classic wartime flagwaver."[5] "Of all the reality-inspired films of WW II, this one really cries out for a remake."[6] **Final Word** While 15 of 16 planes were lost, 71 of the 80 crew members safely returned from the mission. Two 1940s movies, *Destination Tokyo* and *The Purple Heart*, are companion pieces to this story.

Three Kings
1999   USA   color   d. David Russell

Persian Gulf War: Action-Adventure   5.0

Here is a movie that does everything right! It's hip, subversive, funny, fast-paced, full of action, has an intelligent script and is exceptionally well-directed and acted. As far as the war action-adventure genre goes, *Three Kings* is as good as it gets. Kudos to director David Russell. The time is immediately following a cease-fire in the Gulf War, when an American soldier discovers an "Iraqi ass map" (a map between the ass cheeks of an Iraqi POW) showing where Saddam Hussein has hidden tens of millions of dollars in gold bullion stolen from Kuwait. George Clooney plays Maj. Archie Gates, a Special Forces officer who has been passed over for promotion and is now relegated to escorting reporters around the war front. Into the mix come three Army reservists played by Ice Cube, Mark Wahlberg and Spike Jonze who also have knowledge of the map. Together the four hatch a scheme to steal the gold that's only a few hours from their position. Shot in a grainy, bleached out style to capture the intensity of the desert sun, this genre-busting film turns the misfit, caper movie inside out with a serious challenge to the politics of this feel-good victory by "Coalition" forces. When these gold seekers finally get to the bunker, they discover a small town held by Hussein's Republican Guard, who ignore them while they're rounding up rebels and suppressing the civilian population. Clooney is excellent as the cynical and practical leader of this group, and tells them, "You do the thing you're scared shitless of and you get the courage after you do it, not before you do it." What had been a race for the gold has now become a flight to save themselves, rescue their buddy, and save civilians trying to escape certain death. All the characters are quirky and interesting. This is a movie filled with bizarre and violent confrontations, humorous and satirical asides and graphic-realism. What could have been very good escapist entertainment becomes something more poignant, by showing us a civilian population (Kurds and Sunni) that was abandoned for political expediency.

What the critics say Critics rate this movie 4.0 to 4.5. "Discharges black humor, startling action, genre subversion, anarchic attitude and barbed political commentary."[4] "Subversive, chaotic and ultimately satisfying."[5] **Final Word** The best action-adventure movie since the 1930s.

317th Platoon

1965   FRA/SPA b/w   subtitles   d. Pierre Schoendoerffer

French-Indochina War: Infantry Combat   5.0

This is one of the most compelling and riveting portrayals of war ever put on film. Director Pierre Schoendoerffer, himself a veteran of this conflict (shot and captured at Diên Biên Phu in 1954), has created an unparalleled documentary-style film. Shot on location in Cambodia, this film chronicles the final days of the French-Indochina War. These are also the last days of a platoon of Laotian commandos being lead by four French paratroopers in 1954. Ordered to burn their installation at Luong Ba in Cambodia, they have to fight their way to a French base at Tao Tsai, 100 miles south. However, this base is overrun before they can get there, and they are stranded in the jungle and pursued by a division of Vietminh. Over a six-day period, while attempting to carry their wounded, the platoon is engaged in running firefights before being trapped along a river bank and annihilated. Only a few escape to the jungle. The camera focuses on a young and inexperienced French officer, Lt. Torrens (Jacques Perrin), and his combat experienced adjutant, Willsdorf (Bruno Cremer), a nine year veteran of this war and a former Werhmacht veteran. Very little is said as men are wounded and attended to. Their faces and brief comments speak eloquently about their experience. If you were told this film was a documentary, and that what you were seeing was real, you would not doubt it for a moment. The echoing sounds of jungle warfare are haunting, and the battle scenes jolting in their realism. The scenes of men being wounded and dying are horrific. The sheer physical reality of what is taking place is overwhelming as bodies slip from stretchers into streams and the jungle itself becomes a battle. We are shown haunting images of exhausted, desperate men with jittery nerves and fears of dying. Perhaps this film is as close to war as you will ever get without actually being there.

What the critics say Critics rate this movie 3.0 to 4.5. "Capturing both the horrors of battle and the anguish and solitude each solider endures."[3] "An emotionally gripping war drama...portrays this struggle, conflict, and the quiet haunting tension of war with great skill."[5] **Final Word** Schoendoerffer has produced two other excellent films, *Diên Biên Phu* and the Academy Award winning documentary on the Vietnam War, *The Anderson Platoon.*

Tigerland

2000 USA color d. Joel Schumacher

Vietnam War: Combat Training Hell   2.5

This Vietnam War-era movie about Army infantry combat training
has good production values, decent acting and sustained
dramatic tension, but goes way over the top. *Tigerland* is also 15
years too late in finding its target audience. In 1971, at the US
Army's Infantry Training Center at Fort Polk, Louisiana, a platoon
of young draftees go through nine weeks of advanced infantry
combat training, after having completed basic training. From
here, most of the trainees will be shipped directly to 'Nam. As
shown here this training is brutal, sadistic and violent (the
soldiers describe it as a "cluster-fuck"). The action involves a
group of young, under-educated, 18-20 year olds who are at
each others throats when their training sergeants and officers
aren't trying to kill them (all in the name of preparing them for a
war they are soon to enter). With numerous great one-liners and
smart dialogue, the story focuses on two recruits, Bozz (Colin
Farrell) and Paxton (Matthew Davis). Unfortunately, the movie's
over-focus on Bozz is one of its main flaws. Bozz, way too smart-
mouthed, manipulative and cynical (with a good heart) to be
either believable or likable, ultimately conflicts with just about
everyone. While he does a good job of harassing authority, he is
obnoxious. Finally, another recruit tries to kill Bozz during combat
training at "Tigerland," which is a training facility where the Army
attempts to duplicate the real-life conditions in Vietnam. This is a
film full of attitude about everything. As one captain is confronted
by recruits trying to get out of the Army, he asks out loud, "When
did my country right or wrong turn into, fuck that shit?" Where
this movie ultimately goes wrong, and nearly puts itself into the
Vietnam "action-exploitation" movie category, is its stereotypical
portrayal of Vietnam War recruits as unstable, if not outright
crazy, cynical and unpatriotic. Director Joel Schumacher appears
to have opted for violent action over real people in order to
market this film to a younger male audience.

What the critics say Critics rate this movie 2.5 to 3.5. "Original
take on the military."[2] "Familiar story but the ensemble cast is
right on the mark."[5] **Final Word** There's sex, violence and lots of
profanity. The action freaks will find this to be a satisfying and
entertaining movie.

Tobruk

1967 USA color d. Arthur Hiller

WW II: Commando Operation 3.0

Film studios in the 1960s had a fascination with fictional, big-budget, big-name stars in commando-action movies, including *Operation Crossbow, Where Eagles Dare* and *The Guns of Navarone*. While the latter is the best known, *Tobruk*, directed by Arthur Hiller, is probably the better movie. The action is better, and it has a tighter and more realistic script. The setting is North Africa in 1942, and Rommel has captured Tobruk and is driving for the Suez Canal. Rommel's problem is getting fuel to his tanks and trucks 300 miles across the desert from the Mediterranean port of Tobruk in Libya. The contrived plot entails a British commando team of 90 men, that is also comprised of German-Jews disguised as German soldiers, taking British prisoners of war 800 miles across the desert as a ruse to gain access to Tobruk. Once inside, the commandos then participate in a coordinated air/sea assault and take out underground fuel depots. For the most part, this is a predictable movie, particularly during the desert crossing where they encounter enemy tanks and aircraft, mine fields, hostile nomadic Arab horsemen, German spies, and a turncoat among themselves. This movie's only original element is an ongoing subplot about the motives of Jews in this operation. When it becomes clear that the Jews' participation is in anticipation of their resettlement in Palestine and the creation of a Jewish state, British distrust grows. Unfortunately, the film doesn't pursue this subplot in a serious manner. While there are big-name stars such as Rock Hudson, who plays a Canadian geologist, and George Peppard, who portrays a German-Jew, the real star is Nigel Green, as Col. John Harker, who heads the British commando team. Harker is tough, smart, suspicious of everyone and driven to make this operation succeed. Hudson and Peppard come across as lightweights in comparison. The action scenes are outstanding throughout and spectacular at the end when the fuel dump is destroyed

What the critics say Critics rate this movie 1.0 to 3.0. "Quite tough and spectacular but undistinguished."[1] "A colorful, hard-hitting WW II melodrama with plenty of guts and suspense."[4] "An exciting climax, beautiful photography and good performances help offset farfetched script."[6] **Final Word** Better than expected, and should hold the war-action buff's attention.

To End All Wars

2003 GBR color d. David L. Cunningham

WW II: Prisoner-of-War	3.5

This is a thoughtful prisoner of war drama based on the autobiography of Ernest Gordon (*Through the Valley of the Kwai*). Shot on location in Thailand, *To End All Wars* examines the plight of Scottish prisoners of war after the fall of Singapore in 1942. Imprisoned at Kanchanaburi Camp in Thailand are soldiers of the Argyle and Sutherland regiments, along with nearly 61,000 other Allied prisoners. Treading on much of the same ground as *Bridge on the River Kwai*, this film has a grittier realism. It also places the conflict of values between East and West, the British and the Japanese, and Judeo-Christian ethics and Bushido (samurai code of chivalry) at the center of the story, in a philosophical examination of pacifism in the face of violence. Conscripted by the Japanese to build the 420-kilometer Burma-Thailand railroad, British soldiers are of two minds. Major Campbell (Robert Carlyle) is ferocious in his efforts to avenge the murder of their colonel by the Japanese and to escape. Lt. Gordon (Ciarán McMenamin) believes revenge and escape are suicide. Instead, he starts a school dubbed the "jungle university" to help soldiers cope with this horrific experience. However, the story begins to unravel in its belief that it knows the answer to the dilemma of having to choose between violence or pacifism. Gordon truly believes that "to turn the other cheek," and "to love one's enemy" are the answer. Time and again individual soldiers make sacrifices to help their own, while the vengeful Maj. Campbell threatens their survival if he carries out his plan. The film's simplistic morality regarding this complex issues is disconcerting. While it's easier to turn the other cheek and believe you are virtuous when you have almost no other choice, what would Gordon have done if their passivity escalated violence against them? More to the point, why was he in the army? Well-acted, with a thoughtful script that's too dense for its own good, this provocative film raises more questions than it answers.

What the critics say No available reviews. **Final Word** The fact is, survival depends as much upon altruism as it does self-interest. Whether violence or pacifism increases the good of the whole and, therefore, the individual, may be a decision best determined on a case-by-case basis. Gordon may be right in this instance, but for the wrong reasons. Watch and judge for yourself.

To Hell and Back

1955   USA   b/w   d. Jesse Hibbs

WW II: War Hero Biopic	4.5

Audie Murphy enlisted in the US Army in 1942 at the age of 17. Three years later, having served in seven major military campaigns, he was a lieutenant and America's most decorated combat war hero. He was wounded three times and credited with killing more than 200 German soldiers. For this, he received every decoration for valor this nation has to offer, including the Congressional Medal of Honor. What makes this film a particularly compelling war drama is that Audie Murphy stars as himself in the film (which was based on his autobiography). It is interesting to note that Murphy's early life has many parallels with that of Sgt. Alvin York's (the most decorated war hero of World War I). As a war movie "tripper" you want the movie to reflect the reality of war, and I have to believe that what we see here mostly accomplishes this. There are no overly-dramatic acts of heroism, no emotional outbursts, nothing but a steady determination by Murphy to quietly step up each time and do what is in front of him. Murphy was embarrassed by promotions and talk of medals and he often did not feel worthy or educated enough to be commissioned an officer. He does a very credible job of acting, and one does not doubt his self-effacing and quiet nature. Knowing that many of the outstanding combat scenes were based on fact adds to their realism. There's an accurate depiction of Murphy single handedly turning back a German attack of 6 tanks and 250 infantrymen at the "Colmar Pocket." This film transcends the genre by forcing viewers to be careful not to let war be defined by war films or our own prejudices as to what war is or is not. Director Jesse Hibbs' *To Hell and Back* comes across as the real deal, not all of it, but enough to make this an important war movie. (Audie Murphy died in a plane crash at the age of 46.)

What the critics say Critics rate this movie 2.5 to 4.0. "Very good war film...with excellent battle sequences."[2] "This biopic...is gripping drama...and the action is that of a modest, unassuming young man."[4] "Is a much better film than it has any right to be...more importantly, it is not celluloid hero-worship."[6] **Final Word** Every serious war-film savant should interrupt an autistic moment and watch this film. This is an important American war film.

Too Late the Hero

1970   USA   color   d. Robert Aldrich

Directed, produced and written by Robert Aldrich, this movie is a tribute to war-movie producer, director and writer *extraordinaire* Samuel Fuller. Aldrich has the ability to not only rip off the same lame story that Fuller has told over and over, but to invoke the same gory sadism, Buddhist temple, and bizarre plot twists that leave one wondering if the ghost of Fuller has not taken over Aldrich's body. The movie stars Cliff Robertson (Lt. Lawson) as an American Navy radio officer who is fluent in Japanese, and Michael Caine ("Tosh") as a British medical orderly. Lt. Lawson is a shirker who wants nothing but a cushy job in order to avoid combat. However, over his protests, in 1942 he is given a special assignment to New Hebrides, where he's to join a British patrol whose objective is to destroy a Japanese radio station. The lieutenant's job is to radio Japanese command that everything is normal, while an American naval convoy slips through the straits at the north end of the island. From here the story gets truly strange. This British patrol is comprised solely of angry malcontents at each others' throats who are immediately contemplating shooting their commanding officer. They argue and disagree about everything, while continually point their weapons at one another, and actually cut the throat of one of their wounded. (Obviously, these guys don't want to be on this patrol.) Lt. Lawson then makes an unlikely transformation from easygoing desk jockey to hardened veteran before the patrol even begins. Later, in an act of cowardice, he fails to carryout his part of the mission (however, he gets it in the end). In one of the most bizarre moments in war movie history, this motley crew meets its match when a Japanese officer hunts them down by wiring the jungle with speakers in an attempt to talk them into surrendering. You will have to rent the movie to find out if he succeeds.

What the critics say Critics rate this movie 3.5 to 4.0. "Semi-cynical, long and bloody adventure of competence but no great merit."[1] "Action-packed film builds to pulsating finale."[2] "It really doesn't have anything to do with the actual war or the generation who fought it."[8] **Final Word** This is the ultimate cynical take on command. But who cares, it's a bad film that's right up there with *The Long and the Short and the Tall* in depicting soldiers at war with each other.

Top Gun

1986 USA color d. Tony Scott

Military Life: Fighter Pilot Training   3.0

Imagine a slick production with great soundtrack, outstanding aerial photography, beautiful people, and the complete cooperation of the Navy. Unfortunately though this movie is filled with contrived situations, a lack of sexual chemistry between the leads, average performances and an uncompelling story. You would have *Top Gun*. Tom Cruise stars as Lt. Pete "Maverick" Mitchell, an outstanding fighter pilot who's always pushing the limits and trying to prove something to everyone around him. He and his co-pilot, Nick "Goose" Bradshaw (Anthony Edwards) are selected to attend the naval Fighter Weapons School or "Fightertown" in San Diego, California. Here they receive advanced fighter combat tactics training. The best student/flight crew in each graduating class is named the "Top Gun." The competition for this award is between Cruise and Val Kilmer (Lt. Tom "Iceman" Kazanski), and there's no love lost between them. Lt. Mitchell is an in-it-for-himself type of guy and Iceman is strictly a team-player. While they compete with one another in the air, they aren't competing for the attention of Charlotte Blackwood (Kelly McGillis), a beautiful Ph.D. specializing in Soviet fighter design and tactics (only in your dreams). What makes this movie different from most military stories is the psychology of the hero, a self-absorbed 1980s guy who is trying to undo the shame of his father's past. When Maverick becomes depressed over the death of his co-pilot, he loses confidence in himself. (Fair enough.) But he resolves this crisis by jumping into a combat situation and shooting down the "bad" Migs. (This isn't very satisfying.) While this was the standard redemption for the old-style hero, it's not clear that it works for the new self-styled hero of the 1980s. Okay, all the audience really wants is a happy ending, and *Top Gun* has a very happy ending—except for "Goose," who dies in order for Maverick to find himself. A small sacrifice between buddies? Right!

What the critics say Critics rate this movie 2.5 to 3.5. "Young studs vie for glory...contrived beyond belief."[2] "Military jingoism...inane dramatics."[3] "Pretty young people in stylish clothes and non-stop soundtrack."[4] **Final Word** Fighter pilot testosterone rage meets vulnerable, self-absorbed hero in the age of "Reaganomics."

Tora! Tora! Tora!

1970   USA /JAP   color   d. Richard Fleischer/Toshio Masuda

World War II: Big Battle	4.0

At the time this film was made, it was one of Hollywood's biggest-budgeted epics ($25 million), as it recreates the December 7, 1941 attack on Pearl Harbor by Japan. It was also a collaborative effort, with Richard Fleischer directing the American side of the war and Kinji Fukasaku and Toshio Masuda directing the Japanese side. Based on two books, *Tora! Tora! Tora!* (Tiger! Tiger! Tiger!) by Gordon W. Prange and *The Broken Seal* by Landislas Farango, the movie is a careful and elaborately detailed effort to show all the key events leading up to the attack. The film's recreation of the attack is an incredible special effects bonanza. From the Japanese side, it paints a highly sympathetic view of Admiral Yamamoto, Commander and Chief of the Japanese Imperial Navy, and makes the case that America had acted provocatively by moving its Pacific fleet from San Diego to Hawaii. From the American side, the failure to anticipate and detect the attack are attributed to complacency, incompetence, bureaucracy and politics (all the usual suspects). With hindsight, there is no doubt that Japan was extraordinarily lucky, and given all the events that had to go their way to succeed, it was amazingly foolish they even tried. However, the United States lucked out by not having its carriers stationed at Pearl Harbor, which essentially meant the attack failed. It's an interesting drama to watch unfold, as US military intelligence anticipated this attack but couldn't get anyone's attention. Unfortunately, as with many epics, the people get lost in the spectacle. This movie is too overly dependent on the drama of unfolding events to hold viewers attention and fails to create any drama through character and story development. The result is a beautifully staged recreation of the attack during which the viewer's attention may wander.

What the critics say Critics rate this movie 2.0 to 4.5. "Immense, largely studio bound, calcified war spectacle."[1] "Well-made film creates incredible tension."[2] "Notable for its good photography but lacks a storyline equal to its epic intentions."[5] **Final Word** Producer Darryl F. Zanuck placed an ad in the *New York Times* explaining that the film was made in order to make the public aware of the risks of a missile attack and the need for preparedness—public relations or politics?

Torpedo Alley

1953   USA   b/w   d. Lew Landers

Korean War: Submarine-Romance	1.0

This studio "B" movie, directed by Lew Landers, is one of the most lifeless and generic war films ever made. *Torpedo Alley* opens in the South Pacific in 1945, near the end of the war when Navy torpedo bomber pilot and decorated war hero Lt. Bob Bingham (Mark Stevens) freezes and crashes his plane, killing his two crewmen. He states that this is the third time he has done this, but keeps flying. The audience, of course, is supposed to be impressed with his sense of patriotism and duty (he's obviously a walking headcase who should have been grounded years earlier—an irrelevant issue the movie doesn't address). Rescued by a submarine, Lt. Bingham is hospitalized in Hawaii where he meets attractive nurse Susan Peabody (Dorothy Malone). Bingham, guilt ridden about the death of his two crewmen, proceeds to act angrily and obnoxiously towards everyone around him. No effort is made to address the issue of posttraumatic stress disorder (apparently he's just obnoxious and not disordered.) Unable to adapt to civilian life after the war, Bingham retrains in the Navy's submarine school and renews his efforts to romance Ms. Peabody—in an angry, arrogant and aggressive manner that makes this romance closer to stalking than seduction. Upon completion of training (most of this movie looks and feels like a Navy training video), Bingham is stationed on a submarine off the coast of Korea. After successfully conducting a commando raid, he returns to the states where nurse Peabody is waiting for him. There is simply no aspect of this film that rises above mediocrity. But perhaps the most obvious questions raised by this movie are, how and why was Mark Stevens ever cast in a leading role? Stevens comes across as one of the most drab, lifeless figures ever to appear on the screen. These problems are compounded by Lt. Bingham's obnoxious character. No matter how borishly he behaves, everyone appears to forgive him. Basically, this is an actionless movie that better qualifies as a dull romance.

What the critics say Critics rate this movie 1.0. to 3.0. "Typical Korean War actioner."[2] "For next to no budget...(a) tacky piece of regurgitation."[8] **Final Word** If you have read this review, you have already wasted too much time on *Torpedo Alley*.

Torpedo Run
1958 USA color d. Joseph Pevney

World War II: Submarine Warfare   3.5

If you watch enough war movies, you just might come to believe that all submarine commanders are just a little crazy. In this case, there is Lt. Commander Barney Doyle (Glenn Ford), captain of the USS *Grayfish*, in the obsessive pursuit of the Japanese carrier *Shinaru*. This carrier has personal significance to Commander Doyle because it was the lead carrier in the bombing of Pearl Harbor and, therefore, has a great deal of symbolic importance to the Navy and the American war effort. However, in an earlier attempt by Doyle to torpedo this ship he sank a Japanese POW transport ship that was being used as a shield. In an unnecessary and melodramatic plot twist, his wife and child, who had been taken prisoner in Manila, are onboard the transport. Where this movie really unravels is in not providing any motive for Doyle taking a high-risk shot at the *Shinaru*, particularly when he was advised by his executive officer and best friend, Lt. Archer Sloan (Ernest Borgnine), that he was likely to hit the transport ship. Of course, Doyle goes ahead. The rest of *Torpedo Run* plays out in an interesting, if not predictable manner, as Doyle and Sloan clash in Doyle's pursuit of the carrier. Commander Doyle also continues to exercise more bad judgment, but is ultimately succeeds in sinking the carrier. Shot in Technicolor and with wide-angle screen, this movie benefited from having the cooperation of the Navy. The result is excellent special effects and the realistic portrayal of submarine operations. However, the movie did not benefit from casting Ernest Borgnine as a lead, as he is annoying in nearly every scene he appears. For a sub actioner, this film is somewhat slow moving (too many flashbacks of Dole and his family), and has a sloppy script with far too many plot holes to elevate this mildly entertaining movie to the next level.

What the critics say Critics rate this movie 2.0 to 3.0. "Well-staged potboiler with excellent action sequences."[1] "Sluggish WW 2 revenge narrative."[2] "Standard submarine melodramatics ...generally worthwhile."[5] "Tautly exciting WW II mouse-chases-cat story."[7] **Final Word** By 1958 the theme of subs sinking POW ships had already been rendered routine by two 1940s movie efforts, *Prison Ship* and *Submarine Raider*.

To the Shores of Tripoli
1942   USA   b/w   d. H. Bruce Humberstone

| WW II: Classic '40s Flagwaver | 1.0 |

On the surface, this lightweight romantic comedy by director Bruce Humberstone, appears to be a war film. In reality, it's a recruitment vehicle for the Marine Corps. All the action (if one can use that word for this movie) takes place at the Marine Corps Training Center in San Diego, California in 1941, just prior to the bombing of Pearl Harbor. Handsome young man and all around swell, Chris Winters (John Payne) has decided to become a Marine in order to please his father (a former Marine officer). Chris then encounters Sgt. Smith (Randolph Scott), a Marine D.I. who is one of the most understanding guys to be found anywhere in the military. The sergeant patiently explains things in such a calm and rational manner, that it would be hard not to go along with his polite requests. But then, Marine bootcamp is revealed for what it really is—a great place to meet women, socialize with a bunch of fun guys and when required—do a lot of close order drills. That's it; after only eight short weeks—they've made a man out of you. And, in the case of Chris Winters, he gets the girl he has been chasing around the entire time, nurse Mary Carter (Maureen O'Hara). He has also seen the big picture and gets to go off to war and fight the enemy. Equally important, his father couldn't be prouder of him, or Sgt. Smith happier. In fact, as the Marines board the troop transport ship they break into song. Now I have left out a lot of twists and turns in the plot that might leave you concerned for Chris. What are his intentions towards Mary? Will he keep seeing his old girlfriend? Will he take a cushy job in Washington, D.C.? *To the Shores of Tripoli* is obviously filled with the types of primal angst experienced by young men who are being sent off to war. The real question raised by this movie remains unanswered: why was money wasted to colorize this film years after it was made?

What the critics say Critics rate this movie 1.0 to 3.0. "Routine material."[1] "Wartime propaganda in the guise of drama."[5] "Run-of-the-mill US Marine training picture."[8] **Final Word** Former Marine D.I. Sgt. R. Lee Ermey, star of *Boys in Company C*, *Full Metal Jacket* and *The Siege of Firebase Gloria*, would probably put his Colt .45 in his mouth and pull the trigger after watching this movie.

Tour of Duty
1987 USA color tv d. Bill Norton

Vietnam War: Infantry Combat	3.0

While *Tour of Duty* is considerably better than the dozens of Vietnam War exploitation-actioners that litter the video store shelves, it's clearly a notch or two below the best Vietnam War movies. This fictional story opens in Vietnam in 1967, as "Firebase Ladybird" comes under attack from NVA regulars (North Vietnamese Army). The movie focuses on "Bravo" company of the 23rd Infantry Division as it's in the process of getting replacements ("cherries") and conducting patrols "in country." There are vague references to drug use, racial tension, vets versus new recruits, pacifism and the war's politics, but none of the issues are delved into with any energy. While there's an attempt to make the individual soldiers edgy in some manner, they all turn out to be really nice guys. The reason for this is that *Tour of Duty* was a pilot for a TV series. At the center of the story is Sgt." Zeke" (Terence Knox), a veteran now serving his third tour of duty in 'Nam. He's the unofficial leader of the platoon and has to deal with Lt. Goldman (Stephen Caffrey) who wants to lead but lacks the experience or the wisdom to defer. The film's most interesting moment comes in a lengthy sequence about the Vietcong/NVA tunneling throughout the South, and the enormous advantages this gave them in fighting the war. There are some tense and well-done scenes as members of the platoon enter the tunnels to chase the Vietcong and NVA. In a contrived attempt at post-war reconciliation, a Black-American soldier is captured but protected by a Communist Vietnamese doctor (Steve Akahoshi). This movie gives considerable voice to antiwar sentiment but doesn't really try to make a political case. Its focus is on the men and the war in front of them. There's a fairly high-degree of military realism, with numerous Hueys, M-60s, lots of explosions, and well-staged combat scenes. However, the characters, acting and dialogue are simply not as good as the war-realism in the film.

What the critics say Critics rate this movie 2.5 to 3.0. "While the cleanliness hinders the film's credibility, the action scenes make it worth while."[7] **Final Word** There were two Vietnam War television series, and both had movie pilots—*China Beach*, which ran from 1988 to 1991, and *Tour of Duty*, which ran from 1987 to 1990.

The Train

1964   USA /FRA/ITA   b/w   d. John Frankenheimer

World War II: Resistance   4.0

This entertaining film, shot on location in France by director John Frankenheimer and adapted from the book by Rose Valland, stars Burt Lancaster (Labiche) as a railway inspector and resistance leader. The story is straightforward. A German colonel, Von Waldheim (Paul Scofield), is an art lover who has decided to personally loot France of all its modernist treasures (what the Nazis called "degenerate art") and ship them to Berlin by train. The treasures include hundreds of paintings by artist such as Cezanne, Degas, Gauguin, Manet, Matisse, Miro, Monet, Picasso, Renoir, and Van Gogh. The action takes place just days before Paris will be liberated by the Allies in 1944. The effete Von Waldheim is the most interesting character in this movie. When talking about the Nazis' condemnation of this art, he states, "I've often wondered at the curious conceit that would attempt to determine taste and ideas by decree." On the other hand, Von Waldheim is absolutely ruthless in his determination to possess this art (perhaps a metaphor for Nazi Germany). The central question confronting Labiche is whether to risk the lives of men who care nothing about art, art that is described as—"this beauty, this vision of life born out of France (that)...we hold in trust for everyone." Slowly, Labiche is drawn into attempts to stop the train carrying the art from making it to Berlin, As he enters into a *cat and mouse* game with Col. Von Waldheim, Labiche becomes equally obsessed in prevailing. While Lancaster gives a solid, if not understated performance, the real star of this film is the work of director John Frankenheimer in providing a high energy story with a gritty physical realism that adds greatly to the overall suspense. If this film has a major failing, it is the frequent and improbable plot twists that begin to undermine the stories credibility. The constant deception perpetrated on the Germans pretty much makes the outcome a foregone conclusion. One could also tire of the world of trains.

What the critics say Critics rate this movie 4.0 to 5.0. "High powered excitement all the way."[2] "A solid rousing thriller."[3] "A colorful, actionful big-scale adventure opus."[4] "The film can be criticized for going to far with its contrived plot."[6] **Final Word** This is a well-crafted and entertaining film that begins to unravel the longer it plays. Not quite in the highest echelon.

The Trench

1999   FRA/GBR   color   d. William Boyd

WW I: Battle of the Somme   4.0

One hundred thousand British soldiers, along 26 miles of trenches, are poised to "stand to" forty-eight hours before the Battle of the Somme is to begin on July 1, 1916. This is the opening scene of *The Trench*, a small drama set in the British trenches where young soldiers confront the terror of walking into "No Man's Land" and the murderous fire of German machine guns. The British High Command believes that five days of massive artillery bombardment (1.7 million shells were fired) would destroy the German defenses, and that this would result in an easy "walk-over." At 7:30 AM, on a bright summer morning, British troops walk toward the German positions at a pace of 100 yards per minute, carrying 65 lb. kits on their backs. One hour later, 30,000 men are lost; by the days end casualties mounted to 60,000. Six months later total casualties for both sides were 1,200,000 men. Written and directed by William Boyd, this movie poignantly focuses on Billy Macfarlane (Paul Nicholls), an 18-year-old soldier who dreams of having a girlfriend. In one moving scene, he steals the picture of a naked prostitute who looks like a young girl he talked to and fell in love with. Billy has the picture of her face in his hand as he walks into battle—and his immediate death. The British Expeditionary Force of 1916 was composed mostly of young men who enlisted locally in order to fight together. The film focuses on this unusual degree of familiarity between the soldiers in the trenches, who grew up together. The soldiers slowly understand what is to come, as men are wounded by snipers, killed by artillery shells and as veterans tell their stories. The tedium and misery of trench life is interrupted only by a growing realization that they are about to die, and that all their talk about the future is their only future. Well-acted with a high degree of realism, *The Trench* reveals the realities of war as seen through the eyes of young British soldiers.

What the critics say The critics rate this movie 2.0 to 2.5. "There are many better movies than this low budget affair"[1] "Low budget psychological set-piece."[8] **Final Word** Yes! It's time to ignore the critics once again. This movie is not for the action junkie. It's a thoughtful and mournful look at how the young men of an entire generation were sacrificed by outmoded military thinking.

Tunes of Glory

1960   GBR   color   d. Ronald Neame

Peacetime Military: Command Conflict   4.5

An outstanding character study, *Tunes of Glory* is based on the novel/screenplay by James Kennaway and features a brilliant performance by Alec Guinness. Guinness plays Maj. Jock Sinclair, the acting commander of a Scottish Highland regiment that is steeped in a 200+ year old military tradition. Sinclair is a crude, gregarious and sodden WW II hero who came up through the ranks. While he's man's man who's tough, edgy, insecure and bordering on the sadistic at times, he's also liked and respected by the officers he commands. Into the regiment comes a new commander, Lt. Col. Basil Barrow, played by John Mills. The colonel comes from an elite public school education at Oxford and Sandhurst and was a prisoner of war during WW II. Erudite, fragile and introverted, he is obsessive about detail and formality, and is the opposite of Sinclair. What ensues is not just a battle of wills and social class but a thoughtful look inside military society and the lives of men which have been formed by war. Neither officer comes across as particularly likable, but as their stories unfold both become more sympathetic. It's clear that Barrow has never fully recovered from his POW experience, nor Sinclair from the intensity and camaraderie of war. Both men continue to be prisoners of these experiences many years later. The issues between them intensify when, in a drunken moment, Maj. Sinclair strikes a corporal. Barrow has to decide whether to pursue a court-martial. If he does he risks losing the support of his officers and of creating a public black eye for the regiment. Not doing so would open the door to possible scandal and to losing the discipline and authority required to command his men. In a brilliant scene at the end, Sinclair finally comes to realize how lost he was without war, and that he betrayed his ideals as a soldier. *Tunes of Glory* is a tense, thoughtful and well-acted drama about the command of men and the potential for the abuse of authority. The film is also about how much is left emotionally undone after a war.

What the critics say Critics rate this movie 4.0 to 5.0. "Finely acted and well made with memorable confrontation scenes."[1] "Engrossing clash of wills."[2] "Memorable character study."[3] **Final Word** After a while, the kilts begin to look fashionable, and it helps to like bagpipes and a wee Scottish brogue.

The Tuskegee Airmen

1995 USA color tv d. Robert Markowitz

World War II: Black Fighter Pilots	4.0

In 1942 the US Army Air Corps established a segregated base in Tuskegee, Alabama, to train "Negro" fighter pilots. This fact-based movie is taken from a story written by Robert W. Williams, a former Tuskegee airman. It chronicles a struggle against prejudice and racism as the Army Air Corps graduates the first class of Black officers and pilots. These men, and those who followed, formed the 332nd Fighter Group and to flew in combat over Europe from 1943-1945. A highly decorated group, these pilots did not suffer a single bomber loss while providing air escort over Germany. This intense and thoughtful movie has a ring of truth throughout. Lawrence Fishburne gives an outstanding, understated performance as Lt. Hannibal Lee, who is at the center of this story. However, in this movie the war is backdrop to the story of these pilots' struggle to prove themselves. The movie makes it clear that many in American society and the military were not ready to accept Blacks as officers and pilots. At every level attempts were made to thwart the Tuskegee program. The washout rate in basic training was made exceptionally high. Politicians intervened in Washington, D.C., so that these pilots would later only be assigned to ground support missions. Finally, they were required to fly many more combat missions than white pilots before being rotated home. Ultimately, the necessities of war gave the 332 Fighter Group equality. Cuba Gooding Junior (Lt. Billy Roberts) and Andre Braugher as Col. Benjamin O. Davis give accomplished performances. While there are several good air combat scenes, this is not the strength of this movie. The real importance of the film is that it opens the door to an important chapter in American military history and reveals the truth—Black-American soldiers have been performing heroically all along.

What the critics say Critics rate this movie 3.5 to 4.5. "An inspiring story of courage and perseverance."[3] "Cast does a fine job in what turns out to essentially be a standard action/war movie."[5] "Script is a collection of clichés."[6] **Final Word** No doubt this movie would have been better served if there were more story and less preaching. An absorbing drama nonetheless.

Twelve O'Clock High
1949 USA b/w d. Henry King

World War II: Air Combat Command   5.0

Directed by Henry King and adapted from a novel by Sy Bartlett
and Beirne Lay, this movie is an examination of the pressures of
sending pilots into combat. In 1942 the American 8th Air Force
conducted daylight bombing raids over Germany, and tried to
knock out military-related industries with B-17 bombers. This was
an experiment to determine the feasibility of precision daylight
bombing in an attempt to shorten the war. Gregory Peck, starring
as Brig. General Frank Savage, is sent down from headquarters
to take command of the 918th Bombardment Group, which is
taking unusually high casualties. As Savage sets about
reestablishing order and discipline, there ensues a complex and
highly engaging psychological drama about the extraordinary
pressures of command at the highest levels. At one point Savage
tells the pilots, who have begun to believe they are hardluck and
feel sorry for themselves, "Consider yourselves already dead"
and "Stop making plans! Forget about going home!" Savage, a
tough by-the-book officer, slowly begins to identify with his men
and earn their respect as he increases his flying missions. In a
poignant scene at the end, Savage breaks down from the stress
and is unable to climb into his bomber for an important mission.
This film looks at the limits of endurance in combat and the
pressures on officers to send men to their death. Every aspect of
this film is well done—Peck gives one of the best performances
of his career and Dean Jagger, as Maj. Stovall, won the
Academy Award for Best Supporting Actor. There is excellent
attention to military detail, and the use of documentary footage of
B-17s in combat over Germany is well-integrated. If the film has
a flaw, it would be the failure to question military command.
While raising questions about the military's willingness to accept
high casualties, not set mission limits, or establish medical
standards for flying fitness, the film does not question
command's decisions to sacrifice these pilots and air crews.

What the critics say Critics rate this movie 4.5 to 5.0.
"Absorbing character drama, justifiably a big box-office success
of its day."[1] "A thoroughly involving war drama."[3] "Epic drama
about the heroic 8th Air Force...and the strain of military
command."[5] **Final Word** Twelve O'Clock High was also a
competent television series from 1964 to 1967.

Twilight's Last Gleaming

1977 USA/GER color d. Robert Aldrich

Cold War: Nuclear Blackmail 2.0

This low-budget, low-tech (not to mention low-intellect affair) probably represents the nadir of film-making about Cold War paranoia and hysteria over mutually assured destruction (MAD). In a not-so-brilliant twist, on the vulnerability of nuclear weapons to sabotage, a disgruntled former Air Force officer, Gen. Dell (Burt Lancaster), breaks out of prison with three violent and dimwitted felons and seizes control of a Titan nuclear missile silo in Montana. Dell threatens World War III if the US government doesn't declassify documents showing that the Vietnam War was, what?—pretty much what we know it for today—an unwinnable war in which events were manipulated to instigate an armed conflict against North Vietnam. When the mad general insists that the President tell the American people the truth, this Cold War thriller degenerate into a self-righteous, left-wing antiwar rant with messianic overtones as seen in the character of Gen. Dell. The President (Charles Durning), is then briefed on how Gen. Dell, once a Vietnam War prisoner, was set up for a murder conviction in order to stop his efforts to reveal the truth. Unfortunately, too much of the movie is devoted to the President and his war cabinet secretly meeting and negotiating with Gen. Dell. Dell wants twenty million dollars and transport on Air Force One out of the country. He also wants the President as hostage, and the release of classified documents about the war. Just how Dell managed to break out of maximum security prison is never indicated. But this film's greatest unreality is Dell's lame attempt to take over a missile silo, and even more improbable his efforts to disarm security measures in the silo, master launch procedures, and gain access to launch codes. There's even a cynical and paranoid conclusion that the President will be sacrificed in order to suppress the truth from the American people. In a genre of film dedicated to exploring all the improbable possibilities for a nuclear catastrophe—this one does just that.

What the critics say Critics rate this movie 1.0 to 3.0. "Fairly incompetent on its level...distinctly overlong and unlikeable entertainment."[1] "Intricate, intriguing and intelligent drama."[4] "Another maniac-at-the-button doomsday chronicle."[7] **Final Word** Too many logical inconsistencies in the plot to even begin worrying about all the incoherent ideas here. Skip this one.

U-571

2000 USA color d. Jonathan Mostow

WW II: Submarine Adventure   2.5

The bar has been raised high in the submarine war/adventure genre over the past twenty years, with the likes of *Crimson Tide*, *Das Boot* and *Hunt for Red October*. By comparison, *U-571*, written and directed by Jonathan Mostow, is a disappointing submarine movie whose only redeeming feature is good special effects. The story has some factual basis, but few of them are evident in this movie. In 1941 German U-boats sunk over 1,000 Allied ships and were close to successfully blockading Great Britain. However, in 1941, the British successfully boarded a stranded German U-boat and captured a secret coding device called the Enigma machine, which was used for encrypting secret messages between submarines and the German high command. This led to a significant breakthrough in decoding German messages to U-boats in the North Atlantic. This movie tells the fictional story of an American submarine disguised as a German sub that seeks to rendezvous with a stranded German sub waiting to be repaired and resupplied. The Americans hope to get to the stranded sub first and board it, intent on capturing the German's coding machine and the codes themselves. The twist is, how to accomplish this without the Germans knowing that the Americans have captured the Enigma machine. Many phony dramatics and numerous plot twists only add to this movie taking on serious water. What really sinks the film is the lack of real people inhabiting the submarines or the story. The movie appears to be nothing more than a star vehicle for Matthew McConaughey (Lt. Andrew Tyler), who can't get to periscope depth. Oh, in a shocker, the German U-boat captain is a really bad guy. Despite these flaws the movie almost works except that in the second half the action comes to a standstill. A lot of cast members stand around issuing orders and hollering, but nothing happens—deadly for an action movie.

What the critics say Critics rate this movie 3.0 to 3.5. "Agreeably old-fashioned WW 2 submarine drama...but fizzles at the end."[2] "Laden with melodrama and nail-biting tension."[4] "Long on loud and impressive action scenes but short on characterizations and good dialog."[5] **Final Word** Adrenaline junkies with surround-sound systems and mega-subwoofers will like it. Serious war geeks should avoid it.

Underground

1995 FRA/GER/HUN/YUG color subtitles d. Emir Kusturica

Balkans Conflict: Allegorical Fantasy   5.0

Probably nothing in recent American social or political
experience could produce a film of such devastating and
outrageous satiric effect. A entire people's reality has been so
completely distorted by war, that life, death and love have been
reduced to farce. To experience life in any other terms is simply
too painful. This brilliant film, written and director by Emir
Kusturica, depicts in broad allegorical terms the life and death of
Yugoslavia from 1941 to 1992. However, it is not quite that
simple. Two of the wildest characters ever to inhabit the screen,
Marko (Miki Manojlovic) and Blacky (Lazar Ristovski), larger-
than-life gangsters, are trafficking black-market weapons to
Yugoslav partisans. The two war-profiteers are also active
Communist Party members in the fight against the "fucking
fascist motherfuckers!" It's Belgrade, 1941, and with crazed slapstick humor, surreal images and rollicking music, the two
gangsters live larger than life. Blacky is fooling around on his
wife and having an affair with Yugoslavia's most beautiful and
talented actress Natalija (Mirjana Jokovic), who is seducing a
Nazi officer. As the Gestapo closes in, Blacky and the families of
both men hide in a large factory cellar and manufacture
weapons. In an act of betrayal, Marko seduces Blacky's girlfriend
and then perpetrates a forty-year hoax that the war is still
ongoing and that they need to stay put and produce weapons for
the upcoming final battle (he, of course, is making a nice profit
and is now a prominent Communist Party official). In a brilliant
sequence, the entire lie unravels and the men find themselves in
the middle of the Yugoslavian civil war. Blacky leads a militia
army and Marko and Natatija deal arms. Brother is killing brother,
literally and figuratively, and no one can be trusted. The acting is
exceptional and the many fantastic scenes and absurd moments
leaves the viewer "dazed and exhausted."

What the critics say Critics rate this movie 4.0 to 5.0. "Magic
realism, with ghosts from the past still inhabiting the present."[1] "A
remarkable...anarchic comedy and wartime tragedy."[3] "Steam-
roller circus that leaves the viewer dazed and exhausted but
mightily impressed."[4] **Final Word** Natatija tells Marko, "You lie
so beautifully." This movie is about those who lie and those who
want to believe the lie. Don't miss it!

Up Periscope

1959   USA   color   d. Gordon Douglas

WW II: Submarine Action	2.0

It's not easy to make a submarine movie this bad, especially with a real submarine, good special effects, a competent cast, big budget and a novel by Robb White. Which raises the question, Why was this movie made? Perhaps Hollywood saw an opportunity to capitalize on the recent popularity of James Garner's television series *Maverick*. Unfortunately, the worst thing about *Up Periscope* is James Garner. Directed by Gordon Douglas, the story is set in the Pacific, in 1942, aboard the *Barracuda*, commanded by Capt. Stevenson (Edmond O'Brien). He has been ordered on a secret mission to deliver Lt. Braden (Garner) to a Japanese-held island. Trained as a underwater demolitions expert, the lieutenant's job is to obtain Japanese radio codes so that the US can disrupt Japanese submarine activity. Of the number of odd things about this movie, none is stranger than the complete unfeasibility of this mission. First of all, Braden isn't a professional soldier but a "90 day wonder" fluent in Japanese. He has to swim underwater from the sub to the shore as a frogman, make his way as a commando through a heavily garrisoned island, locate the communications center, enter the station without detection, locate the code book, photograph it and then return to the sub within 18 hour or be left behind. Preposterous! The mission almost makes the opening romantic interlude seem reasonable. Prior to selecting a candidate for this mission, military intelligence has a beautiful woman seduce Lt. Braden in order to complete a security background check!? (We should all be so lucky.) Back to the island. The island scenes looks as if they were shot in the producers backyard, with Garner swimming and crawling from here to there so many times it becomes comical. Apparently, the screen writer had no idea how Lt. Braden was going to accomplish this mission either. While the submarine action is good, the conflict between crew members and the captain is tedious and predictable. O'Brien does a good acting job but, unfortunately, plays the stereotypical "strange" sub captain.

What the critics say Critics rate this movie 2.0 to 2.5. "A routine submarine film."[5] **Final Word** This is a lame war movie with an implausible story. Watching James Garner crawl around an island as a lost commando is low camp at best.

Victory at Entebbe

1976   USA   color   tv   d. Marvin J. Chomsky

This was the first of three movies about the hijacking of Air
France Flt. 139 on June 27, 1976 by German and Palestinian
terrorists, and the successful Israeli commando operation to free
its passengers. All three movies, *Operation Thunderbolt* (out of
print), *Raid on Entebbe* and *Victory at Entebbe*, were rushed into
production and the subsequent product reflects this. Except for
the names of the cast, this movie and *Raid on Entebbe* are
identical. They are both empty, generic films that are structured
much like the classic "disaster" flicks *Airport* or *The Poseidon
Adventure*, where we are introduced to dozens of terrified and
hysterical passengers who have brief and meaningless moments
on the screen. Meanwhile, the storyline constantly switches back
and forth between the Israeli cabinet, who debate what to do,
and the anxious passengers. The hijackers ultimately direct the
plane to Entebbe airport in Uganda, and with the covert
assistance of Idi Amin attempt to extort money and the freedom
of imprisoned terrorists. Unfortunately, the raid is carried off in a
low-budget, low-tech fashion in the last few minutes of the film.
Perhaps more silly, given the cheap production values of this
film, is the all-star cast (Burt Lancaster, Kirt Douglas, Anthony
Hopkins, Richard Dreyfuss, Helen Hayes, Elizabeth Taylor) as
each is miscast in their own unique way. If this film had focused
on the politics, the commando operation or the passengers, it
would have been better. But as it stands, it all seems to just rush
by. The two most interesting moments are the debate in the
Israeli cabinet about its policy of not negotiating with terrorists,
and the role of Field Marshal, Doctor Idi Amin Dada, President of
Uganda for Life (Julius Harris), who is a corrupt two-faced thug
and grandstander who tries to milk all the media attention he
could from this event.

What the critics say Critics rate this movie 2.0 to 3.0.
"Docudrama fails to capture the truth of the moment and instead
relies on cardboard characters to tell the story."[7] **Final Word** The
epilogue notes that 4 hostages, 7 terrorists, 20 Ugandan soldiers
and 1 commando were killed. One hundred and three Israeli
passengers were rescued. Today we know that hijacking planes
is an old-fashioned terrorist tactic. Still to come were blowing-up
airplanes, and still later airplane suicide attacks.

Vietnam Home Movies

1984   USA   color   tv

Vietnam War: Documentary   1.0

This documentary consists entirely of converted 8-mm amateur film footage taken by US military personnel stationed in Vietnam during the war. *Vietnam Archives Inc.* has apparently been doing this for many years. The movie is divided into two parts, each comprised of footage and narration by a different soldier. The narration is unscripted and spontaneous, and this is a serious mistake that allows the commentary to ramble in an unfocused manner. Part I, titled "Rifle Company C," takes place in the spring of 1968 and was filmed by 20-year-old Specialist First Class Jeffrey Overton, stationed in the Mekong Delta with the 6th Battalion, 31st Infantry. Part 2, titled "Outpost Legionnaire," was filmed by Sgt. Steven M. White, an artillery surveyor with the 82nd Artillery. Unfortunately, the vast separation between amateur video enthusiasts and professional film makers becomes readily apparent. The quality of these films is poor. For the most part they are dark, grainy and jumpy. Also, there is no sound, except for the matter-of-fact voice-over, which renders the images very empty. In addition, the failure to focus on one individual or group precludes having any sense of who these soldiers are. Finally, what makes this film footage truly uninteresting is the random shots of soldiers reading letters, bathing, smoking, and the occasional supply helicopter landing. Occasionally a 155-mm battery fires in the background or jets drop bombs in the distance, but more importantly, there's no combat footage. The narration provides no insight into soldiers at war. Rather it is comprised of mundane comments about daily activities at a base camp. These home movies have nothing to say about the country of Vietnam, the people of Vietnam, the politics of the war, or the experiences of the men who fought in this war. The images here are strangely empty.

What the critics say No available reviews. **Final Word** This movie could have benefited enormously from a professional sitting down with these two veterans, Overton and White, and helping them find the words to tell their important stories—to make their experiences and these images come alive for viewers.

Vietnam War Story

1987   USA   color   tv   (parts 1, 2, 3)

Vietnam War: Collage of War Stories   4.0

This outstanding HBO series (1987-1988) is comprised of three
films, V*ietnam War Story, Vietnam War Story II* and *Vietnam War
Story III.* Each film, in turn, tells three separate and complete
stories "inspired" by the real-life experiences of Vietnam
veterans. Though small budget productions, these films have
excellent casts and are well written. Unlike many films about
Vietnam, they do not attempt to examine the broader moral
issues or offer a political viewpoint of the war. Their ambition is
more modest—to tell the personal stories of American soldiers
who fought in the war. To this end, the films do an excellent job.
Part of what makes the series effective is the wide range of
stories, of which only two directly involve soldiers in combat,
"The Mine" and "Separated." "Dusk to Dawn" tells the story of a
young Marine about to ship out. In "The Promise" a military nurse
at an EVAC hospital is confronted with seriously wounded
soldiers. The most moving story, "Home," is about a small group
of amputees at a stateside naval hospital who reveal the
difficulties of their lives. As one young Marine puts it, "In here
everyone is so fucked-up, you almost feel normal!" The despair
and the anger the men feel is palpable, and more importantly,
the quiet and simple heroism of surviving shines through. It is a
difficult and heartbreaking subject that is well handled. In another
story, "The Pass," soldiers on I & I (intercourse and intoxication)
visit a brothel. As one of them describes the experience, "You
are drinking gasoline in hell." The series of stories were originally
produced for television and were later packaged for home video.
Each short story immediately involves the viewer and provides
an intense emotional catharsis. These movie are interesting and
involving, and while the raw emotional energy can be overwhelming, what they lack in subtlety is compensated for by their
honesty.

What the critics say Critics rate these movies 4.0. "Poignant
and action packed...each an intimate account straight from the
men who lived them."[5] "All are heart-wrenching...all performances are top-rated."[7] **Final Word** Movie goers who are
interested in the small stories of the Vietnam War should
definitely check these movies out. Not for the "action-freak" who
craves the big screen experience.

Von Richthofen and Brown

1971   USA   color   d. Roger Corman

WW I: Air Combat	3.0

Directed by Roger Corman, *Von Richthofen and Brown* is a pale imitation of *The Blue Max*. On the Western Front from 1916 to 1918 the British 209th fighter squadron tangles with the German Jagdstaffel 11 fighter squadron. Through the real-life characters of Lt. Roy Brown (Don Stroud), a Canadian wheat farmer turned volunteer in the British Royal Flying Corps, and Baron Manfred Von Richthofen, aka the "Red Baron," (John Phillip Law), credited with the most air combat victories (80) during the First World War, the film investigates the changed nature of air war. Both the English and German squadrons are composed of men from the upper classes who are fighting a "gentleman's" war. Lt. Brown quickly looses patience with the class sensibilities of his squadron, and begins to introduce more ruthless air combat tactics. He tells the other pilots—"Just men, no more knights." The Germans respond in kind. However, Von Richthofen continues to champion a more aristocratic approach to combat. This results in increased conflict with the other pilots in his squadron and greater casualties. While Richthofen sees war as a "hunt" with a need to save "those traditions that separate gentlemen from savages," a young Herman Goering rebukes him—"I make war to win." No doubt the movie takes great liberty with the historical record here. In fact, Lt. Roy Brown is credited with shooting down Von Richthofen on April 21, 1918. Unfortunately, the actors in this movie, which has absolutely outstanding aerial combat scenes with SE-5s and Fokker D-VIIs, are as wooden as the planes they fly. The effort to show both sides of the war left too little time to develop the characters and tell their stories.

What the critics say Critics rate this movie 2.0. to 2.5. "The airplanes are nice, but the film is grounded by plot and dialog."[1] "Weak historical drama...aerial work is excellent."[2] **Final Word** The critics are right about this film's problems, but it's better than they suggest. An entertaining movie that is worth watching if you enjoy WW I air combat. Recent reexamination of the evidence strongly suggests that an Australian machine gunner probably shot the Red Baron down.

Von Ryan's Express

1965   USA   color   d. Mark Robson

Directed by Mark Robson and adapted from a novel by David Westheimer, *Von Ryan's Express* is interesting only because of Frank Sinatra. In1943 Col. Joseph Ryan (Frank Sinatra), an American pilot, is shot down and captured by Italian soldiers who protect him from the Germans. They also give him a bottle of wine and take him to an Italian prisoner-of-war camp. (We can only assume his Mafia connections were far more extensive than the tabloids let on.) The part of the movie that works and is a lot of camp fun is Col. Ryan's "attitude." He confronts the corrupt camp commander, Maj. Battaglia (Adolpo Celi), and tells him, "No wonder Italy is losing the war with officers like you." Next, he confronts the British commander of the 9th Fusiliers, Maj. Eric Fincham (Trevor Howard), and in just moments is able to insult the entire history of British POW escape-cinema by suggesting their efforts are stupid, and that the British are obsessed with escaping. As the ranking senior officer, Ryan takes control of the camp and reveals the British tunnel to the Italians in exchange for full-food rations and increased medical care. The British then take to calling him "Von Ryan." Unfortunately, the fun ends, and Ryan attempts a mass escape with 600 prisoners. Eventually, they are recaptured and placed on a train to Germany. Good action follows, as they take over the train and attempt to escape to Switzerland. The movie also becomes boring at times because there's little in the way of subplots. In apparent desperation, a beautiful woman (Raffaella Carrà) is introduced but fails to seduce Ryan. For most of the film, the primary conflict has been a clash of styles and personalities between Col. Ryan and the uptight Maj. Fincham. But once the chase began their conflict changed into mutual respect. Filmed in Italy, this movie has good special effects. During the highly improbably chase, the bullets and the danger are real enough to cast doubt as to how it will all end.

What the critics say Critics rate this movie 3.5 to 4.0. "Exhilarating action thriller with slow spots."[1] "Diverting star vehicle...enjoyable fluff."[6] "First rate WW II tale of escape...a great action story."[7] **Final Word** "The Chairman of the Board" does his thing and it's a lot of fun. The fact that this is a war movie is completely incidental.

Vukovar

1994 YUG/CYP/ITA color subtitles d. Boro Draskovic

Balkans Conflict: Antiwar   4.5

A powerful and disturbing antiwar movie, *Vukovar* takes its name from a Croatian city on the Danube River across from Serbia. With the breakup of Yugoslavia, the numerous republics that comprised this nation—made up of many different ethnic and religious groups—found themselves in civil war as nationalist independence movements arose. With large numbers of Serbs residing in Vukovar and Croatia, war engulfed this region in 1993 and reduced Vukovar to rubble. The film was shot on location and that adds to its stark realism. *Vukovar* is not a combat film. The war is shown through the eyes of Anna (Mirjana Jokovic), a Croat who has married and is deeply in love with Toma (Boris Isakovic), a Serb. Toma is drafted into the Serbian army, while pregnant Anna tries to survive, first with her well-off family who are killed, and then later alone in Vukovar. As the city becomes a war zone, it's soon dominated by militia groups and "dogs of war" who loot and rape. This movie is filled with tension that bursts into random acts of chilling and realistic violence. On one level, the movie is about the fratricide between the Serbs and the Croats. As a program of *ethnic cleansing* overtakes the entire region, Toma's father decides to move stating, "It was all a lie...captivating...and treacherous." Director Boro Draskovic, makes it clear that guns dictate that everyone participate, on both sides, in this conflict. On another level, the film reveals how the war is experienced through the eyes of a woman trying to survive. The life Anna knows is quickly imploding, as every moment becomes a life and death struggle. In several harrowing and brutal scenes, Anna is raped and the reality of war and ethnic hatred separate her and her husband. *Vukovar*, an exceptionally well acted and directed movie, brings home the horrors of this regional conflict and of war in general.

What the critics say Critics rate this movie 4.0 to 4.5. "A disturbing glimpse in the psyche of a war-ravaged nation...its voice is articulate and...images overwhelming."[3] "It's searing, unforgettable portrait of a country devouring itself."[7] **Final Word** Forget the popcorn. No one will ever again idealize war after watching this movie.

Wake Island

1942 USA b/w d. John Farrow

No film better illustrates how the tenor of the times influences its reviews. *Wake Island* chronicles the fall of Wake Island to the Japanese a week after Pearl Harbor was bombed. More importantly, the film shows American audiences the heroic defense of Wake Island by the First Marine Battalion and Marine Fighting Squadron 21. Three hundred and eighty-five Marines stalled a large-scale Japanese invasion force and inflicted heavy casualties on them. Using good special effects and documentary footage, this movie was released only nine months after the actual battle. It was popular at the box-office and as a morale builder for the American public. It was also the first combat film about the war and was nominated for four Academy Awards. Interestingly, the opening credits note seven military advisors to this film (all appear to have been on active duty at the time). Was this movie Hollywood or government propaganda? The answer appears to be both. However, if, just for a moment, one steps out of the historical context, the film emerges as a barely average war movie. The story is about the defense of the island, but what mostly comes across are the silly antics of two Marine jokers (William Bendix and Robert Preston). Fully half the film is consumed with their teasing one another and annoying the men around them. Also included is a construction superintendent (the prototype for John Wayne in *The Fighting Seabees*), who is over-the-top in his disdain for the military, and Major Caton (Brian Donlevy), commander of the Marine battalion, who is responsible for organizing the defense of Wake Island. Maj. Canton makes only one patriotic and sentimental speech that concludes—it's a man's job to "destroy destruction." None of these characters are developed and none have a story to tell. The movie ends, as does *Bataan*, which tells a similar story in a slightly superior manner—with machine guns blazing.

What the critics say Critics rate this movie 3.0 to 4.5. "Terse, well-done flagwaver within its limits."[1] "One of the least dated and more entertaining films of the era."[6] "Important flagwaver ...when news everywhere was so depressing."[8] **Final Word** Directed by John Farrow, *Wake Island* was mostly a continuation of the "buddy movie" that began with the 1926 film *What Price Glory* and the characters of "Flagg and Quint."

A Walk in the Sun

1945   USA   b/w   d. Lewis Milestone

Director Lewis Milestone of *All Quiet on the Western Front* and *Pork Chop Hill* fame clearly had something in mind when he made this movie. Perhaps he was trying to get at the personal side of war, those unpredictable interludes that leave soldiers with only their thoughts and one another—shooting the bull, bantering, carrying on with routines, but always aware that a sniper or errant artillery shell could take their lives at any moment. In an attempt to capture this quieter and more introspective side of war, the story focuses on an Army platoon that lands at Salerno, Italy, in 1943, and makes its way to a bridge and farm house six miles away. Based on the Harry Brown novel, *A Walk in the Sun* is a slow-paced and talkative two-hour movie with almost no action. It features a cast of characters who have nothing interesting to say but won't stop talking. In one ten-minute scene Sgt. Tyne (Dana Andrews) and Pvt. McWilliams (Sterling Holloway) chatter as if they had just met at a bus stop. The director's responsibility is to create a drama, to create interesting characters, situations and dialog that will take the audience beyond the mundane comments and boring interludes that even war produces. Instead, the movie is stuck with an irrelevant, if not annoying narration and a silly song played five times (a sort of soldier's ballad). The result is embarrassingly sentimental and a contradiction of the quiet dignity the movie was striving for. The real war movie begins in the last twenty minutes with the platoon encountering its objective and taking heavy casualties. A semblance of a story surfaces here as an insecure sergeant is forced to take command when his lieutenant is killed. The sergeant's slow disintegration under the pressures of command and the emergence of natural battlefield leaders is interesting—probably what this movie should have been about.

What the critics say Critics rate this movie 4.0 to 5.0. "Vivid war film in a minor key."[1] "Human aspect of war explored."[2] "Has failed to achieve a proper fusing of dialog and situation."[4] "Really gets to the heart of the human reaction to war."[7] **Final Word** While refreshingly free of flagwaving propaganda, the movie is static with nothing interesting to say about the combat soldier.

War and Remembrance

1988   USA   color   tv miniseries   d. Dan Curtis

| WW II: Epic War Drama | 4.0 |

War and Remembrance (parts 1-7) continues the stories and characters introduced in *Winds of War*. Based on novels by Herman Wouk, this epic television miniseries will not make sense if you have not watched the earlier episodes. And you will not find out how it ends if you do not watch *War and Remembrance* (parts 8-12). This wartime drama continues (1941-1943) to follow Capt. "Pug" Henry (Robert Mitchum) and the Henry family, his wife Rhoda (Polly Bergen) and his two naval officer sons, Byron (Hart Bochner) and Warren (Michael Woods). However, the focus of this series shifts to the Jastrow family, Natalie (Jane Seymour) and her aging uncle Aaron (John Gielgud), who are trapped in Europe and are slowly being pulled into the horror of the Nazi attempt to exterminate the Jews. This middle story is better told than the first series and the characters have been upgraded considerably (Jane Seymour replacing Ali MacGraw, Hart Bochner subbing for Jan-Vincent Michael and John Gielgud substituting for John Houseman). While just about everyone is being unfaithful here (which brings a certain voyeuristic satisfaction), this series quickly becomes an intense exploration of the Nazi's attempt to implement a "Final Solution" to the "Jewish Problem" in Europe. With cold calculation we watch the SS efficiently build concentration camps and begin the assembly line killing of millions of Jews. We are shown in graphic detail the mass shootings, cremations and burying and digging up of bodies. No detail too horrifying to be left out. We are also introduced to a Nazi's "Whose Who" as the cold, bureaucratic and calculating Goebbels, Himmler and Eichmann are brought to life here. In the inner-sanctum of the Nazi war machine we watch a tense and fascinating struggle evolve between Hitler and the German generals, who eventually hatch a plot to assassinate Hitler in the hope of negotiating a peace settlement. In between we watch Singapore fall to the Japanese, the Germans get defeated at Stalingrad, a great segment on the battle of Midway as well as outstanding submarine action in the South Pacific.

What the critics say Critics rate this movie 2.5 to 3.5. **Final Word** Ignore the critics. With great special effects, and on-location filming and an apparently unlimited budget, this is a unique viewing experience well worth the time and effort.

War and Remembrance: The Final Chapter

1989   USA   color   tv miniseries   d. Dan Curtis

WW II: Epic War Drama	4.5

This is the third and final installment (parts 8-12) of this epic series (see *Winds of War* and *War and Remembrance* parts 1-7) following the war years 1943 to 1945. Slowly the focus of this series begins to shift to the emotionally significant story being told here about the plight of European Jews. Yes, the war romances continue and Admiral "Pug" Henry (Robert Mitchum) comes to his senses and goes for the younger woman (Victoria Tennant). And, yes, there are too many subplots to mention them all, including the Normandy Invasion, the failed assassination of Hitler, the fall of Berlin, the battle for the Philippines and the dropping of the atomic bomb (all shown with documentary film and great detail). But it's truly the harrowing decent into hell by Natalie (Jane Seymour) and Aaron (John Gielgud) Jastow, first at the show camp termed the "Paradise Ghetto" in Czechoslovakia and later at Auschwitz concentration camp in Poland that's important. Horrific events are shown in graphic detail which leave no doubt about the evil that took place here. Eventually we follow Aaron into the gas chambers for disinfecting and watch as he is poisoned with Zyklon B and then delivered into the crematoriums. Meanwhile, Natalie, separated from her young son, survives as a fragile shell of herself. Terrifying and hard too watch at times, this is compelling movie making and truth telling. A second and equally compelling story also takes center stage. Throughout these series we have been given a captivating look at Hitler. Portrayed as obsessed, narcissistic, paranoid and grandiose, his ability to intimidate his generals is fascinating. This all culminates in his final days at his underground bunker in Berlin. His portrayal by Steven Berkoff is absolutely mesmerizing. Given to impulsive outbursts of rage, he continually berates his generals as incompetent and disloyal, and even threatens to have them killed if they disobey him. His ability to maintain control of the German government, even to the end, is amazing.

What the critics say No available reviews. **Final Word** This is a serious war drama and is not for the action junkies. Sit back, relax and become absorbed in the most epic telling ever of WW II. This is war as seen from a very privileged position at the highest levels of government and military command. War, romance, politics, death—it's all here.

Welcome to Sarajevo

1997　USA/GBR　color　d. Michael Winterbottom

| Balkans Conflict: Antiwar | 5.0 |

An outstanding and powerful antiwar film based on a true story, *Welcome to Sarajevo* was shot on location in Croatia and Macedonia in 1996, just months after the end of the civil war in Bosnia. Based on the book *Natasha's Story* by Michael Nicholson (a war correspondent for British television), he relates what happened inside the war-battered city of Sarajevo between 1992 and 1993. With the breakup of Yugoslavia in 1991, remnants of the Yugoslavian army, dominated by Serbian nationalists, attacked Bosnia when its people attempted to gain independence. Serbian troops surrounded and shelled Sarajevo, the capital of Bosnia. Through the experiences of an international group of journalists, often huddled in bombed out hotels and nightclubs, the film captures their forays out into the city, as they dodge snipers and artillery rounds to document the atrocities perpetrated against the civilian population. British journalist Michael Henderson (Stephen Dillane) quickly became numb to the violence and killing. All the journalists are frustrated that their reports almost never make the news. The American correspondent, Flynn (Woody Harrelson)—risk-taking, boozing and with a dark and humorous take on everything—reflects the cynical despair that has overtaken these journalists and this region of Europe. The story eventually focuses on Henderson's report about an orphanage, when he crosses the line from journalist to activist and seeks to rescue these children. He then attempts to smuggle a child, Emira (Emira Nusevic), an orphaned 11 year old girl, out of the Bosnia to England, where he and his wife adopt her. With a masterful blend of documentary footage and special effects, the films realism is of the highest order. The intelligence and energy of this film is palpable, from its excellent musical score, great photography, to the terrific performances. Director Michael Winterbottom's portrayals of death and violence in Sarajevo are graphic and chilling.

What the critics say Critics rate this movie 4.0 to 4.5. "A fierce polemical drama."[1] "Achingly realistic, unsentimental."[2] "Astonishing film...hard-hitting and extremely well-made...as powerful as it is poignant."[3] **Final Word** The epilogue states that 16,000 children were killed and 35,000 wounded, and that over a million people died in this conflict as Europe yawned.

We Were Soldiers
2002 USA color d. Randall Wallace

Vietnam War: Infantry Combat 3.0

This movie is Hollywood 's best effort to turn the Vietnam War
into WW II ("the last good war"). Directed by Randall Wallace,
this movie is adapted from the book We *Were Soldiers...and
Young* by reporter Joe Galloway and Lt. Col. Harold Moore. The
film chronicles the first major engagement between American
soldiers and the North Vietnamese Army (NVA) in the Ia Drang
Valley in the Central Highlands of S. Vietnam in 1965. Moore
(Mel Gibson) leads 400 infantrymen of the 7th Airborne Cavalry
into a hot LZ and unexpectedly runs into 4,000 NVA soldiers. A
savage battle ensues that marks a major shift in strategies by
both sides, including the use of conventional military forces by
North Vietnam and a commitment to air mobility and massive
involvement on the ground by the US. By conventional military
standards, American soldiers earned a hard-fought victory; but
as ironically noted by the NVA commander, the Americans will
think of this as a victory and take on a greater commitment to the
war. Despite the movie's good intentions, it's a major disappointment. Everything is told too simply. The first half endlessly
foreshadows the events to follow, with frequent reference to
"Custer's Last Stand" and Moore's doubts about US military
tactics and strategies. By not telling the story within its political
context, the sacrifice and heroism of American soldiers is robbed
of its true pathos. Gibson and Sam Elliot (Sgt. Major Plumley)
pretty much come across as video game characters invulnerable
to the war. Gibson is wrapped in an odd religious shroud
throughout the movie, giving his character a messianic quality
that borders on proclaiming the self-righteousness of the
American cause. An occasional nod to the families back home
and to NVA soldiers feels more politically correct than an integral
part of the story. While the combat scenes are realistic, the
conclusion is cryptic, and gives no perspective on what is to
follow. This film appears unable to grasp the ironic outcome of
this battle and the many that followed—that we lost by winning.

the critics say Critics rate this movie 2.5 to 4.5. "Gibson...is
corny (like the film itself—especially in the homefront scenes)."[2]
"The story telling here is powerful and unforgettable."[7] **Final
Word** If John Wayne were alive today, this is the film he would
have wanted to make.

What Price Glory?

1952 USA color d. John Ford

WW I: Buddy-Comedy   1.5

Directed by John Ford, this movie is a remake of the original 1926 silent film "classic" *What Price Glory?* directed Raoul Walsh. Adapted from the antiwar play by Maxwell Anderson and Lawrence Stallings, Walsh discarded the antiwar theme for a "comrade in arms" movie that featured two combative but good hearted Marines who are in love with the same women. More at war with one another than the enemy, this movie is the prototype for every "buddy" movie to follow (spawning three sequels). As a result of this adaptation, almost none of the plays original pacifist sentiments remain. I suspect that despite its box-office success in the late 1920s, the corruption of the original pacifist intent for a romantic-action-comedy didn't wash anymore then than it did in 1952. Featuring James Cagney (Capt. Flagg) and Dan Dailey (Ist Sgt. Quirt) as two Marines, all the action is set bound and takes place in France in 1918. The movie plays out in a slapstick fashion as Flagg and Quirt duke it out over every disagreement, which is over just about everything, including the beautiful Charmaine (Corinne Calvet)—a French tart and chanteuse who innocently seduces both Flagg and Quirt. However, she can't quite decide which one to marry. Cagney, unrelentingly bombastic, quickly becomes tiresome to watch, and why Charmaine finds these two lugs charming is a mystery. By the way, there's a war going on. The director's decision to retain the harsh images of war from the original screenplay simply does not fit with the false heroism of Flagg and Quirt. When in the middle of battle they treat war as a personal competition and by analogy a football game, this movie loses all credibility. This movie appears to be a miserable commercial attempt by John Ford to capitalize on the original film's success. Looking for all the world like it's going to breakout into a musical, this movie sadly fails to reconcile its humor with the deadly realities of war.

What the critics say The critics rate this movie 2.0 to 4.0. "Stagy remake of the celebrated silent film and play."[1] "Classic silent film became shallow Cagney-Daily vehicle."[2] "Offbeat comedy, but it works; masterful direction, good acting."[5] **Final Word** Post WW I audiences had tired of movies showing the horrors of war and wanted more escapist entertainment, which is what Hollywood gave them, right up until December 7, 1941.

When Hell Was in Session
1979 USA color tv d. Paul Krasny

| Vietnam War: Prisoner-of-War | 3.0 |

Seven years after the Vietnam War this movie was the entertainment media's first attempt to tell the story of American POWs. Graphic and violent, it makes clear its belief that American POWs acted courageously but were abandoned by the US government. Based on a book by Cmdr. Jeremiah Denton, it tells his story as well as the efforts of military families to organize and confront the military, the US government and ultimately the American public about the plight of POWs. Unfortunately, this is not a satisfying structure for this movie. Each aspect of the larger story, including the politics at home and the story of the POWs, should probably have been told separately. Denton (Hal Holbrook), a Navy carrier pilot, was on a bombing run over Haiphong Harbor in North Vietnam in 1965, when he was subsequently shot down and imprisoned at Hoa Lo Prison in Hanoi ("Hanoi Hilton"), and held there until his release in 1973. While this movie leaves no doubt about the brutality American servicemen suffered or their heroic efforts to resist being used as propaganda, this movie doesn't do justice to telling their story. The audience is kept at a distance and is never allowed to enter the personal stories. In many ways this movie is closer to a documentary than a war movie. Cmdr. Denton, who was 41 at the time of his capture, is a remarkably courageous individual who defied his captor's demand to "be polite," "cooperate," and "have a proper attitude." After being tortured, he agreed to a public interview in front of Japanese news cameras, where he announced his support for the American war effort and then blinked in Morse code the word "torture." Denton is shown surviving all-manner of degradation, filth, malnutrition, beatings, psychological and physical torture and isolation. But we are not shown how he was able to do this. His continuous efforts to organize resistance are mostly alluded to, yet were key to the POW's emotional resistance. This low-budget effort was poorly written and probably hurried for the fall television schedule.

What the critics say Critics rate this movie 3.5 to 4.0. "Painful and violent."[5] **Final Word** This was the first of three made-for-television movies about American POWs during the Vietnam War—*The Hanoi Hilton* and *In Love and War* followed eight years later and tell nearly identical stories.

When Trumpets Fade

1998   USA   color   tv   d. John Irvin

World War II: Infantry Combat	5.0

Unfortunately, this movie came out about the same time as the more highly publicized *Saving Private Ryan*. For the serious war movie viewer *When Trumpets Fade* is a much better movie. Shortly after the liberation of Paris in August 1944, Allied troops were driving for the German border. In the Battle of Hurtgen Forest that took place along the Belgian-German border just weeks before the Battle of the Bulge, twenty-four thousand Allied troops were killed or wounded. The story centers on a Sgt. Manning (Ron Eldard) and his relationship with five new replacements in his squad as they immediately come in contact with the German lines and take heavy casualties. As Manning tells the replacement—"This is the real fucking deal." His company of 200 men is now down to 50. At every level of command, from battalion to company to squad, conflict mounts as casualties increase. The real bottom line is that men are being asked to die at a horrific rate and no one is to question it. Part of what makes this movie outstanding is the performance of Ron Eldard as Sgt. Manning, as complex a character as one is likely to find in a war movie. At heart Manning is a survivor—that is his mission in this war. The transformation of this character as he attempts to survive his hellish circumstances, and the many conflicts he engenders with his superiors and with other enlisted soldiers, is terrific and realistic. Because Manning survives on the battlefield, he is quickly promoted from private, to sergeant, to lieutenant—as everyone in his company is dying around him. While there is something darkly disturbing about Manning's survivability, it may be what war requires. Directed by John Irvin, this film has many realistic battle scenes, as well as numerous smaller dramatic moments that add to the overall sense of tension. Unlike so many war movies, this one provides not only interesting characters and situations but a sense of immediacy and urgency in nearly every scene.

What the critics say Critics rate this movie 3.0 to 5.0. "A searing indictment of war's senseless brutality."[5] "A brilliant, complex performance by Ron Eldard."[6] **Final Word** To quote Sgt. Manning, "This is the real fucking deal." Go rent this move immediately! Now!

Where Eagles Dare

1968   GBR   color   d. Brian G. Hutton

WW II: British Commandos   1.5

This is yet another adaptation from a best selling novel by Alistair MacLean (*Guns of Navarone*). *Where Eagles Dare* is one of the most boring and mindless action-adventure war movies ever produced! Directed by Brian Hutton, Richard Burton (Major Smith) and Clint Eastwood (Lt. Schaffer) sleep-walk through their parts as members of a British commando team that has parachuted into the Bavarian Alps. Their mission is to gain access to Schloss Adler ("Castle of the Eagles"), which is being used by the German secret police to interrogate prisoners. Once in, the team will attempt to rescue a "phony" American general who crash-landed on purpose to make it look like he was shot down. As the Allies were attempting to plant disinformation about the upcoming Normandy Invasion, they hoped the rescue team would convince the Germans that the general is the real deal (all the while the whole thing is a ruse to discover German moles in the British MI-6 intelligence operation). Got that! It takes the entire movie to unravel this convoluted and ill-conceived plot. For the first forty-five minutes absolutely nothing happens. The commando team is not introduced; they plod around in the snow while Burton acts mysterious as team members keep getting murdered. Once the team gets near the castle, they head for the nearest Bavarian beer garden (a good way to keep a low profile). The last half of the movie is obsessed with stabbings, explosions, machine gun fire and action of such unbelievability that the end doesn't really matter—they "all" escape from a castle high in the mountains, accessible only by cable lifts, with thousands of German soldiers in pursuit. They commandeer a bus, careen to an airport where a fake German plane picks them up and, in the final moments, Major Smith (Burton) reveals the real spy. This long, boring, implausible movie—silly and without much tension—is shot in a dark, monochromatic style that makes everything hard to see—great!

What the critics say Critics rate this movie 3.0 to 4.0. "Schoolboy adventure, rather unattractively photographed but containing a sufficient variety of excitement."[1] "It's preposterous but fun...completely satisfying if predictable and derivative."[6] (Say that again!) **Final Word** Avoid all war movies that have the word *Eagle* in the title.

The Wild Geese
1978 GBR color d. Andrew V. McLaglen

Post-Colonial Africa: Mercenaries	2.5

Post-colonial mercenary adventurism in Africa has never before been told on this bloated scale. Based on a Daniel Carney novel and featuring Richard Burton, Richard Harris and Roger Moore (all quite miscast, particularly the aging Burton), *The Wild Geese* is an overblown big-budget, all-star epic that tells a predictable story of greed, power and betrayal. However, a potentially good action movie inhabits this film. Burton stars as Gen. Allen Faulkner, a mercenary soldier hired by a British industrialist (Stewart Granger) to rescue an African president (Winston Ntshona) who is secretly being held prisoner in a neighboring country. Once the president is restored to office, the industrialist hopes to gain copper mining rights in this unnamed East African nation ("greed" and "good" working together the way they're suppose to). With interminable introductions to the main characters and long recruitment and training segments too cute and humorous for their own good, much of this film's energy dissipates before the action even begins. Shot on location in the Northern Transvaal, the 60-man mercenary expedition is double-crossed when the plane that was supposed to extract them is ordered to leave without them. From here, they have to fight their way out with a wounded African president in tow. As they are on the run they take heavy casualties, but eventually come across a bush transport plane and a means of escape. With lots of well-staged and realistic firefights and with most the sympathetic characters killed off, Gen. Faulkner survives to hunt down the banker who betrayed them. Unfortunately, the hard edges and cynicism of this film simply don't match the story being told. When the mercenaries use cyanide gas to kill sleeping African soldiers, it probably goes too far. Besides, In the real world the industrialist loses stock equity margins, while the general's body is picked at by jackals on the veldt.

What the critics say Critics rate this movie 2.5 to 3.0. "Silly but entertaining action yarn."[2] "Fails to meld its comedy, adventure, pathos, violence, heroics—or even its political message—into a credible whole."[4] "Too much training...too long; too much dialogue."[5] **Final Word** Col. "Mad Mike" Hoare, consultant to this film, operated a mercenary unit in the Belgian Congo in the early 1960s.

Winds of War

1983   USA   color   tv miniseries   d. Dan Curtis

WW II: Epic War Drama   4.0

This monumental television production and outstanding drama is a unique viewing experience that has no equivalent. Thirty-eight hours long (19 volumes), it covers WW II from 1939 to 1945. Originally shown in three segments, *Winds of War* (parts 1-7) in 1983, *War and Remembrance* (parts 1-7) in 1988 and *War and Remembrance* (parts 8-12) in 1989, this series is based on two Herman Wouk novels, *The Winds of War* and *War and Remembrance*. (This is one continuous work that should be viewed from beginning to end.) At the time of its release, critics were relatively harsh in their reviews. However, watching all 19 volumes without commercial interruption provides a significantly different viewing experience. Produced and directed by Dan Curtis, this is simply one of the best war dramas ever, with a scope that has never been attempt before or since. Part war drama, part soap opera, *The Winds of War* is about the years leading up to America's direct involvement in World War II, 1939-41. While its a lavish production, there's a good war story here and a lot of guilty viewing pleasures, in which war and romance get equal time. At the center of this sprawling story is Capt. "Pug" Henry (Robert Mitchum) and his family. There's also a related story about the Jastrow family, who are Polish Jews residing in Italy. This is all tied together when Capt. Henry's son, Byron (Jan-Michael Vincent), courts and eventually marries Natalie Jastrow (Ali MacGraw). In 1939 "Pug" is naval attaché to the US embassy in Berlin. His reports catch the attention of President Roosevelt and for the next two years Pug becomes Roosevelt's "eyes and ears" in Europe, as he meets with Hitler, Churchill, Mussolini, Stalin and with Roosevelt himself. In between, he is an observer on an Atlantic convoy, and participates in a bombing run over Berlin, observes the Russian front, and provides us a bird's-eye view of the winds of war coming America's way. The portrayals of Hitler (Günter Meisner) and Roosevelt (Ralph Bellamy) are truly outstanding, and the politics swirling around them makes this movie extraordinary at times.

What the critics say Critics rate this movie 2.5 to 3.5. "Excruciatingly long and dull television miniseries."[5] "Mega WW II epic...spared no expense."[7] **Final Word** A unique viewing experience that's both intelligent and entertaining.

Windtalkers
2002   USA   color   d. John Woo

| WW II: Navajo Code Talkers | 2.0 |

Director John Woo, previously known for his empty action movies, has now created an empty, retro-Hollywood flagwaver filled with self-congratulatory sentiment and choreographed violence that is heavy on explosions. This move is supposedly about Navajo soldiers who were recruited during WW II to code battlefield communications using their mostly unknown language. Instead, the story turns on a completely miscast Nicolas Cage as Sgt. Joe Enders who, while suffering posttraumatic stress disorder from earlier combat, now mumbles, grimaces and hallucinates his way through the invasion of Saipan in 1944. Sgt. Enders also runs around with a submachine gun mowing down "Japs" in a stretch of combat bravado that would embarrass video-game makers. His job is to protect Pvt. Ben Yahzee (Adam Beech), the code talker assigned to him, or, if necessary, kill him to keep him from being captured by the Japanese. This melodramatic plot twist, while not historically accurate, has been added to give dramatic tension to a movie that has none. In fact, it's not clear if the Japanese even knew who the Navajo were. In one of the worst moments in war movie history, Pvt. Yahzee dresses in a Japanese uniform and marches Sgt. Enders toward the Japanese lines where they then shoot their way into the command center, grab a radio, and relay a message to American artillery to stop shelling American forces (enough said). Director Woo would have his viewers believe that every grenade, mortar or bazooka explosion is the equivalent of igniting a fuel dump, and that Americans routinely shot ten Japanese dead for every casualty they suffered. The movie has no real story to tell, develops no real characters, and reveals nothing about war or combat. Worst of all, it patronizes the Navajo.

What the critics say Critics rate this movie 2.0 to 2.5. "Clichéd dialogue with...endless shots of gruesome combat violence."[2] "Squanders a promising premise...characters are trite and the violence a bit overwhelming."[5] **Final Word** While all the stories of this war deserve to be told, you can't do more than die in a war. The fact that the Navajo were able to capitalize on their language is interesting, but all the self-congratulatory media hype surrounding the release of this movie is embarrassing.

Wing and a Prayer
1944 USA b/w d. Henry Hathaway

WW II: Classic '40s Flagwaver	3.0

Of all the 1940s combat classics, *Wing and a Prayer* is the most beautifully filmed. Directed by Henry Hathaway, the film editors did an outstanding job of combining exceptional documentary footage with great special effects, resulting in a treat to the eye. The action takes place aboard "Carrier X" in the South Pacific, just months after the bombing of Pearl Harbor. (The designation "Carrier X" is not real and was only used to add some mystery to this fact-based story.) The US Navy did, in fact, utilize an unidentified carrier to mislead Japanese intelligence about the strength and location of their carrier task forces. The story follows a recently trained TBF torpedo bomber squadron from its arrival on the carrier through the decisive battle of Midway in June 1942. This battle became the turning point of the war in the Pacific, when the Japanese lost three aircraft carriers to American planes. Though much of the film is cliché—young pilots turn the carrier into a frat house, with singing, silly antics and overly sentimental moments—when the pilots are flying, this movie is at its best. While a tough, no-nonsense air officer, Cmdr. Harper (Don Ameche), and a concerned squadron commander, Lt. Cmdr. Moulten (Dana Andrews), conflict over their mission—to not engage Japanese forces but to act as a decoy—most the characters are pretty familiar. In the movie's most dramatic scene, an angry exchange erupts between pilots and the squadron commander, when a plane is allowed to crash rather than to break radio silence. Much of the Battle of Midway is only heard as it is broadcasted to the carrier crew. The broadcast dramatically conveys what the pilots and air crews faced. Visual integrity, even by today's standards, makes this film well worth watching. While too much of this movie is familiar, good action and a several honest emotional scenes make this film a cut above most the 1940s war movies.

What the critics say Critics rate this movie 2.0 to 4.0. "Fine WW 2 actioner." "Excellent use is made of real combat footage."[1] "Better than average...excellent unsentimental direction."[5] "One of the most successful propaganda films to be released during WW II."[7] "Substandard...actioner."[8] **Final Word** This is my personal favorite among classic 1940s flagwavers.

The Winter War

1989   FIN   color   subtitles   d. Pekka Parikka

| World War II: Infantry Combat | 3.0 |

This Finnish television miniseries, re-edited for the big screen, documents the heroic efforts of the Finnish people who repel an invasion by the Soviet Union in 1939. The Soviets were seeking to gain a Baltic seaport, but after 105 days of intensive fighting, they gave up. Filmed in color, but shot in dark or faded snow scenes, this modestly budgeted movie, directed by Pekka Parikka and adapted from a novel by Antti Tuuri, has a monochromatic appearance that makes it difficult at times to tell what is happening on screen. The film presents an infantry view of the war, and is based on the military journals of the 23rd Infantry Regiment. As a result, the politics and military strategy (the big picture) behind this invasion is limited. The film also has a highly patriotic backdrop, and is filled with religious hymns, martial music and strong speeches to inspire the troops. Initially, the story follows two brothers who are part of a small, ragtag group of poorly equipped and disorganized reservists who left their farms and villages to fight the Soviets. Combat quickly settles into trench warfare, whereby waves of Soviet troops unsuccessfully attempt to overwhelm the Finns. The combat scenes have a superior realism, and, at times, a gruesome edge in their graphic depiction of the violence. A significant problem is this movie does not have a story to tell other than this battle and its message. The viewer is unable to identify with the individual characters, and the direction and photography are full of cuts and lurches that add to the general incoherence. All the elements of a good combat movie are here—but not put together as well as they could have been. The result is a somewhat slow-moving film that never fully engages the viewer. The best line is uttered by a Finnish soldier who complains, "If it gets colder—we'll need dynamite to break up the cheese." It appears that the director's primary goal was to document the heroic efforts of Finnish soldiers and the brutality of the short war they fought—a task accomplished, but unfortunately, without inspiration.

What the critics say No available reviews. **Final Word** Beware, it's subtitled, which adds some difficulty in following the action. For the hardcore war movie junkies who prefer realism to drama, this sincere Finnish tribute will provide more than enough action to keep you involved.

The Wooden Horse

1950 GBR b/w d. Jack Lee

WW II: Prisoner-of-War	3.0

This is another straightforward British POW film that doesn't have time for character development or subplots. In the British tradition, the Germans are dunderheads while the superior British go about organizing prison camp life and escape activities with an adolescent zeal. Directed by Jack Lee and adapted from the book *The Tunnel Escape* by Eric Williams, the film follows the true-life events of three British pilots who escape Stalag Luft III in the fall of 1943, and successfully make their way to neutral Sweden. While the escape itself is ingenious—they tunnel from under a gymnastics horse placed in the exercise yard—this action proves to be laborious and uninteresting to watch. Only so much drama can be rung from removing 120 pounds of dirt a day from a tunnel for three months. However, there's no doubt that these men were persistent and able to improvise under extremely difficult and dangerous circumstances. This movie comes alive after the officers (Leo Genn, David Tomlinson and Anthony Steel) successfully escape. They make their way on forged identification papers and very little money, and eventually contact members of the French underground who assist in their escape through Denmark to Sweden. The tension is high as the pilots are constantly close to being discovered, and one gets a real sense of how difficult it was for outsiders to blend into such a highly controlled society (identification paper, travel passes, work permits, limited fluency in the language, almost no money, and authorities continually checking hotels and trains). Unfortunately, too much of the film is shot in the dark, making it less interesting to watch. Also none of the characters are really developed, so they are pretty much interchangeable. Action is limited and the story often plods ahead, conforming to the facts.

What the critics say Critics rate this movie 3.0 to 4.0. "Set the tone for all British prison camp movies to follow: stiff upper lip and all that."[5] "The near-classic British escape picture...here the public school dorm replaces the unpalatable squalor and degradation of the reality of POW life."[8] **Final Word** The Geneva Convention of 1929 gives POWs the right to escape and not be harshly punished. They are also to be housed and fed no worse than the garrisoned troops guarding them.

World War III

1982 USA color tv d. David Greene/Boris Sagal

Titling this movie WW III just about guarantees that directors David Greene and Boris Sagal can't deliver. This made-for-TV nuclear confrontation between the Soviet Union and the United States attempts to expose the fallacies inherent in a nuclear balance of power. The prologue states that the story takes place sometime in "The Future," which looks suspiciously like the 1980s. The politics of brinkmanship escalate into nuclear war as the West, led by the US, institutes a grain embargo against the Soviet Union. In retaliation, the Soviets insert a "cold weather strike force," unknown to the Communist Secretary General (Brian Keith), to capture an oil pipeline "launching valve" in Alaska, with the intention of demolishing thirty miles of pipeline. In effect, the Soviets are seeking to blackmail the US into ending the embargo in return for not destroying the pipeline. The head of the KGB enters into political gamesmanship with the US in the belief that this would never escalate into a nuclear confrontation. The President (Rock Hudson), however, appears to be increasingly trapped in Cold War logic and is unwilling to back down on the issue of the Soviet's intrusion on American soil. Much of the story plays out in the war room but also in Alaska where Col. Caffey (David Soul) leads a group of "weekend warriors" (National Guard) who are on a training mission and, because of severe weather conditions, are the only American force available to interdict the Soviets. For the most part, this overly-long, slow-moving and talkative film has more plot holes than there are crevasses in Alaska. In the end, the "good" soldiers realize the madness of what is occurring and mutually decease hostilities, but the "bad" politicians are unable to compromise. (If someone has to be blamed, the politicians are generally a good choice.) While the acting is lackluster, there are a few decent combat scenes and some genuine drama as negotiations flounder. The issues raised here are legitimate. However, with so many more probable scenarios for a nuclear holocaust, why resort to this tortured plot?

What the critics say Critics rate this movie 3.0 to 3.5. "The battle scenes are intense and effective. It's long but certainly worth a view."[7] **Final Word** It's my sincere hope that the world will end on simpler terms, such as an asteroid.

The Young Lions

1958   USA   b/w   d. Edward Dmytryk

The Young Lions is a slow-moving WW II melodrama without much heart and with no story to tell. Director Edward Dmytryk patch-worked together one of Irwin Shaw's epic blockbuster novels. The film tells the story of three soldiers, two American GIs (Dean Martin and Montgomery Clift) and one German officer (Marlon Brando), that intersect at the end of this long movie. The only truly interesting character is that of Lt. Christian Diestl (Brando), a young German officer (apparently this role was rewritten larger for Brando). While Lt. Diestl is not a Nazi, he has generally supported Hitler's efforts to remake Germany into the Third Reich. Slowly, he confronts his own pacifism and reluctance to participate in the killing. He tells his commanding officer (Maximilian Schell), while witnessing the Gestapo torturing a young man, "I do not think it possible to remake this world from the basement of a dirty, little police station." While Brando is handsome and mesmerizing on the screen, he brings an understated posing to this role, with limited dramatic impact. As for Dean Martin—his casting in this film is a joke and a self-parody, as are all his roles. His character and relationship with his girlfriend (Barbara Rush) get very little screen time and essentially revolve around their conflict over his indifference to the war and being in the service. Montgomery Clift reprises a character he has played throughout his career—a fragile, sensitive individual who brings about his own problems. This character would be better served with therapy than continuing to get beat up in the army. But somehow a woman (Hope Lange) falls for his act. A few limited but irrelevant combat scenes stretch this move to "epic" status but add nothing to the story itself. In retrospect, this movie would have been better without the Martin and Clift characters, rather focusing on Lt. Diestl's coming to grips with the realities of the war and the criminality of what was happening.

What the critics say Critics rate this movie 3.0 to 4.0. "Well-mounted and generally absorbing."[1] "One of the all-time best WW 2 studies."[2] "A   canvas...of scope and stature."[4] "A slow moving but always absorbing adaptation."[8] **Final Word** While it's fun watching Brando do his thing, there's only the spent shell-casing of an interesting movie here.

Zeppelin

1971 GBR color d. Etienne Perier

WW I: Big Blimp Actioner   2.5

Zeppelin is probably closer to a fantasy-adventure film than a war movie. With most of the story devoted to the cruising of a giant air machine above the clouds (1950s movie matinee style), it's a lot of fun and hooey at the same time. A young Michael York (Lt. Richter) is at the center of a plot that is much too improbable for your average fantasy fare however. Lt. Richter was born in Germany but raised by his family in Scotland. Now a lieutenant in the British army in 1915, he's seduced by a beautiful woman who also happens to be a German spy. She's supposedly able to get him to defect after an extremely brief sexual tryst (obviously very "good" in a May West sort of way). Unknown to the Germans, Lt. Richter has reported this to British intelligence and they have now recruited him as a double-agent. Their goal is to obtain intelligence about a bigger and better Zeppelin being developed. So far so good. However, German intelligence wants to use his knowledge of the Scottish country-side to land the newest Zeppelin near an isolated castle, where England has stored all its most treasured documents in a hardened underground bunker. A German commando team then plans to rob Great Britain of its "history," particularly the Magna Carta, as part of a wartime propaganda stunt. There's also Lt. Ricter's innocent flirtation with the beautiful Dr. Frau Ericka Altschul (whom most of us know as Elke Sommer). She's a research scientist assisting in the development of the Zeppelin (the odds of this makes this movie look like a documentary). Their flirtation is as innocent as this movie. In the end, there's a lot of competent action and the inevitable big explosion. With excellent special effects and the right adolescent spirit, this movie can be entertaining at times.

What the critics say Critics rate this movie 3.0 to 3.5. "Undistinguished but entertaining period actioner."[1] "Colorful cast and atmosphere...entertaining story."[2] "Settles for being just another wartime melodrama, with some good aerial sequences."[4] **Final Word** The Zeppelins were a terrifying sight. Their first raid on England took place on January 19, 1915, but by the end of 1916 they were hopelessly obsolete. Zeppelin raids resulted in the death of 557 people, having dropped nearly 5,800 bombs.

Zero
1984 Japan color dubbed d. Toshio Masuda

WW II: Air Combat   1.0

This movie tells the heroic story of the Japanese Zero fighter plane, from its early development in the 1930s until it became obsolete at the end of WW II. A surprisingly bad movie, *Zero* operates at two levels. One level tells the story of two young naval officers, one a fighter pilot and the other the head of an air crew, who remain best friends throughout the war. The story is uninteresting and poorly acted (and the dubbed English voices are terrible). The special effects are nothing more than Japanese anime (cartoons) and RC controlled planes. However, a second movie operating here is interesting and shows how the Japanese portray this war to themselves—never stating how the war started or making mention of Japanese aggression. The movie simply portrays Zero fighter pilots as highly successful against Japan's enemies in Southeast Asia. Early in the movie comes the statement, "The world used to laugh at the Japanese for imitating others. But now we've designed something of our own which is vastly superior to anything else." The idea of this plane's superiority appears to be at the heart of the movie's intention in telling the story of WW II. As the war begins to turn against Japan, the Japanese Imperial Navy's failure to improve the Zero is disclosed. America standardized parts production, and their ability to mass produce planes is compared with Japan's slow and unstandardized production methods. While the Americans focused on producing heavy armor and emphasized pilot survivability, the Japanese navy accepted pilot loss as a means of maintaining the Zero's long-range capability and combat performance. The film shows us how the Zero's armament was ineffective against American heavy bombers. By the war's end, the Zero is characterized as a "has been" and "flying coffin." This movie exhibited a high level of criticism towards the Japanese military establishment for sacrificing pilots and perceiving them as expendable. The movie doesn't say how the war ends, but shows the bombing of Japan by B-29s, as heroic and honorable Zero pilots attempt to protect Japan.

What the critics say No available reviews. **Final Word** Interesting for the students of war and war films. The rise and fall of the Zero is made into a metaphor for Japan's early success and its eventual defeat during WW II.

WAR MOVIE TABLES

"The only people who ever loved war for long were profiteers, generals, staff officers and whores."
Ernest Hemmingway

Best War Satire

Black and White in Color *1977 FRA et al. WW I 4.0* Satirical antiwar tale of French colonials at a remote African trading post who decide to attack a nearby German fort. AA for Best Foreign Film.

Catch 22 *1970 USA WW II 5.0* Powerful and subversive black antiwar comedy of WW II bomber pilots caught up in the surreal absurdities of war.

Dr. Strangelove *1964 GBR Cold War 5.0* AFI top 100. Outrageous, satirical Cold War send-up in a cinematic masterpiece by Stanley Kubrick.

Funny Dirty Little War *1983 ARG Civil War 4.0* Witty and dark farce, as petty rivalries between Marxists and Peronistas in a small Argentine town erupt into all-out civil war.

Good Morning, Vietnam *1987 USA Vietnam War 4.5* Robin Williams ad libs great comic moments as a reluctant armed forces radio DJ serving in Vietnam in 1965.

The King of Hearts *1967 GBR/FRA WW I 4.5* Whimsical antiwar allegory about a WW I Scottish soldier who enters a deserted French village inhabited by the escapees from a nearby asylum—who make him king.

M*A*S*H *1970 USA Korean War 4.0* Irreverent comedy about the outrageous antics and havoc created by a group of surgeons at a Korean War mobile air surgical hospital.

Mediterraneo *1991 Italy WW II 4.5* Light-hearted, affectionate look at eight Italian soldiers garrisoned on an out-of-the-way Greek island, and how life proceeds just fine without war. Won the AA for Best Foreign Film.

A Midnight Clear *1992 USA WW II 4.5* Antiwar comedy-drama that is closer to fable than reality, as bumbling American soldiers on reconnaissance encounter German soldiers wanting to surrender.

No Man's Land *2001 BOS-HRZ/SLO Balkans Conflict 4.5* Dark and ironic satire of three soldiers trapped in a trench between lines, and who cannot find peace even if it means their survival.

Underground *1997 SER/FRA Balkans Conflict 5.0* Wild and dark allegorical satire of the fate of the Yugoslavian people from Nazism to Communism, as two pals attempt in very different ways to survive war and dictatorships.

War in the Balkans

These films represent the highest state of film making and together have redefined the war film genre.

No Man's Land *2001 BOS-HRZ/SLO et al. 4.5* Dark, witty and ironic satire of three soldiers trapped in a trench between Serbian and Croatian lines who cannot find peace, as journalists and peacekeepers make everything worse.

Pretty Village, Pretty Flame *1996 GRE/YUG 5.0* Savage look at the mindless violence that overtook Bosnia after the breakup of Yugoslavia in 1991. Focuses on two childhood friends, one Muslim and the other Serb, as they engage in violent firefights and acts of revenge and hatred.

Savior *1997 USA 5.0* The true story of an American who becomes a mercenary for the Serbian army after his wife and child are killed in a terrorist bombing. An emotionally devastating film that's impossible to forget, as one man attempts to salvage his humanity.

Shot Through the Heart *1998 USA/CAN tv 4.5* Powerful story of two childhood friends, one Serb and the other Croat, who end up becoming snipers on opposite sides in the Bosnian civil war. A mind-bending decent into the hell that engulfed the city of Sarajevo from 1992-1995.

Underground *1997 SER/FRA. 5.0* Wild and dark allegorical satire of the fate of the Yugoslavian people from Nazism to Communism, as two pals attempt in very different ways to survive war and dictatorships.

Vukovar *1994 YUG/ITA 4.5* Gut-wrenching antiwar drama in the Bosnian city of Vukovar, as a Serbian family seeks to survive in a city reduced to ruble and is governed by renegade militias engaged in a program of ethnic cleansing.

Welcome to Sarajevo *1997 USA 5.0* In 1992 international journalists in Sarajevo struggle to make sense of the ferocious ethnic violence all around them. This is the true story of one journalist's attempt to redeem the "world" by rescuing a young girl.

Other outstanding films include: *The Beast, Beautiful People, Before the Rain, Café Balkans, The Gaze of Ulysses, Prisoner of the Mountain, Requiem for Dominic,* and *An Unforgettable Summer.*

Best Sub Movies

The Bedford Incident *1965 USA Cold War 4.5* Richard Widmark plays a paranoid American destroyer captain obsessed with hunting down Soviet submarines in a "thinking man's Cold War thriller.

Crimson Tide *1995 USA Cold War 4.5* Denzel Washington instigates mutiny on a nuclear submarine commanded by Gene Hackman, in a confrontation that could lead to a nuclear war.

Das Boot *"The Boat" 1981 GER WW II 5.0* Survival on a German U-boat in the North Atlantic. This decent into a claustrophobic hell is one of the great war films of all time.

The Enemy Below *1957 USA WW II 4.0* Robert Mitchum is the commander of a destroyer in an exciting cat-and-mouse chase with U-boat commander Curt Jürgens.

Hunt for Red October *1990 USA Cold War 4.5* Cold War thriller starring Sean Connery as a Soviet nuclear submarine commander seeking to defect to the US.

K-19: The Widowmaker *2002 USA/GBR/GER Cold War 3.5* Harrison Ford and Liam Neeson conflict in this semi-factual story of a Soviet sub with a damaged nuclear power plant.

Run Silent, Run Deep *1958 USA WW II 4.0* Clark Gable and Burt Lancaster clash as Gable is obsessed with revenge and the sinking of a Japanese destroyer.

Torpedo Run *1958 USA WW II 3.0* Glen Ford and Ernest Borgnine chase down and sink the Japanese carrier that led the attack on Pearl Harbor.

Until the 1940s the submarine was mostly an artifact of another story—espionage, sabotage, passengers on a ship about to be torpedoed. Since the 1940s there have been nearly 30 sub movies of mostly minor distinction, including—*Above Us the Waves, Battle of the Coral Sea, Crash Dive, Destination Tokyo, Full Fathom Five, Gray Lady Down, Hellcats of the Navy, The Hunley, Ice Station Zebra, Up Periscope, Sub Down, Submarine Attack, Submarine Command, Submarine D-I, Submarine Patrol, Submarine Raider, Submarine Seahawk, Submarine X-1, Torpedo Alley, U-571, We Dive at Dawn.*

"John Wayne" Goes to War

Back to Bataan *1945 USA 1.5* The "Duke" organizes resistance to the Japanese in the Philippines.

The Fighting Seabees *1944 USA 2.5* Wayne's most entertaining war movie as he leads a Navy construction battalion against the Japanese in the Pacific and wins.

Flying Leathernecks *1951 USA 2.5* The "big guy" is the tough commander of a Marine Flying Squadron over Guadalcanal.

Flying Tigers *1942 USA 2.0* Wayne joins Chennault's Air Volunteer Group in China to take on the Japanese.

The Green Berets *1968 USA 1.0* Propaganda effort does not scare the North Vietnamese.

In Harm's Way *1965 USA 3.0* Shares the war with an all-star cast in a WW II soap opera.

Jet Pilot *1957 USA 1.0* Falls in love with a Russian jet pilot who is, fortunately, a woman.

The Longest Day *1962 USA 2.0* How is it possible, in an all-star salute to the D-Day invasion of Europe, that JW is only a blustering Lt. Col. in a small role?

Operation Pacific *1951 USA 2.5* The Duke is a submarine commander in the Pacific who can't miss.

Reunion in France *1942 USA 1.0* Paris dress designer (not Wayne) helps allied airman (Wayne) back to England during WW II.

Sands of Iwo Jima *1949 USA 3.0* As Sgt. John Stryker, John Wayne gives his best performance in a war film.

The Sea Chase *1955 USA 1.5* Wayne plays a WW II German (?) freighter captain, with hot romance on board.

They Were Expendable *1945 USA 2.5* Patriotic salute to PT-boat commanders in the South Pacific.

Wayne's war record is best summed up as long and honorable but without distinction.

Best Military Legal Dramas

The Andersonville Trial *1970 USA tv 4.0* True story of the war-crime trial against the Confederate superintendent of the Andersonville military prison.

Breaker Morant *1980 AUS 5.0* A riveting fact-based courtroom drama set in S. Africa in 1901 as three Australian soldiers are tried for war crimes during the Boer War.

The Caine Mutiny *1954 USA 3.5* Naval officers mutiny against an obsessive Humphrey Bogart as Capt. Queeg.

The Court-Martial of Billy Mitchell *1955 USA 3.5* Gary Cooper stars in the 1925 court-martial of an American general for challenging the establishment.

A Few Good Men *1992 USA 3.5* Tom Cruise and Jack Nicholson star in a tense courtroom melodrama of Marines accused of murder and a cover-up.

The Incident *1989 USA tv 3.5* During WW II, in a small Colorado town, a German prisoner of war at a nearby POW camp is accused of murder.

Judgment at Nuremburg *1961 USA 5.0* An outstanding and powerful story about the international trial of Nazi war criminals, starring Spencer Tracy and Maximilian Schell.

Judgment: The Court-Martial of Lieutenant William Calley *1975 USA tv 3.0* Stanely Kramer's painful examination of the My Lai massacre during the Vietnam War in 1969.

Paths of Glory *1957 USA 4.0* Kirt Douglas is a WW I French officer assigned to defend soldiers charged with cowardice, in a show-trial by the French army. Early Kubrick film.

Prisoner of Honor *1991 USA tv 3.5* "The Dreyfus Affair," an anti-Semitic scandal in 19th century France, in which a Jewish French army officer is scapegoated and court-martialed.

Prisoners of the Sun *1990 AUS. tv 5.0* In a powerful statement about justice, a military attorney prosecutes Japanese officers responsible for the death of Australian POWs.

A Soldier's Tale *1984 USA 4.5* During WW II a Black Army attorney defends an unpopular Black sergeant on murder charges in a complex examination of racism. This is an outstanding drama.

Fact-Based Military Scandals

The Affair *1995 USA tv 3.5* WW II drama of a Black-American soldier's involvement with a married white English woman and the social and legal consequences they faced.

Afterburn *1992 USA tv 3.5* When an F-16 fighter pilot is killed in a plane crash, his wife investigates and sues General Dynamics.

Assault at Westpoint *1994 USA tv 3.0* The first Black West Point Cadet is court-martialed and expelled for supposedly beating himself unconscious.

The Court-Martial of Jackie Robinson *1990 USA tv 4.5* This famous athlete faces a court-martial for refusing to take a backseat on a bus.

The Execution of Private Slovick *1974 USA tv 4.0* The execution of an American soldier for desertion during WW II. The first since the Civil War.

Gary Powers: The True Story of the U-2 Spy Incident *1976 tv 4.0* An Air Force pilot is shot down and captured during a spy mission over the Soviet Union in 1960, leading to a international scandal.

A Glimpse of Hell *2001 USA 4.0* Examines the peacetime explosion of a gun turret onboard the battleship *Iowa* in 1989, and the Navy's attempt to scapegoat a sailor for its negligence.

Mission of the Shark *1991 USA tv 4.0* In 1945 the cruiser USS *indianapolis* was sunk by a Japanese sub and the Navy court-martials its commander Charles McVay.

Mutiny *1999 USA tv 3.0* In 1944 a ship explodes and fifty Black munition workers refuse to work in unsafe conditions. The Navy charges them with mutiny.

The Pentagon Wars *1998 USA tv 4.5* A satiric look at a whistle-blower who exposes the Army's cover-up of the flawed Bradley armored troop transport.

Sergeant Matlock vs. the US Air Force *1978 USA tv 3.0* Serviceman's attempt to remain in the Air Force after admitting his homosexuality.

Serving in Silence *1995 USA tv 2.5* Story of Col. Margarethe Cammermeyer, a decorated Army nurse, who was discharged from the service due to her sexual orientation.

Thanks of a Grateful Nation *1998 USA tv 3.0* Searing indictment of the DOD and VA for stone-walling treatment of veterans suffering from Gulf War Syndrome.

Best POW Movies

Andersonville *1996 USA tv Civil War 4.5* A powerful fact-based Civil War movie about captured Union soldiers and their inhumane treatment at a Confederate POW camp.

Hanoi Hilton *1987 USA tv Vietnam War 4.5* The true story of American POWs during the Vietnam War. A graphic, hard-hitting testament to their will to survive.

The Hill *1965 GBR WW II 4.5* Sean Connery is sentenced to a British military prison camp in North Africa, in a tense and well-acted drama about the sadistical abuse of authority.

The Human Condition Part 3. "Soldier's Prayer" *1961 JAP WW II 4.5* Part three of Kobayashi's epic and sorrowful antiwar trilogy tells of Japanese soldiers escaping from a Russian POW camp and perishing in the wilderness.

In Love and War *1987 USA tv Vietnam War 4.0* The story of Navy pilot Commander Jim Stockdale, a North Vietnamese POW for eight years. It also shows the efforts of his wife to get the American government to negotiate the return of POWs.

King Rat *1965 USA/GBR WW II 4.0* James Clavell novel of an opportunistic and cynical American in a Japanese POW camp who bribes guards to live better.

A Man Escaped *1956 FRA WW II 4.5* The remarkable and true story of a French resistance officer's determination to escape from a German prison days before his execution.

The McKenzie Break *1970 IRE/GBR WW II 3.5* In a taut battle of wits, a German U-boat commander attempts to lead a mass escape from a British POW camp.

The One That Got Away *1957 GBR WW II 3.5* An exciting, true-life adventure about the escape attempts of a German fighter pilot from British POW camps. Almost too unbelievable to be true.

Prisoner of the Mountain *1996 RUS Chechen Revolt 4.5* Ironic, humorous and ultimately a tragic story of two Russian soldiers captured by Chechen rebels and the relationships that develop.

When Hell Was in Session *1979 USA tv Vietnam War 3.0* True story chronicling the physical and psychological torture of Navy pilot Commander Jeremiah Denton during his seven years as a North Vietnamese POW.

Perhaps no subgenre of war movies is as filled with nonsense as the POW movie. False drama and phony heroism have rendered the most popular films in this category an empty spectacle. These are the best.

Holocaust Experiences

Au Revoir les Enfants *1987 FRA 5.0* Autobiographical story of how the friendship of two teenage boys is torn apart when the Gestapo discovers one is Jewish.

The Boat Is Full *1981 SWI 4.5* A harrowing account of prejudice and fear as a group of Jewish refugees seeking asylum in Switzerland pose as a family. Won AA for Best Foreign Film.

Diamonds of the Night *1964 CZE 5.0* A haunting and surreal account of two Jewish boys escaping a train bound for Auschwitz and attempting to survive in the countryside.

Europa, Eruopa *1991 GER/RUS 4.5* The mind-bending true story of a German-Jewish teenage boy who poses as Aryan to escape persecution.

Escape from Sobibor *1987 USA tv 4.0* The suspenseful true story of the largest prisoner escape from a Nazi death camp.

Holocaust *1978 USA tv miniseries 4.5* An outstanding movie about what happens to two German families, one Jewish and one Aryan, during the Nazi reign from 1935-1945.

Life is Beautiful *1997 ITA 5.0* A funny, touching and ultimately heartbreaking fable about love of family and life set in a concentration camp.

Partisans of Vilna *1986 FRA doc. 4.5* A powerful film showing Jewish youth in the Vilna ghetto resisting the Nazis.

Shoah *1985 FRA/GER/POL doc. 5.0* An epic, two-part, 8-hour documentary on the human dimension of the Holocaust through interviews with survivors and oppressors.

The Shop on Mainstreet *1965 CZE 5.0* The heartbreaking story of a Slovak man and a elderly Jewish woman and the relationship that forms and is torn apart. Won AA for Best Foreign Film.

The Sorrow and the Pity *1970 FRA 5.0 doc.* A wrenching examination of French collaboration with the Nazis in persecuting Jews.

Voyage of the Damned *1976 GBR 4.0* Based on true events, Jewish refugees are refused asylum in Havana, Cuba in 1939 and are forced to return to Nazi Germany.

There are more outstanding films in this genre than in any other two combined. The ones selected here are among the best and attempt to reflect a range of experiences.

Nazism

Berlin Alexanderplatz *1980 GER 4.0* Epic by Fassbinder explores the rise of Nazism through the life of a transit worker who tumbles into the Berlin underworld.

Cabaret *1972 USA 4.5* Outstanding musical-drama about the decadent night life of Berlin, foreshadowing the rise of nationalism and Fascism in 1931.

The Damned *1969 ITA/GER 4.0* Shows the rise of Nazism through the destructive narcissism and decadence of a self-destructive upper-class German family.

Hanussen *1989 HUN/GER 4.5* A magician and clairvoyant cooperates with the Nazis, even though he foresees the rise and fall of the Third Reich. Compelling story telling here.

The Harmonists *1999 GER 5.0* A rich, multilevel film about the rise of anti-Semitism in Germany in the 1920s and 1930s, as a popular vocal harmony group performs throughout Europe.

Hitler: The Last Ten Days *1973 GBR/ITA 2.5* Based on eyewitness accounts, Alec Guinness portrays Hitler during his final days, also see *The Death of Adolf Hitler* (1984).

Inside the Third Reich *1982 USA tv miniseries 3.0* Details the rise to power of Albert Sheer, architect and confidant to Hitler.

Mephisto *1981 HUN 4.5* Outstanding film that delivers a powerful message of conscience, as an ambitious actor barters his soul with the Nazis for artistic success. AA for Best Foreign Film.

The Ogre *1996 GER/FRA/GBR 3.5* A misfit who believes he has special powers is used by the Nazis to recruit young men to military service.

The Tin Drum *1979 GER 5.0* Günter Grasse's realistic-fantasy about a young boy who refuses to grow up when the Nazis take power in Germany. AA for Best Foreign Film.

The Wannsee Conference *1984 GER 5.0* Reenactment of the January 20, 1942 conference at which the Nazis outlined their plan for the "final solution" to the "Jewish problem."

Action guys may want to check out *Apt Pupil, The Boys From Brazil, Eye of the Needle, Fatherland, Mother Night, Marathon Man, The Night of the Generals, The Odessa Files, The Quiller Memorandum, The Salzburg Connection.*

Black-American Soldiers

The Affair *1995 USA tv 3.5* A Black GI (Courtney Vance) has an affair with a married English woman during WW II, with social and legal consequences. Based on true events.

All the Young Men *1960 USA 2.5* Sidney Poitier is put in command of a combat patrol, which leads to a racial confrontation during the Korean War.

Antwone Fisher *2000 USA 2.5* Denzel Washington is a Navy psychiatrist who helps Fisher (Derek Luke) overcome anger and a history of family dysfunction to succeed in the service.

Assault at Westpoint *1994 USA tv 4.0* Fact-based drama about the first Black West Point Cadet who is court-martialed and expelled for supposedly beating himself unconscious.

Buffalo Soldiers *1997 USA 4.0* Danny Glover is a first sergeant in the all Black 10th US cavalry regiment, in the 1880s, as they attempt to subdue Apaches in the southwest.

The Court-Martial of Jackie Robinson *1990 USA tv 4.5* Jackie Robinson (of baseball fame) faces court-martial charges as an Army officer in 1944 for refusing to sit at the back of a bus. Outstanding performance by Andre Braugher.

Glory *1989 USA 5.0* A towering movie with outstanding battle scenes, tells the story of America's first Black regiment, the 54th Massachusetts Volunteers, formed by the North during the Civil War.

Home of the Brave *1949 USA 3.5* James Edwards stars in this WW II psychological drama about a soldier breaking down under the stress of war and racism.

Men of Honor *2000 USA 2.5* Cuba Gooding, Jr. stars as the real-life Navy diver Carl Brashear, who overcomes racism and a physical handicap to realize his dream.

Mutiny *1999 USA tv 3.0* In 1944 a ship explodes at Port Oakland and fifty Black munition workers refuse to work in unsafe conditions, in this fact-based story.

A Soldier's Story *1984 USA 4.5* An outstanding drama adapted from a Pulitzer Prize-winning play about the murder of a Black sergeant on a southern army base in the 1940s.

Tuskegee Airmen *1995 USA tv 4.0* A docudrama about the formation of the 99th Fighter Squadron (332 Fighter Group), the first Black fighter squadron during WW II.

A small number of "B" war movies have been made that primarily featured Black actors telling Black stories—*Black Brigade, The Red, White and Black, Sergeant Rutledge, The Walking Dead.*

Best War Romances

And a Nightingale Sang *1989 GBR tv WW II 3.5* A charming and bittersweet Masterpiece Theater production of family strength and romance during the bombing of London.

Ballad of a Soldier *1960 RUS WW II 4.5* The journey of a young Russian soldier, on leave for his heroism, who meets a young women, only to encounter tragedy.

The Cranes Are Flying *1957 RUS WW II 4.5* A poignant and unsentimental story of a young Russian women whose lover goes off to war. Beautifully photographed and acted.

The English Patient *1996 USA WW II 4.0* Intelligent and passionate romance, told in flashbacks, about a man and a woman thrown together during war.

From Here to Eternity *1953 USA WW II 3.5* Smoldering, hard-hitting look at the seamier side of military life and relationships.

D-Day, the Sixth of June 1956 USA WW II 3.0 A married American officer falls in love with a young English girl whose fiancé is serving in North Africa. A touching and bittersweet war romance.

In Harm's Way *1965 USA WW II 3.0* A hard-hitting melodrama by Otto Preminger, starring John Wayne, that weaves the scope of the early war in the Pacific with jaded romances.

Summer of My German Soldier *1978 USA tv WW II 4.0* In a small Georgia town a young Jewish girls secretly begins a friendship with an escaped German POW.

A Town Like Alice *1981 USA/AUS tv miniseries WW II 4.05* English woman and Australian soldier meet in a Japanese POW camp and fall in love. Separated, they meet years later in the Australian outback.

We'll Meet Again *1982 GBR 13 part tv miniseries WW II 4.0* Chronicles the relationships that form in 1943 when a quiet English town is overtaken by American pilots of the 8th Air Force.

Winds of War *1983 USA 19 part tv miniseries WW II 4.5* This is the great nostalgic melodrama of WW II, on a scale no other war movie has ever attempted. A must see series.

There is probably only one great war romance movie—Casablanca. While many pre-1950 films are still critically admired—*A Farewell to Arms, For Whom the Bells Toll,* and *Waterloo Bridge*—they have dimmed considerably over time.

War Journalism

Before the Rain *1994 GBR/FRA 4.0* A trio of interwoven stories comes to a powerful and bitter conclusion as a photojournalist returns home to war-torn Macedonia.

Harrison's Flowers *2000 USA 2.5* Newsweek photojournalist Harrison Lloyd, who is wounded during the Yugoslavian civil war in 1991, is rescued by his wife Sarah.

Kandahar *2001 IRA/FRA 2.5* A woman journalist returns to her native Afghanistan to rescue her sister, and witnesses firsthand the oppression and destruction by the Taliban.

The Killing Fields *1984 USA GBR 5.0* An emotionally jarring account of the genocide committed by the Khmer Rouge under the Pol Pot regime in Cambodia, as witnessed by a newspaper correspondent.

Missing *1982 USA 4.0* A tense, fact-based look at the 1973 military coup in Chile by Gen. Pinochet, and the search for a young American writer by his father (Jack Lemmon).

The Quiet American *2002 USA 2.5* The second unremarkable movie based on Graham Greene's novel about political intrigue and romance during the French-Indochina War.

Salvador *1986 USA 4.0* Semiautobiographical account of photojournalist Richard Boyle (James Wood) uncovering covert US support for the ruling right-wing junta and death squads in El Salvador.

Under Fire *USA 1983 4.5* Three foreign correspondents struggle to stay neutral while covering the conflict between the right-wing Somoza government and the left-wing Sandanista rebels in Nicaragua in 1979. Stars Nick Nolte.

Ulysses' Gaze *1995 GRE 4.0* The beautifully filmed odyssey of an exiled Greek filmmaker (Harvey Keitel), as he travels across the war-torn Balkans in search of early documentary film of the region.

Welcome to Sarajevo *1997 USA 5.0* International journalists in Sarajevo struggle to make sense of the ferocious ethnic violence all around them in 1992.

The Year of Living Dangerously *USA 1982 4.5* Mel Gibson and Sigourney Weaver star as an Australian foreign correspondent and British diplomat during the 1965 military coup in Indonesia.

War journalism has slowly emerged as an important war story. Also see—*Angkor: Cambodia Express, Circle of Deceit, Deadline, Hors La Vie, The Last Plane Out, Live From Baghdad, War Stories.*

TV War Series

Baa Baa Black Sheep *1976-1978* Marine fighter squadron during WW II in the Pacific, led by Maj. "Pappy Boyington (Robert Conrad).

Call to Glory *1984-1985* Cold War story of military life for the family of a U-2 pilot during the 1960s.

China Beach *1988-1991* Army nurse (Dana Delany) experiences the trauma of the Vietnam War at a forward hospital.

Combat *1962-1967* Provides a realistic look at an Army infantry platoon in Europe during WW II. A very popular series.

Combat Sergeant *1956* Story about an Army sergeant operating behind enemy lines in N. Africa during WW II.

Gallant Men, The *1962-1963* A knock-off "Combat" directed by Robert Altman about a squad of combat soldiers in Europe.

Garrison's Gorillas *1967-1968* The Army recruits convicts to operate behind German lines in exchange for post-war paroles.

Gomer Pyle USMC *1964-70* Stars Jim Nabors as a bumbling but good hearted Marine recruit who frustrates his drill sergeant.

The Gray Ghost *1957* Thirty-nine episodes about Civil War hero Maj. John Mosby, a Confederate "raider."

Hogan's Heroes *1965-1971* Comedy about American POWs in a German prison camp, starring Bob Crane.

JAG *1995-2004* Navy attorneys confront all the contemporary political and military issues of the day in a superior drama.

M*A*S*H *1972-1983* Outstanding comedy about a mobile army surgical hospital during the Korean War, starring Alan Alda.

McHale's Navy *1962-1966* Misadventures of a PT-boat crew during WW II in the Pacific, starring Ernest Borgnine.

Mister Roberts *1965* A comedy based on a popular play and motion picture about Navy slackers during WW II.

Navy: NCIS *2003* Crime drama series about a naval criminal investigator solving crimes using forensic evidence.

No Time for Sergeants *1964* A naive and bumbling Air Force recruit is too literal and too honest. Based on a very funny 1958 movie.

The Rat Patrol *1966-1968* A 4 man commando team of American soldiers operating in N. Africa during WW II.

Sergeant Bilko *(aka Phil Silvers Show) 1955-1959* Comedy about an army motor pool run by a con artist.

The Silent Service *1957* American submarine action in the Pacific during WW II.

Tour of Duty *1987-1991* An American army platoon in Vietnam, starring Terence Knox and Stephen Caffrey.

Twelve O'Clock High *1964-1967* Based on the original movie about an American bomber group flying daylight raids over Germany. Excellent drama.

Victory at Sea *1952 doc.* Twenty-six episodes of WW II naval combat. "Famous for its music score, eloquent narration and combat footage."

Best Action Adventure

Every movie on this list is a must-see for serious war movie viewers. Note, however, that movies predating 1930 were not considered. For the true film cognoscenti, this is a grievous and probably unforgivable decision, but for most moviegoers it reflects reality.

1. **Lawrence of Arabia** *1962 USA*
2. **Ran** *1985 JAP*
3. **Henry V** *1989 GBR*
4. **Ben Hur** *1959 USA*
5. **Aguirre, Wrath of God** *1972 GER*

6. **Braveheart** *1995 USA*
7. **Gunga Din** *1939 USA*
8. **Zulu** *1964 GBR*
9. **Spartacus** *1960 USA*
10. **War and Peace** *1968 RUS*

11. **Dances with Wolves** *1990 USA*
10. **Lives of a Bengal Lancer** *1935 USA*
13. **Gladiator** *2000 USA*
14. **Beau Geste** *1939 USA*
15. **The Man Who Would Be King** *1975 GBR*

16. **Four Feathers** *1939 GBR*
17. **The Fall of the Roman Empire** *1964 USA/SPA*
18. **El Cid** *1961 USA*
19. **Waterloo** *1970 RUS/ITA*
20. **Charge of the Light Brigade** *1936 USA*

21. **Quo Vadis** *1951 USA*
22. **Last of the Mohicans** *1992 USA*
23. **Taras Bulba** *1962 USA*
24. **The Alamo** *1960 USA*
25. **Damn the Defiant** *1962 GBR*

Belle & Blade's Top Ten Sellers

Civil War

Alvarez Kelly
Birth of a Nation
Civil War, The (Ken Burns)
Gettysburg
Glory
Gods and Generals
Great Locomotive Chase, The
Horse Soldiers
Red Badge of Courage, The
Shenandoah

WW I

All Quiet on the Western Front
ANZACS
Big Parade, The
Blue Max, The
Dawn Patrol, The
Hell's Angels
Lost Battalion
Stosstrup 1917
Trench, The
Westfront 1918

WW II

Attack and Retreat
Band of Brothers
Battleground
Bridge, The
Come and See
Cross of Iron
Stalingrad (1958)
Stalingrad (1992)
When Trumpets Fade
Winter War, The

Modern

Apocalypse Now
Beast, The
Black Hawk Down
Full Metal Jacket
Hamburger Hill
Lost Command
Platoon
317th Platoon
We Were Soldiers
Wild Geese

Aviation

Battle of Britain
Bridges at Toko-Ri, The
Dambusters
God Is My Co-Pilot
Piece of Cake
Reach for the Sky
Spitfire
Thirty Seconds Over Tokyo
Tora! Tora! Tora!
Twelve O'Clock High

Naval

Battle of the River Platte
Das Boot (The Boat)
Cruel Sea, The
Enemy Below, The
Fighting Sullivans, The
In Harm's Way
In Which We Serve
Sharks and Little Fish
Silent Enemy, The
Up Periscope

ABOUT WAR MOVIES:
WW I to Vietnam

"I'm not saying we wouldn't get our hair mussed, but I do say no more than ten to twenty million, tops, depending on the breaks."
George C. Scott as Gen. "Buck" Turgidson in Dr. Strange Love

World War I Movies

"War is a series of catastrophes which results in victory."
George Clemenceau

The "Great War," "The war to end all wars," has basically faded from the consciousness of the movie-going public. The most recent major American film about WW I was *The Blue Max*, released in 1966. In the past 50 years Hollywood has produced only one other non-romantic film about WW I, Kubrick's 1957 antiwar statement *Paths of Glory*. Having been eclipsed by WW II, and with the passing of the last of its veterans, there's very little living memory of the first world war. Prior to 1940, more than 300 films were made about this war. From 1940 until today that number is about 70, of which maybe only 15 would be included on any list of outstanding war films.

Perhaps the truth is, that WW I was never really America's war. The US entered in late 1917 and engaged in only 110 days of heavy fighting, with casualties of approximately 116,516 (fewer than in the Korean and Vietnam wars). Total casualties for this war reached 35.5 million.

War movies have left two enduring images of WW I—the grim life of the infantrymen in the trenches and the semi-romantic images of biplanes dueling across the skies. For most contemporary viewers, it's this later image that forms film memories of WW I, including movies such as *Aces High, Aces of Aces, The Blue Max, Dawn Patrol, Hell's Angels* and *Wings*.

The great enduring legacy of the first world war, however, is the antiwar consciousness that arose from it. Every major army that participated in the war since 1914, including the British, French, Russian and German—was near collapse and mutiny. The loss of an entire generation of young men from Europe sowed the seeds for a new understanding that modern warfare was basically absurd and immoral as conducted on the battle-fields of Europe. This legacy has been passed down to all of us today.

WW I changed people's consciousness of war forever. Films from the 1930s, including films such as *All Quiet on the Western Front, The Big Parade, The Grand Illusion, Hell's Angeles,*

J'Accuse, Journey's End and *Westfront 1918* helped keep this consciousness alive. Today the antiwar consciousness of the First World War informs nearly all modern war films.

Special mention is in order for three contemporary Australian films about WW I—*ANZACS, Gallipoli* and *The Lighthorsemen.* These films make strong antiwar statements—statements that continue to raise questions that are ultimately at the heart of "total war," as it has been practiced in some form for the last 2,000 years in the West. Is this cause worth dying for? Can you trust those who are commanding you to risk your life? These questions still haunt the European psyche today. How did commanders order 2.5 million men to die on battlefields that never changed position for more than a few miles over the course of a year (1916)? There are many answers to this question but none of them are satisfactory. This issue arises for the first time in American history during the Vietnam War, and it's not going away anytime soon.

The British have also done their part to keep the consciousness of WW I alive, but in a quieter manner. Films such as *All the King's Men, Behind the Lines, An Indecent Obsession, The King of Hearts, Oh! What a Lovely War, The Trench* and *The Unknown Soldier* show the quiet reality that emerged from this war. These films show modern war as a shattering psychological experience for many soldiers, as well as the limits to what human beings can endure. WW I tested these limits in a way no prior or subsequent war has. Many of the films set during this time examine the damage of war on the human psyche and how soldiers try to cope with the enormous brutality of the war experience.

With the exception of two so-called "classics," *All Quiet on the Western Front* and *Sergeant* York, WW I films are increasingly difficult to find in video stores. While the modern WW I movies are among the best war films available, the public consciousness of this war has been eclipsed by the wars that followed it. Listed on the following page are the best of the pre-1940 WW I movies.

"Classic" WW I Movies

Ace of Aces *1933 GBR*

All Quiet on the Western Front *1930 USA*

The Big Parade *1924 USA silent*

Dawn Patrol *1930/1938 USA*

A Farewell to Arms *1932 USA*

The Fighting 69th *1940 USA*

Four Horsemen of Apocalypse *1921 USA silent*

Grand Illusion *1937 FRA*

Hell's Angels *USA 1930*

J' Accuse *1933 FRA*

Journey's End *1930 GBR/USA*

The Lost Patrol *1934 USA*

Nurse Edith Cavell *1939 USA*

The Road to Glory *1936 USA*

Sergeant York *1941 USA*

Tell England *1931 GBR*

Westfront 1918 *1930 GER*

What Price Glory *1926/1952 USA*

Wings *1927 USA silent*

From 1914 to 1940 over three hundred films were made about WW I. Today only a small handful standout or are available to contemporary audiences.

World War II Movies

"Bob...I want you to take Burma, or not come back alive."
Gen. Douglas MacArthur, to General Robert Eichelberger

There are more movies about World War II than about any other war, which is why so many of them are reviewed for this book.

First and foremost, it helps to understand that WW II was not just another war, but rather was the avatar of all wars. In all of human history, no war has ever been fought on this scale, involved the death of so many people (55+ million), crossed so many oceans, been fought on so many continents, involved so many nations or consumed so many human and material resources. The scope of WW II transcends all wars and all previous ideas about the nature and cause of war. As a result, what films have to tell about the Second World War is important. However, the final telling of this war will probably not be known for hundreds, and perhaps even thousands of years.

The point is, World War II is the first great mythic story of the modern age. Just as every great culture has its mythic stories by which it comes to define itself, it is likely that many centuries from now, twentieth-century culture (the world's first universal culture) will be understood by the images and symbols of this great cataclysm. It is in this light that the following discussion about the WW II film should be viewed.

WW II is the only war depicted on film that encompasses the entire human experience. No one who understands this war is immune to what war is truly about. Decade by decade, generation by generation, our understanding of this overwhelming human experience is evolving and changing, and movies play an essential role in this process.

Patriotizing the Nation (1940-1950s) All the early WW II films are properly called "flagwavers" and, by some, wartime "propaganda." They were not so much about depicting the "everyman" as a hero, as is typically seen in the action-adventure movie, Rather, the focus was on everyone doing his or her duty regardless of the cost or sacrifices required of each individual. These films basically served to provide moral support for the war effort, and appropriately so, as seen in *Air Force, Bataan, Guadalcanal Diary, Sahara, Wake Island* and *A Wing and a Prayer.* This early war movie formula of patriotism and propaganda still remains the staple of most war movies today—and for the foreseeable future.

Irony and Personal Conflict (1950-1960s) By the 1950s and early 1960s patriotic war themes had begun to transform into a closer inspection of the conflicts inherent in command, as seen in *Command Decision* and *Twelve O'Clock High.* The complaints and fears of the soldiers making the sacrifices began to surface in movies such as *Attack!* and *Home of the Brave.* By the 1960s, soldiers were portrayed as at war with one another, as seen in *The Long and the Short and the Tall* and *Too Late the Hero.* However, the early versions of *Stalingrad* and *The Thin Red Line* probably represent the best of the familiar WW II formula, while *From Here to Eternity*, which reflects this new level of antagonism, was probably the rawest and best of the war-romance themed movies.

Parody and Spectacle (1960-1970s) America's immediate consciousness of World War II had waned, and no doubt the Vietnam War partially accounts for this. People stopped wanting to watch war; as a result, WW II films became mostly a parody of war. Take the absurdist *The Big Red One*, the semiserious, if not camp *Cross of Iron*, the antisocial *The Dirty Dozen* and the downright silly and amoral *Kelly's Heroes.* Still other films portrayed large-scale heroic and unbelievable action-adventure stories, including *The Guns of Navarone, Operation Crossbow* and *Tobruk.* Even better, they become spectacular, star-driven large-scale and impersonal stories of great battles, as seen in *The Battle of Britain, Battle of the Bulge, A Bridge Too Far, The Longest Day* and *Midway.* Certainly *Tora! Tora! Tora!* stands out as a superior movie in this group.

WW II as Nostalgia (1970-1980s) In 1943 no one ever described WW II as the "last good war." This is *nostalgia*, a trick of the mind that romanticizes the past as a better time and place. WW II as nostalgia has been emerging right from the beginning and has not yet stopped. Early films that best epitomize this are *The Best Years of Our Lives, Casablanca* and *Mrs. Miniver.* For over sixty years filmmakers have been trying to capture the essence of these nostalgic memories and package it for audiences. For the most part, they have failed. At the forefront of this has been the war-romance. The best of the nostalgic-war romances include the Russian films *Ballad of a Soldier* and *The Cranes are Flying*; the British miniseries *A Nightingale Sang* and *We'll Meet Again*, and the epic miniseries *Winds of War* and *War and Remembrance*. These are all at the top of their class. With a few spectacular exceptions, including *Come and See*, *Das Boot* and *Patton*, the WW II film does not reemerge as an important film subject, free of nostalgia, for nearly thirty years.

The New War "Reality" (1990-2000+) Infused with the "new realism" of Vietnam War era movies, a few WW II films strove to tell compelling and highly realistic stories about this war. This was aided by the realization that the soldiers of this era were passing, and that all the important stories had not been told. Movies such as *Band of Brothers*, *Stalingrad*, *The Thin Red Line* and *When Trumpets Fade* stand out here. Nostalgic WW II films also strongly re-emerged in the 2000s, with films like *Dark Blue World*, *Enemy at the Gate*, *Hart's War* and *The Windtalkers*. In retrospect, it is clear that the best WW II movies did not begin to emerge until nearly twenty-five years after the war. Many believe that the best are yet to come.

Ultimately, these WW II films are about mythologizing the greatest, heroic war adventures of our culture. WW II is in the process of becoming myth, a cultural tale that will be told for centuries to come. There is the great music and dance, the fashions and styles, the desperate romances, the men in uniform, the great collision of good and evil on a scale that dwarfs all that preceded it. It's a story of personal heroism and sacrifice and great national ideals. In time, it will take its place in the psyche of all cultures. In the meantime, a lot of effort is being made to make sure every-one's role is redeemed.

Late Night Action from the '40s

Action in the North Atlantic *1943 USA*
Air Force *1943 USA*
Back to Bataan *1945 USA*
Bataan *1943 USA*
Battleground *1949 USA*
Bombardier *1943 USA*
Burma Convoy *1941 USA*
Command Decision *1948 USA*
Commandos Strike at Dawn *1942 USA*
Crash Dive *1943 USA*
Convoy *1941 USA*
Corregidor *1943 USA*
Corvette K-225 *1943 USA*
Day Will Dawn, The *1942 GBR*
Days of Glory *1944 USA*
Desperate Journey *1942 USA*
Destination Tokyo *1943 USA*
Destroyer *1943 USA*
Dive Bomber *1941 USA*
Eagle Squadron *1942 USA*
Fighter Squadron *1948 USA*
Fighting Seabees, The *1942 USA*
Fighting Sullivans, The *1942 USA*
Flying Tigers *1942 USA*
God Is My Co-Pilot *1945 USA*
Guadalcanal Diary *1943 USA*
Gung Ho! *1943 USA*
Home of the Brave *1949 USA*
Immortal Battalion, *1944 GBR*
Immortal Sergeant , The *1943 USA*
In Which We Serve *1943 GBR*
Jungle Patrol *1948 USA*
Lion Has Wings, The *1940 GBR*
Marine Raiders *1944 USA*
Objective, Burma! *1945 USA*
Sahara *1943 USA*
Salute to the Marines *1943 USA*
Sands of Iwo Jima *1949 USA*
Spitfire *1942 GBR*
Story of G.I. Joe, The *1945 USA*
Task Force *1949 USA*
They Were Expendable *1945 USA*
Thirty Seconds Over Tokyo *1944 USA*
To the Shores of Tripoli *1942 USA*
Twelve O'Clock High *1949 USA*
Wake Island *1942 USA*
Walk in the Sun, A *1946 USA*
We Dive at Dawn *1943 GBR*
Wing and a Prayer *1944 USA*
Yank in the RAF, A *1941 USA*

Korean War Movies

"Glory is being shot and having your name
misspelled in the papers."
Maj. Gen. Oliver O. Howard

The fact that there are no outstanding Korean War movies may help explain why this war is often referred to as the "forgotten war." It is very hard to say exactly why this is. Critics have speculated that the Korean War followed the Second World War too closely, and that the Korean War was a small, highly political war in a part of the world that was obscure and unknown to most Americans. Others have offered the opinion that the movie-going public simply had no interest in war movies following WW II and the glut of war movies it produced.

Big-budget Hollywood studio attempts to address the Korean War were limited and primarily "romance-based," with the war appearing almost as a backdrop. The three best known Korean War films are *The Bridges at Toko-Ri* starring William Holden, *The Hunters* starring Robert Mitchum, and *Men of the Fighting Lady* with Van Johnson. They all featured romance and the glitter of jet pilots and jet aircraft in Technicolor. Two of these films featured the spectacle of aircraft carriers.

All other Korean War films were low-budget, black and white productions. Surprisingly, nearly 60 of these films were made. While none of them can be characterized as "good," many had good moments or did some things well. For the most part, these films were what critics have come to term "standard war actioners." Among this group of films, critics have continually praised *Pork Chop Hill*, starring Gregory Peck. While it does not stand out as a superior film, in this reviewer's judgment, it does, however, offer criticism of politics and military command. Most Korean War films portray war as hell by simply recasting the WW II movie formula to fit a new war—and without success.

None of the Korean War films really attempts to deal with the politics of this politically complex war, and as a result, they feature WW II veterans called up from reserve status who simply want to be with their families, or young men fighting and dying because they are there and that's what soldiers do. And mostly, the films consist of "unit dramas" that focus on the soldier rather than on the war.

The most difficult part of reviewing Korean War movies was finding them. They simply are not available for rent at major nor independent local video stores. With the exception of the films mentioned above, it is nearly impossible to find any other Korean War movies without going to specialty outlets.

Why the Korean War was Forgotten!

These Korean War combat films are what reviewers call "low budget" actioners. Most are out of print.

All the Young Men *1960*
Battle Circus *1953*
Battle Flame *1959*
Battle Hymn *1957*
Battle Taxi *1954*
Battle Zone *1952*
Combat Squad *1953*
Dragonfly Squadron *1954*
Field of Honor *1984*
Fixed Bayonets *1951*
Glory Brigade, The *1953*
Hell in Korea *1956*
Hell's Horizon *1955*
Hold Back the Night *1956*
Inchon *1981*
Iron Angel *1965*
Jet Attack *1958*
Korea Patrol *1951*
McConnell Story, The *1955*
Marines Let's Go *1961*
Men in War *1957*
Mission Over Korea *1953*
One Minute to Zero *1952*
Pork Chop Hill *1959*
Rack, The *1956*
Reluctant Heroes *1971*
Retreat, Hell! *1952*
Saber Jet *1953*
Sergeant Ryker *1968*
Sky Commando *1953*
Sniper's Ridge *1961*
The Steel Helmet *1951*
Submarine Command *1951*
Tank Battalion *1958*
Target Zero *1955*
Torpedo Alley *1953*
War Hunt *1962*
War is Hell *1963*
Wonsan Operations *1978*
Yank in Korea, A *1951*
The Young and the Brave *1963*

Vietnam War Movies

"My country right or wrong" is like saying,
"My mother drunk or sober."
G.K. Chesterton

There are basically two types of Vietnam War movies. The most popular and largest group is the exploitation-actioner. Here the themes are primarily angry revenge and violent justice. *Missing in Action*, starring Chuck Norris, and *First Blood*, starring Sylvester Stallone as "Rambo," best represent this group. The popularity of these films appears to have faded as movies about Delta Forces and Navy SEALs have succeeded them. However, there is a second group of films that are legitimately trying to tell the story of this war. This book will focus on these films, and they include films such as *84 Charlie MoPic, Platoon* and *A Rumor of War*.

The Vietnam War movie brought a new war-realism that had not been seen before in war movies. There were the views from the Huey gunships, complex characters and situations, a wise-cracking, cynical view of the war, and blunt, profane language. These films had a willingness to show new and complex issues: racial problems, drug and alcohol abuse, the morality of killing and the soldiers' complex relationships with one another and to the civilian population. There were also very direct expressions of antiwar sentiment and attacks on military authority.

This war was told almost exclusively from the viewpoint of the soldier in the field or at low levels of command. Films with a command viewpoint raised too many uncomfortable political and military questions. Because there was nothing nostalgic about the public image of the war, studios were not willing to venture into war romances (thank goodness). There were no heroic stories, only stories of survival and disaffection on the homefront. (*We Were Soldiers* is a recent exception.)

The Vietnam War was called the first TV war, so perhaps we shouldn't be surprised that television was the medium that best told the story of this war. Movies such as *A Bright Shining Lie, Dear America: Letters Home from Vietnam, A Rumor of War* and *Vietnam War Story* probably provided the best and most balanced view of the war and of men in combat.

While most of the publicity, acclaim and awards went to *Apocalypse Now, The Deer Hunter, Full Metal Jacket* and *Platoon*, in this reviewer's judgment, they did not live up to their hype. Yes, each of these films is well made and entertaining, but they tried to tell a story that made the movie larger than the war and the men who served in it.

In *Apocalypse Now* there's a descent into inner-madness; in *The Deer Hunter* there's a crazed obsession with death in games of Russian roulette; *Full Metal Jacket* showed the primitive blood lust that war sets loose in soldiers; and *Platoon* featured a battle between the good and evil in each of us. Each of these films peels away the thin veneer of not just what constitutes a society but a person. Unable to look directly at this war, the films' directors created dark, fantastic allegories about the experiences of war. The result, in every instance, was a very distorted view of war based on fictional contrivances to drive home a point.

However, there was a second tier of Hollywood movies that did an excellent job, but unfortunately failed to capture the public's attention. These include *Casualties of War, 84 Charlie MoPic, Go Tell the Spartans* and *Hamburger Hill*. The audience for a lost war was clearly not there. It's also obvious, looking back, that there was an audience for fantastic movies that were more entertaining than the stories of war.

Vietnam is the only American war, to my knowledge, where the madness of the war itself began to become infused with the image of the soldier. The screen images of Vietnam soldiers as unstable, rebellious, undisciplined, unpatriotic, drug-using and even as "psycho" are disturbing. The media appears to have stigmatized the soldier in an attempt to blame the war for everything wrong in America. There is still something profoundly disturbing about this war that America has never fully addressed.

Does war creates its own madness, and dying for an unpopular war create an even greater madness in the psyche of the soldier and the culture? For Americans the real question became, how do we remain patriotic but question the war? In this case the soldier carried the burden of this conflict, partly because America did not emerge the victors in this war, and also because America had reached the limits of questioning authority in the 1960s and 1970s. Movies about why America went to war and how the war was conducted may never be made, or at least not for many years to come.

Vietnam War Exploitation-Actioners

Behind Enemy Lines *1986*
Beyond the Call of Duty *1992*
Braddock: Missing in Action *1988*
Chain of Command *1993*
Charlie Bravo *1980*
China Gate *1957*
Crossfire *1989*
Eye of the Eagle *1987*
Eye of the Eagle 2 *1988*
Eye of the Eagle 3 *1993*
Expendables, The *1989*
Fatal Mission *1990*
Field of Fire *1992*
Fighting Mad *1977*
Final Mission *1984*
Firehawk *1992*
First Blood *1982*
Heated Vengeance *1987*
Hell on the Battleground *1987*
How Sleep the Brave *1981*
In Gold We Trust *1991*
Kill Zone *1993*
Last Hunter, The *1986*
Missing in Action *1984*
Missing in Action 2: The Beginning *1985*
Nam Angels *1988*
Night Wars *1988*
No Dead Heroes *1986*
Operation 'Nam *1985*
Operation War Zone *1989*
P.O.W. Death Camp *1989*
P.O.W.: Escape *1986*
Rambo First Blood Part II *1985*
Rambo III *1988*
Rolling Thunder *1977*
Saigon Commandos *1987*
Search and Destroy *1981*
Soldier Boyz *1995*
Strike Commando *1987*
To the Shores of Hell *1966*
Violent Breed, The *1983*
Violent Zone *1989*
Walking Dead, The *1995*
War Bus *1985*
Yank in Vietnam, A *1964*

WAR MOVIE INDEX

"An Admiral has to be put to death now and then to encourage others."

Voltaire

War Movie Index

American Civil War

Andersonville *1996 USA*
Andersonville Trial *1970 USA*
The Blue and the Gray *1982 USA*
Civil War, The *1990 USA doc.*
Gettysburg *1993 USA*
Glory *1989 USA*
Gods and Generals *2003 USA*
Horse Soldiers, The *1959 USA*
Hunley, The *1990 USA*
Ironclads *1991 USA*
North and South *1985 USA*
Red Badge of Courage, The *1951 USA*

World War I

Aces High *1976 GBR*
All Quiet on the Western Front *1930 USA*
All the King's Men *1999 GBR*
ANZACS *1985 AUS*
Behind the Lines *1997 GBR*
Black and White in Color *1976 FRA/SWI/IVC*
Blue Max , The *1966 USA*
Capitaine Conan *1996 FRA*
Fighting 69th, The *1940 USA*
Gallipoli *1981 AUS*
Guns of August, The *1964 USA doc.*
King of Hearts *1966 FRA/ITA*
Lafayette Escadrille *1958 USA*
Lighthorsemen, The *1987 AUS*
Lost Battalion, The *2001 USA*
Paths of Glory *1957 USA*
Sergeant York *1941 USA*
Trench, The *1999 FRA/GBR*
Von Richthofen and Brown *1971 USA*
What Price Glory? *1952 USA*
Zeppelin *1971 GBR*

World War II: Europe and North Africa

Above Us the Waves *1955 GBR*
Action in the North Atlantic *1943 USA*
Affair, The *1995 USA*
Anzio *1968 ITA*
Attack! *1956 USA*
Attack and Retreat *1965 ITA/RUS/USA*

Band of Brothers *2001 USA*
Battle Force *1977 GER/YUG*
Battleground *1949 USA*
Battle of Britain, The *1969 GBR*
Battle of the Bulge *1965 USA*
Battle of the Last Panzer, The *1968 SPA/ITA*
Big Red One, The *1980 USA*
Breakthrough *1978 GER*
Bridge, The *1959 GER*
Bridge at Remagen, The *1969 USA*
Bridge Too Far, A *1977 GBR/USA*
Captain Corelli's Mandolin *2001 USA*
Castle Keep *1969 USA*
Catch 22 *1970 USA*
Cockleshell Heroes *1955 GBR*
Colditz Story, The *1954 GBR*
Come and See *1985 RUS*
Command Decision *1948 USA*
Commandos Strike at Dawn *1942 USA*
Cross of Iron *1977 GBR/GER/YUG*
Cruel Sea, The *1953 GBR*
Dam Busters, The *1954 GBR*
Darby's Rangers *1958 USA*
Dark Blue World *2001 CZE*
Das Boot *1981 GER*
D-Day, the Sixth of June *1956 USA*
Desert Fox , The *1951 USA*
Desert Rats, The *1953 USA*
Desperate Journey *1942 USA*
Devil's Brigade, The *1968 USA*
Dieppe *1993 CAN*
Dirty Dozen, The *1967 USA*
Dunkirk *1958 GBR*
Eagle Has Landed, The *1976 GBR*
Enemy at the Gates *2001 USA/GER/GBR/IRE*
Enemy Below, The *1957 USA*
Enigma *2001 USA*
Execution of Private Slovik, The *1974 USA*
Fighter Attack *1953 USA*
Fireball Forward *1972 USA*
Force of Arms *1951 USA*
Force 10 From Navarone *1978 GBR*
Glory at Sea *1952 GBR*
Go For Broke *1951 USA*
Great Escape, The *1963 USA*
Guns of Navarone, The *1961 GBR/USA*
Hart's War *2002 USA*
Hell is for Heroes *1962 USA*
Heroes of Telemark, The *1965 GBR*
Hill, The *1965 GBR*

Immortal Battalion *1944 GBR*
Immortal Sergeant, The *1943 USA*
In Which We Serve *1942 GBR*
Is Paris Burning *1966 FRA/USA*
Kelly's Heroes *1970 USA/YUG*
Longest Day, The *1962 USA*
Man Escaped, A *1956 FRA*
McKenzie Break, The *1970 GBR*
Mediterraneo *1991 ITA*
Mein Krieg *1993 GER doc.*
Memphis Belle *1990 GBR*
Midnight Clear, A *1992 USA*
Mosquito Squadron *1969 GBR*
One That Got Away, The *1957 GBR*
Operation Crossbow *1965 GBR*
Patton *1970 USA*
Piece of Cake *1988 GBR*
Pursuit of the Graf Spee *1956 GBR*
Raid on Rommel *1971 USA*
Reach for the Sky *1956 CAN/GBR*
Red Ball Express *1952 USA*
Sahara *1943 USA*
Saving Private Ryan *1998 USA*
Sea Shall Not Have Them, The *1954 GBR*
Sink the Bismarck! *1960 GBR*
633 Squadron *1964 GBR*
Soldier of Orange *1977 NET*
Stalag 17 *1953 USA*
Stalingrad *1958 GER*
Stalingrad *1993 GER*
Story of G.I. Joe, The *1945 USA*
Tanks are Coming, The *1951 USA*
Tobruk *1966 USA*
To Hell and Back *1955 USA*
Train, The *1964 USA*
Tuskegee Airmen, The *1995 USA*
Twelve O'Clock High *1949 USA*
U-571 *2000 USA*
Von Ryan's Express *1965 USA*
Walk in the Sun, A *1946 USA*
War and Remembrance (parts 1-7) *1988 USA*
War and Remembrance (parts 8-12) *1989 USA*
When Trumpets Fade *1998 USA*
Where Eagles Dare *1968 USA*
Winds of War (parts 1-7) *1983 USA*
Winter War, The *1989 FIN*
Wooden Horse, The *1950 GBR*
Young Lions, The *1958 USA*

WW II: Pacific

Above and Beyond *1952 USA*
Air Force *1943 USA*
Attack Force Z *1982 USA*
Away All Boats *1956 USA*
Back to Bataan *1945 USA*
Bataan *1943 USA*
Battle Cry *1955 USA*
Battle for Blood Island, The *1960 USA*
Between Heaven and Hell *1956 USA*
Bridge on the River Kwai, The *1957 GBR*
Burmese Harp, The *1956 JAP*
Caine Mutiny, The *1954 USA*
Corregidor *1943 USA*
Death of a Soldier *1986 AUS*
Deep Six, The *1958 USA*
Destination Tokyo *1943 USA*
Empire of the Sun *1987 USA*
Enola Gay *1980 USA*
Farewell to the King *1989 USA*
Fat Man and Little Boy *1989 USA*
Fighting Seabees, The *1944 USA*
Fighting Sullivans, The *1944 USA*
Fires on the Plain *1959 JAP*
First to Fight *1967 USA*
Flat Top *1952 USA*
Flying Leathernecks *1951 USA*
Flying Tigers *1942 USA*
From Here to Eternity *1953 USA*
Gallant Hours, The *1960 USA*
Guadalcanal Diary *1943 USA*
Gung Ho! *1943 USA*
Halls of Montezuma *1950 USA*
Hellcats of the Navy *1957 USA*
Hell in the Pacific *1968 USA*
Hell to Eternity *1960 USA*
Home of the Brave *1949 USA*
Human Condition, The (parts 1, 2, 3) *1959 JAP*
Imperial Japanese Empire, The *1985 JAP*
In Harm's Way *1965 USA*
King Rat *1965 USA*
Long and the Short and the Tall, The *1960 GBR*
Marine Raiders *1944 USA*
Merrill's Marauders *1962 USA*
Merry Christmas, Mr. Lawrence *1983 GBR/JAP*
Midway *1976 USA*
Mission of the Shark *1991 USA*
Mister Roberts *1955 USA*
Naked and the Dead, The *1958 USA*

Never So Few *1959 USA*
No Man is an Island *1962 USA*
None But the Brave *1965 USA/JAP*
Objective, Burma! *1945 USA*
Operation Pacific *1951 USA*
Paradise Road *1997 USA/AUS*
Pearl Harbor *2001 USA*
Prisoners of the Sun *1990 AUS*
PT109 *1963 USA*
Purple Heart, The *1944 USA*
Run Silent, Run Deep *1958 USA*
Sands of Iwo Jima *1949 USA*
Task Force *1949 USA*
They Were Expendable *1945 USA*
Thin Red Line, The *1964 USA*
Thin Red Line, The *1998 USA*
Thirty Seconds Over Tokyo *1944 USA*
To End All Wars *2003 USA*
Too Late the Hero *1970 USA*
Tora! Tora! Tora! *1970 USA/JAP*
Torpedo Run *1958 USA*
To the Shores of Tripoli *1942 USA*
Up Periscope *1959 USA*
Wake Island *1942 USA*
Windtalkers *2002 USA*
Wing and a Prayer, A *1944 USA*
Zero *1984 JAP*

Korean War

All the Young Men *1960 USA*
Battle Circus *1953 USA*
Battle Hymn *1957 USA*
Bridges at Toko-Ri, The *1954 USA*
Dragonfly Squadron *1954 USA*
Field of Honor *1984 HOL*
Hell in Korea *1956 GBR*
Hunters, The *1958 USA*
Korea: The Forgotten War *1987 USA doc.*
Manchurian Candidate, The *1962 USA*
M*A*S*H *1970 USA*
McConnell Story , The 1955 *USA*
Men in War *1957 USA*
Men of the Fighting Lady *1954 USA*
Pork Chop Hill *1959 USA*
Reluctant Heroes *1971 USA*
Retreat, Hell! *1952 USA*
Sergeant Ryker *1968 USA*
Steel Helmet, The *1951 USA*
Torpedo Alley *1953 USA*

Vietnam War

Anderson Platoon, The *1967 FRA doc.*
Apocalypse Now *1979 USA*
Bat 21 *1988 USA*
Born on the Fourth of July *1989 USA*
Boys in Company C, The *1978 USA*
Bright Shining Lie, A *1998 USA*
Cadence *1991 USA*
Casualties of War *1989 USA*
Dear America: Letters Home From Vietnam *1988 USA doc.*
Deer Hunter, The *1978 USA*
84 Charlie MoPic *1989 USA*
Flight of the Intruder *1991 USA*
Full Metal Jacket *1987 USA*
Gardens of Stone *1987 USA*
Good Morning, Vietnam *1987 USA*
Go Tell the Spartans *1978 USA*
Green Berets, The *1968 USA*
Hamburger Hill *1987 USA*
Hanoi Hilton *1987 USA*
In Love and War *1987 USA*
Iron Triangle, The *1989 USA*
Odd Angry Shot, The *1979 AUS*
Platoon *1986 USA*
Platoon Leader *1988 USA*
Rumor of War, A *1980 USA*
Siege of Firebase Gloria, The *1989 USA*
Tigerland *2000 USA*
Tour of Duty *1987 USA*
Vietnam Home Movies *1984 USA doc.*
Vietnam War Story *(parts 1, 2, 3) 1987 USA*
We Were Soldiers *2002 USA*
When Hell Was in Session *1979 USA*

Cold War

Battle Hell *1957 GBR*
Bedford Incident, The *1965 GBR*
Bombers B-52 *1957 USA*
By Dawn's Early Light *1990 USA*
Call to Glory *1984 USA*
Crimson Tide *1995 USA*
Dr. Strangelove *1963 GBR*
Fail Safe *1964 GBR*
Full Fathom Five *1990 USA*
Gathering of Eagles, A *1963 USA*
Gray Lady Down *1978 USA*
Hunt for Red October, The *1990 USA*

Ice Station Zebra *1968 USA*
Jet Pilot *1957 USA*
K-19: The Widowmaker *2002 USA /GBR/GER*
Manchurian Candidate, The *1962 USA*
On the Beach *1959 USA*
Red Dawn *1984 USA*
Seven Days in May *1964 USA*
Strategic Air Command *1955 USA*
Thirteen Days *2001 USA*
Twilight's Last Gleaming *1977 USA/GER*
World War III *1982 USA*

Wars Around the World

Ay, Carmela! *1990 SPA/ITA* Spanish Civil War 1936-1939
Beast, The *1988 USA* Soviet-Afghanistan Campaign 1979-1989
Battle for Port Arthur, The *1980 JAP* Russo-Japanese War 1904-1905
Battle for the Falklands *1984 GBR* British Falklands War 1982
Battle of Algiers, The *1965 ITA/ALG* Algerian Independence 1954-1962
Behind Enemy Lines *2001 USA* Balkan Conflict 1991-1995
Black Hawk Down *2001 USA* Somalia Operations 1992-1995
Bravo Two Zero *1999 RSA* Persian Gulf War 1990-1991
China Gate *1957 USA* French-Indochina War 1946-1954
Dark of the Sun *1968 GBR* Post-Colonial Africa c. 1960
Dogs of War, The *1980 GBR* Post-Colonial Africa c. 1980
Field of Honor *1987 HOL* Franco-Prussian War 1870-1871
Funny Dirty Little War *1983 ARG* Argentine Civil War 1974
Heartbreak Ridge *1986 USA* Invasion of Grenada 1983
Heroes of Desert Storm, The *1991 USA* Persian Gulf War 1990-1991
No Man's Land *2001 BOS-HRZ* Balkan Conflict 1991-1995
One Man's Hero *1999 USA/SPA/MEX* Mexican War 1846-1948
Pretty Village, Pretty Flame *1996 GRE/YUG* Balkan Conflict 1991-1995
Prisoner of the Mountains *1996 RUS* Chechen Revolt 1994-1996
Raid on Entebbe *1977 USA* Israeli-Palestinian Conflict 1922-2002
Rough Riders *1997 USA* Span-Am War 1898
Savior *1998 USA* Balkan Conflict 1991-1995
Shot Through the Heart *1998 USA/CAN* Balkan Conflict 1991-1995
Tears of the Sun *2003 USA* African Civil War
Three Kings *1999 USA* Persian Gulf War 1990-1991
317th Platoon *1965 FRA* French-Indochina War 1946-1954
Underground *1995 FRA/GER/HUN* Yugoslavian Civil War 1943-1995
Victory at Entebbe *1976 USA* Israeli-Palestinian Conflict 1922-2002
Vukovar *1994 YUG/ITA* Balkans Conflict 1991-1995
Welcome to Sarajevo *1997 USA/GBR* Balkans Conflict 1991-1995
Wild Geese, The *1978 GBR* Post-Colonial Africa

Military Life

Beau Travail *1999 FRA*
Best Years of Our Lives, The *1946 USA*
Bombers B-52 *1957 USA*
Born on the Fourth of July *1989 USA*
Buffalo Soldiers *1997 USA*
Cadence *1991 USA*
Call to Glory *1984 USA*
D.I., The *1957 USA*
From Here to Eternity *1953 USA*
Gardens of Stone *1987 USA*
G.I. Jane *1997 USA*
Great Santini, The *1979 USA*
Heartbreak Ridge *1986 USA*
In Harm's Way *1965 USA*
In Pursuit of Honor *1995 USA*
Last Detail, The *1973 USA*
Men of Honor *2000 USA*
Officer and a Gentleman, An *1982 USA*
Pentagon Wars, The *1998 USA*
Soldier's Story, A *1984 USA*
Strategic Air Command *1955 USA*
Tigerland, *2000 USA*
Top Gun *1986 USA*
To the Shore of Tripoli *1942 USA*
Tunes of Glory *1960 GBR*
Tuskegee Airmen, The *1995 USA*

Military Justice

Affair, The *1995 USA*
Afterburn *1992 USA*
Andersonville Trial *1970 USA*
Assault at West Point *1994 USA*
Breaker Morant *1980 AUS*
Caine Mutiny, The *1954 USA*
Capitaine Conan *1996 FRA*
Carrington V.C. *1955 GBR*
Courage Under Fire *1996 USA*
Court-Martial of Billy Mitchell, The *1955 USA*
Court-Martial of Jackie Robinson, The *1990 USA*
Death of a Soldier *1986 AUS*
Execution of Private Slovik, The *1974 USA*
Few Good Men, A *1992 USA*
Glimpse of Hell, A *2001 USA*
Hill, The *1995 GBR*
Judgment at Nuremberg *1961 USA*
Last Castle, The *2001 USA*

Men of Honor *2000 USA*
Mission of the Shark *1991 USA*
Mutiny *1999 USA*
One Man's Hero *1999 USA*
Paths of Glory *1957 USA*
Prisoners of the Sun *1990 AUS*
Rules of Engagement *2000 USA*
Sergeant Rutledge *1960 USA*
Sergeant Ryker *1968 USA*
Serving in Silence *1995 USA*
Soldier's Story, A *1984 USA*
Thanks of a Grateful Nation *1998 USA*

POW

Andersonville *1996 USA*
Bridge on the River Kwai, The *1957 GBR*
Colditz Story, The *1954 GBR*
Empire of the Sun *1987 USA*
Great Escape, The *1963 USA*
Hanoi Hilton *1987 USA*
Hart's War *2002 USA*
Hill, The *1965 USA*
Human Condition, The (parts 1-3) *1959 JAP*
In Love and War *1987 USA*
King Rat *1965 USA*
Last Castle, The *2001 USA*
Man Escaped, A *1956 USA*
McKenzie Break, The *1970 IRE/GBR*
Merry Christmas, Mr. Lawrence *1983 GBR/JAP*
One That Got Away, The *1957 GBR*
Paradise Road *1997 USA/AUS*
Prisoner of the Mountains *1996 USA*
Prisoners of the Sun *1990 AUS*
Purple Heart, The *1944 USA*
Stalag 17 *1953 USA*
To End All Wars *2003 GBR*
Von Ryan's Express *1965 USA*
When Hell was in Session *1979 USA*
Wooden Horse, The *1950 USA*

REFERENCES

Atlas of World War II, Richard Natkiel, Barnes & Noble Books, NY 1985

The Dictionary of Modern War, Edward Luttwak and Stuart L. Koehl, editors, Gramercy Books, NY 1998

Encyclopedia of American War Films, Editors, Larry Langman and Ed Borg, Garland Publishing Company, NY 1989

The First War Planes, William E. Barrett, Fawcett Book, NY 1960

Great Battlefields of the World, John MacDonald, MacMillan Publishing Co., NY 1984

A History of Warfare, John Keegan, Vintage Books, NY 1993

The Military Quotation Book, James Charlton, editor, Thomas Dunne Books, NY 2002

The Oxford Companion to American Military History, John Whiteclay Chambers, II, Editor, Oxford University Press, UK 2001

The Oxford Companion to Military History, Richard Holmes, Editor, Oxford University Press, UK 2001

The Oxford Essential Dictionary of the US Military, Berkley Books, NY 2001

Listed below are the eight movie video guides consulted for the **What the critics say** section of the reviews.

1. *Brassey's Guide to War Films*, Alun Evans, Brassey's, Washington, D.C. 2000.

2. *Halliwell's Film and Video Guide 2001*, John Walker, editor, Harper Resource, NY 2003

3. *Leonard Maltin's 2001 Movie and Video Guide*, Leonard Maltin, Plume, NY 2004

4. *TLA Film and Video Guide (2000-2001)*, David Bleiler, editor, St. Martin's Griffin, NY 1999

5. *Variety Movie Guide 2000*, Derek Elley, editor, A Perigee Book, NY 2003

6. *Videohound's Golden Movie Retriever 2001*, Jim Craddock, editor, Visible Ink, NY 2004

7. *Videohound's War Movies: Classic Conflict Films* (1999), Mike Mayo, Visible Ink, NY 1999

8. *Video Movie Guide 2001*, Mick Martin and Marsha Porter, Balantine Books, NY 2004

1884